CURRENT PERSPECTIVES IN FORENSIC PSYCHOLOGY AND CRIMINAL BEHAVIOR

FOURTH EDITION

Current Perspectives in Forensic Psychology and Criminal Behavior

Fourth Edition

Curt R. Bartol
Anne M. Bartol

Editors

Los Angeles | London | New Delhi
Singapore | Washington DC

Los Angeles | London | New Delhi
Singapore | Washington DC

FOR INFORMATION:

SAGE Publications, Inc.
2455 Teller Road
Thousand Oaks, California 91320
E-mail: order@sagepub.com

SAGE Publications Ltd.
1 Oliver's Yard
55 City Road
London EC1Y 1SP
United Kingdom

SAGE Publications India Pvt. Ltd.
B 1/I 1 Mohan Cooperative Industrial Area
Mathura Road, New Delhi 110 044
India

SAGE Publications Asia-Pacific Pte. Ltd.
3 Church Street
#10-04 Samsung Hub
Singapore 049483

Printed in the United States of America

A catalog record of this book is available from the Library of Congress.

ISBN 978-1-4833-7621-9

This book is printed on acid-free paper.

Acquisitions Editor: Jerry Westby
Editorial Assistant: Laura Kirkhuff
Production Editor: Libby Larson
Copy Editor: Megan Granger
Typesetter: C&M Digitals (P) Ltd.
Proofreader: Laura Webb
Cover Designer: Janet Kiesel
Marketing Manager: Terra Schultz

14 15 16 17 18 10 9 8 7 6 5 4 3 2 1

ANNOTATED CONTENTS

PREFACE

The articles in this book are offered as supplementary readings to accompany the main text in a variety of undergraduate and graduate courses, such as introduction to forensic psychology, criminology, psychology and criminal justice, psychology and law, victimology, and similar courses. All articles were originally published after 2000, most within the past 5 years. All are new to this fourth edition, but most of the articles from the three previous editions of this reader can be found on the SAGE website.

We have subdivided the readings into six units: an introductory section and five sections that reflect different specializations in forensic psychology. These subsections are not mutually exclusive, and the topics of the articles often overlap. As but one example, a reading on hate crimes is included in the victimology section but could just as easily have been placed in the section on criminal and delinquent behavior. Although there is logic to our placement of the articles, which we hope will be evident from the introductory commentary for each unit, instructors, students, and other readers should have no difficulty shifting the order.

As in past editions, we have edited—often reluctantly—many of the original works. Ellipses indicate that sentences have been removed, and asterisks mark the deletion of one or more paragraphs. When substantial portions of an article have been omitted, we indicate that in a footnote at the beginning of the article. In addition, abstracts, authors' notes, most footnotes and endnotes, appendices, recommended readings, and many figures and tables have been removed. Although authors understandably would prefer that their articles be reprinted intact, space limitations necessitate editing. Complete citations are included at the end of each article, including citations in sections that may have been removed. We emphasize that the length of the original article, not its quality, was the dominant criterion applied for this editing process. In addition, we decided to omit complex statistical analyses from some articles, knowing that readers could access these by retrieving the original articles.

ACKNOWLEDGMENTS

We are grateful for the continuing encouragement and support of acquisitions editor Jerry Westby. Production editor Libby Larson and editorial assistant Laura Kirkhuff responded cheerfully and efficiently to multiple requests for guidance at various stages of this project. We also appreciate the competence and professionalism of copy editor Megan Granger during the last phases of production, as well as the work of marketing manager Terra Schultz and the help of many individuals behind the scenes whom we did not meet but could not do without. Finally, we thank the researchers and scholars whose articles are reprinted herein for their significant contributions to the literature.

UNIT 1

INTRODUCTION

INTRODUCTION AND COMMENTARY

Students with serious interests in careers in psychology know that they will likely pursue graduate education—if not immediately after obtaining an undergraduate degree, soon thereafter. A college degree is a first step to an entry-level professional position, but a master's or doctoral degree should be the ultimate goal. In most states, a person with a master's degree in psychology cannot use the title "psychologist" in clinical practice, and the PhD or PsyD is the minimum degree required in many forensic contexts, such as testifying as an expert or conducting forensic mental health assessments. In addition to obtaining a formal degree, the value of "hands-on" experiences, such as volunteer positions and internships, cannot be overestimated.

The two articles in this introductory section provide helpful information for students considering graduate work in forensic psychology and correctional psychology, but they are relevant to other fields as well. Forensic psychology, broadly defined, has grown rapidly over the past two decades, and many students find it a fascinating career option. An ever-increasing number of programs and courses within programs have been developed, and career opportunities are expanding.

Burl, Shah, Filone, Foster, and DeMatteo (2012) provide an excellent review of the content and requirements of numerous graduate programs that confer master's and doctoral degrees, the latter including both the research-and-clinical–oriented PhD and the more clinical-oriented PsyD. We have not included a lengthy table listing programs and schools because the list is ever changing, particularly with respect to new offerings; however, the article offers websites for additional career information. A table indicates the types of courses typically offered in forensic psychology graduate programs.

The article by Morgan, Beer, Fitzgerald, and Mandracchia (2007) reports on a survey of 175 advanced graduate students in counseling and clinical psychology who provided feedback on their education thus far. Undergraduate advisors and many practitioners often recommend that students obtain broad graduate degrees, such as clinical and counseling psychology degrees, rather than enroll in programs that are specifically geared to forensic psychology. Morgan and his colleagues were interested in exploring the extent to which counseling and clinical programs addressed specifically the needs of students who might want careers in forensic and/or correctional psychology, but especially the latter. As the authors note, there are numerous professional opportunities in that field, especially at the doctoral level, and positions often go unfilled. Morgan et al. found that the broad programs—while of high quality—rarely provide students with courses in correctional psychology. Of particular note is the fact that few faculty members in these broad programs had research interests or practical experiences in corrections. Nevertheless, there were ample internship opportunities in correctional spheres, such as juvenile facilities and community correctional programs.

These articles are just two of many available to students who are interested in both law and the behavioral and social sciences. The list of references included with each article will provide readers with additional career resources.

1

A Survey of Graduate Training Programs and Coursework in Forensic Psychology*

Jeffrey Burl

Sanjay Shah

Sarah Filone

Elizabeth Foster

David DeMatteo

Forensic psychology encompasses the activities of psychologists, both clinical and non-clinical, who apply the science of psychology to questions and issues related to the law and legal system (American Board of Forensic Psychology, 2009). For example, psychologists interested in the relationship between psychology and law may participate in a variety of psycholegal activities, such as conducting forensic mental health assessments of criminal defendants and civil litigants, studying the reliability of eyewitness testimony and jury decisions, or providing mental health services in correctional settings. The American Psychological Association recognized forensic psychology as specialty area in 2001, indicating that the field is defined by a discrete body of knowledge and set of practice competencies (Otto & Heilbrun, 2002).

*This article was published in *Teaching of Psychology, 39,* 48–53 (2012). We have removed a table listing programs by degree type as well as brief sections on limitations and future research.

Although the field of forensic psychology dates to the early 1900s, formal training programs in forensic psychology have only developed during the last 35 years. The University of Nebraska established the first training opportunity in forensic psychology in 1973, followed by the creation of 14 more forensic psychology programs over the next 20 years (Ogloff, Tomkins, & Bersoff, 1996). Since then, the field has seen a rapid expansion in the number of training programs being offered at the undergraduate, graduate, and post-doctoral levels of education (DeMatteo, Marczyk, Krauss, & Burl, 2009). At the graduate level specifically, students can now receive training in both master's and doctoral programs, as well as in joint-degree programs that allow students to pursue a law degree and a master's or doctoral degree simultaneously.

Students interested in pursuing graduate training in forensic psychology must not only be aware of the different degree paths available to them, they must also develop an understanding of the variations in educational foci across programs. Students should arguably receive training in seven core competency areas during their graduate training: (1) substantive psychology; (2) research design/methodology and statistics; (3) conducting research; (4) legal knowledge; (5) integrative law-psychology knowledge; (6) ethics and professional issues; and (7) clinical forensic training (DeMatteo et al., 2009). However, given the numerous intersections between psychology and law, as well as the diversity in current forensic research and practice, the available law and psychology course-work can potentially vary considerably across programs. The range of forensic course-work offered by graduate programs adds another layer of complexity to the daunting task that faces the growing number of students interested in pursuing a graduate degree in forensic psychology.

Undergraduate academic advisors who are familiar with the current graduate training opportunities in forensic psychology can better assist students with accessing relevant information and can indicate what type of training students can expect to receive at the graduate level. The purposes of this study are to assist undergraduate faculty who advise students interested in forensic psychology graduate training and to provide information that will allow students to make informed decisions about which forensic psychology graduate program will best meet their professional needs. To achieve these complementary goals, this study provides advisors and students with three descriptive sources of information. First, this study attempts to identify all current graduate programs offering training in forensic psychology, and second, to categorize them according to degree type. Third, this study aims to identify the categories of integrative law-psychology course-work, a core competency for students and practitioners in forensic psychology, offered by these programs. Understanding the variety of forensic training programs available to students, as well as the breadth of coursework offered in these graduate programs, will help advisors more effectively steer students toward programs that offer training consistent with each student's professional goals.

METHOD

Two previously compiled lists of forensic psychology graduate programs served as the sources used to identify programs reported in this study. We defined graduate forensic psychology programs as those that were included (a) on the website of the American Psychology-Law Society (AP-LS [n.d.]; Division 41 of the American Psychological Association) or (b) in the Guide to Graduate Programs in Forensic and Legal Psychology (2007–2008), which was created by the Teaching, Training, and Careers Committee of AP-LS (AP-LS, 2008). Using these lists, we categorized programs according to the degree offered: master's, clinical PhD (defined as both clinical and counseling programs), non-clinical PhD (e.g., social, developmental), PsyD, and joint-degree (combining a law degree with a graduate degree in psychology).

After identifying the current graduate programs in forensic psychology, we then conducted a thorough online search to identify integrative law-psychology course offerings in each program. Using the definition provided by DeMatteo et al. (2009, p. 189), this study classified law-psychology knowledge as "Introductory/overview foundational courses on forensic psychology, and knowledge of research in psycholegal areas such as eyewitness testimony, jury decision-making, admissibility of scientific testimony, forensic assessment measures and techniques, and the treatment of offender populations."The selected courses were then divided into specific categories based on course titles. To the authors' knowledge there are no defined and established categories for law-psychology coursework. Therefore, categories were created for this study when it was determined that at least 10% of all training programs offered coursework in a specific area (e.g., introductory courses, treatment courses, assessment courses, etc.). Although this inevitably excluded courses that some programs offered, this rule was necessary to limit the number of groupings. In addition, when programs offered multiple courses in a single category, only one course was incorporated into the data, which was sufficient to indicate the program offered some training in the respective category. Courses that were a part of the general graduate psychology curriculum (e.g., research methods) were excluded because this study focused exclusively on the forensic specialty. Law school curricula in joint-degree programs were also excluded because the goal of this study was to focus solely on the offerings of psychology departments.

We used the Internet as our exclusive means of obtaining information about various schools, programs, and coursework. Programs are motivated to keep websites up to date because of the Internet's increasing role as the initial (and even primary) information source for prospective students (Fauber, 2006). Using the Internet to examine graduate programs is therefore an ecologically valid way of researching graduate training options. For this reason, we believe that the Internet was an appropriate data source for this exploratory study.

RESULTS

Forensic Psychology Training Programs

Using the AP-LS website and the Guide to Graduate Programs, we initially identified 41 institutions that offered training in forensic psychology through 64 different programs. The discrepancy between these numbers reflects that several institutions offer more than one training program (e.g., PhD and JD/PhD programs). During the course search, however, we also found that some institutions offered one or more degree programs not listed on the AP-LS website or in the Guide to Graduate Programs. These programs were added to the initial results and included in the study. Therefore, after closely examining each institution offering graduate training in forensic psychology, we identified a total of 41 institutions that offered training through 68 programs. The 68 programs included 15 clinical PhD programs, 10 PsyD programs, 15 non-clinical PhD programs, 12 joint-degree programs (i.e., JD/PhD, JD/PsyD, and JD/master's), and 16 master's programs. . . .

Forensic Coursework

Using the approach described above, we identified the following 10 broad categories of forensic psychology coursework offered throughout the various training programs: Introductory/General Forensic Psychology, Forensic Assessment, Forensic Treatment, Social Psychology and the Law, Juvenile Offending, Psychology of Criminal Behavior, Law and Mental Health, Ethical Issues in Forensic Psychology, Victimology, and Socio-Cultural Issues in Forensic Psychology. In this section, we explain each of the 10 categories and identify examples of such courses. Table 2 identifies the percentage of programs within each degree type that offer courses in each of the 10 identified categories.

Table 2 Percentage of Programs Offering Training in Integrative Law-Psychology Categories

Course Category	Clinical PhD	PsyD	Non-Clinical PhD	Joint Programs	Master's	Total
Introductory	87	100	87	100	100	94
Forensic Assessment	67	70	40	50	75	60
Forensic Treatment	20	60	13	8	75	35
Social Psychology	7	0	47	0	19	16
Juvenile Offending	33	60	33	33	63	44
Psychology of Criminal Behavior	27	30	27	17	94	41
Mental Health Law	33	20	20	33	31	28
Ethics	13	10	0	8	50	18
Victimology	13	0	13	0	38	15
Socio-Cultural	0	0	7	25	31	13

Note: The values represent percentages of schools within each degree program offering a course in each course category.

Introductory/General Forensic Psychology. Courses in this category provide a general overview of the integration of psychology and law (civil and/or criminal law). They typically do not focus on any specific psycholegal area or population, although the scope of content appears to vary somewhat. Examples of such courses include Psychology and Law; Law, Psychology, and Policy; Civil Forensic Psychology; and Criminal Forensic Psychology. These courses were well represented across program websites. Depending on the degree type, the surveyed websites showed that between 87% and 100% offered at least one course in this category.

*****

Forensic Assessment. Courses in this category focus on clinical mental health assessment in forensic settings, which may include such activities as reviewing records, interviewing offenders/litigants and collateral informants, and testing offenders/litigants. Such courses include Forensic Assessment; Forensic Diagnostics; and Psycholegal Assessment, Diagnosis, and Testimony. At least half of the program websites for each type of degree, with the exception of non-clinical PhD programs, offered a course in forensic assessment.

Forensic Treatment. Courses in this category focus on the rehabilitation and treatment of individuals involved in the legal system, or more broadly focus on the means to reduce recidivism among offenders. However, we excluded courses having to do with the treatment of a specific subgroup of individuals (e.g., juvenile, sex offender); these courses were placed in other categories. Examples of courses in this category include Evaluation and Treatment of the Adult; Correctional Psychology; Psycholegal Intervention and Treatment; and Probation, Parole, and Community Corrections. The majority of master's and PsyD program websites indicated the presence of treatment-oriented courses (75% and 60%, respectively).

Social Psychology and the Law. This category is defined by courses that focus on social psychology research relevant to the legal system, such as eyewitness testimony and jury decision making. Such courses include Psychology of Juries, Actual Innocence and Wrongful Conviction, Contemporary American Jury, Jury Decision-Making and Jury Selection, and Psychology of Eyewitness Testimony. As Table 2 indicates, non-clinical PhD programs had the largest representation of these courses (47%).

Juvenile Offending. This category explores child and adolescent offending, including the evaluation and treatment of juvenile offenders. Such courses included Juvenile Delinquency, Evaluation and Treatment of the Juvenile Offender, and Juvenile Offenders. The percentage of program websites showing a course in this category ranged from 33% (clinical PhD, non-clinical PhD, and joint-degree programs) to 63% (master's programs).

Psychology of Criminal Behavior. Courses in this category generally deal with efforts to understand both general and violent offending and specific forms of criminal behavior. Examples include Psychology of Criminal Behavior; Sex Offender Evaluation and Treatment; White Collar Crime; Terrorism; and Family Violence and Disputes. The percentage of programs offering courses in this category ranged from 17% (joint-degree programs) to 94% (master's programs).

Law and Mental Health. These are courses that examine issues relevant to psychological science and practice in mental health law. Mental health law encompasses a variety of topics relevant to criminal and civil forensic psychology, including civil commitment, various competencies (e.g., competence to stand trial), and criminal sentencing. Examples include Mental Health Law; Mental Health Issues in Policing; and Mental Health Law and Policy. Across degree types, one-third or fewer of the programs offered coursework in law and mental health.

Ethical Issues in Forensic Psychology. This category includes courses dealing with ethics in a forensic psychology context or the specific ethical guidelines pertaining to forensic psychology. Titles of such courses are Advanced Ethics, Legal, and Clinical Issues in Professional Practice in Psychology; and Counseling and Forensic Ethics. Half of master's degree programs offered coursework in this category, but 13% or fewer of all other degree types offered a course in forensic ethics.

Victimology. This category is defined by courses focusing on the psychology of victims of criminal behavior. Such courses include Victimology; Legal Policy and Analysis in Victimology; and Assessment, Diagnosis, and Treatment of the Victim. Master's degree programs had the largest representation of such courses (38%), with other degree types indicating either very little (13% in PhD and non-clinical PhD programs) or no exposure to victimology coursework.

Socio-Cultural Issues in Forensic Psychology. Courses in this category deal specifically with race, ethnicity, or gender in a forensic psychology context. Examples include Psychology, Gender, and Law; Race, Crime, and Justice; and Sociocultural Issues in Forensic Psychology. Program websites indicated that this category was offered the least with just 13% of programs offering coursework across all degree types.

DISCUSSION

The growth of forensic psychology graduate training programs during the last 35 years has been an important development in the field of psychology and law, but it may present a challenge for undergraduate academic advisors and interested students who are less familiar with this specialty area. This project sought to compile a list of current forensic psychology graduate programs, categorize the programs by degree type, and identify the content of psychology-law courses that are offered within these programs. Although the results revealed a wide array of options in forensic psychology graduate training, these findings should provide a foundation for faculty who advise their students on graduate programs.

Students can presently seek graduate training at 68 forensic psychology programs housed in 41 different institutions. To put this in context with two other specialty areas in psychology, Clinical Neuropsychology and Industrial and Organizational Psychology currently list 35 doctoral programs and 243 graduate programs, respectively, on their division websites (Division of Clinical Neuropsychology, 2011; Society for Industrial and Organizational Psychology, 2011). This study identified both master's level and doctoral level (PhD, PsyD, and joint law-psychology degree) forensic psychology programs, with several institutions offering more than one training program. Results indicate that most integrative law-psychology course-work in these programs falls into 1 of 10 identified categories. The data revealed that these content areas varied considerably across the different degree types, with master's programs offering the greatest selection in forensic coursework, but with most categories made up of courses offered by less than half of all the programs.

Students—and faculty advising them—should be aware of the variability in graduate forensic training. These findings suggest that forensic coursework at the master's level is quite varied and exposes students to a wide range of topics in psychology and law. In contrast, the focus at the doctoral level appears to be on developing a general competency in psychology research and practice (which is consistent with APA's view that specialization should occur primarily at the post-doctoral level), with specialized forensic coursework being more limited and based on specific areas emphasized by each program. For example, PsyD programs tend to place more importance on treatment coursework over social psychology content, whereas non-clinical PhD programs have the opposite focus. An understanding of these differences between degree types and programs will better prepare advisors to guide students in their search for advanced training that best fits their academic and professional goals.

REFERENCES

American Board of Forensic Psychology. (2009). *ABFP brochure.* Retrieved from http://www.abfp.com/brochure.asp

American Psychology-Law Society. (2008). *Guide to graduate programs in forensic and legal psychology (2007–2008).* Southport, NC: Author.

American Psychology-Law Society. (n.d.). Graduate programs. Retrieved from http://www.ap-ls.org/academics/programsIndex.html

DeMatteo, D., Marczyk, G., Krauss, D. A., & Burl, J. (2009). Educational and training models in forensic psychology. *Training and Education in Professional Psychology, 3,* 184–191.

Division of Clinical Neuropsychology. (2011). *Training programs.* Retrieved from http://www.div40.0rg/training/index.html

Fauber, R. L. (2006). Graduate admissions in clinical psychology: Observations on the present and thoughts on the future. *Clinical Psychology: Science and Practice, 13,* 227–234.

Ogloff, J. R. P., Tomkins, A. J., & Bersoff, D. N. (1996). Education and training in law/criminal justice: Historical foundations, present structures, and future developments. *Criminal Justice and Behavior, 23,* 200–235.

Otto, R. K., & Heilbrun, K. (2002). The practice of forensic psychology: A look toward the future in light of the past. *American Psychologist, 57,* 5–18.

Society for Industrial and Organizational Psychology. (2011). *Graduate training programs.* Retrieved from http://www.siop.org/gtp/ GtpLookup.asp

2

Graduate Students' Experiences, Interests, and Attitudes Toward Correctional/Forensic Psychology*

Robert D. Morgan

Amanda M. Beer

Katherine L. Fitzgerald

Jon T. Mandracchia

The past decade has witnessed unprecedented growth in the U.S. prison population. With the incarcerated population within the United States rapidly reaching 2 million (Fagan, 2003) and prisons expanding at an alarming rate (see Lawrence & Travis, 2004), resources within criminal justice systems have become taxed. Combined with the disproportionate increase in the number of mentally ill and substance-abusing offenders, there is an increased need for mental health professionals, including correctional and forensic psychologists, at all levels of the criminal justice system. Although overlapping in many regards, a simplistic distinction can be drawn

*This article was published in *Criminal Justice and Behavior*, *34*, 96–107 (2007). We have deleted portions of the literature review on graduate training, part of the procedures section, and a table reporting frequency and descriptive statistics within the results section.

9

between correctional and forensic psychology specialties based on the populations served. For purposes of this study, correctional psychology is the application of psychological principles to individuals convicted of a crime and sentenced to serve time in a correctional setting (including community corrections), whereas forensic psychology (specifically, criminal forensic psychology for purposes of this article) is the application of psychological principles to individuals charged with a crime but who remain in the judicial process (i.e., have not been convicted of the crime with which they are charged).

Although there has been a rise in the total number of mental health professionals throughout corrections, increased staffing has not been proportionate to the rising prison population and lags behind current mental health service needs (Boothby & Clements, 2002; Magaletta & Boothby, 2003). In fact, mental health services are so direly needed that psychologists appear to have become integral components in the criminal justice system with their contributions now regarded as essential rather than optional (Turnbo & Murray, 1997). As a result, there is increased need for well-trained, motivated, and competent psychologists in correctional and forensic settings (Harowski, 2003). . . .

*****

. . . (T)he purpose of the current study was to investigate current correctional and forensic training opportunities available to doctoral students in clinical and counseling psychology programs. More specifically, this study sought to identify the availability of practicum experiences in criminal justice settings, availability of academic coursework related to issues in correctional and forensic psychology, access to mentors and faculty with research interests in these areas, and students' interest in such training opportunities. Finally, this study sought to investigate graduate students' attitudes toward inmates as well as offender-based mental health services.

METHOD

Participants

Participants for this study were 175 advanced graduate student volunteers from APA accredited counseling and clinical psychology programs. Advanced students were defined as those graduate students within 2 years of applying for predoctoral internship. The counseling doctoral students were recruited from the 77 APA-accredited counseling doctoral programs. The clinical doctoral students were recruited from 77 randomly selected APA-accredited clinical psychology doctoral programs. Of the 77 clinical doctoral programs participating in this study, 65 (84%) offer the Ph.D. and 12 (16%) offer the Psy.D. degree. It should be noted that the percentage of Psy.D. programs in this study (i.e., 16%) is a slight underrepresentation of the total percentage of clinical doctoral programs offering the Psy.D. programs (25%; APA, n.d.).

There were 37 (21%) male participants and 136 (79%) female participants in this study (data were missing for 2 participants). It should be noted that this gender distribution is generally consistent with recent graduate school demographics, where approximately 71% of doctoral students are women (APA, 2005). The participants had a mean age of 29.1 (SD = 5.4) and were predominantly Caucasian (n = 137, 79%); however, other ethnic/racial groups were represented in this sample, including Hispanic/Latino(a) (n = 10, 5.7%), African American (n = 8, 4.6%), Asian/Asian American (n = 8, 4.6%), multi/biracial (n = 8, 4.6%), and American Indian/Native American (n = 1, 0.6%). Two (1.1%) individuals defined themselves as Other. There were 86 (49.7%) participants from clinical Ph.D. programs, 65 (37.1%) participants from counseling Ph.D. programs, and 22 (12.7%) participants from clinical Psy.D. programs. Approximately one third of the participants' training programs (n = 121, 69.1%) were within Departments of Psychology, 42 (24%) were within Departments of Education, and 12 (6.9%) departments were listed as other. The majority of participants reported a M.S./M.A. (n = 139, 79.9%) as their highest degree earned, whereas 30 (17.2%) reported a B.S./B.A. as their highest degree earned, 2 (1.1%) participants reported a Ph.D./Psy.D. as their highest degree earned, and 3 (1.7%) listed their highest degree earned as other. The mean total months of graduate school completed for the participants was 47.06 (SD = 17.94), whereas the mean total months completed in the participants' current program was 36.64 (SD = 14.95).

Materials

A two-page survey was developed by the first two authors to assess what training experiences students have available to them through their program of study. The survey consisted of four sections. Section 1 inquired about demographic data (e.g., age, race/ethnicity, marital status, years in graduate school, years in program, highest degree earned, field of highest degree) and program characteristics (i.e., type of program, academic housing of department, average number of years for students to complete the program). Section 2 assessed previous practicum experiences, including correctional and forensic experiences, as well as client characteristics such as client history of juvenile delinquency, antisocial personality disorder, and/or time spent in secure facilities. Section 3 inquired about academic program and training opportunities in correctional and forensic psychology (e.g., "How many faculty at your program engage in research pertaining to forensic/correctional psychology?" "How many graduate-level courses at your program cover topics related to forensic/correctional psychology?"). Finally, section 4 implemented a Likert-type scale format (1 = *disagree strongly*, 3 = *undecided*, 5 = *agree strongly*) to assess graduate students' educational opportunities and potential interest in professional and career opportunities with offender and antisocial populations. Sample questions included the following: "I would like to receive training in forensic/correctional psychology," "I have been or plan to be involved in research pertaining to forensic/correctional psychology," "I will consider applying to forensic/correctional psychology internship programs," "Working with an offender population would be professionally satisfying," and "I think working with offenders would be interesting and challenging work."

The Attitudes Toward Prisoners scale (ATP; Melvin, Gramling, & Gardner, 1985) was also used in this study to assess students' general attitudes toward offenders/prisoners. The ATP scale includes 36 items using a Likert-type format (1 = *disagree strongly*, 3 = *undecided*, 5 = *agree strongly*). Scores range from 36 to 180, with higher scores indicative of more favorable attitudes toward prisoners. Initial investigation of the ATP scale demonstrated moderate to high reliability (test-retest reliability of .82 and split-half reliability in two samples of .84 and .92) as well as adequate validity as evidenced by a contrasted groups method and the relationship between attitudes toward prisoners and dogmatism (Melvin et al., 1985). A subsequent investigation assessed the psychometric properties of the ATP scale and concluded the instrument has high reliability (test-retest and internal consistency) as well as adequate construct and criterion related validity (Ortet-Fabregat, Perez, & Lewis, 1993).

Procedure

Training directors from all 77 counseling psychology programs and from the random sample of 77 clinical psychology programs were contacted via e-mail requesting their participation in this project. The training directors were informed that their participation would involve providing the researchers with the number of advanced graduate students (i.e., previously defined as advanced graduate students within 2 years of applying for pre-doctoral internship) currently enrolled in their program, followed by the distribution of survey packets to these students at a later date. Training directors willing to assist with the distribution of research materials were asked to reply to the e-mail with the number of graduate students meeting the previously defined criteria.

*****

RESULTS

Practicum Experiences and Opportunities

Graduate student participants, on average, completed 5.4 ($SD = 2.67$) semester hours of practicum, for an average of 546 (mode = 500, $SD = 453$) direct client contact hours. Students earned practicum credit in a variety of settings, including (mean number of semesters and percentage of participants in parentheses) in-house clinics (1.9, $SD = 2.8$; 53%), community mental health centers (0.7, $SD = 1.1$; 40%), university counseling centers (0.8, $SD = 1.4$; 40%), private outpatient clinics (0.2, $SD = 0.7$; 10%), state/county hospitals (0.3, $SD = 0.4$; 13%), private psychiatric hospitals (0.9, $SD = 0.4$; 6%), medical schools (0.2, $SD = 1.1$; 8%), armed forces medical centers and/or Veterans' Administrative hospitals (VAs; 0.2, $SD = 0.6$; 9%), school districts (0.2, $SD = 0.5$; 13%), prison/jail facilities (0.3, $SD = 0.9$; 15%), secure forensic hospitals (0.03, $SD = 0.2$; 2%), other secure facilities (0.03, $SD = 0.3$; 2%), and other facilities (0.5; $SD = 1.1$; 30%).

Forty-six participants (26% of sample) completed a practicum in a correctional or forensic setting. Of these participants, 9 (20%) worked with juveniles, 16 (35.6%) with adults, and 19 (42.2%) with a combination of juveniles and adults (these data were missing for two participants). In addition, the majority of these practicum experiences were with both male and female offenders ($n = 29$, 63%); however, some were limited to experience with male ($n = 13$, 28.3%) or female ($n = 3$, 6.5%) offenders.

Although only 26% of graduate students are receiving practicum experiences in correctional or forensic settings, the majority are receiving experience with clients with a history of juvenile delinquency, criminal behavior, antisocial personality disorder, or a history of confinement. Participants' responses regarding client characteristics and caseloads were prearranged to assess three primary categories: current or most recent experience in a secure setting, current or most recent experience in all other settings, and accumulated practicum experiences in all settings. In regard to nonsecure settings, graduate students reported having one or more clients on their current (or most recent) practicum caseload with a history of juvenile delinquency (64% of participants), charged or convicted of a crime (48% of participants), who meet the diagnostic criteria for antisocial personality disorder (30% of participants), and/or confined for criminal behavior (57%). It should be noted that overlap exists between participants' responses regarding (a) clients who have a history of juvenile delinquency and/or adult charges or convictions and (b) responses regarding the issue of incarceration (i.e., the question of time spent in jail, prison, or other secure facilities was independent of the questions regarding percentage of client caseload with a history of juvenile delinquency or history of criminal behavior). See Table 1 for the percentage of graduate students' caseloads consisting of current and accumulated clients with a history of juvenile delinquency, charges or convictions for an offense, history of confinement, and meeting the diagnostic criteria for antisocial personality disorder.

Academic Program and Training

Graduate students were asked about the availability of research mentors and coursework in correctional and/or forensic psychology. Approximately one half ($n = 79$, 48%; data missing for 11 participants) of the participants have at least one faculty member conducting research in the area of correctional or forensic psychology. Overall, participants reported an average of approximately 1 ($M = 0.96$, $SD = 1.4$) faculty member in their programs who conducts research in these areas. In addition, 42% of students reported that at least one faculty member was involved in the delivery of mental health services to offenders.

Regarding academic coursework, 42% of graduate students reported the availability of

Table 1 Descriptive Statistics for Graduate Students' Practicum Caseloads

Current or Most Recent Practicum Case Load Not Including Secure Facilities (e.g., Jail, Prison, Secure Forensic Mental Health Unit)	M	Mdn	SD	N
Percentage of clients with a history of juvenile delinquency	20.63	8.0	29.3	161
Percentage of clients who have been charged or convicted of a crime as an adult	13.03	0.0	26.01	155
Percentage of clients diagnosed with antisocial personality disorder	4.4	0.0	11.61	156
Percentage of clients who have spent time in a jail, prison, or other secure facility	15.75	2.0	26.76	160
Accumulated Practicum Caseload (Including Practica Completed in Secure Facilities)	M		SD	N
Percentage of clients with a history of juvenile delinquency	24.4	10.0	31.2	159
Percentage of clients who have been charged or convicted of a crime as an adult	18.68	5.0	29.05	155
Percentage of clients diagnosed with antisocial personality disorder	7.71	0.0	16.27	154
Percentage of clients who have spent time in a jail, prison, or other secure facility	20.63	5.0	30.34	160

Note: Categories are not mutually exclusive, so overlap exists between participants' responses to the respective questions.

graduate courses covering topics related to correctional and/or forensic psychology in their programs, with an average of 1 ($M = 1.15$, $SD = 2.8$) course available. Twenty-five percent ($n = 42$, data missing from 5 participants) of the participants completed at least one academic class offering topics related to correctional and/or forensic psychology. In addition to academic coursework, students had attended an average of 1 ($M = 1.13$, $SD = 2.26$) symposium or workshop on topics related to correctional or forensic psychology, with a total of 68 (40%) participants seeking such opportunities.

Professional Interests and Career Plans

Table 2 [not included here] presents participants' perceptions, opportunities, and interests in correctional and forensic psychology. . . . graduate students are interested in receiving training in forensic and correctional psychology (52% of respondents reported they would like to receive training as well as have additional training opportunities in forensic and correctional psychology; 37% desired to complete a practicum in a correctional or forensic setting). Also of interest, many students (i.e., approximately 28%) are interested in pursuing forensic or correctional psychology as a specialty area, and even more (44%) would like to complete a more generalized practicum that affords experience working with offenders.

Although the majority of students do not plan to apply to correctional or forensic internships (61%, 15% undecided), a sizable percentage of students plan to apply to such internships or will consider applying to such programs (24% and 32%, respectively). A career in correctional or forensic psychology is a consideration for 27% of participants and a career plan for 17% of graduate students participating in this study. It is not surprising that safety is an important consideration for a large percentage (71%) of students when considering working in a secure facility; however, approximately half (52%) of the graduate students would not be concerned about having a therapy caseload that included offenders or clients with antisocial personality disorder. Lastly, it is noted … that graduate students harbor generally positive attitudes toward offenders and inmates as they see such work as interesting and challenging (77% of participants), provision of services to this population as meaningful (87% of participants), and inmates as a population in need of social advocacy efforts (70% of participants).

*****

Graduate Students Attitudes Toward Prisoners

Graduate students, on average, maintain positive attitudes toward prisoners, as measured by the ATP scale ($M = 130.88$, $SD = 17.55$). This total score is impressive when compared to scores reported by the developers of the instrument (Melvin et al., 1985) obtained from groups of reform/rehabilitation counselors ($M = 108.3$, $SD = 15.31$), prisoners ($M = 109.5$, $SD = 12.41$), undergraduate students ($M = 90.5$, $SD = 16.33$), community sample ($M = 87.4$, $SD = 18.47$), correctional officers ($M = 90.7$, $SD = 15.55$), and law enforcement officers ($M = 67$, $SD = 16.6$).

Hierarchical regression analysis was used to assess the influence of participants' training opportunities and experiences in predicting attitudes toward prisoners, as measured by the ATP. Specifically, we were interested in training experiences specific to forensic/correctional populations. Hierarchical analysis was used for two primary reasons: (a) We wanted to use sets of variables to represent proposed constructs, and (b) we wanted to control for the potential impact of general training or experience in predicting participants' attitudes toward prisoners. The construct of general training or experience was represented by number of months in graduate school and total client contact hours. The construct of specific applied training with forensic/correctional populations was represented by four items assessing percentage of clients (accumulated) presenting histories or current issues relevant to forensics/corrections (i.e., juvenile delinquency, charges or convictions of a crime, antisocial personality disorder, jail or prison time). Educational training was defined by responses to two items: "How many courses have you taken focusing on topics related to forensic/correctional psychology?" and "How many symposia/workshops focused on forensic/correctional psychology or working with offenders have you attended?"

A hierarchical regression analysis was conducted, entering general training experience in the first step, educational training in forensics/corrections in the second step, and specific applied training or experience in forensics/corrections in the third step. Scores on the ATP scale served as the dependent variable. Results of the analyses revealed that none of the three sets of variables accounted for a significant amount of variance in ATP scores: $R^2 = .05$, $F(2, 100) = 2.48$, $p > .05$ for general training; $\Delta R^2 = .01$, $\Delta F(2, 98) = .61$, $p > .05$ for educational training in forensics/corrections, and $\Delta R^2 = .01$, $\Delta F(4, 94) = .33$, $p > .05$, for specific applied training with forensic/correction populations. According to the current study, neither amount of general training/experience, nor specific training/experience in corrections/forensics was predictive of students' attitudes toward prisoners.

DISCUSSION

The purpose of this study was to investigate the correctional and forensic training opportunities available to graduate students in clinical and counseling psychology, their experiences in related coursework and practica, and graduate students' attitudes toward offender populations. Results indicated that almost one half of the participants in this study have access to mentors with specialized skills and research interests in correctional and forensic psychology, as well as training opportunities, including practica, in correctional and/or forensic psychology. In fact, although in-house psychology clinics, community and mental health centers, and university counseling centers appear to provide the majority of practicum experiences, correctional and forensic psychology practicum experiences appear to be as common as other specialty practicums, such as private practice settings, medical centers and medical schools, VA settings, private psychiatric hospitals, and educational (school) settings.

Furthermore, although some students do not have such specialty experiences available, the majority of students have worked with clients with a history of juvenile delinquency, criminal behavior, history of confinement, or who meet the diagnostic criteria for antisocial personality disorder. This finding indicates that although students may not be afforded specific training opportunities in correctional or forensic psychology, they are nevertheless gaining experience with related clientele. Thus, they may be more likely to enter correctional and forensic settings with an appreciation and understanding of the clinical dynamics and issues presented by offender clients. Consistent with Morgan et al. (2004), this finding also highlights the likelihood that students in varied settings will encounter clients with a criminal history. Thus,

graduate students could benefit from specialty training in issues relevant to working with offenders. Furthermore, approximately one half of the participants indicated they would like additional training in correctional and/or forensic psychology, even though many of these students have no interest in pursuing correctional or forensic psychology specialties or careers.

Given concerns regarding staffing limitations (Boothby & Clements, 2002; Magaletta & Boothby, 2003), it was encouraging to find that approximately 17% of graduate students planned to pursue a career in correctional or forensic psychology and approximately 27% indicated they would consider such a career. Even more impressive, 24% of students indicated they plan to pursue predoctoral internships in correctional or forensic psychology, and approximately 32% indicate they will consider such internship possibilities. Given current estimates that only 6% of psychologists (in California) are employed in correctional settings (Pingitore, Scheffler, Haley, Sentell, & Schwalm, 2001), the student responses in this study may indicate greater willingness to pursue such careers. Additionally, the finding that approximately 32% of graduate students are open to consider correctional and/or forensic psychology predoctoral internships bodes well for recruiting efforts given that prior interns have been satisfied with their correctional experiences (Pietz et al., 1998).

Of particular relevance for criminal justice recruiting purposes, an important issue in corrections (Harowski, 2003), graduate students, regardless of previous experiences with offenders, generally have positive attitudes toward inmates. Furthermore, they generally perceive mental health work with offenders as interesting and challenging, believe such services are meaningful, and believe that inmates are disadvantaged and in need of social advocacy efforts. However, graduate students also appear to be concerned about safety issues in working with correctional and forensic populations. Although correctional and forensic institutions are dangerous environments in which to work (e.g., Magaletta & Boothby, 2003), it is possible that graduate students are overestimating potential dangerousness. Recruiting efforts may be more effective if criminal justice administrators and academicians educate students about some of the societal myths about penal institutions and present data regarding the dangers of working in criminal justice settings compared to other settings (e.g., psychiatric hospitals, VA hospitals, private practice). As students already maintain positive attitudes toward work with inmates, it is possible that demystifying some safety issues purportedly inherent in correctional and forensic work will increase recruiting efforts.

Although results of this study are promising for the future of correctional and forensic psychology fields, this study is not without limitations. Although the response rate is acceptable, participants may consist of an overrepresentation of students with interests in correctional and/or forensic psychology. In other words, students who elected to participate may be more favorable toward correctional and/or forensic psychology than their nonparticipating peers. Although not all participants in this study indicated interests in these specialty areas (and a sizeable number indicated no such interests), it is nevertheless possible that the results of this study are somewhat inflated toward positive interests in correctional and/or forensic psychology. Another limitation of this study is the focus on correctional and/or forensic psychology training opportunities simultaneously rather than separately. Because we combined correctional and forensic psychology in the survey, information about the specific training opportunities in correctional psychology versus forensic psychology is not available. This is an issue of relevance given previous findings of disproportionate emphasis in forensic psychology when compared to correctional psychology training (Ax & Morgan, 2002). To account for these limitations, future research should investigate training opportunities in correctional and forensic psychology separately. This may be more efficiently accomplished via Internet surveys, which may increase the response rate and decrease possible response bias. Additionally, future research should contrast programs that

self-identify as having correctional and forensic specialty training with those that do not elucidate differences between specialty and generalist training as well as to further identify training in generalist programs.

*****

REFERENCES

American Psychological Association. (2005). *Demographic shifts in psychology*. Retrieved December 15, 2005, from http://research.apa.org/general07.html

American Psychological Association. (n.d.). *What is the difference between a Ph.D. and a Psy.D.?* Retrieved July 13, 2004, from http://www.apa.org/ed/graduate/faqs.html

Ax, R. K., & Morgan, R. D. (2002). Internship training opportunities in correctional psychology: A comparison of settings. *Criminal Justice and Behavior, 29*, 332–347.

Bersoff, D. N., Goodman-Delahunty, J., Grisso, J. T., Hans, V. P., Poythress, N. G., Jr., & Roesch, R. G. (1997). Training in law and psychology: Models from the Villanova Conference. *American Psychologist, 52*, 1301–1310.

Boothby, J. L., & Clements, C. B. (2000). A national survey of correctional psychologists. *Criminal Justice and Behavior, 27*, 716–732.

Boothby, J. L., & Clements, C. B. (2002). Job satisfaction of correctional psychologists: Implications for recruitment and retention. *Professional Psychology: Research and Practice, 33*, 310–315.

Fagan, T. J. (2003). Mental health in corrections: A model for service delivery. In T. J. Fagan & R. K. Ax (Eds.), *Correctional mental health handbook* (pp. 3–19). Thousand Oaks, CA: Sage.

Fagan, T. J., & Ax, R. K. (2003). Introduction. In T. J. Fagan & R. K. Ax (Eds.), *Correctional mental health handbook* (pp. xiii–xvi). Thousand Oaks, CA: Sage.

Farrington, D. P. (1980). The professionalization of English prison psychologists. *Professional Psychology: Research and Practice, 11*, 855–862.

Harowski, K. J. (2003). Staff training: Multiple roles for mental health professionals. In T. J. Fagan & R. K. Ax (Eds.), *Correctional mental health handbook* (pp. 237–249). Thousand Oaks, CA: Sage.

Lawrence, S., & Travis, J. (2004). *The new landscape of imprisonment: Mapping America's Prison Expansion* (Justice Policy Center Publication CPR04 0121). Washington, DC: Justice Policy Center.

Magaletta, P., & Boothby, J. (2003). Correctional mental health professionals. In T. J. Fagan & R. K. Ax (Eds.), *Correctional mental health handbook* (pp. 21–37). Thousand Oaks, CA: Sage.

Magaletta, P. R., & Verdeyen, V. (2005). Clinical practice in corrections: A conceptual framework. *Professional Psychology: Research and Practice*, *36*, 37–43.

Melvin, K. B., Gramling, L. K., & Gardner, W. M. (1985). A scale to measure attitudes toward prisoners. *Criminal Justice and Behavior*, *12*, 241–253.

Morgan, R. D., Rozycki, A. T., & Wilson, S. (2004). Inmate perceptions of mental health services. *Professional Psychology: Research and Practice*, *35*, 389–396.

Ortet-Fabregat, G., Perez, J., & Lewis, R. (1993). Measuring attitudes toward prisoners: A psychometric assessment. *Criminal Justice and Behavior*, *20*, 190–198.

Otto, R. K., & Heilbrun, K. (2002). The practice of forensic psychology: A look toward the future in light of the past. *American Psychologist*, *57*, 5–18.

Otto, R. K., Heilbrun, K., & Grisso, T. (1990). Training and credentialing in forensic psychology. *Behavioral Sciences & the Law*, *8*, 217–231.

Pietz, C., DeMier, R. L., Dienst, R. D., Green, J. B., & Scully, B. (1998). Psychology internship training in a correctional facility. *Criminal Justice and Behavior*, *25*, 99–108.

Pingitore, D., Scheffler, R., Haley, M., Sentell, T., & Schwalm, D. (2001). Professional psychology in a new era: Practice-based evidence from California. *Professional Psychology: Research and Practice*, *32*, 585–596.

Turnbo, C., & Murray, D. W., Jr. (1997). The state of mental health services to criminal offenders. In T. R. Watkins & J. W. Callicutt (Eds.), *Mental health policy and practice today* (pp. 298–311). Thousand Oaks, CA: Sage.

UNIT 2

POLICE AND PUBLIC SAFETY PSYCHOLOGY

INTRODUCTION AND COMMENTARY

Police and public safety psychology is a rapidly expanding field of research and practice. About 14,000 agencies in the United States qualify as public law enforcement agencies. In addition, there is a wide range of private and public safety agencies, including private security enterprises, campus police, and public safety departments housed in hospitals and other health care facilities. Psychologists play a vital role in this sphere, as in-house employees, consultants, and researchers conducting studies in topics relevant to police work. The six articles in this section offer illustrations.

The first article, by Gershon, Barocas, Canton, Li, and Vlahov (2009), reports the results of an extensive survey of police officers in a large urban department, focusing on perceived stress and how it is handled. Prior research has documented that policing is a stressful occupation, taking its toll on physical and psychological health and, often, on police families. Over the past two decades, many agencies have initiated stress management workshops, hired consultants, and set up peer counseling programs and early warning systems to address stress and prevent negative outcomes, but there are few large-scale studies to identify the sources of this stress. Gershon and her fellow researchers obtained completed questionnaires from more than 1,000 officers from various ranks. In line with other research—amply cited in the article—they learned that the greatest sources of police stress came not from dealing with critical incidents but, rather, from organizational stressors, such as perceived lack of support from supervisors. The article provides good insight into police work, what it entails, and how officers cope. Officers with the highest levels of perceived stress also tended to adopt ineffective methods of coping, such as avoiding confrontation with other officers and engaging in negative behaviors such as substance abuse and smoking more than usual. Perceived stress also was associated with adverse health outcomes. In addition, officers reporting high levels of police stress also admitted to being short-tempered and aggressive, findings that lead to concerns about family abuse and intimate partner violence. These findings are consistent with other research that finds a positive association between police work and these negative issues. Psychologists who consult with or work in-house with police agencies provide a valuable service by helping police cope with stress, whatever its source.

The five remaining articles in this section focus on topics that have received avid research attention: interviewing and interrogation techniques, false confessions, mistakes in eyewitness identification, the merits of sequential and simultaneous lineups, and detecting deception in persons being interviewed. Each article offers a concise summary of the recent findings. A common theme is that findings from the research literature have not been adequately disseminated to police and integrated into law enforcement practices.

Snook, Luther, Quinlan, and Milne (2012) take a close look at styles of police interrogation by studying transcripts of 80 interviews that Canadian police officers conducted with suspects accused of crimes ranging from fraud to murder. The traditional way of interrogating criminal suspects in both the United States and Canada has been accusatory; that is, police go into the interview session believing that the suspect is guilty and hoping to obtain a confession or, at the least, information that will lead them to better evidence than they have at hand. This approach, though, is at odds with professional literature on interviewing, which has long identified "best practices" in a wide range of situations. Among these best practices are asking open-ended questions, not doing most of the talking, and practicing active listening without interrupting. This is believed to be the best way of drawing out an interviewee and obtaining accurate information.

Snook et al. hypothesized that police interrogation would violate best practices, primarily because police have generally not been taught to use that approach. The transcripts confirmed their suspicions, at least for this field sample. Very few (less than 1%) of the questions police asked were open-ended—the vast majority were closed questions requiring a yes or no answer. In only 14% of the interviews were the suspects encouraged to provide a free narrative. The researchers also found that the interviewers did most of the talking and often gave opinion statements, speculating as to how a criminal event might have happened. Much current research on police interrogation suggests that, although these tactics typically result in information gained from the suspect, the information is not necessarily accurate. The interviewees merely tell police what they think police want to hear or provide false information based on "facts" supplied by the interviewer. "Let them talk," Snook and his fellow researchers plead.

Closely related to the above is the issue of false confession, the topic of the article by Kassin, Bogart, and Kerner (2012). Substantial research evidence shows that many suspects confess to crimes they did not commit. This sometimes occurs at the instigation of police, though not necessarily. For example, innocent people may confess to protect the guilty party or because they see themselves in a hopeless situation. Kassin et al.'s article, however, focuses on the collateral damage that a false confession can cause. Examining actual cases from the files of convicted people who were later exonerated, the researchers found that those cases in which false confessions occurred had other errors as well, and most of these errors occurred *after* a confession had been obtained. Specifically, in two thirds of the false-confession cases, bad forensic science (e.g., invalid or improper techniques) also occurred. False-confession cases also were accompanied by questionable polygraphy results and problems with eyewitness testimony, such as overconfidence of the witness in what he or she saw. Kassin et al. emphasize that a false confession should not be viewed as a harmless error in the eyes of the law.

Next, Frenda, Nichols, and Loftus (2011) summarize more than 30 years of research on "misinformation effects" relative to eyewitness testimony. Misinformation refers to the misleading or distorting information that eyewitnesses receive after they have witnessed an event. Memory is malleable, and its accuracy can be affected in many ways. Witnesses may receive information from other witnesses or from the police and then incorporate that information into their own accounts of the event. Although no one is immune to having his or her memory distorted in this way, individual personality characteristics may make an individual more susceptible. Frenda et al. review these characteristics. The researchers also note that certain interviewing techniques minimize the likelihood that misinformation effects will occur. These techniques include the cognitive interview, which has many of the same features as those mentioned in the Snook et al. article summarized above. In general, this concise article reminds us that the reports of eyewitnesses, though welcomed and valuable to police, also must be viewed cautiously.

Police lineups, using both live individuals and photographs, are a common method of identifying perpetrators of a crime. The article by Wells (2014)—one of the foremost psychological experts on lineups—considers the relative merits of the sequential versus the simultaneous lineup. In the sequential lineup, individuals (including the suspect) are viewed one at a time; in the simultaneous lineup, individuals are viewed as a group. Wells and other researchers have long promoted the sequential lineup, arguing that it is the most likely to produce accurate identification and also most likely to avoid fingering an innocent person. Critics of the procedure maintain that it is most likely to result in a guilty person not being identified, because the witness must view each person in turn and make a yes or no decision. In this article, Wells addresses these criticisms, and he issues an interesting challenge to the next generation of eyewitness researchers.

In the last article in this section, Vrij, Granhag, Mann, and Leal (2011) tackle the important topic of detecting deception in persons being interviewed. They note that many interviewers believe that they know when people are lying (e.g., by their nonverbal communication) and that many scholars have tried to teach lie-detection strategies, with little success. On the basis of their extensive research, Vrij et al. suggest strategies that might be more effective, including imposing a greater cognitive load on the person being interviewed and asking questions that the interviewee would not anticipate. When evidence is available to the interviewers, a strategic approach to using that evidence in framing questions is a promising technique.

Working in the laboratory as well as in the field, psychologists have valuable information to offer the law enforcement profession. As a group, the above articles illustrate the practical application of research findings in this important area.

3

Mental, Physical, and Behavioral Outcomes Associated With Perceived Work Stress in Police Officers*

Robyn R. M. Gershon

Briana Barocas

Allison N. Canton

Xianbin Li

David Vlahov

Perceived work stress has been defined as the degree to which workers "feel strain" associated with their jobs (Karacek & Theorell, 1990). Work that is both physically and emotionally demanding, as well as lacking in flexibility and control, has been characterized as particularly stressful (Grosch & Sauter, 2005; Hurrell & Aristeguieta, 2005; Murphy & Sauter, 2004; Quick, Quick, Nelson, & Hurrell, 1997). Although certain levels of work stress are inevitable in almost any occupation, unremitting high levels of work stress are a concern because, as

---

*This article was published in *Criminal Justice and Behavior*, *36*, 275–289 (2009). We have deleted analyses and limitations sections as well as portions of other sections, as indicated. We have also removed a table on interactions between stress and avoidance behavior.

numerous empirical studies have shown, a number of negative outcomes at both the individual and organizational levels can result (Cropanzano, Rupp, & Byrne, 2003; Podsakoff, LePine, & LePine, 2007).

Law enforcement has long been recognized as a high stress and high strain profession (Brown & Campbell, 1994; Horn, 1991; Kroes, 1976; Kroes & Hurrell, 1975; Raiser, 1974; Reilly & DiAngelo, 1990; Violanti & Marshall, 1983). Police stress is known to be associated with certain health problems, such as cardiovascular disease and depression, both of which are prevalent in police populations (Brown & Campbell, 1990; Collins & Gibbs, 2003; Franke, Ramsey, & Shelly, 2002; Franke, Cox, Schultz, & Franke, 1997). Police stress has also been associated with maladaptive and antisocial behavior, such as problem drinking and hyper-aggressiveness and violence, both on and off the job (Kohan & O'Connor, 2002; Paton, Violanti, & Schmuckler, 1999; Violanti, Marshall, & Howe, 1985). Although suicide rates are commonly believed to be high in law enforcement, careful analysis and comparison with comparable demographic groups (i.e., White males 25 to 54 years old) indicate that this is a misconception (Aamodt, 2008; Loo, 2003). However, research by Violanti (2004) on suicide ideation and alcohol use in law enforcement noted an increased risk among officers reporting both . . . .

Police stressors have been well characterized, with many of these common in other types of jobs as well. These include ineffective workplace communication, rigid organizational structure, shift work, excessive overtime, heavy workload, variable and intermittent work pace, lack of opportunities for advancement, workplace discrimination and/or harassment, poor working conditions, and frequent interaction with the general public (Brown & Campbell, 1994; Violanti & Aron, 1994).

Other stressors, however, are more specific to policing, such as the threat of physical danger and potential exposure to disturbing, even horrific events. The death or injury of a fellow officer in the line of duty is known to be especially stressful for officers (Finn & Tomz, 1997; Gershon, Lin, & Li, 2002; Jermier, Gaines, & McIntosh, 1989; Violanti & Aron, 1994). Increasingly, response to or the threat of terrorism is viewed as an important police stressor (Dowling, Moynihan, Genet, & Lewis, 2006; Paton, 1997; Paton & Smith, 1996). The effects of routine police stressors along with exposure to critical incidents or traumatic stressors may result in physiological, psychological, and/or behavioral problems (Everly & Smith, 1987; Jaffe, 1995; Quick et al., 1997; Violanti, 1981; Violanti, Marshall, & Howe, 1983). More recent research has assessed PTSD in police officers (Violanti et al., 2007). The impact of these stressors may be exacerbated in some officers who may be especially vulnerable to stress, such as those without supportive family or friends and those lacking the necessary coping skills for dealing with a stressful job (Dewe & Guest, 1990; Latach & Havlovic, 1992; Thompson, Kirk, & Brown, 2005; Violanti et al., 1985). Moreover, prior life experiences that result in unresolved personal and family issues may also predispose police officers to greater vulnerability in responding to conflicts (Kirschman, 2006; Reese & Scrivner, 1994).

From the organizational perspective, negative outcomes associated with police stress can seriously undermine the effectiveness of law enforcement agencies through poor productivity, excessive rates of turnover, difficulties in recruitment, and high absenteeism, health care utilization, and workers' compensation costs (Tang & Hammontree, 1992). Certain police stress–related problems, such as hyper-aggression and violence, can lead to public distrust and erosion of support for law enforcement agencies in general. Thus, police stress has both public safety and public health implications.

The purpose of this study is to examine the impact of a wide range of police stressors on potential health outcomes while controlling for various coping strategies in a large sample of urban police officers.

METHOD

Participants

Project SHIELDS (the Study to Help Identify, Evaluate and Limit Department Stress) represented a collaborative effort among the Baltimore Chapter of the Fraternal Order of Police, the Baltimore Police Department, and the study team. Study participants were recruited from the Baltimore Police Department, which provides law enforcement services to 700,000 residents of Baltimore, Maryland. The department serves nine different precincts and covers a total of nearly 81 sq. mi., primarily urban and inner city.

*****

The majority of the respondents were White (64.6%) and men (85.7%), with a mean age of 36 years (range = 20 to 66). Most respondents (62.5%) indicated that they were either married or with a long-term partner. The majority of respondents (84.8%) reported having at least some college education, and 35.4% reported prior military service. Most respondents (62.5%) were officers, though 37.5% were reportedly supervisors. The average tenure on the force was nearly 12 years, with a range of less than 1 to 44 years on the force. Respondents' characteristics were generally similar to the force as a whole (data not shown).

Sampling Strategy

Sample recruitment took place during roll call at each of the department's nine districts as well as at three other major divisions, including headquarters. Officers completed the questionnaires prior to going out on their shift....

Questionnaire

A five-page, 132-item survey instrument was designed to address four major study constructs: police stressors, perceived work stress, coping strategies, and adverse outcomes. The development of the questionnaire, which was prepared at a 10th grade reading level to facilitate its rapid completion, was guided by qualitative data generated through in-depth interviews and focus groups and then further refined through two additional procedures, cognitive testing and pilot testing. Wherever possible, well-defined and well-characterized scales were used, and all scales underwent psychometric validation. Copies of the study questionnaire, coding information, and psychometric data may be obtained by contacting the corresponding author.

Measurements

Police stressors. A 25-item police stressors scale, based on Beehr, Johnson, and Nieva's (1995) Police Stress Scale, factored into five subscales as follows: (a) inequities at work or organizational unfairness (e.g., "Promotions are not tied to ability and merit"), (b) discrimination at work (e.g., "Compared to my peers, I find that I am likely to be more criticized for my mistakes; I feel that I am less likely to get chosen for certain assignments because of who I am [e.g., race, gender, sexual orientation, physical characteristics]"; "Female officers are held to a higher standard than male officers"), (c) lack of cooperation from fellow officers (e.g., "There is good and effective cooperation between units"; "I can trust my work partner"), (d) lack of job satisfaction (e.g., "It is likely that I will look for another full-time job outside this department within the next year"; "I view my work as just a job—it is not a career"), and (e) exposure to critical incidents ("making a violent arrest"; "shooting perpetrator or suspect"; "internal affairs investigations"). Officers were asked to rate each item (except the critical incident questions) using a 5-point Likert-type scale (Likert, 1932). The scale was dichotomized into *"high"* exposure (5) and *"low"* exposure (1) stressors, with the upper quarter defined as "high" and the bottom three quartiles as "low" exposure. Officers who experienced a critical incident rated the emotional impact of this using a 3-point scale ranging from *low exposure* (1) to *high exposure* (3). Mean scores and other descriptive statistics were calculated for each subscale.

Perceived stress. A work stress scale, originally developed for health care workers by Revicki, Whitley, and Gallery (1993) and Revicki and Gershon (1996) and later modified and validated by Gershon, Vlahov, Kelen, Conrad, and Murphy (1995) and Gershon et al. (1999) to measure work stress in both health care and public service worker populations, was revised for use in this study. The scale consists of 11 items rated on a 4-point scale bounded by *never* and *always*. The scale was dichotomized into *high stress* (above median) and *low stress* (below median). Sample items included, "I want to withdraw from constant demands and my time and energy at work," "I feel negative, futile, or depressed at work," and "I think that I am not as effective at work as I should be." The original scales had alpha coefficients of .85 to .91.

Coping strategies. A 14-item modification of the Billings and Moos (1981) Coping Scale and the Police Coping Scale developed by Beehr et al. (1995) was used to assess coping strategies. The scale factored into four subscales as follows: (a) cognitive (problem-solving) strategies (e.g., "draw on your past experiences from a similar situation you have been in before"; "make a plan of action and follow it"; "talk with your spouse, relative, or friend about the problem"), (b) faith-based strategies (e.g., "rely on your faith in God to see you through this rough time"), (c) avoidance (e.g., "stay away from everyone"; "you want to be alone"; "act as if nothing is bothering you"), and (d) negative behavioral (e.g., "smoking, gambling, aggression, alcohol consumption"). The items were rated on a 4-point scale ranging from *never* (1) to *always* (4). Major coping style was determined by the subscale with the highest score.

Adverse outcomes. Several different scales were used to measure each of three adverse outcome domains, including (a) psychological (using a

modification of the Symptom Check List-90; Beehr et al. [1995] published the use of the revised scale in police officers), with subscales relating to anxiety (four items), depression (nine items), somatization (six items), posttraumatic stress symptoms (PTSS; three items), and burnout (using Maslach's Burnout Scale; three items); (b) physiological, with a health outcomes subscale (nine items; 0 = *no*, 1 = *yes*); and (c) behavioral, including subscales relating to alcohol use (using a modified alcohol dependency scale; three items), interpersonal family conflict (three items), serious accidents on or off the job (one item), aggressive behavior (four items), and spouse abuse (one item) (Cronbach, 1951, Derogatis, 1981; Maslach & Jackson, 1986). Several of these scales were originally developed and evaluated by Beehr et al. (1995) in a study conducted on police families and crossover stress. All scales are self-reported.

*****

RESULTS

Police Stressors

Of the five police stressor subconstructs, exposure to critical incidents (M = 2.00, SD = 0.44, possible score range = 1 to 3, á = .79) and job dissatisfaction (M = 3.35, SD = 0.54, possible score range = 1 to 5, á = .36) had the highest scores, followed by perceived organizational unfairness (M = 3.22, SD = 0.67, possible score range = 1 to 5, á = .39) (e.g., "the administration does not support officers who are in trouble"), discrimination (M = 3.16, SD = 0.66, possible score range = 1 to 5, á = .44), and a lack of cooperation and trust (M = 2.40, SD = 0.80, possible score range = 1 to 5, á = .55). Exposure to critical incidents was high, with 92.7% of respondents reporting one or more exposures. The frequency of exposure to various critical incidents and its perceived impact are shown in Table 1. Attendance at police funerals had the greatest emotional impact (66.4%), followed by needlestick injury (54.3%), being subjected to an internal affairs

Table 1 Critical Incidents in Policing

Type of Incident	Exposure to Critical Incident		Percentage Reporting "High Emotional Affect" From Incident
	n	%	%
Attending police funeral	886	82.6	66.4
Needle stick injury or other exposure to bloody and body fluids	584	54.5	54.3
Being the subject of an internal affairs investigation	696	64.9	51.7
Shooting someone	275	25.7	32.4
Personally knowing a victim	607	56.6	28.7
Making a violent arrest	960	89.5	21.4
Responding to a bloody crime scene	970	90.5	16.9
Being involved in a hostage situation	633	59.0	13.3
Responding to a call related to a chemical spill	502	46.8	9.2

Note: $N = 1,072$

investigation (51.7%), and shooting someone in the line of duty (32.4%).

Perceived Work Stress

The perceived work stress scale had an overall mean score of 1.68 ($SD = 0.48$, possible range = 1 to 4, á = .89). For the analyses, we assigned officers to either a high or low stress category, depending on whether their stress score fell above or below the median score. Demographic variables associated with perceived work stress included education level ($p < .05$), with higher stress levels reported by officers without a college degree than by those with a college degree, and race ($p < .05$), with membership in a racial/ethnic minority group associated with higher levels of perceived work stress. Perceived work stress was not associated with other demographic characteristics, including gender.

Frequency scores were particularly high for certain items on the perceived stress scale. For example, 84% of respondents reported that they sometimes or more often felt "tired at work even with adequate sleep," 70% felt "moody, irritable, or impatient over small problems," 63% frequently felt that they were "not as efficient at work as I should be," 62% reported that they "wanted to withdraw from the constant demands" of their time and energy at work, 56% reported that they sometimes or more often agreed with the statement, "When I ask myself why I get up and go to work, the only answer that occurs to me is that I have to," 54% often felt "physically, emotionally, and spiritually depleted," 52% reported that they sometimes

Table 2 Relationship Between Perceived Work Stress and Coping Strategy

Percentage Reporting	Univariate		Multivariate		
	OR	95% CI	AOR	95% CI	High Stress
Coping strategy					
Cognitive	41.4	0.75	0.59, 0.96	ns	-----
Faith based	43.2	ns	----	ns	-----
Avoidance	70.7	4.25	3.18, 5.69	2.68	1.94, 3.70
Negative behavior	63.8	3.72	2.88, 4.80	2.70	2.03, 3.60

Note: OR = odds ratio; CI = confidence interval; AOR = adjusted odds ratio. Adjusted for demographic variables.

or more often felt "negative, futile, or depressed about work," and 45% sometimes or more often felt "uncaring about the problems and needs of the public when I am at work." Of the officers, 21% reported that they would likely look for another job within the coming year.

Coping Strategies

Officers commonly reported the following cognitive problem-solving coping strategies ($M = 2.43$, $SD = 0.54$, range = 1 to 4, á = .71) to deal with the stress of their work: making a plan of action and following through (45%), drawing on past experiences (40%), and talking to family members or professionals when they felt stressed (39%). Faith-based strategies ($M = 1.35$, $SD = 0.96$, range = 1 to 4, á = .31) included relying on their faith in God (39%) and praying (32%). Examples of commonly used avoidance ($M = 2.00$, $SD = 0.58$, range = 1 to 4, á = .49) or negative strategies ($M = 1.32$, $SD = 0.34$, range = 1 to 4, á = .49) included acting as if nothing was bothering them when they were feeling stressed (27%), smoking more than usual (12%), yelling at others, such as family members (6%), and going to bars with fellow officers (5%). The percentage of officers who reported high stress for each of the different coping subscales is reported in Table 2. A greater proportion of

officers who used problem-solving and faith-based coping strategies reported lower perceived stress, whereas a higher percentage of officers who used avoidance or negative coping behaviors reported higher perceived stress ($p < .05$).

Adverse Outcomes

Psychological symptoms. Of a possible range of 1.00 to 4.00 (*never, sometimes, often, always*), the mean scores for the stress-related psychological subscales were as follows: PTSS symptoms = 1.53 ($SD = 0.41$, á = .89), burnout = 1.51 ($SD = 0.38$, á = .80), depression = 1.47 ($SD = 0.40$, á = .85), somatization = 1.39 ($SD = 0.38$, á = .76), and anxiety = 1.27 ($SD = 0.36$, á = .67). For individual items related to psychological symptoms, the most commonly reported were low energy (81%), feeling blue (64%), headaches and pressure in the head (58%), self-blame (47%), stomach pains (47%), no interest in things (46%), and pains or pounding in the chest (46%). Also, 7% reported that they sometimes thought about ending their life.

Symptoms of posttraumatic stress were common. For example, 33% of the respondents reported that they had intrusive or recurrent thoughts, memories, or dreams about distressing work events, 24% felt detached from people and activities that they believe were related to the stressful event, and 23% avoided anything related to the stressful event.

Frequency scores for specific items on the burnout scale were as follows: 33% were on "automatic pilot most of the time," 31% stated that they felt "burned out" from the job, 14% "treat the public as if they were impersonal objects," and 9% stated that they "are at the end of (their) rope."

Physical symptoms. The most commonly reported physical symptom included chronic lower back pain (35%). This was followed by foot problems (23%), migraines (20%), and chronic insomnia (15%).

Behavioral symptoms. Several behaviors previously linked to work stress were also commonly reported by officers. In all, 34% reported that they sometimes drank more than they had planned, 30% reported that they currently smoke tobacco products, 14% felt worried or guilty about their alcohol consumption, and 14% stated that they sometimes did not remember what happened when they were drinking. The mean score for the alcohol dependence scale was 0.62 (*SD* = 0.92, range = 0 to 1, á = .87). Nearly 9% of respondents stated that they had experienced a serious injury on or off the job within the previous 6 months. Regarding aggressive behavior, 15% of the respondents admitted that they sometimes "smashed things" to relieve their stress. Officers also acknowledged sometimes "getting physical," that is, by pushing, shoving, grabbing, and hitting their pets (8%), fellow officers (7%), spouse or significant other (7%), or children (7%).

Relationship Between Job Stressors and Perceived Work Stress

In Table 3, it is noteworthy that all five major categories of stressors (exposure to critical incidents, job dissatisfaction, perceived organizational unfairness, discrimination, and a lack of cooperation and trust) that were measured were significantly associated at the univariate level with perceived work stress. The strongest associations were for lack of organizational fairness (OR = 3.29), followed by job dissatisfaction (OR = 3.21). After

Table 3 Association Between Job Stressors and Perceived Work Stress Among Police

| | Percentage Reporting | | | | | |
| | Work Stress | | Univariate | | Multivariate | |
Job Stressors	High Stress	Low Stress	OR	95% CI	AOR[a]	95% CI
Poor cooperation	54.0	46.0	1.99	1.56, 2.54	1.47	1.11, 1.97
Lack of organizational fairness	59.7	40.3	3.29	2.56, 4.24	1.92	1.42, 2.59
Discrimination	57.9	42.1	2.71	2.12, 3.47	1.64	1.21, 2.21
Job dissatisfaction	57.4	42.6	3.21	2.48, 4.14	1.93	1.44, 2.60
Critical incidents exposure	55.9	44.1	2.21	2.21, 2.82	1.62	1.21, 2.15

Note: OR = odds ratio; CI = confidence interval; AOR = adjusted odds ratio.

[a]Each stressor is adjusted for age, gender, race, education, rank, and past military service.

adjustments for demographic variables, perceived work stress remained significantly associated with each of the job stressor subscales in the regression model (see Table 3).

Relationship Between Perceived Work Stress and Adverse Outcomes

Psychological outcomes. At the univariate level, all of the psychological symptoms were associated with perceived work stress, including depression (OR = 9.91), anxiety (OR = 6.12), burnout (OR = 5.82), somatization (OR = 5.44), and PTSS (OR = 3.25). At the multivariate level, both anxiety and burnout were no longer significantly associated with perceived work stress after controlling for demographics and coping variable, although depression (OR = 7.50), somatization (OR = 3.93), and PTSS (OR = 2.49) remained in the model (see Table 4).

Table 4 Adjusted Odds Ratio of Adverse Outcomes by Perceived Sources of Work Stress

Outcome Variable	% Reporting		Univariate		Multivariate[a]	
	High Stress	Low Stress	OR	95% CI	OR	95% CI
Psychological						
Depression	70.6	29.4	9.91	7.46, 13.15	7.50	5.51, 10.21
Anxiety	65.9	34.1	6.12	4.68, 7.99	ns	ns
Somatization	69.6	30.4	5.44	4.16, 7.10	3.93	2.94, 5.27
PTSS	62.2	37.8	3.25	2.52, 4.19	2.49	1.89, 3.30
Burnout	63.9	36.1	5.82	4.45, 7.63	ns	ns
Physical						
Chronic back pain	62.6	37.4	2.89	2.22, 3.75	2.36	1.77, 3.14
High blood pressure	51.8	48.2	ns	—	ns	—
Migraine	63.5	36.5	2.49	1.83, 3.41	1.99	1.40, 2.84
Foot problems	61.9	38.1	2.36	1.76, 3.17	1.88	1.36, 2.60
Heart disease	63.9	36.1	2.17	1.09, 4.34	ns	—
Behavioral						
Alcoholism	60.4	39.6	2.67	2.07, 3.44	1.76	1.31, 2.36
Aggression	69.2	30.8	3.47	2.52, 4.76	2.63	1.86, 3.70
IPV	68.8	31.2	2.84	1.73, 4.68	1.94	1.11, 3.38
Interpersonal conflict	65.2	34.8	4.27	3.30, 5.52	2.74	2.06, 3.65

Note: OR = odds ratio; CI = confidence interval; AOR = adjusted odds ratio; PTSS = posttraumatic stress symptoms; IPV = intimate partner violence.

[a]Adjusted for demographic and coping variables

Physiological outcomes. Perceived work stress was associated at the univariate level with all the adverse health outcomes, with the exception of high blood pressure. At the multivariate level, the findings were similar with the addition of heart disease, which was no longer associated after controlling for demographics and coping.

Behavioral outcomes. All five categories of negative behaviors were associated with perceived work stress at both the univariate and multivariate levels. The strongest association was with aggression (OR = 2.63) and interpersonal conflict (OR = 2.74).

Relationship Between Perceived Work Stress and Coping Strategy

Perceived work stress was strongly associated with avoidant (OR = 4.25) and negative coping (OR = 3.72) behaviors, whereas cognitive problem-solving coping behavior was inversely related to perceived work stress at the univariate level, although this association did not remain at the multivariate level. As shown in Table 2, both avoidant and negative coping remained strongly associated with perceived stress at the multivariate level. Faith-based coping was unassociated with perceived stress.

Relationship Among Perceived Work Stress, Coping, and Health Outcomes

The evidence of interaction between perceived work stress and coping styles on psychological outcomes was assessed. A significant interaction was found between perceived work stress and avoidant coping…; officers reporting high work stress and who relied on avoidant coping mechanisms were more than 14 times more likely to report anxiety and more than 9 times more likely to report burnout than were officers who did not rely on avoidance as a coping strategy.

DISCUSSION

Like a number of other police studies (e.g., Brown & Campbell, 1990; Brown, Cooper, & Kirkcaldy, 1996; Davidson & Veno, 1980), our study found that organizational stressors, *not* critical incidents, are most strongly associated with perceived police stress. This could be explained by officers expecting that line-of-duty critical incidents will occur but not expecting to be treated unfairly by their department. It may be seen as a betrayal of the trust that officers place in their leadership; in high-risk jobs such as policing, trust in senior leadership might be especially important.

Similar to a number of other police studies, including an earlier report on an older cohort of police officers, we noted that police officers who reported high levels of police stress were at an increased risk for a number of adverse health outcomes, especially depression, anxiety, burnout, somatization, and PTSS. These findings have been found in other recent studies as well (Martinussen, Richardsen, & Burke, 2007). It is surprising that we did not observe a relationship between police stress and high blood pressure (Gershon et al., 2002). This may be because officers with this health problem were unavailable to complete the survey (selection bias or survivor bias).

As other studies have shown, we also detected a strong association between police stress and negative behavioral outcomes, such as spousal abuse, aggression, and increased use of alcohol (Beehr et al., 1995; Burke, 1993; Johnson, Todd, & Subramanian, 2005; Violanti et al., 1983; Violanti et al., 1985). This is an important finding, as it addresses an area of concern that is disturbing and thus often overlooked. Given that officers have access to lethal weapons as well as training on aggression, this particular finding is troubling. Other community-based studies on intimate partner violence (IPV) have noted a correlation among alcohol, IPV, and abuse of other family members and even pets (Ascione et al., 2007; Walton-Moss, Manganelo, Frye, & Campbell, 2005). A study conducted on IPV in police families also supported these findings (Gershon, Tiburzi, Lin, & Erwin, 2005).

There are two paths to improvement: One is to improve the coping mechanisms of officers who may be exposed to stress as a part of their job, and the other is to identify and address modifiable stressors associated with policing. Both of these approaches can help to mitigate the effects of work stress among police officers. Similar to the results from He, Zhao, and Archibold (2002) and Violanti (1992), this study found that avoidant coping in the presence of high stress not only was ineffective but also led to increased scores on anxiety and burnout measures. These results differ from the recent findings of Morash et al. (2008) in a study of South Korean police officers. In that study, the authors did not find that various coping strategies influenced stress, which they suggested might be a reflection of cultural differences in communications and family dynamics common in members of a collective culture. The present findings, however, suggest an important role for cognitive problem solving skills building in law enforcement. Other innovative approaches might include Alcoholics Anonymous programs strictly limited to officers and their families and couples' retreats led by experienced police counselors. Stress inoculation training also offers a promising approach for promoting and cultivating resiliency among individuals exposed to multiple occupational stressors (Meichenbaum, 1985). Utilizing a cognitive behavioral framework, the stress inoculation approach is designed to strengthen coping skills and enhance stress tolerance by systematically desensitizing individuals to events perceived as stressful.

With respect to modifying police stressors, many unique and effective programs have been developed during the past two decades to address these. For example, several departments have police peer support programs, which seek to address work-related stress among officers (Robinson & Murdoch, 2003). These programs are staffed by carefully selected, well-trained officers recruited from the organizations they serve. The underlying assumption is that peers are in the best position to assist other peers in recognizing and acknowledging work-related stress and facilitating an intervention if necessary (Finn & Tomz,

1997; Robinson & Murdoch, 2003). Thus far, only anecdotal data have supported the finding that departments that actively address the concerns of their workforce are less likely to experience high turnover and poor relations with the general public.

*****

CONCLUSION

Employers in general are increasingly aware of the quality of work-life needs of their workforce to stay competitive and productive and to retain workers in an increasingly restricted and aging labor market. Consequently, programs on conflict resolution and workplace wellness are more prevalent, especially in some of the high-risk industries and workforces (Stokols, 1991). Similarly, it may be advisable for police departments to continue to find opportunities to improve the work environment of officers and to find new and effective mechanisms for addressing stressors in policing. Progressive police departments favor this approach and actively implement innovative strategies (e.g., providing peer counselors, encouraging officers and couples to enter confidential counseling, making structural administrative changes, adding diversity programs, changing hiring and training practices, adding critical incident management programs, etc.) to help minimize the risk of work stress among police officers. The present study's results underscore the need to reevaluate police training of recruits at the police academy to ensure they get the training necessary to meet the daily challenges and demands of police work.

REFERENCES

Aamodt, M. G. (2008). Reducing misconceptions and false beliefs in police and criminal psychology. *Criminal Justice and Behavior, 35*, 1231–1240.

Ascione, F. R., Weber, C. V., Thompson, T. M., Heath, J., Maruyama, M., & Hayashi, K. (2007). Battered pets and domestic violence: Animal abuse reported by women experiencing intimate violence and by nonabused women. *Violence Against Women, 13*, 354–373.

Beehr, T. A., Johnson, L. B., & Nieva, R. (1995). Occupational stress: Coping of police and their spouses. *Journal of Organizational Behavior, 16*, 3–25.

Billings, A. G., & Moos, R. H. (1981). The role of coping responses and social responses in attenuating the stress of life events. *Journal of Behavioral Medicine, 4*, 139–157.

Brown, J., & Campbell, E. (1990). Sources of occupational stress in police. *Work & Stress, 4*, 305–371.

Brown, J. M., & Campbell, E. A. (1994). *Stress and policing: Sources and strategies*. New York: John Wiley.

Brown, J., Cooper, C., & Kirkcaldy, B. (1996). Occupational stress among police officers. *British Journal of Psychology, 87*, 31–41.

Burke, R. J. (1993). Work-family stress, conflict, coping and burnout in police officers. *Stress Medicine, 9*, 171–180.

Collins, P. A., & Gibbs, A. C. C. (2003). Stress in police officers: A study of the origins, prevalence and severity of stress-related symptoms within a county police force. *Occupational Medicine, 53*, 256–264.

Cronbach, L. J. (1951). Coefficient alpha and the internal structure of tests. *Psychometrika, 16*, 297–334.

Cropanzano, R., Rupp, D. E., & Byrne, Z. S. (2003). The relationship of emotional exhaustion to work attitudes, job performance, and organizational citizenship behaviors. *Journal of Applied Psychology, 88*, 160–169.

Davidson, M. J., & Veno, A. (1980). Stress and the policeman. In C. L. Cooper & J. Marshall (Eds.), *White collar and professional stress* (pp. 131–166). Chichester, UK: Wiley.

Derogatis, L. R. (1981). *Description and bibliography for SCL-90*. Baltimore: Johns Hopkins University Press.

Dewe, P. J., & Guest, D. E. (1990). Methods of coping with stress at work: A conceptual analysis and empirical study of measurement issues. *Journal of Occupational Behavior, 11*, 135–150.

Dowling, F. G., Moynihan, G., Genet, B., & Lewis, J. (2006). A peer-based assistance program for officers with the New York City Police Department: Report of the effects of Sept. 11, 2001. *American Journal of Psychiatry, 163*, 151–153.

Everly, G. S., & Smith, K. (1987). Occupational stress and its management. *Human Stress: Current Selected Research, 2*, 235–246.

Finn, P., & Tomz, J. E. (1997). *Developing a law enforcement stress program for officers and their families*. Washington, DC: U.S. Department of Justice, Office of Justice Programs, National Institute of Justice.

Franke, W. D., Cox, D., Schultz, D., & Franke, W. (1997). Coronary heart disease risk factors in employees Iowa's Department of Public Safety compared to a cohort of the general population. *American Journal of Industrial Medicine, 31*, 733–737.

Franke, W., Ramsey, S. L., & Shelly, M. C. (2002). Relationship between cardiovascular disease morbidity, risk factors, and stressors in a law enforcement cohort. *Journal of Occupational and Environmental Medicine, 44*, 1182–1189.

Gershon, R. R. M., Karkashian, C., Vlahov, D., Kummer, L., Kasting, C., Green-McKenzie, J., et al. (1999). Compliance with universal precautions in correctional health care facilities. *Journal of Occupational and Environmental Medicine, 41*, 181–189.

Gershon, R. R. M., Lin, S., & Li, X. (2002). Work stress in aging police officers. *Journal of Occupational and Environmental Medicine, 44*, 160–167.

Gershon, R. R. M., Tiburzi, M., Lin, S., & Erwin, M. (2005). Reports of intimate partner violence made against police officers. *Journal of Family Violence, 20*, 13–19.

Gershon, R. R., Vlahov, D., Kelen, G., Conrad, B., & Murphy, L. (1995). Review of accidents/injuries among emergency medical service workers in Baltimore, Maryland. *Prehospital and Disaster Medicine, 10*, 14–18.

Grosch, J., & Sauter, S. (2005). Psychologic stressor and work organization. In L. Rosenstock, M. Cullen, C. Brodkin, & C. Redlich (Eds.), *Textbook of clinical occupational and environmental medicine* (2nd ed., pp. 931–942). Philadelphia: Elsevier.

He, N., Zhao, J., & Archibold, C. A. (2002). Gender and police stress: The convergent and divergent impact of work environment, work-family conflict, and stress coping mechanisms of female and male police officers. *Policing: An International Journal of Police Strategies and Management, 24*, 687–708.

Horn, J. (1991). Critical incidents for law enforcement officers. In J. Reese & C. Dunning (Eds.), *Critical incidents in policing* (pp. 143–148). Washington, DC: Government Printing Office.

Hurrell, J. J., & Aristeguieta, C. (2005). Occupational stress. In B. Levy, D. Wegman, S. Baron, &

R. Sokas (Eds.), *Occupational and environmental health: recognizing and preventing disease and injury* (5th ed., pp. 382–396). Philadelphia: Lippincott Williams & Wilkins.

Jaffe, D. T. (1995). The healthy company: Research paradigms for personal and organizational health. In L. R. Murphy & S. L. Sauter (Eds.), *Organizational risk factors for job stress* (pp. 13–40). Washington, DC: American Psychological Association.

Jermier, M. J., Gaines, J., & McIntosh, N. J. (1989). Reactions to physically dangerous work: A conceptual and empirical analysis. *Journal of Organizational Behavior, 10,* 15–23.

Johnson, L. B., Todd, M., & Subramanian, G. (2005). Violence in police families: Work-family spillover. *Journal of Family Violence, 20,* 3–12.

Karacek, R., & Theorell, T. (1990). *Healthy work: Stress, productivity, and the reconstruction of working life.* New York: Basic Books.

Kirschman, E. (2006). *I love a cop: What police families need to know.* New York: Guilford.

Kohan, A., & O'Connor, B. P. (2002). Police officer job satisfaction in relation to mood, well-being, and alcohol consumption. *Journal of Psychology, 136,* 307–318.

Kroes, W. H. (1976). *Society's victim, the policeman: An analysis of job stress in policing.* Springfield, IL: Charles C Thomas.

Kroes, W. H., & Hurrell, J. (1975). *Job stress and the police officer.* Washington, DC: National Institute of Justice.

Latach, J. C., & Havlovic, S. J. (1992). Coping with job stress: A conceptual evaluation framework for coping measures. *Journal of Organizational Behavior, 13,* 479–508.

Likert, R. (1932). A technique for the measurement of attitudes. *Archives of Psychology, 140,* 1–55.

Loo, R. (2003). A meta-analysis of police suicide rates: Findings and issues. *Suicide and Life-Threatening Behavior, 33,* 313–325.

Martinussen, M., Richardsen, A. M., & Burke, R. J. (2007). Job demands, job resources, and burnout among police officers. *Journal of Criminal Justice, 35,* 239–249.

Maslach, C., & Jackson, S. E. (1986). *Maslach Burnout Inventory manual* (2nd ed.). Palo Alto, CA: Consulting Psychologists Press.

Meichenbaum, D. (1985). *Stress inoculation training.* New York: Pergamon.

Morash, M., Kwak, D., Hoffman, V., Lee, C. H., Cho, S. H., & Moon, B. (2008). Stressors, coping resources and strategies, and police stress in South Korea. *Journal of Criminal Justice, 36,* 231–239.

Murphy, L. R., & Sauter, S. L. (2004). Work organization interventions: State of knowledge and future directions. *Sozial-und Praventivmedizin, 49,* 79–86.

Paton, D. and Violanti, J. (1997). Long term exposure to traumatic demands in police officers: Behavioural addiction and its management. In G. Habermann (ed.), *Looking back, moving forward: fifty years of New Zealand psychology.* (pp. 194–201). Wellington, New Zealand: Psychological Society.

Paton, D., & Smith, L. M. (1996). Psychological trauma in critical occupations: Methodological and assessment strategies. In D. Paton & J. M. Violanti (Eds.), *Traumatic stress in critical occupations: Recognition, consequences, and treatment* (pp. 125–139). Springfield, IL: Charles C Thomas.

Paton, D., Violanti, J., & Schmuckler, E. (1999). Chronic exposure to risk and trauma: Addiction and separation issues in police officers. In J. M. Violanti & D. Paton (Eds.), *Police trauma: Psychological aftermath of civilian combat* (pp. 78–87). Springfield, IL: Charles C Thomas.

Podsakoff, N. P., LePine, J. A., & LePine, M. A. (2007). Differential challenge stressor-hindrance stressor relationships with job attitudes, turnover intentions, turnover, and withdrawal behavior: A meta-analysis. *Journal of Applied Psychology, 92,* 438–454.

Quick, J. C., Quick, J. D., Nelson, D. L., & Hurrell, J. J. (1997). *Preventive stress management in organizations.* Washington, DC: American Psychological Association.

Raiser, M. (1974). Some organizational stress on policemen. *Journal of Police Science and Administration, 2,* 156–159. Reese, J. T., & Scrivner, E. (1994). *Law enforcement families: Issues and answers.* Washington, DC: Government Printing Office.

Reilly, B. J., & DiAngelo, J. A. (1990). Communication: A cultural system of meaning and value. *Human Relations, 4,* 129–140.

Revicki, D. A., & Gershon, R. R. (1996). Work-related stress and psychological distress in emergency medical technicians. *Journal of Occupational Health Psychology, 1,* 391–396.

Revicki, D. A., Whitley, T. W., & Gallery, M. E. (1993). Organizational characteristics, perceived work stress, and depression in emergency medicine residents. *Behavioral Medicine, 19,* 74–81.

Robinson, R., & Murdoch, P. (2003). *Establishing and maintaining peer support programs in the workplace* (3rd ed.). Elliot City, MD: Chevron.

Stokols, D. (1991, August). *Conflict-prone and conflict resistant organizations in helping, coping and health.* Paper presented at the American Psychological Association meeting, Washington, DC.

Tang, T. L., & Hammontree, M. L. (1992). The effects of hardiness, police stress, and life stress on police officers illness and absenteeism. *Public Personnel Management, 21,* 493–510.

Thompson, B. M., Kirk, A., & Brown, D. F. (2005). Work based support, emotional exhaustion, and spillover of work stress to the family environment: A study of policewomen. *Stress and Health, 21,* 199–207.

Violanti, J. M. (1981). *Police stress and coping: An organizational analysis.* Unpublished doctoral dissertation, State University of New York at Buffalo.

Violanti, J. M. (1992). Coping strategies among police recruits in a high-stress training environment. *Journal of Social Psychology, 132,* 717–729.

Violanti, J. M. (2004). Predictors of police suicide ideation. *Suicide and Life-Threatening Behavior, 34,* 277–283.

Violanti, J. M., Andrew, M., Burchfiel, C. M., Hartley, T. A., Charles, L. E., & Miller, D. B. (2007). Post-traumatic stress symptoms and cortisol patterns among police officers. *Policing: An Internal Journal of Police Strategies and Management, 30,* 189–202.

Violanti, J. M., & Aron, F. (1994). Ranking police stressors. *Psychological Reports, 75,* 824–826.

Violanti, J. M., & Marshall, J. R. (1983). The police stress process. *Journal of Public Science and Administration, 11,* 389–394.

Violanti, J. M., Marshall, J. R., & Howe, B. H. (1983). Police occupational demands, psychological distress and the coping function of alcohol. *Journal of Occupational Medicine, 25,* 455–458.

Violanti, J. M., Marshall, J. R., & Howe, B. H. (1985). Stress, coping, and alcohol use: The police connection. *Journal of Police Science and Administration 13,* 106–110.

Walton-Moss, B. J., Manganelo, J., Frye, V., & Campbell, J. C. (2005). Risk factors for intimate partner violence and associated injury among urban woman. *Journal of Community Health, 30,* 377–389.

4

Let 'em Talk!

A Field Study of Police Questioning Practices of Suspects and Accused Persons*

Brent Snook

Kirk Luther

Heather Quinlan

Rebecca Milne

Investigative interviewing researchers tend to agree, for the most part, on the questioning practices required to conduct professional and ethical information-gathering interviews (e.g., Fisher & Geiselman, 1992; Lamb, Hershkowitz, Orbach, & Esplin, 2008; Milne & Bull, 2003; Shepherd, 2007). A common observation made from examinations of real-life witness and suspect interviews, however, is that interviewers use best questioning practices rarely (e.g., Baldwin, 1993; Clarke, Milne, & Bull, 2011; Fisher, Geiselman, & Raymond, 1987; Snook & Keating, 2010; Wright & Alison, 2004). Even more disconcerting is that trained interviewers also struggle to implement best practices (Soukara, Bull, Vrij, Turner, & Cherryman, 2009). The failure to use best practices raises serious concerns about the ability of investigators to obtain complete and accurate information that is needed to conduct criminal investigations successfully and efficiently.

What constitutes best practices with respect to questioning practices? Granted, the answer to this question can be intricate because of the many components that compose professional questioning skills. However, there are a few core components that most researchers and trained practitioners would likely agree on as being fundamental for conducting thorough, efficient,

*This article was published in *Criminal Justice and Behavior*, *39*, 1328–1339 (2012). Portions of the literature review, and the discussion and a section on interrater reliability have been deleted.

and professional information-gathering interviews. For instance, most would agree that interviewers should ask as many open-ended questions as possible (see Lamb et al., 2008; Milne & Bull, 2003; Read, Powell, Kebbell, & Milne, 2009). It is also best practice to listen actively (and not to interrupt) once an open-ended question is asked so that central topics can be noted for further exploration within the questioning phases of the interview (Beune, Giebels, Adair, Fennis, & Van Der Zee, 2011). Active listening also helps the interviewer avoid repeating unnecessary questions. It is also pertinent not to violate an 80–20 talking rule (where the interviewer talks for 20% of the interview), thus supporting the "less is more" axiom with respect to investigative interviewing. ...

Despite practitioners and academics agreeing on what constitutes best practices, field studies of police interviews—especially where the officers have not been afforded training, supervision, or feedback—have shown that most real-life interviews contain many undesirable practices. For instance, research has shown that investigative interviewers tend to ask many more inappropriate rather than appropriate questions (Myklebust & Alison, 2000; Smith & Ellsworth, 1987; Walsh & Milne, 2008). In one of the first field studies exploring witness interviewing practices, Fisher et al. (1987) analyzed 11 video-recorded witness interviews and found that questions consisted mostly of closed yes–no questions—described as being delivered in a staccato style—and only three open-ended questions were asked per interview. On average, only 10% of questions composing an interview consisted of open-ended questions. Similarly, Clifford and George (1996) found that 73% of the questions asked by untrained investigators were closed yes–no questions, and only 2% were open-ended. This inappropriate style of questioning has also been documented routinely since those seminal studies (e.g., Clarke et al., 2011; Griffiths & Milne, 2006; Griffiths, Milne, & Cherryman, 2011; Snook & Keating, 2010; Walsh & Milne, 2008).

Related to the types of questions asked is the requesting of a free narrative at the beginning of an interview. The use of free narratives is encouraged when extracting information from interviewees because the free recall phase of the interview has been shown to procure the most accurate form of remembering with the best quality of detail (e.g., Lipton, 1977). Free recall provides approximately one third to one half of all information extracted during the entire interview (see Milne & Bull, 2003). It is this initial phase that allows the interviewer an insight into the interviewee's mental representation of the event, which in turn helps the interviewer structure the subsequent questioning of the interview (Milne, Shaw, & Bull, 2007). However, the extent to which a free narrative is used tends to vary dramatically across interviewers. Fisher et al. (1987), for instance, found that only approximately 30% of the witness interviews contained the use of a free narrative. Yet, more recently, Snook and Keating (2010) observed the use of a free narrative in approximately 70% of the witness interviews they examined. Although free narratives have historically been associated with witness interviewing (presumably because of the perceived cooperativeness of a witness or victim), the requesting of a free narrative is also encouraged for suspect interviews because they also enable investigators to collect information that is checkable and verifiable when searching for the truth (see Shepherd, 2007).

Overtalking on the part of the interviewer is also of concern in investigative interviews. It is generally accepted that interviewers should talk around 20% of the time during interviews (Fisher, 1995; Shepherd, 2007). There is no doubting that the time occupied when the interviewer is talking is time that the interviewee is not providing information. Myklebust and Alison (2000) reported that interviewers spent about as much time talking as the children who were interviewed. In studies of adult witness interviewing practices, Wright and Alison (2004) found that interviewers spoke, on average, 33% of the time, and Snook and Keating (2010) also found that interviewers spoke, on average, 36%

of the time. Snook and Keating also reported that the interviewers actually spoke more than the witness in 16% of the interviews analyzed. Talking too much on the part of the interviewer can lead to a reduction in the cognitive effort employed by interviewees, which may reduce the likelihood of their provision of a complete account. Overtalking may also result in the interviewer providing too much guidance or information to the interviewee (Wright & Alison, 2004). Of course, the amount of talking time by the interviewer will need to vary according to the level of cooperativeness exhibited by the interviewee (e.g., when using a conversation management model; see Shepherd, 2007). Officers may need to talk more when interviewing uncooperative than when interviewing cooperative interviewees. Given that the goal of an interview is to extract as much complete and accurate information as possible, and the fact that the interviewer was not present at the offence, it remains imperative—regardless of level of cooperation—that the majority of the talking be done by the interviewee.

*****

The limited knowledge about the current questioning practices (which we contrast with interrogation tactics and techniques) being utilized in interrogation rooms in North America provided the impetus for the current study. The goal of the current field study was to add to this body of knowledge by examining the questioning practices employed by Canadian police officers when interviewing suspects and accused persons. More specifically, our goal was to replicate Wright and Alison's (2004) and Snook and Keating's (2010) research on witness interviewing using a sample of suspect interviews. Given the lack of (and often insufficient) interview training provided to Canadian police officers (see Snook, House, MacDonald, & Eastwood, in press) and knowledge about the questioning practices used by police officers in the United Kingdom, it is expected that best interviewing practices would be observed infrequently.

METHOD

Sample

A convenience sample ($N = 80$) of police interviews with suspects was obtained from a Canadian police organization. The interviews were conducted between 1999 and 2008. The types of crimes the suspects were interviewed about were fraud (20.0%), assault (16.3%), sexual assault (11.3%), robbery (8.8%), theft and break and enter (7.5%), homicide (6.3%), and a range of other crimes (i.e., uttering threats, solicitation, mischief, verbal harassment, attempted murder, possession of stolen property, property damage, breach of security, Internet luring of a child, sexual interference, child abuse, and hit and run all occurred 5.4% or less). In 46 of the interviews (57.5%), there was one interviewer present, with two interviewers present in the remaining interviews. Of the primary interviewers, 64 (79.0%) were men. A total of 37 different primary officers composed the sample; the most interviews any one interviewer did was seven. The mean age of the primary interviewers was 42.09 years ($SD = 5.05$, range = 24–52), and the average years of policing experience for the primary interviewers was 18.96 ($SD = 5.84$, range = 2–28). A total of 76 (95%) primary interviewers held the rank of constable at the time of the interview. The mean age of the suspects was 24.48 ($n = 60$, $SD = 17.59$, range = 18–62), and 71 (88.8%) of the suspects were male.

Procedure

The interviews were transcribed by clerical staff at the participating police organization and provided to the researchers on compact discs. A coding guide and content dictionary were developed. In the current study, we coded the types of questions asked, response length for each question type, whether or not a free narrative was requested, and talking time by interviewer and interviewee. The total number of words spoken by the interviewer(s) and the interviewee, along with the length of response to each question, was determined by using the word count feature in Microsoft Word 2010.

The following nine question types were coded:

Open-ended: These questions encourage interviewees to provide answers from free recall memory. They allow for a wide range of responses, and typically start with "tell," "explain," or "describe." For example, "Tell me about the argument with your wife" would constitute an open-ended question.

Probing: These questions tap into cued recall memory and tend to generate answers that are narrower in scope compared to those provided from open-ended questions. They usually commence with "who," "what," "why," "where," "when," or "how." An example of a probing question would be, "What part of her body hit the ground first?"

Closed yes–no: These questions tap into cued recall as well, but are typically answered with a "yes" or "no" response. An example of a closed yes–no question would be, "Did he have his face covered?"

Leading: This type of question also taps into cued recall memory but suggests an answer to the interviewee. That is, the desired answer is embedded in the question. For example, the question "You were drunk, right?" constitutes a leading question.

Forced-choice: This type of question only offers the interviewee a limited number of possible responses. "Did you kick or punch the other woman?" would be an example of a forced-choice question.

Opinion/statement: This involves posing an opinion or puts statements to an interviewee. For example, "I think you assaulted Mr. Eastwood" would be classified as an opinion/statement.

Multiple: This question type involves the interviewer asking several questions at once, without giving the interviewee a chance to respond after each question. An example of this would be, "How did you get there? What did you do inside? When did you first decide to steal the car?"

Re-asked: This question type involves the interviewer asking any question that was asked earlier in the interview.

Clarification: These question types involve the interviewer repeating what the interviewee has said but forming it as a question. An example of a clarification question would be as follows: "Interviewee:

John said he went to a movie. Interviewer: Okay, so John went to a movie? Interviewee: Yes, that's right."

The aforementioned question types were coded as they appear frequently in the scientific literature on investigative interviewing (see, e.g., Griffiths & Milne, 2006; Snook & Keating, 2010; Wright & Alison, 2004), thus allowing for consistency in the interpretation of results across studies.

*****

RESULTS

The average number of questions per interview was 96.90 (SD = 70.94, 95% CI = 81.11, 112.69). The mean percentage of questions asked and associated 95% confidence intervals for each of the nine question types are shown in Figure 1. On average, 39.98% of all questions asked by interviewing officers were closed yes–no (SD = 11.81, CI = 37.35, 42.61) and 29.26% were probing (SD = 9.95, CI = 27.05, 31.47). Clarification-based questions composed 8.07% of all questions asked (SD = 5.66, CI = 6.81, 9.33).

Opinions/statements accounted for 7.40% of all questions asked (SD = 7.44, CI = 5.74, 9.06). Multiple questions composed 5.65% (SD = 4.35, CI = 4.68, 6.62), re-asked questions composed 3.15% (SD = 3.29, CI = 2.39, 3.91), forced-choice questions composed 2.84% (SD = 3.07, CI = 2.16, 3.52), and leading questions composed 2.78% (SD = 3.21, CI = 2.07, 3.49) of all questions asked, respectively. Open-ended questions composed 0.95% all questions asked (SD = 1.40, CI = 0.64, 1.26), and such a question type was never used in 49 (61.25%) of the interviews. In addition, 23 of the 37 (62.16%) interviewers asked open-ended questions. Of the 49 interviews where time of day was reported at the beginning and end of the transcripts, it was determined that the average length of interview was 33.49 minutes (SD = 25.09, CI = 26.28, 40.70).

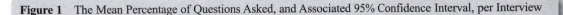

Figure 1 The Mean Percentage of Questions Asked, and Associated 95% Confidence Interval, per Interview

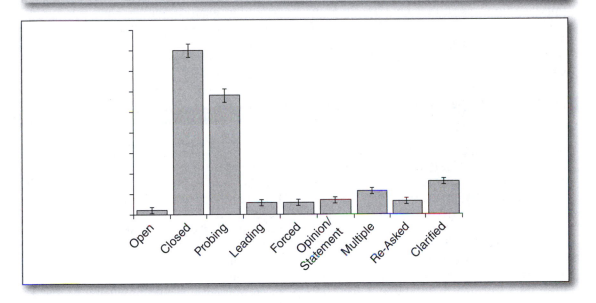

On average, 3.09 questions were asked each minute (*SD* = 1.59, CI = 2.63, 3.55).

The average length of response for each type of question asked is shown in Figure 2. The average length of response for all open-ended questions was 90.98 words (*SD* = 190.81, CI = 42.70, 139.26). When free narratives were removed, the average response for open-ended questions

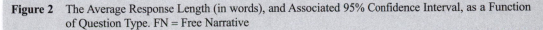

Figure 2 The Average Response Length (in words), and Associated 95% Confidence Interval, as a Function of Question Type. FN = Free Narrative

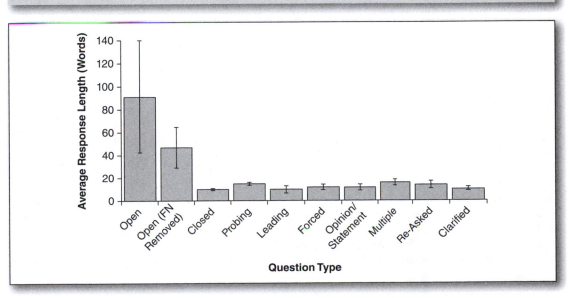

was 47.16 words (SD = 62.58, CI = 29.64, 64.68). The average length of response for multiple questions was 16.18 words (SD = 29.52, CI = 13.58, 18.78), followed by 15.22 words (SD = 28.01, CI = 14.03, 16.42) for probing questions. The average response length for closed yes–no questions was 10.24 words (SD = 20.85, CI = 9.43, 11.05). Average length of response for clarification questions was 10.62 words (SD = 17.83, CI = 9.19, 12.05), 12.10 words (SD = 16.59, CI = 9.75, 14.46) for forced-choice questions, 10.14 words (SD = 26.05, CI = 7.06, 13.21) for leading questions, 11.90 words (SD = 27.65, CI = 9.55, 14.24) for opinion/statement questions, and 13.98 words (SD = 17.83, CI = 10.67, 17.29) for re-asked questions.

On average, 55.58% (CI = 51.76%, 59.40%) of the words spoken in an interview were attributed to the interviewers. The 80–20 talking rule was violated in 100% of the interviews. Moreover, a 70–30 rule was violated in 95% of interviews, and a 60–40 rule was violated in 75% of interviews. In 47 of the interviews (58.75%), the interviewers spoke more than the interviewee.

A free narrative was requested in 11 interviews (13.8%) by nine different interviewers. From those 11 free narratives, 10 (90.91%) were requested solely at the beginning of the interview. The average length of response for the free narratives was 286.18 words (SD = 380.39, CI = 61.39, 510.97).

DISCUSSION

Our analysis of questioning practices in a sample of interviews with suspects and accused persons showed that best practices are not being followed often. In general, the overarching finding is that interviewers failed to use practices that allow suspects or accused persons to talk and provide information freely. Rather than using practices to facilitate the extraction of information, interviewers tended to ask many short-answer questions, asked few open-ended questions, dominated the

talking time, and requested free narratives infrequently. These findings suggest that there is much room for improvement in how investigators gather information from suspects and accused persons.

Consistent with previous findings, we found that interviewers almost never asked open-ended questions starting with "tell," "explain," or "describe" (e.g., Fisher et al., 1987; Griffiths & Milne, 2006; Wright & Alison, 2004). This finding may simply be because of the fact that these words are not a common part of our vernacular used to form questions in everyday life and thus may be difficult to use. It may also be because of the fact that these investigators were never trained to ask open-ended questions according to the way researchers define them. What is somewhat intriguing, however, is the discrepancy between the percentage of open-ended questions in our study and those reported in previous field studies of witness interviews. Specifically, Snook and Keating's (2010) field study of witness interviews showed that around 6% of all questions asked in an interview were open-ended, but we found that open-ended questions composed less than 1% of all questions asked to suspects. Such differences in the proportion of open-ended questions asked within witness and suspect interviews may simply be the result of random fluctuations. Nevertheless, such differences raise questions about the mind-set of interviewers when dealing with different types of interviewees.

There is much consensus among investigative interviewing researchers that all interviews—regardless of type of interviewee—should be an exercise in gathering complete and accurate information (Read et al., 2009). Previous studies have shown that open-ended questions elicit the most information from an interviewee (see Milne & Bull, 2003). Our analysis of response lengths from open-ended questions and requests for free narratives also supports this notion. The very infrequent use of open-ended questions may also be the result of a self-fulfilling prophecy where interviewers have a preconceived idea that suspects will be unwilling to provide an account on their own accord, thus they do not ask the questions that would result in a free and extensive account being provided. Some support for this speculation comes from research showing that the types of questions asked vary if there are preexisting expectations (for an example of how preconceptions of guilt lead to the use of confirmation-seeking questions by investigators, see, e.g., Kassin, Goldstein, & Savitsky, 2003).

In contrast to an expectation that suspects will always be unwilling to talk, research with offenders suggests that they may be willing to provide information if they are treated in a humane and ethical manner. In a recent study by Vanderhallen, Vervaeke, and Holmberg (2011), 126 interviewees completed a questionnaire about the perceptions of the interviewer's approach and a measure of working alliance. They found a positive correlation between working alliance and humanitarian interviewing style, empathy, respect, and interview clarity. By contrast, there was a negative correlation between working alliance and a dominating interviewing style and feelings of anxiety (for similar findings, see Beune, Giebels, & Taylor, 2010; Kebbell, Alison, Hurren, & Mazerolle, 2010; O'Connor & Carson, 2005). Future experimental research should examine how the level of responsiveness expected from an interviewee influences the types of questions (e.g., open-ended vs. closed yes–no) that interviewers ask.

In terms of the other types of questions asked, we found, as have other researchers, that nearly half of all questions asked tended to be either closed yes–no or probing (e.g., Griffiths & Milne, 2006; for how such questions may be used intentionally by interviewers to control the interview, also see Griffiths et al., 2011). The use of probing and closed yes–no question types at appropriate points in an interview is acceptable (e.g., after open-ended questions have been used). However, the overuse of and reliance on probing and closed yes–no questions to extract the majority of information is problematic because it is a sign of a controlling interview strategy, and the elicited information is tied to the specific request that often generates shorter responses than those obtained from open-ended questions (Fisher et al., 1987; Griffiths et al., 2011). Our results showed that, on average, open-ended questions (including free narratives) produced 6 times more information as probing questions and 9 times more information as closed yes–no questions. As a consequence, unsolicited information is generated rarely from closed yes–no questions, and the information gathered might ultimately narrow the scope of the investigation and provide little guidance as to whether the suspect is lying and/or is guilty (for how information-gathering interviews are useful for the Strategic Use of Evidence (SUE) technique, see Granhag, Stromwall, & Hartwig, 2007).

*****

In comparison to studies of witness interviews, the results from the current study showed that the interviewers tended to express their opinions/statements about the events in question relatively frequently. For instance, we found nearly 7 times more opinions/statements being used than what Snook and Keating (2010) reported in their study of witness interviews. We postulate that relatively more opinions and statements were used because of the traditional confession culture in countries, such as Canada and the United States, where accusatorial interviewing approaches are ubiquitous. Interviewers using an accusatorial approach try to convince the interviewees that it is in their best interests to confess their wrongdoing (for a comprehensive account of the link between accusatorial interviews and false confessions, see Lassiter & Meissner, 2010). A natural corollary of the accusatorial methods is the use of opinions and/or statements (e.g., "I have no doubt that you are responsible for the assault") to persuade an interviewee who is perceived to be uncooperative to become cooperative. It is possible that the use of opinions/statements may cause interviewees to become defensive and uncooperative if the interviewer's expressed attitudes are factually incorrect, accusatorial, and/or judgmental. Research suggests that suspects and accused persons are more inclined to deny offences and to be uncooperative when they perceive the interviewer to be domineering (see, e.g., Beune et al., 2010; Holmberg & Christianson, 2002; Kebbell et al., 2010; O'Connor & Carson, 2005; Vanderhallen et al., 2011). Even if our speculations are wrong, the expression of opinions/statements is not conducive to effective information extraction.

In general, the officers asked relatively few leading, multiple, forced-choice, and re-asked questions. It is important to note that these questions should not be asked at all during an interview because they are not conducive to maximizing the amount of information gathered. Furthermore, misunderstandings and memory contamination, which decrease the reliability of the elicited information, can occur easily. For instance, leading questions suggest an answer to an interviewee, multiple questions make it difficult to ascertain which question the interviewee is meant to answer, and forced-choice questions cause interviewees to guess the answer by selecting one of the options given (which may or may not be the correct answer), thus potentially resulting in incorrect information being brought into an investigation (Milne & Bull, 2003).

Another important finding was that the interviewers talked too much and often talked more than the interviewee. The finding that interviewers talked more than 50% of the time is substantially higher than Wright and Alison's (2004) and Snook and Keating's (2010) findings that Canadian interviewers spoke, on average, slightly more than 30% of the time during a witness interview. The domination of talking time may also be related to the confession culture, where the interviewer monopolizes the time to convince suspects of guilt and to minimize the speaking time given to the interviewee to obtain a psychological advantage over the individual (see Inbau, Reid, & Buckley, 2004). As mentioned above, it may also be the case that the assumption that suspects are not going to talk much leads the interviewer to talk the majority of the interview to persuade the suspects to confess. Alternatively, the overtalking on the part of the interviewer may also be a reaction to the interviewee's perceived unwillingness to talk, whereby the interviewer has made the decision that they will have to engage in extensive conversation to extract the desired information.

Contrary to the observations from witness interviews, free narratives were almost never requested. The 14% of interviews that contained a request for a free narrative is around half of the percentage reported by Fisher et al. (1987) and dramatically lower than the 70% found by Snook and Keating (2010). Again, this finding may be a result of the interviewing officer's belief that suspects will not talk and will likely be uncooperative. These findings are troubling because research by Lipton (1977) showed that more than one third of the information obtained in a witness interview is gathered from the free narrative. It is likely that the amount of information obtained using a free narrative with a suspect will be lower than that obtained with a cooperative witness. However, it is still likely that the use of a free narrative with suspects will lead to the collection of more information than when using other question types. In fact, we found that the average response for the 11 free narratives that were requested was, on average, 24 times longer than that provided for all other question types (excluding open-ended questions). The free narrative also represented approximately 10% of the interviewee's talking time, whereas each of the other question types generated just less than 1% of the interviewee's talking time (i.e., there was an average of 97 questions per interview). Regardless of one's belief about the cooperativeness of an interviewee, every attempt should be made to obtain a free narrative of the events in question.

There are two potential limitations of the current study. One limitation is that a convenience sample of transcripts was used . . . . Another limitation is that the current study examined only transcribed interviews. Reading transcribed interviews eliminates the context provided by many verbal and physical cues. The transcribed interviews prevent the researchers from hearing the intonation of the officer's voice during the interview . . . . As always, we encourage replication of our research, especially research that is able to examine questioning practices through the use of audio- and video-recorded interviews.

There is no doubting the fact that interviewing suspects is a key aspect of every police investigation and subsequent legal proceedings. The results of this field study showed that, for at least one police organization, best practices for eliciting complete and accurate accounts were not being followed when interviewing suspects and accused persons. In particular, the take-home message from the current findings is that investigators do not engage in interviewing practices that facilitate effective information gathering from suspects and accused persons . . . .

REFERENCES

Baldwin, J. (1993). Police interview techniques: Establishing truth or proof? *British Journal of Criminology, 33*, 325–352.

Beune, K., Giebels, E., Adair, W. L., Fennis, B. M., & Van Der Zee, K. I. (2011). Strategic sequences in police interviews and the importance of order and cultural fit. *Criminal Justice and Behavior, 38*, 934–954.

Beune, K., Giebels, E., & Taylor, P. (2010). Patterns of interaction in police interviews: The role of cultural dependency. *Criminal Justice and Behavior, 37*, 904–925.

Bull, R., & Soukara, S. (2010). Four studies of what really happens in police interviews. In G. D. Lassiter & C. A. Meissner (Eds.), *Police interrogations and false confessions: Current research, practice, and policy recommendations* (pp. 81–69). Washington, DC: American Psychological Association.

Clarke, C., Milne, R., & Bull, R. (2011). Interviewing suspects of crime: The impact of PEACE training, supervision, and the presence of a legal advisor. *Journal of Investigative Psychology and Offender Profiling, 8*, 149–162.

Clifford, B. R., & George, R. (1996). A field evaluation of training in three methods of witness/victim investigative interviewing. *Psychology, Crime and Law, 2*, 231–248.

Cohen, J. (1960). A coefficient for agreement for nominal scales. *Educational and Psychological Measurement, 20*, 37–46.

Feld, B. C. (2006). Police interrogation of juveniles: An empirical study of policy and practice. *Journal of Criminal Law & Criminology, 97*, 219–316.

Fisher, R. P. (1995). Interviewing victims and witnesses of crime. *Psychology, Public Policy and Law, 1*, 732–764.

Fisher, R. P., & Geiselman, R. E. (1992). *Memory enhancing techniques for investigative interviewing: The cognitive interview*. Springfield, IL: Charles C Thomas.

Fisher, R. P., Geiselman, R. E., & Raymond, D. S. (1987). Critical analysis of police interview techniques. *Journal of Police Science and Administration, 15*, 177–185.

Granhag, P. A., & Stromwall, L., & Hartwig, M. (2007). The SUE technique: The way to interview to detect deception. *Forensic Update, 88*, 25–29.

Griffiths, A., & Milne, R. (2006). Will it all end in tiers? Police interviews with suspects in Britain. In T. Williamson (Ed.), *Investigative interviewing: Rights, research, regulation* (pp. 167–189). Cullompton, UK: Willan.

Griffiths, A., Milne, R., & Cherryman, J. (2011). A question of control? The formulation of suspect and witness interview question strategies by advanced interviewers. *International Journal of Police Science and Management, 13*, 255–267.

Holmberg, U., & Christianson, S. (2002). Murderers' and sexual offenders' experiences of police interviews and their inclination to admit or deny crimes. *Behavioral Sciences and the Law, 20*, 31–45.

Inbau, F. E., Reid, J. E., & Buckley, J. P. (2004). *Criminal interrogation and confessions* (4th ed.). Burlington, VT: Jones & Bartlett.

Kassin, S. M., Goldstein, C. C., & Savitsky, K. (2003). Behavioral confirmation in the interrogation room: On the dangers of presuming guilt. *Law and Human Behavior, 27*, 187–203.

Kassin, S. M., Leo, R. A., Meissner, C. A., Richman, K. D., Colwell, L. H., Leach, A., & La Fon, D. (2007). Police interviewing and interrogation: A self-report survey of police practices and beliefs. *Law and Human Behavior, 31*, 381–400.

Kebbell, M., Alison, L., Hurren, E., & Mazerolle, P. (2010). How do sex offenders think the police should interview to elicit confessions from sex offenders? *Psychology, Crime and Law, 16*, 567–584.

King, L., & Snook, B. (2009). Peering inside the Canadian interrogation room: An examination of the Reid model of interrogation, influence tactics, and coercive strategies. *Criminal Justice and Behavior, 36,* 674–694.

Lamb, M. E., Hershkowitz, I., Orbach, Y., & Esplin, P. W. (2008). *Tell me what happened: Structured investigative interviews of child victims and witnesses.* Chichester, UK: Wiley.

Landis, R., & Koch, G. (1977). The measurement of observer agreement for categorical data. *Biometrics, 33,* 159–174.

Lassiter, G. D., & Meissner, C. A. (2010). *Police interrogations and false confessions: Current research, practice, and policy recommendations.* Washington, DC: American Psychological Association.

Leo, R. A. (1996). Inside the interrogation room. *Journal of Criminal Law & Criminology, 86,* 266–303.

Lipton, J. (1977). On the psychology of eyewitness testimony. *Journal of Applied Psychology, 62,* 90–95.

Meyer, J. R., & Reppucci, N. D. (2007). Police practices and perceptions regarding juvenile interrogation and interrogative suggestibility. *Behavioral Sciences and the Law, 25,* 757–780.

Milne, R., & Bull, R. (2003). *Investigative interviewing: Psychology and practice.* Chichester, UK: Wiley.

Milne, B., Shaw, G., & Bull, R. (2007). Investigative interviewing: The role of research. In D. Carson, B. Milne, F. Pakes, K. Shalev, & A. Shawyer (Eds.), *Applying psychology to criminal justice* (pp. 65–80). Chichester, UK: Wiley.

Myklebust, T., & Alison, L. J. (2000). The current state of police interviews with children in Norway: How discrepant are they from models based on current issues in memory and communication? *Psychology, Crime and Law, 6,* 331–351.

O'Connor, T., & Carson, W. (2005). Understanding the psychology of child molesters: A key to getting confessions. *Police Chief, 72,* 70–74,76.

Read, J. M., Powell, M. B., Kebbell, M. R., & Milne, R. (2009). Investigative interviewing of suspected sex offenders: A review of what constitutes best practice. *International Journal of Police Science and Management, 11,* 442–459.

Shepherd, E. (2007). *Investigative interviewing: The conversation management approach.* Oxford, UK: Oxford University Press.

Smith, V. L., & Ellsworth, P. C. (1987). The social psychology of eyewitness accuracy: Misleading questions and communicator expertise. *Journal of Applied Psychology, 72,* 294–300.

Snook, B., House, J. C., MacDonald, S., & Eastwood, J. (2012). Police witness interview training, supervision, and feedback: A survey of Canadian police officers. *Canadian Journal of Criminology and Criminal Justice, 54,* 363–372.

Snook, B., & Keating, K. (2010). A field study of adult witness interviewing practices in a Canadian police organization. *Legal and Criminological Psychology, 16,* 160–172.

Soukara, S., Bull, R., Vrij, A., Turner, M., & Cherryman, J. (2009). What really happens in police interviews of suspects? Tactics and confessions. *Psychology, Crime and Law, 15,* 493–506.

Vanderhallen, M., Vervaeke, G., & Holmberg, U. (2011). Witness and suspect perceptions of working alliance and interviewing style. *Journal of Investigative Psychology and Offender Profiling, 8,* 110–130.

Walsh, D. W., & Bull, R. (2010). What really is effective in interviews with suspects? A study comparing interviewing skills against interviewing outcomes. *Legal and Criminological Psychology, 15,* 305–321.

Walsh, D. W., & Milne, R. (2008). Keeping the PEACE? A study of investigative interviewing practices in the public sector. *Legal and Criminological Psychology, 13,* 39–57.

Wright, A. M., & Alison, L. J. (2004). Questioning sequences in Canadian police interviews: Constructing and confirming the course of events? *Psychology, Crime and Law, 10,* 137–154.

5

CONFESSIONS THAT CORRUPT

Evidence From the DNA Exoneration Case Files*

SAUL M. KASSIN

DANIEL BOGART

JACQUELINE KERNER

In the criminal justice system, confession evidence is so powerful that once a suspect is induced to confess, additional investigation often stops, and the suspect is almost invariably prosecuted and convicted. Although confessions from offenders help to solve crimes in an efficient manner, roughly 25% of all exonerations based on DNA evidence uncover false confessions—and this sample represents the mere tip of an iceberg (Gudjonsson & Pearse, 2011; Kassin et al., 2010; Kassin & Gudjonsson, 2004).

Research on the impact of confessions on decision makers is unequivocal. Mock-jury experiments have shown that confessions influence verdicts even when the confessions are seen as coerced (Kassin & Sukel, 1997), and this finding has recently been replicated in a study of experienced judges (Wallace & Kassin, 2012). Confessions influence verdicts even when the confessor is said to have psychological illness or to have been under stress (Henkel, 2008), and even when the confession is reported second-hand by an informant motivated to lie (Neuschatz, Lawson, Swanner, Meissner, & Neuschatz, 2008).

One explanation of the power of confession is that generalized common sense leads people to trust confessions and use them to infer guilt (Henkel, Coffman, & Dailey, 2008; Leo & Liu, 2009; Levine, Kim, & Blair, 2010). But basic research suggests a second, more troubling mechanism by which confessions may exert influence: by tainting the perceptions of lay and expert witnesses entrusted to provide independent other

*This article was published in *Psychological Science*, *23*, 41–45 (2012).

evidence. Over the years, a good deal of research has revealed that top-down influences inform human judgment. Classic studies showed that prior exposure to images of a face or a body, an animal or a human, or letters or numbers can bias what people see in an ambiguous figure (Bruner & Minturn, 1955; Bugelski & Alampay, 1961; Fisher, 1968; Leeper, 1935). Similarly, people detect more resemblance between an adult and a child when led to believe that the two are parent and offspring (Bressan & Dal Martello, 2002), and people hear more incrimination in degraded speech recordings when led to believe that the speaker was a criminal suspect (Lange, Thomas, Dana, & Dawes, in press). The presence of objective evidence may even exacerbate the effects of preexisting biases (Darley & Gross, 1983).

In a forensic context, recent experiments have suggested the similarly corruptive potential of confessions in influencing the judgments of experienced polygraph examiners (Elaad, Ginton, & Ben-Shakhar, 1994), latent-fingerprint experts (Dror, Charlton, & Peron, 2006), and eyewitnesses to a staged crime (Hasel & Kassin, 2009)—a set of findings that may well extend to other types of visual similarity judgments (Dror & Cole, 2010). But does this phenomenon, amply demonstrated in the laboratory, occur in the high-stakes venue of actual cases? One means of addressing this question is to compare the evidentiary errors made in wrongful-conviction cases involving a false confession with those made in wrongful-conviction cases without a confession in evidence. To test the hypothesis that confessions can corrupt other evidence, we conducted an archival analysis of DNA exoneration cases from the Innocence Project case files. Founded in 1992, the purpose of the Innocence Project is to assist prisoners who could be proven innocent through DNA testing. As of August 2011, the Innocence Project's Web site (http://www.innocenceproject.org/) indicated that 273 people in the United States, including 17 who served time on death row, had been exonerated in this way. On average, they had served 13 years in prison before their release.

Drawing from the Innocence Project's sample of wrongful convictions, approximately one quarter of which involved false confessions, we tested the corruptive-confessions hypothesis by asking three questions: (a) Are confession cases more likely than nonconfession cases to contain multiple other evidence "errors"? (b) What other types of errors are likely to appear in confession cases, and how prevalent are they? (c) In confession cases with multiple errors, which evidence was collected first— the confession or the other errors?

METHOD

At the time we first delved into the case files, in July of 2009, the Innocence Project had assisted in 241 DNA exonerations over a period of 17 years. This constituted the population on which our analysis at the time was based. Data concerning the types of evidence that contributed to conviction in each case were available from the Innocence Project Web site. Information concerning the temporal order of the items of evidence was gleaned from the actual case files, most of which include police reports, witness statements, trial testimony, and other court records. In coordination with the Innocence Project, Winston & Strawn LLP digitized this repository and made it available to us for this study.

Two independent coders counted whether different types of "contributing causes" were present or absent in each case, as listed by the Innocence Project. The coders then separately counted the frequency with which the cases specifically involved an erroneous eyewitness, bad forensic-science evidence, and an informant. In confession cases with multiple types of errors, the coders used the case documents to determine the order in which the confessions and other evidence were collected. Nonevidentiary contributing causes— notably, government misconduct and bad defense lawyering—were also noted by the Innocence Project, but because these factors were unrelated to our hypothesis concerning the nonindependence of evidence, we did not examine them. The coding did not require subjective judgment. If the Innocence Project listed a mistaken eyewitness, a forensic-science error, or an informant as a contributing cause in a particular case, the coders listed it. Hence, there were no disagreements between the two coders.

RESULTS

Overall, 59 of the 241 DNA exonerations (24.48%) contained false confessions as a contributing cause (in 46 cases, the person who was later exonerated had confessed; in 13 cases, that person was implicated in the confession of an alleged accomplice). In order of frequency, the other contributing causes were eyewitness misidentifications ($N = 180$, 74.69%), invalid or improper forensic-science evidence ($N = 124$, 51.45%), and government informants and snitches ($N = 30$, 12.45%).

If confessions have a tendency to corrupt other evidence, then false-confession cases should contain more additional errors than nonconfession cases. Out of the 240 cases for which we had data on contributing causes, 59 contained false confessions, and 181 did not. Overall, 131 of the 240 cases (54.58%) contained multiple types of errors. A comparison of the confession and nonconfession sets revealed that multiple types of errors were present in 46 of the 59 confession cases (77.97%) and in only 85 of the 181 nonconfession cases (46.96%); the difference in frequency between the two sets of cases was significant, Yates-corrected $\chi^2(1, N = 240) = 16.03, p < .0001$, Cramer's V = .27. Within the full set of confession cases, 45.76% were accompanied by one type of nonconfession error, and 32.21% were accompanied by two types of nonconfession errors. Only 22.03% contained no additional errors. In order of frequency, false confessions were most often accompanied by invalid or improper forensic science, eyewitness identification mistakes, and informants.

A gross comparison of the total number of errors in confession and nonconfession cases does not provide an appropriate test of the corruptive-confessions hypothesis. However, more specific comparisons showed that the 59 confession cases were more likely than the 181 nonconfession cases to contain invalid or improper forensic-science evidence (62.71% vs. 48.07%), $\chi^2(1, N = 240) = 3.82, p < .05$, Cramer's V = .13, and marginally more likely to contain an informant (18.64% vs. 10.50%), $\chi^2(1, N = 240) = 2.70, p < .10$, Cramer's V = .11. In contrast, the confession cases were less likely than the non-confession cases to contain a mistaken eyewitness (28.81% vs. 90.05%), $\chi^2(1, N = 240) = 89.0, p < .0001$, Cramer's V = .61.

By far, the most common source of error in wrongful convictions is mistaken eyewitness identification—a phenomenon of considerable interest to psychologists. Are eyewitness identifications associated with other evidentiary errors as frequently as confessions are? To answer this question, we compared "pure" eyewitness cases ($n = 163$) and pure confession cases ($n = 42$) by excluding the 17 cases that contained both eyewitness identifications and confessions. We found that pure confession cases contained more additional types of errors ($M = 0.91$ per confession case; $M = 0.51$ per eyewitness case). More specifically, pure confession cases were significantly more likely than pure eyewitness cases to be accompanied by forensic-science errors (67% vs. 45%), $\chi^2(1, N = 205) = 6.04, .02$, Cramer's V = .17, and also more likely to be accompanied by informant errors (24% vs. 6%), $\chi^2(1, N = 205) = 11.2, p < .001$, Cramer's V = .25 (see Table 1).

Although confession cases overall were more likely than eyewitness cases to contain one or more other errors (77.97% vs. 53.89%), $\chi^2(1, N = 239) = 9.74, p < .001$, Cramer's V = .21, they were *less* likely to contain multiple types of errors than were the 124 cases containing forensic-science errors (94.55%), $\chi^2(1, N = 183) = 8.08, p < .005$, Cramer's V = .23, and the 30 cases containing informant errors (96.67%), $\chi^2(1, N = 89) = 3.93, p < .05$, Cramer's V = .24. Hence, we wondered whether the forensic-science and informant errors

Table 1 Percentage of False-Confession and Eyewitness-Misidentification Cases in Which Other Errors Were Involved

Case error	Forensic-science error	Informant error	No other Errors
Confession ($n = 42$)	67	24	31
Eyewitness ($n = 163$)	45	6	52

Note: The cases in this analysis excluded those involving both false confessions and eyewitness misidentifications. Within each column, the percentages are significantly different, $p < .05$.

preceded or followed the confessions. We predicted that confessions taint other forms of evidence, rather than the other way around. To test this temporal-order hypothesis, two of the authors independently combed through the case files of the 46 cases in which there was a confession and one or more other errors (17 also contained an eyewitness error, 37 involved improper or invalid forensic science, and 11 involved an informant error). In each case, we indicated whether each item of evidence came first, second, or third in the sequence (no case contained all four kinds of errors). In 30 of these cases (65.22%), the confession was the first item of evidence collected; in 15 (32.61%), it was second; in 1 (2.17%), it was third.

Finally, we compared the temporal distributions of the four kinds of errors via a 4 (evidence type: confession, eyewitness, forensic science, informant) × 3 (temporal order: first, second, third) test of significance. Temporal ordering differed significantly across the evidence types, $\chi^2(6, N = 111) = 46.43, p < .0001$. Table 2 shows that false confessions and eyewitness errors were most likely to be obtained first (mean placements = 1.37 and 1.35, respectively), whereas forensic-science errors and informant errors were more likely to be obtained second or third (mean

placements = 2.32 and 2.09, respectively). Specific comparisons confirmed that confessions were more likely to precede than to follow both forensic-science errors, $\chi^2(2, N = 83) = 38.58, p < .0001$, Cramer's V = .68, and informant errors, $\chi^2(2, N = 57) = 14.07, p < .001$, Cramer's V = .49.

DISCUSSION

Confessions are highly incriminating, leading fact finders to infer guilt even when the confessions are retracted and alternative attributions are available. Basic research suggests that confessions may exert influence not only by tainting jurors' perceptions of the defendant, but also by corrupting lay and expert witnesses. Experiments have shown that a confession can bias professional polygraph examiners, fingerprint experts, and mock eyewitnesses. To determine if this phenomenon might also occur in actual cases, we compared wrongful convictions that did and did not contain a confession. Results were consistent with the corruption hypothesis: Multiple errors were more likely to exist in confession cases than in eyewitness cases; in order of frequency, confessions were accompanied by invalid or improper forensic science, eyewitness misidentifications, and informant errors; and in cases containing multiple errors, confessions were more likely to be obtained first rather than later in the investigation.

Confessions are not the only form of evidence persuasive enough to corrupt. Since the first wave of DNA exonerations, it has been clear that eyewitness mistakes constitute the most common problem (Wells, Memon, & Penrod, 2006; Wells et al., 1998). In our sample, it is striking that many cases contained not one but two or more mistaken witnesses. In some instances, multiple errors could have occurred independently, especially when the suspect physically resembled the perpetrator. In other instances, however, eyewitnesses may have influenced one another (Gabbert, Memon, & Allan, 2003; Shaw, Garven, & Wood, 1997; Skagerberg, 2007). To further complicate matters, eyewitnesses tainted

Table 2 Temporal Order of the Evidence in the 46 Multiple-Error Cases Containing a Confession

Evidence type	Obtained first	Obtained second	Obtained third	Mean sequential position
Confession	30	15	1	1.37$_a$
Eyewitness	12	4	1	1.35$_a$
Informant	3	4	4	2.09$_b$
Forensic science	1	23	13	2.32$_c$

Note: Cell entries represent numbers of cases. Means not sharing a common subscript are significantly different, $p < .05$.

by extrinsic information cannot accurately estimate the extent of that influence, which suggests that self-report cannot be used to diagnose corruption once it occurs (Charman & Wells, 2008).

It is interesting and disturbing that the most common means of corroboration for false confessions comes from bad forensic science—which was present in nearly two thirds of the confession cases we examined. As a result of scandalous improprieties in several crime laboratories and the frequency with which forensic-science errors had surfaced in wrongful convictions, the National Academy of Sciences (2009) was highly critical of a broad range of forensic disciplines, such as ballistics, hair and fiber analysis, impression evidence, handwriting analysis, and even fingerprint analysis. The academy concluded that there are problems with standardization, reliability, accuracy and error, and the potential for contextual bias. Clearly, the presence of a confession constitutes the kind of strong contextual bias that can skew expert judgments in these domains.

In cases in which a confession preceded other erroneous evidence, the mechanism of influence—if one is to be inferred from these correlations—is not known. One possibility is that subsequent witnesses were corrupted by mere knowledge of the confession and the cognitive confirmation biases resulting from the consequent belief in the suspect's guilt. A second possibility is

that knowledge of the confession increased their motivation to help police and prosecutors implicate the presumed-guilty suspect. Indeed, recent studies indicate that just as people tend to see what they expect to see, they also tend to see what they *want* to see (Balcetis & Dunning, 2006). A third possibility is that police and prosecutors sought out support for previously taken, recanted, and disputed confessions. This mechanism is suggested by research showing that nonblind mock investigators (i.e., those who know which lineup member is the suspect) often lead witnesses, albeit inadvertently, to falsely identify their suspect within a lineup (Greathouse & Kovera, 2009). Without delving into the often unknown details of the cases in our sample and making subjective judgments about the mental states of investigators and witnesses, it is not possible to tease apart these possible sources of influence.

We have reason to believe that the present analysis may have underestimated the more general problem of evidence corruption in two important ways. First, confessions might spawn incriminating evidence of sorts that we did not address in our study (e.g., additional confessions by codefendants). Moreover, false confessions may serve to suppress exculpatory evidence—an effect that would not be detectable in our study. At present, only anecdotal data are available on this point. In one case, for example, John Kogut, who was eventually exonerated on the basis of DNA evidence, had alibi witnesses who withdrew their support once told by police that he had confessed. In a second case, Barry Laughman confessed to rape and murder. When two witnesses insisted that they had seen the victim alive after the confessed murder, police sent them home and said that they must have seen a ghost. Additional systematic research is needed to determine the prevalence with which exculpatory evidence is suppressed by confession.

A second way in which our analysis may have underestimated the problem is in our exclusive and unidirectional focus on confessions as a corruptive agent. Confessions are powerfully persuasive. As noted earlier, however, many wrongful-conviction cases involve mistaken eyewitnesses, and often more than one per case. Therefore, it might be useful to examine DNA exoneration cases to determine whether different witnesses were corrupted by one another. Our analyses also revealed that eyewitness mistakes often precede false confessions when the two co-occur, thus suggesting the broader conclusion that strong evidence of any sort can corrupt judgments, testimony, and even confessions themselves. This latter notion in particular receives anecdotal support from numerous cases in which innocents were induced to confess to police by the true or false presentation of an eyewitness, physical evidence, failed polygraph, or other incriminating evidence (Gudjonsson & Pearse, 2011; Kassin et al., 2010).

It is important to note that this study was based on a dynamic and fluid data set. In drawing from DNA exoneration case files, we took an archival "snapshot" of 241 cases in which the contributing causes of conviction were identified by the Innocence Project. As the numbers of DNA exoneration cases have increased, there has been a great deal of consistency in the data (e.g., the percentages of false confessions and eyewitness errors have remained stable over time). Precise frequencies and patterns may fluctuate from one snapshot to another, however, whenever new cases are added to the data set and new information about old cases is discovered. For this reason, researchers who use this database should consider periodic reexamination of their results.

Finally, our findings have profound implications for criminal law and the safety nets designed to prevent miscarriages of justice. In a pretrial rule founded in common law in England, many states require that confessions be corroborated by independent evidence as a precondition for admissibility. At the appellate level, courts may determine that although a confession was coerced and erroneously admitted at trial, the conviction may stand if that error was "harmless"—as measured by whether the remaining evidence alone was sufficient to support a jury's conviction. Both corroboration and harmless error rest on the assumption that the other evidence on record is independent of the confession. Yet our results suggest that this assumption is incorrect, that the other evidence may be tainted, and that the appearances of corroboration and sufficiency may be more illusory than real.

REFERENCES

Balcetis, E., & Dunning, D. (2006). See what you want to see: Motivational influences on visual perception. *Journal of Personality and Social Psychology, 91*, 612–625.

Bressan, P., & Dal Martello, M. F. (2002). *Talis pater, talis filius:* Perceived resemblance and the belief in genetic relatedness. *Psychological Science, 13*, 213–218.

Bruner, J. S., & Minturn, A. L. (1955). Perceptual identification and perceptual organization. *Journal of General Psychology, 53*, 21–28.

Bugelski, B. R., & Alampay, D. A. (1961). The role of frequency in developing perceptual sets. *Canadian Journal of Psychology, 15*, 205–211.

Charman, S. D., & Wells, G. L. (2008). Can eyewitnesses correct for external influences on their lineup identifications? The actual/counterfactual assessment paradigm. *Journal of Experimental Psychology: Applied, 14*, 5–20.

Darley, J., & Gross, P. H. (1983). A hypothesis confirming bias in labeling effects. *Journal of Personality and Social Psychology, 44*, 20–33.

Dror, I. E., Charlton, D., & Peron, A. (2006). Contextual information renders experts vulnerable to making erroneous identifications. *Forensic Science International*, *156*, 74–78.

Dror, I. E., & Cole, S. A. (2010). The vision in "blind" justice: Expert perception, judgment, and visual cognition in forensic pattern recognition. *Psychonomic Bulletin & Review*, *17*, 161–167.

Elaad, E., Ginton, A., & Ben-Shakhar, G. (1994). The effects of prior expectations and outcome knowledge on polygraph examiners' decisions. *Journal of Behavioral Decision Making*, *7*, 279–292.

Fisher, G. (1968). Ambiguity of form: Old and new. *Perception & Psychophysics*, *4*, 189–192.

Gabbert, F., Memon, A., & Allan, K. (2003). Memory conformity: Can eyewitnesses influence each other's memories for an event? *Applied Cognitive Psychology*, *17*, 533–543.

Greathouse, S. M., & Kovera, M. B. (2009). Instruction bias and lineup presentation moderate the effects of administrator knowledge on eyewitness identification. *Law and Human Behavior*, *33*, 70–82.

Gudjonsson, G. H., & Pearse, J. (2011). Suspect interviews and false confessions. *Current Directions in Psychological Science*, *20*, 33–37.

Hasel, L. E., & Kassin, S. M. (2009). On the presumption of evidentiary independence: Can confessions corrupt eyewitness identifications? *Psychological Science*, *20*, 122–126.

Henkel, L. A. (2008). Jurors' reactions to recanted confessions: Do the defendant's personal and dispositional characteristics play a role? *Psychology, Crime & Law*, *14*, 565–578.

Henkel, L. A., Coffman, K. A. J., & Dailey, E. M. (2008). A survey of people's attitudes and beliefs about false confessions. *Behavioral Sciences & the Law*, *26*, 555–584.

Kassin, S. M., Drizin, S. A., Grisso, T., Gudjonsson, G. H., Leo, R. A., & Redlich, A. D. (2010). Police-induced confessions: Risk factors and recommendations. *Law and Human Behavior*, *34*, 49–52.

Kassin, S. M., & Gudjonsson, G. H. (2004). The psychology of confession evidence: A review of the literature and issues. *Psychological Science in the Public Interest*, *5*, 35–69.

Kassin, S. M., & Sukel, H. (1997). Coerced confessions and the jury: An experimental test of the "harmless error" rule. *Law and Human Behavior*, *21*, 27–46.

Lange, N. D., Thomas, R. P., Dana, J., & Dawes, R. M. (2011). Contextual biases in the interpretation of auditory evidence. *Law and Human Behavior*, *35*, 178–187.

Leeper, R. (1935). A study of a neglected portion of the field of learning: The development of sensory organization. *Journal of Genetic Psychology*, *46*, 41–75.

Leo, R. A., & Liu, B. (2009). What do potential jurors know about police interrogation techniques and false confessions? *Behavioral Sciences & the Law*, *27*, 381–399.

Levine, T. R., Kim, R. K., & Blair, J. P. (2010). (In) accuracy at detecting true and false confessions and denials: An initial test of a projected motive model of veracity judgments. *Human Communication Research*, *36*, 81–101.

National Academy of Sciences. (2009). *Strengthening forensic science in the United States: A path forward*. Washington, DC: National Academies Press.

Neuschatz, J. S., Lawson, D. S., Swanner, J. K., Meissner, C. A., & Neuschatz, J. S. (2008). The effects of accomplice witnesses and jailhouse informants on jury decision making. *Law and Human Behavior*, *32*, 137–149.

Shaw, J. S., Garven, S., & Wood, J. M. (1997). Co-witness information can have immediate effects on eyewitness memory reports. *Law and Human Behavior*, *5*, 503–521.

Skagerberg, E. M. (2007). Co-witness feedback in lineups. *Applied Cognitive Psychology*, *21*, 489–497.

Wallace, D. B., & Kassin, S. M. (2012). Harmless error analysis: How do judges respond to confession errors? *Law and Human Behavior*, *36*, 151–157.

Wells, G. L., Memon, A., & Penrod, S. D. (2006). Eyewitness evidence: Improving its probative value. *Psychological Science in the Public Interest*, *7*, 45–75.

Wells, G. L., Small, M., Penrod, S., Malpass, R., Fulero, S., & Brimacombe, C. A. E. (1998). Eyewitness identification procedures: Recommendations for lineups and photospreads. *Law and Human Behavior*, *22*, 603–647.

6

CURRENT ISSUES AND ADVANCES IN MISINFORMATION RESEARCH*

STEVEN J. FRENDA

REBECCA M. NICHOLS

ELIZABETH F. LOFTUS

Twenty-five people died when a Metrolink commuter train collided with a Union Pacific freight train near Los Angeles in September of 2008 (Steinhauer, 2008). With millions of dollars in lawsuit payouts at stake, federal accident authorities began an investigation of the deadly crash and had to decide a key issue: Did the conductor pass legally through a green light, as four eyewitnesses maintained? Or did he sail through a red light, distracted by sending and receiving text messages? The conductor died in the crash, so he could not be asked. If he were at fault, the railroad company that was responsible for hiring and supervising him would be liable. If the signal malfunctioned, another company would be on the hook. After an extensive investigation, the authorities decided the eyewitnesses were wrong. The signal was red, and the engineer's text messaging was a major contributor to the accident. Is it possible that four eyewitnesses—including a conductor, a security guard, and two railroad enthusiasts—were all mistaken about such a crucial detail? The answer is yes. Eyewitnesses make mistakes, multiple eyewitnesses can all be wrong, and their erroneous testimony can have enormous consequences.

How is it possible that so many witnesses could all be so wrong? Eyewitnesses are called upon not only to remember details of events but also to describe what people look like and to decide how confident they are in the accuracy of their memories. They are often asked to remember things they saw in extremely stressful circumstances, sometimes months or even years after the fact. They are frequently bombarded with information following the event they witnessed, such as other witnesses' reports, investigator feedback, leading questions, and pressures to be both accurate and helpful. In the

*This article was published in *Current Directions in Psychological Science*, 20, 20–23 (2011).

face of these challenges, eyewitnesses misremember. In a recent discussion of the distorting effect witnesses have on the memory of other witnesses, Wright, Memon, Skagerberg, and Gabbert (2009) proposed three accounts of why eyewitnesses come to report incorrect information. First, a witness's report may be altered due to normative social influence. That is, a witness may decide that the cost of disagreeing with law enforcement—or with other witnesses—is too high, and so he adjusts his report accordingly. A second possibility is that through informational social influence processes, a witness comes to endorse a version of events that is different from what he remembers because he believes it to be truer or more accurate than his own memory. Finally, a witness's memory can become distorted, sometimes as the result of being exposed to incorrect or misleading information. This third possibility, known as the misinformation effect, is the focus of the current review. Advances in misinformation research concerning individual differences, neurophysiological correlates, cognitive interviewing, and related research paradigms are reviewed.

What Is the Misinformation Effect?

In the wake of more than 30 years of research, an ever-growing literature continues to demonstrate the distorting effects of misleading postevent information on memory for words, faces, and details of witnessed events (see Loftus, 2005, for a review of the misinformation effect). In a typical misinformation experiment, research subjects are shown materials (e.g., photographs) and are then exposed to deliberately misleading information about what they saw. In a final testing phase, many subjects will inadvertently incorporate elements from the misleading information into their memory for the original source material. For example, Stark, Okado, and Loftus (2010) showed subjects a series of photographs that depicted a man stealing a woman's wallet and hiding it in his jacket pocket. Later, subjects heard recorded narratives describing the slides. Embedded in the narratives were several pieces of misleading information (e.g., "Then the man hid the wallet in his pants pocket"). Finally, subjects were asked questions about details from the photographs, such as "Where did the thief hide the woman's wallet?" A substantial number of those subjects not only reported that the thief hid the wallet in his pants pocket but they also reported that they remembered that information from the photographs, not the narratives.

Who Is Vulnerable?

Nobody is immune to the distorting effects of misinformation. Building on the adult literature, misinformation effects have been obtained in myriad subject samples, including infants (Rovee-Collier, Borza, Adler, & Boller, 1993), and even animals (e.g., Schwartz, Meissner, Hoffman, Evans, & Frazier, 2004). Nonetheless, there is evidence that certain types of people are especially vulnerable to misinformation effects. For instance, very young children and the elderly are more susceptible to misinformation than adolescents and adults (see Davis & Loftus, 2005). Also especially vulnerable are subjects who report lapses in memory and attention (Wright & Livingston-Raper, 2002). What do these findings tell us about the underlying mechanisms driving the misinformation effect? One argument is that a poverty of cognitive resources necessitates an increased reliance on external cues to reconstruct memories of events. As Loftus (2005) points out, misinformation effects are easier to obtain when subjects' attentional resources are limited. Similarly, people who perceive themselves to be forgetful and who experience memory lapses may be less able (or willing) to depend on their own memories as the sole source of information as they mentally reconstruct an event.

Recently, two major studies containing more than 400 subjects have explored cognitive ability and personality factors as predictors of susceptibility to misinformation. In each study, subjects viewed slides of two crimes and later read narratives of the crimes that contained misinformation.

Those subjects who had higher intelligence scores, greater perceptual abilities, greater working memory capacities, and greater performance on face recognition tasks tended to resist misinformation and produce fewer false memories (Zhu et al., 2010a). Certain personality characteristics were also shown to be associated with false memory formation, particularly in individuals with lesser cognitive ability. Specifically, individuals low in fear of negative evaluation and harm avoidance, and those high in cooperativeness, reward dependence, and self-directedness were associated with an increased vulnerability to misinformation effects (Zhu et al., 2010b). In other words, it seems that personality variables may be helpful in understanding the processes underlying memory distortion following exposure to misinformation but less so in individuals with superior cognitive ability. These interactions may help explain why individual difference results have not always replicated in false memory research.

MISINFORMATION AND NEUROIMAGING

Relatively new but increasingly popular tools for exploring the effects of postevent information on memory include a set of highly specialized neuroscientific methods which include functional magnetic resonance imaging, or fMRI. In a typical fMRI-based behavioral experiment, subjects undergo traditional experimental procedures in an MRI scanner, during which functional images of oxygenated blood flow in the brain are collected. The resulting images can be analyzed and interpreted as differential brain activation associated with particular tasks. Functional MRI, therefore, is a useful and noninvasive tool for examining the neurobiological correlates of behavior.

Scientists have begun to investigate brain activity associated with the misinformation effect. In a recent study (Stark et al., 2010), subjects were shown a series of photographs and later listened to an auditory narrative describing them, which included misleading information. Soon afterward, they were placed into an MRI scanner and given a test of their memory for the photographs. Functional neuroimaging data revealed similar patterns of brain activity for true and false memories, but the true memories (formed by visual information) showed somewhat more activation in the visual cortex while the false memories (derived from the auditory narrative) showed somewhat more activation in the auditory cortex. As the researchers noted, these results are congruent with the sensory reactivation hypothesis (Slotnick & Schacter, 2004, 2006), which in part proposes that the same sensory regions activated in the brain during encoding will be reactivated during retrieval. These results suggest that there may be differing brain activation patterns for true and false memories when they are encoded in different sensory modalities.

Research that involves neuroimaging and other neuroscientific measurement techniques are promising for discoveries about the effects of misinformation on memory: They can provide glimpses into how different neurological processes underlie true and false memories. At the present time, however, it would be wise to err on the side of caution in the application of these findings. Although some differences were found, the patterns of brain activation associated with true and false memories in Stark et al.'s (2010) study were not reliably distinct, and other small differences in brain activation (unrelated to the sensory reactivation hypothesis) were not fully accounted for. Furthermore, data from fMRI studies are often averaged both within and across participants, which makes interpretation at the individual level of analysis difficult. Although functional neuroimaging is elaborate and cutting edge, it has yet to provide a sure-fire way to confidently judge whether or not a particular person's memory is accurate.

PROTECTING AGAINST MISINFORMATION EFFECTS

Not surprisingly, some effort has been focused on ways to protect against the distorting effect of misinformation. One technique for improving the accuracy and completeness of an eyewitness's recollection is known as the cognitive interview, a set of rules and guidelines for interviewing eyewitnesses (see Wells, Memon, & Penrod, 2006, for a review). The CI recommends, for example, the use of free recall, contextual cues, temporal ordering of events, and recalling the event from a variety of perspectives (such as from a perpetrator's point of view). Also, the CI recommends that investigators avoid suggestive questioning, develop rapport with the witness, and discourage witnesses from guessing. In one recent study, subjects viewed an 8-minute film depicting a robbery (Memon, Zaragoza, Clifford, & Kidd, 2009). Later, subjects were given either a CI or a free-response control interview, followed by suggestive questioning about events not depicted in the film. Results indicated that, consistent with earlier findings, the CI produced more correct details than did the free-response procedure. One week after the interview procedure, subjects were given a recognition test for items in the video, and subjects incorporated details from the suggestive questioning into their memory for the event. Results showed that the CI deterred the effects of suggestion, but only when it came before the suggestive interview. Though the investigative process would ideally be free of all suggestive influence, a properly implemented cognitive interview may help protect the integrity of an eyewitness's memory.

RELATED LINES OF RESEARCH

In addition to the classic misinformation paradigm, researchers have developed other ways to demonstrate that even the subtlest suggestions can produce astonishing false witness reports. For instance, a handful of studies have emerged in which subjects are simply asked if they have seen video footage of well-known news events, when in fact no such video footage exists. One study found that 40% of a British sample was willing to report having seen nonexistent footage of a bus exploding in the 2005 London terrorist attacks (Ost, Granhag,

Udell, & Hjelmsäter, 2008). Of the subjects who claimed they saw the footage, 35% described memories of details that they could not have seen. Another study (Sjödén, Granhag, Ost, & Hjelmsäter, 2009) found that 64% of a Swedish sample claimed to have seen nonexistent video footage of an attack on the Swedish foreign minister, and 19% went on to describe details in the form of written narratives. The ease with which these studies elicited blatantly false memory reports is striking.

Research has also shown that suggestion can also shape autobiographical memory. Beginning with Loftus and Pickrell's Lost in the Mall study (1995), a series of studies have successfully used personalized suggestion (or other suggestive techniques) to plant false memories of traumatic childhood events (Porter, Yuille, & Lehman, 1999), receiving a painful enema (Hart & Schooler, 2006), and even impossible events such as meeting Bugs Bunny—a Warner Brothers character—at Disneyland (Braun, Ellis, & Loftus, 2002). These lines of research represent a broad area in their own right, with controversies and applications that are beyond the scope of this paper. However, they show that misleading postevent information has implications beyond merely mistaking a green traffic light for a red one or misremembering where a pickpocket hid a woman's wallet. If suggestion can cause us to remember experiences that never occurred, what does this say about the reliability of eyewitness evidence in general? If merely asking people if they have seen events they could not possibly have witnessed represents a strong enough suggestion to cause such staggering errors, what are the implications for witnesses who were present at a crime scene but never saw a perpetrator's face, only to hear it described later? Researchers continue to investigate what conditions lead to memory distortion, which types of people are most susceptible, and how best to prevent the distorting effects of postevent information. Unfortunately, in spite of recent scientific advances, many eyewitness errors continue to go undetected and can have devastating consequences.

REFERENCES

Braun, K. A., Ellis, R., & Loftus, E. F. (2002). Make my memory: How advertising can change our memories of the past. *Psychology & Marketing*, *19*, 1–23.

Davis, D., & Loftus, E. F. (2005). Age and functioning in the legal system: Perception memory and judgment in victims, witnesses and jurors. In I. Noy & W. Karwowski (Eds.), *Handbook of forensic human factors and ergonomics*. London, England: Taylor & Francis.

Hart, R. E., & Schooler, J. W. (2006). Increasing belief in the experience of an invasive procedure that never happened: The role of plausibility and schematicity. *Applied Cognitive Psychology*, *20*, 661–669.

Loftus, E. F. (2005). Planting misinformation in the human mind: A 30-year investigation of the malleability of memory. *Learning and Memory*, *12*, 361–366.

Loftus, E. F., & Pickrell, J. E. (1995). The formation of false memories. *Psychiatric Annals*, *25*, 720–725.

Memon, A., Zaragoza, M., Clifford, B. R., & Kidd, L. (2009). Inoculation or antidote? The effects of cognitive interview timing on false memory for forcibly fabricated events. *Law and Human Behavior*, *34*, 105–117.

Ost, J., Granhag, P., Udell, J., & Hjelmsäter, E. R. (2008). Familiarity breeds distortion: The effects of media exposure on false reports concerning media coverage of the terrorist attacks in London on 7 July 2005. *Memory*, *16*, 76–85.

Porter, S., Yuille, J. C., & Lehman, D. R. (1999). The nature of real, implanted, and fabricated memories for emotional childhood events: Implications for the recovered memory debate. *Law and Human Behavior*, *23*, 517–537.

Rovee-Collier, C., Borza, M. A., Adler, S. A., & Boller, K. (1993). Infants' eyewitness testimony: Effects of postevent information on a prior memory representation. *Memory and Cognition*, *21*, 267–279.

Schwartz, B. L., Meissner, C. M., Hoffman, M. L., Evans, S., & Frazier, L. D. (2004). Event memory and information effects in a gorilla. *Animal Cognition*, *7*, 93–100.

Sjödén, B., Granhag, P. A., Ost, J., & Hjelmsäter, E. R. (2009). Is the truth in the details? Extended narratives help distinguishing false "memories" from false "reports." *Scandinavian Journal of Psychology*, *50*, 203–210.

Slotnick, S. D., & Schacter, D. L. (2004). A sensory signature that distinguishes true from false memories. *Nature Neuroscience*, *7*, 664–672.

Slotnick, S. D., & Schacter, D. L. (2006). The nature of memory related activity in early visual areas. *Neuropsychologia*, *44*, 2874–2886.

Stark, C. E. L., Okado, Y., & Loftus, E. F. (2010). Imaging the reconstruction of true and false memories using sensory reactivation and the misinformation paradigms. *Learning and Memory*, *17*, 485–488.

Steinhauer, J. (2008, September 12). At least 18 killed as trains collide in Los Angeles. *The New York Times*. Retrieved from http://www.nytimes.com/2008/09/13/us/13crash.html

Wells, G. L., Memon, A., & Penrod, S. D. (2006). Eyewitness evidence: Improving its probative value. *Psychological Science in the Public Interest*, *7*, 45–75.

Wright, D. B., & Livingston-Raper, D. (2002). Memory distortion and dissociation: Exploring the relationship in a non-clinical sample. *Journal of Trauma & Dissociation*, *3*, 97–109.

Wright, D. B., Memon, A., Skagerberg, E. M., & Gabbert, F. (2009). When eyewitnesses talk. *Current Directions in Psychological Science*, *18*, 174–178.

Zhu, B., Chen, C., Loftus, E. F., Lin, C., He, Q., Chen, C., et al. (2010a). Individual differences in false memory from misinformation: Cognitive factors. *Memory*, *18*, 543–555.

Zhu, B., Chen, C., Loftus, E. F., Lin, C., He, Q., Chen, C., et al. (2010b). Individual differences in false memory from misinformation: Personality characteristics and their interactions with cognitive abilities. *Personality and Individual Differences*, *48*, 889–894.

7

EYEWITNESS IDENTIFICATION

Probative Value, Criterion Shifts, and Policy Regarding the Sequential Lineup*

GARY L. WELLS

Eyewitness-identification evidence obtained from lineup procedures was never subjected to empirical tests of reliability until psychologists began conducting lineup experiments in the mid-to-late 1970s. It was not until the mid-1990s that the U.S. legal system began to take the issue seriously. A turning point was the advent of forensic DNA testing. Approximately 75% of the innocent people who have been exonerated by DNA testing have been associated with cases that involved mistaken eyewitness identification (Innocence Project, 2013). These exoneration cases include people such as Kirk Bloodsworth, a man who had never been in trouble with the law but who was convicted of murder on the basis of mistaken eyewitness identification and sentenced to Maryland's death chamber. He was eventually exonerated by DNA testing, and the actual murderer has now been determined (Junkin, 2004). These exonerated people are the lucky ones because few crimes leave behind DNA-rich biological evidence.

The legal system's newfound concern with the eyewitness-identification problem relates closely to the message that psychological scientists have been delivering for nearly 40 years, namely, that the tendency to believe eyewitness-identification evidence tends to exceed its probative value. *Probative value* refers to the strength of the relationship between the proffered evidence at trial and the proposition sought. Probative value is a revered term in the legal system and represents the extent to which a piece of evidence makes it more probable that a proposition (e.g., that this is the person who committed the offense) is true. For eyewitness-identification evidence, probative value is reflected in likelihood ratios or probabilities that an identification of the defendant offered at trial was accurate or mistaken. In eyewitness-identification experiments, the ratio of accurate to

*This article was published in *Current Directions in Psychological Science*, *23*, 11–16 (2014).

mistaken identifications obtained under some set of conditions, typically referred to as diagnosticity, is considered an index of the probative value of an identification (Wells & Lindsay, 1980).

The legal system's interest in improving the probative value of eyewitness-identification evidence dovetails with eyewitness researchers' focus on system variables, which are variables that affect the accuracy of eyewitness-identification evidence over which the justice system has control (Wells, 1978). The research presented here addresses some of the issues surrounding one system variable, namely, simultaneous versus sequential lineup procedures.

A simultaneous lineup is the traditional type of lineup in which the witness views all lineup members at once. A sequential lineup is one in which the witness views lineup members one at a time without knowing the number to be viewed. Meta-analyses have shown that the probative value of the sequential procedure is higher than is the probative value of the simultaneous procedure (Clark, 2012; Steblay, Dysart, & Wells, 2011). Gronlund, Wixted, and Mickes (2014) argued that this result is due to the fact that the sequential procedure is a more conservative test (an upward shift in the decision criterion) rather than that the sequential procedure is an improvement in discriminability over the simultaneous procedure. This is not a new point about the sequential procedure (e.g., see Meissner, Tredoux, Parker, & MacLin, 2005; Palmer & Brewer, 2012), and I agree that the empirical evidence is consistent with this argument. Palmer and Brewer (2012), for example, analyzed 22 experiments and concluded that although the sequential procedure does not increase discrimination, it does promote a less-biased criterion setting.

My aim in the present research was to place the Gronlund et al. (2014) article in a broader context, counter some questionable claims, and consider the policy implications. First, the sequential-superiority argument in the literature has always been made on the basis of an assessment of its probative value for identifications. Even if this better probative value comes from a criterion shift, an identification obtained from a sequential lineup can be better trusted than can one from a simultaneous lineup. Of course, if the increase in the probative value of identifications is due to an increase in the decision criterion (rather than to a change in discrimination), then there will be a decrease in identifications of the culprit along with a decrease in identifications of the innocent. This pattern was observed in simultaneous versus sequential lineup comparisons from the outset (Lindsay & Wells, 1985), and the pattern holds in meta-analyses (Steblay, Dysart, Fulero, & Lindsay, 2001; Steblay et al., 2011).

The simple way to think about this distinction is that eyewitnesses are less likely to make an identification with the sequential procedure than with the simultaneous procedure, but when they do make an identification with a sequential procedure, it is more trustworthy for the prosecutor, the judge, and the jury. At the same time, of course, the more conservative sequential procedure will produce more "misses" (failure to identify the culprit) than will the simultaneous procedure. But it should be kept in mind that a miss does not necessarily mean that a culprit will go free. People are convicted in great numbers without the aid of eyewitness-identification evidence because guilty people tend to have other evidence against them even if there is no eyewitness. Nevertheless, this distinction between the two procedures inevitably raises policy discussions about the relative weights that ought to be attached to the errors of identifying the innocent versus not identifying the guilty.

THE PROBATIVE ADVANTAGE OF THE SEQUENTIAL LINEUP

Gronlund et al. (2014) occasionally questioned whether there is a probative value (diagnosticity) advantage for the sequential procedure, but they did so by pointing to a few selected contrasts in a few studies rather than by relying on broad meta-analyses. All literatures have some outliers. The better probative value of the sequential lineup is well documented by meta-analyses and reviews of the extant literature. Steblay et al. (2001) and

Steblay et al. (2011) meta-analyzed 72 tests of simultaneous versus sequential lineups from 23 labs involving more than 13,000 participant witnesses. Across these studies, the accurate-to-inaccurate identification ratio (probative value) for the sequential procedure was 6.3, whereas the ratio for the simultaneous procedure was 5.5. In a subanalysis that included only the 27 studies in which researchers employed the full design and did not have ceiling or floor effect problems, the sequential ratio was 7.7 and the simultaneous ratio was 5.8. Clark (2012) used slightly different methods and a slightly different set of studies and reported accurate and inaccurate identification rates across 51 tests of sequential and simultaneous procedures that correspond to ratios of 4.8 and 3.6, respectively.

Palmer and Brewer (2012) analyzed 22 simultaneous versus sequential studies and, as with the other meta-analyses, the ratio of accurate to mistaken identifications (probative value) was greater for the sequential procedure. But Palmer and Brewer also calculated both d (a measure of discrimination) and c (a measure of response bias or decision criterion). There was no significant difference in discrimination, but there was a significant difference in response bias. A c score of 0 indicates unbiased responding, and negative values indicate a bias to identify. "Although responding was markedly lenient for both presentation modes, witnesses—on average—set a less-biased response criterion for sequential lineups [$c = -.41$] than for simultaneous lineups [$c = -.94$]" (Palmer & Brewer, 2012, p. 252). In other words, witnesses were too eager to make identifications with both procedures but less so with the sequential lineup.

Is There Evidence That Eyewitness Decision Criteria Are Too Low in Actual Cases? Archival Data

Should the decision criterion be raised for eyewitness-identification evidence? That is, of course, a policy issue. Relevant to this question, however, are eight published archival analyses of actual lineups conducted in various locations in the United States and the United Kingdom. Because a proper lineup contains known-innocent fillers who are included in the lineup for the purpose of maintaining a procedure that is fair to the suspect, researchers are able to count how often witnesses do not identify anyone and how often witnesses identify known-innocent fillers. For example, in an archival study in the United Kingdom, researchers analyzed more than 1,000 lineups and found that 65% of witnesses made an identification of someone and that among those witnesses who made an identification, 40% identified an innocent filler (Horry, Memon, Wright, & Milne, 2012).

Table 1 lists and provides identification outcomes for all eight published studies in which researchers have examined how often witnesses in serious criminal cases identify a known-innocent filler. Overall, one of every three witnesses who made an identification chose a filler, even though the witnesses were clearly instructed that the culprit might not be present and, thus, the witnesses could (and should) have made no identification. Although fillers will not be charged with a crime, any one of those fillers could have been an innocent suspect. Moreover, it is unknown how often the suspect in those lineups was innocent; thus, the filler identification rate is an underestimate of the actual error rate among those witnesses who made an identification.

Given that at least one third of actual eyewitnesses to serious crimes who make an identification are choosing a known-innocent lineup member, a reasonable person could conclude that eyewitnesses' criteria for choosing are too lax and that a more conservative procedure is an appropriate policy response to this problem. Receiver operating characteristic curves are a nice statistical tool, but they cannot answer an important question that policymakers face in this situation: Should we use a more conservative procedure that will improve the ratio of accurate to mistaken identifications?

IDENTIFICATIONS AND NONIDENTIFICATIONS: THE POLICY ISSUE

Any suggestion that the ratio of accurate to mistaken identifications is not better with the sequential procedure seems unfounded given the meta-analyses that have shown otherwise. Gronlund et al. (2014) are on safer grounds, however, when they point out that a better ratio of hits to mistaken identifications resulting from the sequential procedure appears to be due to a criterion shift rather than to a change in discrimination. As a result, improvement in the ratio of accurate to mistaken identifications will be accompanied by a poorer ratio of correct to false rejections. How have policymakers dealt with this issue?

Many U.S. jurisdictions now use sequential lineup procedures, including the states of New Jersey, Connecticut, and North Carolina, as well as individual cities and counties, such as Dallas, Boston, Denver, and Santa Clara County, California.[1] During the process of deciding whether to adopt the sequential procedure, were these jurisdictions misunderstanding what the data showed? Definitely not. Having worked with most of these jurisdictions, I know that the primary data they used at that time was the Steblay et al. (2001) meta-analysis, which showed very clearly the trade-off between accurate and mistaken identification rates inherent to the sequential procedure. Far from being cavalier about the simultaneous versus sequential issue, the policymakers engaged in deep discussions and displayed considerable sophistication in their thinking.

Table 1 Identification Outcomes for Published Archival Studies of Lineups

Study	Percentage of witnesses making an ID	Percentage of IDs that are of the suspect	Percentage of IDs that are of a known-innocent filler
Behrman and Davey (2001)	74	68	32
Behrman and Richards (2005)	67	78	22
Horry, Halford, Brewer, Milne, and Bull (2014)	64	72	28
Horry, Memon, Wright, and Milne (2012)	65	60	40
Memon, Havard, Clifford, Gabbert, and Watt (2011)	86	51	49
Valentine, Pickering, and Darling (2003)	62	66	34
Wright and McDaid (1996)	59	66	34
Wright and Skagerberg (2007)	79	73	27
Average across studies	70	67	33

The Status Quo Effect

Policymakers are quite aware of the status quo effect. Accordingly, when they ask whether they should adopt a new procedure (sequential) that reduces mistaken identifications but increases the chances that the guilty might not be identified, they always try to "flip the status quo." Specifically, they also ask, What if we had always used a sequential procedure and then someone came along and said we should use a simultaneous procedure? The question then becomes, Should we adopt a new procedure (simultaneous) that increases the chances that the guilty might be identified but also increases the chances of mistaken identification?

THE MISTAKEN IDENTIFICATION/ NONIDENTIFICATION ASYMMETRY

Although value judgments come into play, policymakers are well aware of a natural asymmetry between not identifying the guilty and mistaken identifications of the innocent that is not in and of itself a value judgment. Specifically, a failure to identify the guilty party creates one potential error, namely, that a guilty person might go free. But the identification of an innocent suspect creates two potential errors: an innocent person could be convicted and a guilty person might go free. This asymmetry is a very interesting one because it is not a value judgment that places greater weight on one type of error as opposed to another. Instead, it is a judgment that one error (a false rejection) cannot be as serious as that same error (a false rejection) plus another error (a false alarm).

The Second-Lap Policy

Because they recognize that the sequential procedure could result in an eyewitness failing to identify the culprit, every U.S. jurisdiction that has adopted the sequential procedure has included a proviso that the witness can view the sequence a second time if the witness explicitly requests to see the lineup members again. Of course, any second lap through the sequential lineup is a matter of record that must be disclosed to the defense, and it could be argued that a second lap regresses to the functional equivalent of a simultaneous procedure for that witness. However, this compromise is interesting because it separates witnesses who were able to make their identification before knowing what the other lineup members looked like from those witnesses who felt that they had to see the remaining lineup members to make a decision. The proviso is similar to the observation made by Steblay et al. (2011) that you can always perform a sequential procedure followed by a simultaneous procedure but it makes no sense to do the reverse.

Additional Policy Considerations

Policymakers look well beyond the data to include such things as the cost of lawsuits associated with wrongful conviction, the need for greater probative value in evidence, and the cost that convicting the innocent has on the public's confidence in the justice system.

FINAL REMARKS

Gronlund et al. (2014) were correct to suggest that receiver operating characteristic analyses are the best way to determine whether the simultaneous/sequential difference is a criterion shift. But equality of receiver operating characteristic curves does not negate the fact that probative value is greater for the sequential procedure. When it comes to considering lineup reforms, the primary concern of policymakers has been that witnesses too often make mistaken identifications, not that they too often fail to identify the culprit. The sequential lineup is one tool that some jurisdictions have decided is a useful one for the goals they have in mind.

It is important to note that the argument that the sequential procedure increases the decision criterion is not an explanation but instead is a mere redescription of the data. Psychologically, it remains quite viable to argue that the sequential procedure is more conservative (a higher criterion) precisely because witnesses have to make an identification decision before knowing what the other lineup members look like (a more absolute decision rather than a relative decision); that is, the sequential procedure prevents witnesses from using a lax criterion of simply deciding which lineup member, compared with the other lineup members, looks most like the culprit (which would lead to a mistake whenever the culprit is not in the lineup). Within the sequential procedure, the witnesses know that there might be someone later in the sequence who looks even more like the culprit. What should one make of a witness who got to the fourth lineup member in a sequential procedure and said, "Can I see the rest before I decide whether this is the person I want to identify as the murderer?" Given the powerfully incriminating nature of eyewitness-identification evidence, it seems that eyewitnesses ought to be able to show that they can identify the culprit if they see the person without needing to see the remaining lineup members.

I agree with Gronlund et al. (2014) that the goal should be to find even better eyewitness-identification procedures (see Brewer & Wells, 2011). If the traditional lineup did not already exist, a wholly different approach probably would be developed, perhaps one involving eye movements, pupil dilation, event-related potential patterns, response latencies, implicit memory tests, and other potential indicia of recognition. Bringing psychological science to bear on the serious problem of eyewitness identification ought to mean much more than manipulating whether photos are shown as groups versus one at a time. The next generation of eyewitness researchers should throw out the traditional lineup approach and bring more creative tools to bear.

Note

1. A recent national survey estimated that 32% of U.S. law enforcement agencies use the sequential procedure (see Police Executive Research Forum, 2013).

REFERENCES

Behrman, B. W., & Davey, S. L. (2001). Eyewitness identification in actual criminal cases: An archiva analysis. *Law and Human Behavior, 25,* 475–491.

Behrman, B. W., & Richards, R. E. (2005). Suspect/foil identification in actual crimes and in the laboratory: A reality monitoring analysis. *Law and Human Behavior, 29,* 279–301.

Brewer, N., & Wells, G. L. (2011). Eyewitness identification. *Current Directions in Psychological Science, 20,* 24–27.

Clark, S. E. (2012). Costs and benefits of eyewitness identification reform: Psychological science and public policy. *Perspectives on Psychological Science, 7,* 238–259.

Gronlund, S. D., Wixted, J. T., & Mickes, L. (2014). Evaluating eyewitness identification procedures using ROC analyses. *Current Directions in Psychological Science, 23,* 3–10.

Horry, R., Halford, P., Brewer, N., Milne, R., & Bull, R. (2014). Archival analyses of eyewitness identification test outcomes: What can they tell us about eyewitness memory? *Law and Human Behavior, 38,* 94–108.

Horry, R., Memon, A., Wright, D. B., & Milne, R. (2012). Predictors of eyewitness identification decisions from video lineups in England: A field study. *Law and Human Behavior, 36,* 257–265.

Innocence Project. (2013). *Understand the causes: Eyewitness misidentification.* Retrieved from http://www.innocen ceproject.org/understand/Eyewitness-Misidentification.php

Junkin, T. (2004). *Bloodsworth: The true story of the first death row inmate exonerated by DNA.* Chapel Hill, NC: Algonquin Books.

Lindsay, R. C., & Wells, G. L. (1985). Improving eyewitness identifications from lineups: Simultaneous versus sequential lineup presentation. *Journal of Applied Psychology, 70,* 556–564.

Meissner, C. A., Tredoux, C. G., Parker, J. F., & MacLin, O. H. (2005). Eyewitness decisions in simultaneous and sequential lineups: A dual-process signal detection theory analysis. *Memory & Cognition, 33,* 783–792.

Memon, A., Havard, C., Clifford, B., Gabbert, F., & Watt, M. (2011). A field evaluation of the VIPER system: A new technique for eliciting eyewitness evidence. *Psychology, Crime & Law, 17,* 711–729.

Palmer, M. A., & Brewer, N. (2012). Sequential lineup presentation promotes less-biased criterion setting but does not improve discriminability. *Law and Human Behavior, 36,* 247–255. doi:10.1037/h0093923

Police Executive Research Forum. (2013). *A national survey of eyewitness identification processes in law enforcement agencies.* Retrieved from http://policeforum.org/library/eyewitness-identification/NIJEyewitnessReport.pdf

Steblay, N. K., Dysart, J., Fulero, S., & Lindsay, R. C. L. (2001). Eyewitness accuracy rates in sequential and simultaneous lineup presentations: A meta-analytic comparison. *Law and Human Behavior, 25,* 459–474.

Steblay, N. K., Dysart, J. E., & Wells, G. L. (2011). Seventy- two tests of the sequential lineup superiority effect: A meta-analysis and policy discussion. *Psychology, Public Policy, and Law, 17,* 99–139.

Valentine, T., Pickering, A., & Darling, S. (2003). Characteristics of eyewitness identification that predict the outcome of real lineups. *Applied Cognitive Psychology, 17,* 969–993.

Wells, G. L. (1978). Applied eyewitness testimony research: System variables and estimator variables. *Journal of Personality and Social Psychology, 36,* 1546–1557.

Wells, G. L., & Lindsay, R. C. L. (1980). On estimating the diagnosticity of eyewitness non-identifications. *Psychological Bulletin, 88,* 776–784.

Wright, D. B., & McDaid, A. T. (1996). Comparing system and estimator variables using data from real lineups. *Applied Cognitive Psychology, 10,* 75–84.

Wright, D. B., & Skagerberg, E. M. (2007). Post-identification feedback affects real eyewitnesses. *Psychological Science, 18,* 172–178.

8

OUTSMARTING THE LIARS

Toward a Cognitive Lie Detection Approach*

ALDERT VRIJ

PÄR ANDERS GRANHAG

SAMANTHA MANN

SHARON LEAL

Five decades of lie detection research have shown that people's ability to detect deception by observing behavior and listening to speech is limited—with, on average, 54% of truths and lies being correctly classified (C. F. Bond & DePaulo, 2006). To improve accuracy rates, researchers have attempted to unravel the strategies used by certain individuals identified as having extraordinary lie detection skills, so-called wizards (O'Sullivan & Ekman, 2004). Is it the case that less sophisticated lie catchers can learn from these wizards? Some scholars doubt whether these identified individuals are real wizards (C. F. Bond & Uysal, 2007), and to date, no publication has emerged about the strategies these alleged wizards use (G. D. Bond,

2009). Other researchers have taught investigators "diagnostic"cues to deceit. The success of such training programs has been limited, with only a few percentage points, on average, gained in accuracy (Frank & Feeley, 2003).

The problem is that cues to deception are typically faint and unreliable (DePaulo et al., 2003). One reason is that the underlying theoretical explanations for why such cues occur— nervousness and cognitive load—also apply to truth tellers. That is, both liars and truth tellers can be afraid of being disbelieved and may have to think hard when providing a statement. Can interviewers ask questions that actively elicit and amplify verbal and nonverbal cues to deceit? Efforts in the past (e.g., Reid's Behavior Analysis

*This article was published in *Current Directions in Psychological Science*, 20, 28–32 (2011).

Interview) have concentrated on eliciting and amplifying emotions (Vrij, 2008), but it is doubtful whether questions that will necessarily raise more concern in liars than in truth tellers can be asked (National Research Council, 2003).

We will demonstrate, however, that it is possible to ask questions that raise cognitive load more in liars than in truth tellers. This cognitive lie detection perspective consists of two approaches. The imposing-cognitive-load approach aims to make the interview setting more difficult for interviewees. We argue that this affects liars more than truth tellers, resulting in more, and more blatant, cues to deceit. The strategic-questioning approach examines different ways of questioning that elicit the most differential responses between truth tellers and liars.

THE IMPOSING-COGNITIVE-LOAD APPROACH

Lying can be more cognitively demanding than truth telling (Vrij et al., 2008). First, formulating the lie may be cognitively demanding. A liar needs to invent a story and must monitor their fabrication so that it is plausible and adheres to everything the observer or observers know or might find out. Moreover, liars must remember what they have said to whom in order to maintain consistency. Liars should also refrain from providing new leads. Second, liars are typically less likely than truth tellers to take their credibility for granted. As such, liars will be more inclined than truth tellers to monitor and control their demeanor in order to appear honest to the investigator, and such monitoring and controlling is cognitively demanding. Third, because liars do not take credibility for granted, they may also monitor the investigator's reactions carefully in order to assess whether they appear to be getting away with their lie, and this too requires cognitive resources. Fourth, liars may be preoccupied with the task of reminding themselves to role-play, which requires extra cognitive effort.

Fifth, liars also have to suppress the truth while they are fabricating, and this is also cognitively demanding. Finally, while activation of the truth often happens automatically, activation of the lie is more intentional and deliberate, and thus requires mental effort.

A lie catcher could exploit the different levels of cognitive load that truth tellers and liars experience in order to discriminate more effectively between them. Liars who require more cognitive resources than truth tellers will have fewer cognitive resources left over. If cognitive demand is further raised, which could be achieved by making additional requests, liars may not be as good as truth tellers in coping with these additional requests.

One way to impose cognitive load is by asking interviewees to tell their stories in reverse order. This increases cognitive load because (a) it runs counter to the natural forward-order coding of sequentially occurring events, and (b) it disrupts reconstructing events from a schema (Gilbert & Fisher, 2006). Another way to increase cognitive load is by instructing interviewees to maintain eye contact with the interviewer. When people have to concentrate on telling their stories—like when they are asked to recall what has happened—they are inclined to look away from their conversation partner (typically to a motionless point), because maintaining eye contact is distracting (Doherty-Sneddon & Phelps, 2005). In two experiments, half of the liars and truth tellers were requested to recall their stories in reverse order (Vrij et al., 2008) or to maintain eye contact with the interviewer (Vrij, Mann, Leal, & Fisher, 2010), whereas no instruction was given to the other half of the participants. More cues to deceit emerged in the reverse-order and maintaining-eye-contact conditions than in the control conditions. Observers who watched these videotaped interviews could distinguish between truths and lies better in the reverse-order condition and maintaining-eye-contact conditions than in the control conditions. For example, in the reverse-order experiment, 42% of the lies were correctly classified in the control condition, well below that typically found in verbal and nonverbal lie detection research, suggesting that the lie detection task was difficult. Yet, in the experimental condition, 60% of the lies were correctly classified, more than typically found in this type of lie detection research.

STRATEGIC-QUESTIONING APPROACH

Unanticipated questions. A consistent finding in deception research is that liars prepare themselves when anticipating an interview (Hartwig, Granhag, & Strömwall, 2007). Planning makes lying easier, and planned lies typically contain fewer cues to deceit than do spontaneous lies (DePaulo et al., 2003). However, the positive effects of planning will only emerge if liars correctly anticipate which questions will be asked. Investigators can exploit this limitation by asking questions that liars do not anticipate. Though liars can refuse to answer unanticipated questions, such "I don't know" or "I can't remember" responses will create suspicion if the questions are about central (but unanticipated) aspects of the target event.

To test the unanticipated-questions technique, pairs of liars and truth tellers were interviewed individually about having had lunch together at a restaurant (Vrij et al., 2009). While the truth tellers did have lunch together, the liars did not but were instructed to pretend that they had. All pairs were given the opportunity to prepare for the interview. The interviewer asked conventional opening questions (e.g., "What did you do in the restaurant?"), followed by questions about spatial details (e.g., "In relation to where you sat, where were the closest diners?") and temporal details (e.g., "Who finished their food first, you or your friend?"). Further, they were asked to sketch the layout of the restaurant. The spatial questions and drawing requests came as a surprise to interviewees (this was established after the interview). Based on the overlap in responses between the two pair members to the anticipated questions, the liars and truth tellers were

not classified above chance level. However, based on the responses to the unanticipated questions, up to 80% of pairs of liars and truth tellers were correctly classified (i.e., the answers to spatial questions and the answers to drawings were less alike for the pairs of liars than pairs of truth tellers). Asking unanticipated questions about central topics therefore elicited cues to deceit.

Asking unanticipated questions can also be effective when assessing individual interviewees rather than pairs of interviewees. An interviewer could ask the same question twice. When liars have not anticipated the question, they have to fabricate an answer on the spot. A liar's memory of this fabricated answer may be more unstable than a truth teller's memory of the actual event. Therefore, liars may contradict themselves more than do truth tellers. This approach probably works best if the questions are asked in different formats. Truth tellers will have encoded the topic of investigation along more dimensions than liars will have. Truth tellers should therefore be able to recall the event more flexibly (along more dimensions) than liars. When asked to verbally describe and sketch the layout of a restaurant, truth tellers' verbal answers and drawings showed more overlap than liars' verbal answers and drawings (Leins, Fisher, Vrij, Leal, & Mann, 2011).

Drawings have never been used before as a lie detection tool, but they have potential, as demonstrated in two further experiments. Moreso than a verbal request, the request to sketch forces the interviewee to convey spatial information. That is, including an object within a drawing requires that object to be spatially located. By comparison, verbally describing an object in a room can be done without indicating its spatial location. If a liar has not experienced an item in a particular location, he or she may still verbally describe the object but will do so without referring to its location to avoid the risk of misplacing it. Such a "masking strategy" is not possible when asked to sketch. As a result, a liar may instead decide against sketching the object. In an occupations experiment, truth tellers discussed their real occupations, whereas liars discussed occupations they pretended to have. When asked to verbally describe the layout of their office, truth tellers' and liars' answers were equally detailed; however, when asked to sketch the layout of their offices, liars' drawings were less detailed than were those of truth tellers (Vrij, Mann, Leal, & Fisher, 2012).

In a second experiment, 31 "agents" were sent on a mission during which they had to collect a decoder from another agent (Vrij, Leal, et al., 2010). After delivering the decoder, they were asked to (a) verbally describe and later to (b) sketch what they could see at the location where they had received the decoder. Half of the agents were requested to lie and half to tell the truth. The liars were asked to pretend to have been on a different mission in which they received the decoder at a different location. Only 2 out of 16 (12.5%) liars included an agent from whom they pretended to have received the decoder in their drawing, whereas 12 out of 15 truth tellers (80%) included the real agent in their drawing. In their verbal descriptions, again 2 out of 16 (12.5%) liars mentioned the other agent, whereas 8 out of 15 (53%) truth tellers did so. In other words, like the occupations experiment, truth tellers' and liars' drawings differed more from each other than did truth tellers' and liars' verbal recalls. Liars were inclined to omit the agent from the sketch and verbal description for two possible reasons: First, the agent had not been present at the location they sketched/ described, and therefore did not think about including him/her. Second, liars may have been reluctant to include people in their drawings/descriptions for fear of triggering further questions about who those people actually were. Note that more truth tellers sketched (80%) than verbally described the agent (53%), demonstrating why drawings were more informative about deception than verbal recalls. After sketching the stable elements, the truth tellers probably noticed that the agent was missing from the drawing. Liars, however, will have been less aware of this during their verbal recall, because of difficulties in building a complete mental picture of their verbal recall.

Devil's-advocate approach. Spatial and drawing requests are unsuitable when examining lying about opinions. Determining the veracity of such conceptual representations can be important in security settings, as demonstrated by the loss of seven CIA agents in Afghanistan. They were killed via a suicide attack by a man they believed was going to give them information about Taliban and al-Qaeda targets in Pakistan's tribal areas. The CIA was aware that he had posted extreme anti-American views on the Internet but believed these to be part of a cover (Leal, Vrij, Mann, & Fisher, 2010).

The devil's-advocate technique aims to detect deception in expressing opinions. Interviewees are first asked an opinion-eliciting question that invites them to argue in favor of their personal view ("What are your reasons for supporting the U.S. in the war in Afghanistan?"). This is followed by a devil's-advocate question that asks interviewees to argue against their personal view ("Playing devil's advocate, is there anything you can say against the involvement of the U.S. in Afghanistan?").

People normally think more deeply about, and are more able to generate, reasons that support rather than oppose their beliefs (Ajzen, 2001). Therefore, truth tellers are likely to provide more information in their responses to the true opinion-eliciting question than to the devil's-advocate question. This pattern is unlikely to occur in liars, as for them, the devil's advocate question is more compatible with their beliefs than is the opinion-eliciting question. In effect, for liars, the devil's-advocate approach is a setup wherein they first lie when answering the opinion-eliciting question and then are lured into telling the truth when answering the devil's-advocate question. In an experiment, participants were asked to tell the truth or lie about their views regarding issues they felt strongly about, including the war in Afghanistan. Truth tellers' opinion-eliciting answers were longer than their devil's-advocate answers, whereas no differences emerged in liars' answers to the two types of questions (Leal et al., 2010). Based on this principle, 75% of truth tellers and 78% of liars could be classified correctly.

The Strategic Use of Evidence (SUE). Lying and truth-telling suspects enter police interviews in different mental states (Granhag & Hartwig, 2008). A guilty suspect will often have unique knowledge about the crime, which, if recognized by the interviewer, makes it obvious that he or she is the perpetrator. The guilty suspect's main concern will be to ensure that the interviewer does not gain that knowledge. Innocent suspects face the opposite problem, fearing that the interviewer will not learn or believe what they did at the time of the crime. These different mental states result in different strategies for liars and truth tellers (Hartwig et al., 2007). Guilty suspects are inclined to use avoidance strategies (e.g., in free recall, avoiding mentioning where they were at a certain time) or denial strategies (e.g., denying having been at a certain place at a certain time when directly asked). In contrast, innocent suspects neither avoid nor escape but are forthcoming and "tell the truth like it happened" (Granhag & Hartwig, 2008).

In the SUE technique, the investigator aims to detect these differential strategies via a strategic use of the available evidence (e.g., possible incriminating information). The purpose of SUE is to ask open questions (e.g., "What did you do last Sunday afternoon?") followed by specific questions (e.g., "Did you or anyone else drive your car last Sunday afternoon?") without revealing that evidence (e.g., closed-circuit TV images of the interviewee's car driven in a specific location on that Sunday afternoon). Truth tellers are likely to mention driving the car on that Sunday afternoon either spontaneously or after being prompted (e.g., "tell the truth like it happened" strategy). Liars are unlikely to mention driving the car spontaneously (e.g., avoidance) or after being

prompted (e.g., denial). A denial will contradict the evidence.

Hartwig, Granhag, Strömwall, and Kronkvist (2006) experimentally tested the SUE technique. Prior to the experiment, half of the interviewers were SUE trained and were instructed to interview the suspect using the SUE technique. The remaining interviewers were instructed to interview the suspect in the style of their own choice. The untrained interviewers obtained 56.1% accuracy (similar to that typically found in nonverbal and verbal lie detection research), whereas the SUE-trained interviewers obtained 85.4% accuracy. Guilty suspects contradicted the evidence more often than did innocent suspects, particularly when questioned by SUE-trained interviewers.

FINAL THOUGHTS

The lie detection techniques that we have discussed can be employed in various settings. SUE can be used when evidence is available, and the devil's-advocate technique can be employed when examining the veracity of opinions. The other techniques can be employed to determine the veracity of statements about past activities but, in theory, also to determine the veracity of statements about future activities (intentions). We have shown that the unanticipated questions technique can be employed to identify deceit in both individuals and networks (multiple liars). Future research should examine whether the techniques are sensitive to countermeasures—that is, liars' attempts to fool investigators. The unanticipated-question technique should be immune to this, as its method is to ask questions that a liar has not anticipated and therefore not prepared answers for. Due to individual differences in people's responses, within-subjects lie detection techniques are preferred because they control for such individual differences. The unanticipated-questions and devil's-advocate techniques are within-subjects techniques.

REFERENCES

Ajzen, I. (2001). Nature and operation of attitudes. *Annual Review of Psychology, 52*, 27–58.

Bond, C. F., & DePaulo, B. M. (2006). Accuracy of deception judgements. *Personality and Social Psychology Review, 10*, 214–234.

Bond, C. F., & Uysal, A. (2007). On lie detection "wizards." *Law and Human Behavior, 31*, 109–115.

Bond, G. D. (2009). Deception detection expertise. *Law and Human Behavior, 32*, 339–351.

DePaulo, B. M., Lindsay, J. L., Malone, B. E., Muhlenbruck, L., Charlton, K., & Cooper, H. (2003). Cues to deception. *Psychological Bulletin, 129*, 74–118.

Doherty-Sneddon, G., & Phelps, F. G. (2005). Gaze aversion: A response to cognitive or social difficulty? *Memory and Cognition, 33*, 727–733.

Frank, M. G., & Feeley, T. H. (2003). To catch a liar: Challenges for research in lie detection training. *Journal of Applied Communication Research, 31*, 58–75.

Gilbert, J. A. E., & Fisher, R. P. (2006). The effects of varied retrieval cues on reminiscence in eyewitness memory. *Applied Cognitive Psychology, 20*, 723–739.

Granhag, P. A., & Hartwig, M. (2008). A new theoretical perspective on deception detection: On the psychology of instrumental mind-reading. *Psychology, Crime & Law, 14*, 189–200.

Hartwig, M., Granhag, P. A., Strömwall, L., & Kronkvist, O. (2006). Strategic use of evidence during police interrogations: When training to detect deception works. *Law and Human Behavior, 30*, 603–619.

Hartwig, M., Granhag, P. A., & Strömwall, L. (2007). Guilty and innocent suspects' strategies during interrogations. *Psychology, Crime & Law, 13*, 213–227.

Leal, S., Vrij, A., Mann, S., & Fisher, R. (2010). Detecting true and false opinions: The devil's advocate approach as a lie detection aid. *Acta Psychologica, 134*, 323–329.

Leins, D., Fisher, R. P., Vrij, A., Leal, S., & Mann, S. (2011). Using sketch-drawing to induce inconsistency in liars. *Legal and Criminological Psychology, 16*, 253–265.

National Research Council, Committee to Review the Scientific Evidence on the Polygraph. (2003). *The polygraph and lie detection*. Washington, DC: The National Academies Press.

O'Sullivan, M., & Ekman, P. (2004). The wizards of deception detection. In P. A. Granhag & L. A. Strömwall (Eds.), *Deception detection in forensic contexts*. (pp. 269–286). Cambridge, England: Cambridge University Press.

Vrij, A. (2008). *Detecting lies and deceit: Pitfalls and opportunities*, second edition. Chichester, England: John Wiley and Sons.

Vrij, A., Leal, S., Granhag, P. A., Mann, S., Fisher, R. P., Hillman, J., & Sperry, K. (2009). Outsmarting the liars: The benefit of asking unanticipated questions. *Law and Human Behavior, 33*, 159–166.

Vrij, A., Leal, S., Mann, S., Warmelink, L., Granhag, P.A., & Fisher, R. P. (2010). Drawings as an innovative and successful lie detection tool. *Applied Cognitive Psychology, 4*, 587–594.

Vrij, A., Mann, S., Fisher, R., Leal, S., Milne, B., & Bull, R. (2008). Increasing cognitive load to facilitate lie detection: The benefit of recalling an event in reverse order. *Law and Human Behavior, 32*, 253–265.

Vrij, A., Mann, S., Leal, S., & Fisher, R. (2010). "Look into my eyes": Can an instruction to maintain eye contact facilitate lie detection? *Psychology, Crime & Law, 16*, 327–348.

Vrij, A., Mann, S., Leal, S., & Fisher, R. (2012). Is anyone out there? Drawings as a tool to detect deception in occupations interviews. *Psychology, Crime & Law, 18*, 377–388.

UNIT 3

LEGAL PSYCHOLOGY

INTRODUCTION AND COMMENTARY

*L*egal psychology is a descriptive term for the interaction between psychology and the law. In some literature, the terms *legal* and *forensic psychology* are used interchangeably, while in other literature legal psychology is a category of forensic psychology. Legal psychologists consult with lawyers and judges, conduct research that is directly relevant to judicial issues, and testify in court proceedings, among other activities.

The first article in this section focuses on psychological expert testimony. The legal system has long called on experts who have specialized knowledge in matters before criminal and civil courts. Cutler and Kovera (2011) provide a concise overview of the topics on which psychologists testify, as well as the criteria they must meet before their testimony is accepted. The authors emphasize that the psychologist's sole responsibility is to educate the judge and jury about a content area—such as the credibility of eyewitness testimony or the effects of employment discrimination. Cutler and Kovera also review some of the research on expert testimony, such as the extent to which it influences the decisions of jurors. They assert, though, that despite the fact that expert testimony should possess scientific reliability, the legal system itself often cannot adequately identify whether it does or does not. Therefore, the psychological profession must monitor itself to ensure that only high-quality expert testimony reaches the courts. In addition, psychology must continue to conduct research to help the courts recognize the difference between reliable and unreliable testimony.

Next, Murrie, Boccaccini, Guarnera, and Rufino (2013) report on a unique experimental study designed to assess bias among forensic psychologists and psychiatrists conducting evaluations and possibly offering subsequent expert testimony. The researchers wondered whether these professionals demonstrated bias toward the side that hired them. Participants were clinicians who volunteered for a 2-day training period involving two measures, the PCL-R and the Static-99R. Their attitudes toward sexual offenders also were measured. Three weeks later, the participants returned and scored case files that consisted of four real but deidentified records of sex offenders. Participants were told that they were hired by either the prosecution or the defense. You will have to read the article to learn what the researchers found. Many field studies have been done on this topic, but here the authors conducted a laboratory experiment, which adds considerably to the existing research in this area.

In the next article, Brainerd (2013) looks at research on children as witnesses, particularly on the reliability of their memory. It is often assumed that children's memory is less reliable than that of adults and that memory progressively improves as children reach adulthood. Therefore, children are thought to be more likely than adults to remember things that did not happen. Brainerd disputes this, citing recent research on developmental reversals in memory indicating that false memories can actually increase between childhood and adulthood. Thus, Brainerd states, it should not be assumed that the testimony of children cannot be trusted because their memory is unreliable. The reading represents a different slant on ever-expanding research on children's eyewitness testimony.

One of the most common tasks of forensic psychologists is to assess whether a defendant meets the criteria for competency to stand trial—basically, can the defendant understand the proceedings and help his or her lawyer? Put another way, can he or she play the role of a defendant? In the next article, Zapf and Roesch (2011)—each of whom has conducted extensive research on competency to stand trial—focus on what occurs when an adult defendant has been found incompetent. Which defendants are restorable, and how is restoration to be accomplished? The authors note that less emphasis should be placed on a person's diagnosis and more on his or her competency-related abilities—what are the person's deficits, and can they be fixed? The authors also recognize that medication—the predominant approach to restoring competency—may be important for some individuals. But they also note that educational treatment and cognitive remediation should not be overlooked. They review some research suggesting that informing the person of how the legal system works and improving cognitive functions such as reasoning or focusing attention has had some success.

Scientific jury selection (SJS) is a fascinating topic for many readers. Can psychologists or jury consultants help attorneys choose jurors who are likely to be favorable to their case? Most of the commentary in this area has concluded that jury decisions cannot be predicted on the basis of juror attitudes or demographics. In his review of the research, Lieberman (2011) acknowledges that SJS has earned mixed reviews in studies of both mock trials and actual trials. Studies on demographic factors and attitudes have shown little success in prediction of verdicts. However, he argues that many of the studies have had notable methodological flaws, and no conclusions can be drawn about the overall effectiveness of SJS techniques; they are still murky, as the title of his article indicates. Lieberman is not ready to give up on SJS, particularly in light of evidence that trial consultation is a lucrative business with increasingly more resources at its disposal.

The final article in this section takes us down a very different path. Legal psychologists often perform child custody evaluations for courts when they must decide on issues of child custody, visitation, and relocation. To perform these evaluations effectively and professionally, evaluators must be aware of the research findings on divorce and children's adjustment. Lansford (2009) provides an extensive review of the literature on numerous topics. She looks at research focusing on age of the children, their adjustment prior to the divorce, the effect of conflict between parents, and remarriage, among many factors. This lengthy article was shortened significantly for the purposes of this book of readings, but Lansford's summary section was kept intact and her long list of references should be of great help to students wanting to delve further into this topic.

As a group, the readings in this section remind forensic psychologists and other mental health practitioners who interact with the courts to remain informed about developments in their profession and to exercise caution in their interpretations and use of various assessment measures. Many courts are not familiar with scientific methods and are dependent on scientists to monitor themselves by providing reliable testimony. Nevertheless, as legal professionals such as judges and lawyers become more sophisticated in their understanding of psychological principles and research, they also may demand more accountability on the part of the mental health professionals and ask more probing questions in their cross-examinations.

9

Expert Psychological Testimony*

Brian L. Cutler

Margaret Bull Kovera

Expert psychological testimony refers to the offering of expert psychological knowledge and opinions in court hearings and trials. The range of expert domains in which psychologists testify is vast. Clinical psychologists testify about past and present mental states that arise in cases in which competence (e.g., competence to stand trial, to consent to treatment, to share parenting responsibilities) is questioned, risk to oneself or to others must be assessed, the insanity defense is raised, or disabilities or damages must be assessed. Neuropsychologists testify about assessment and treatment of traumatic brain injury in cases involving injury assessment. Social and cognitive psychologists testify in court about such issues as the reliability of and factors affecting eyewitness memory and the impact of pretrial publicity on jury decision making. Developmental psychologists testify about memory and suggestibility of child witnesses. Industrial and organizational psychologists testify about adverse impact in employment discrimination cases and hostile work environments in sexual harassment cases. The purpose of this article is to provide an overview of the wide range of issues associated with expert psychological testimony and to provide examples of the empirical research addressing these issues.

Psychologists who testify as experts are normally retained by a party to the case (plaintiff, prosecution, defense), but sometimes the judge, rather than one of the adversaries in the case, appoints the expert. In all cases, the expert's role is to provide assistance to the triers of fact—either the judge or a jury—in the form of an opinion based on some type of specialized knowledge, education, or training. Prior to testifying in court, the expert may have been required to submit a report for review by both parties and the judge and may have testified

*This article was published in *Current Directions in Psychological Science*, *20*, 53–57 (2011).

under oath in a less formal setting to inform the parties of the expert's conclusions and opinions (i.e., deposed). If admissibility of the expert testimony is challenged, the psychologist might testify in an admissibility hearing and thus preview the proffered testimony for the judge who must make an admissibility decision. After a hearing to establish his or her qualifications to testify as an expert witness, the expert testifies under oath in response to questions on direct and cross-examination and may also take questions from the judge.

Some forms of expert testimony allow the expert to give an opinion about a party to the case. For example, a forensic clinical psychologist may offer an opinion about whether a defendant is competent to stand trial. In other expert domains, the expert's sole responsibility is to educate the judge and jury about the content area and is not expected or sometimes not even allowed to offer an opinion about how the case should be decided. For example, eyewitness experts testify about how factors associated with the viewing of a crime and characteristics of the procedures used to elicit an identification influence the risk of false identification, but generally they are not allowed to give an opinion about the accuracy of an eyewitness, for it is the jury's responsibility to determine whether the identification was accurate.

ADMISSIBILITY OF EXPERT PSYCHOLOGICAL TESTIMONY

Given the specialized nature of expert testimony and the risk of abuse (e.g., representing scientific knowledge in an incomplete or false manner), lawmakers have developed safeguards in the form of admissibility standards in their attempts to maximize the inclusion of legitimate scientific knowledge and to exclude "junk science." The courts treat expert psychological testimony as any other form of expert, scientific, or technical testimony. One party proffers the expert testimony, and the other party may challenge its admission in court (in practice, the admissibility of many forms of expert psychological testimony is not challenged). The judge then applies the appropriate admissibility criteria and decides whether the expert testimony will be admitted into court. In the United States federal courts, the "*Frye* test"(*Frye v. United States,* 1923) guided admissibility decisions for many years, and some states' rules of evidence still use this test to guide admissibility decisions. In *Frye*, the defendant proffered an expert witness who would testify about a lie detection test, but the expert's testimony was disallowed and Frye was convicted of murder. When considering Frye's appeal, the court developed the *Frye* test: Novel scientific evidence must be generally accepted within the relevant scientific community to be admissible.

Some 50 years later, the U.S. congress adopted the Federal Rules of Evidence (FRE; 1975), which included different admissibility criteria. According to FRE Rule 702, expert testimony will be ruled admissible if the specialized knowledge will "assist the trier of fact" and the expert has been qualified based on "knowledge, skill, experience, training, or education." In a series of U.S. Supreme Court cases in the 1990s (principal among them *Daubert v. Merrell Dow Pharmaceuticals, Inc.*, 1993), the Supreme Court affirmed that the FRE supplanted the *Frye* test and further articulated the admissibility criteria for expert testimony in federal courts. Specifically, the Court developed a two-prong admissibility test: Judges must decide whether the proffered testimony is relevant and, if relevant, whether the testimony is reliable. Judges admit the proffered expert testimony only if they determine that the testimony is both relevant and reliable. Specifically, the Court held that testimony must be scientifically reliable, which has been interpreted to encompass both reliability and validity. The major change from *Frye* to *Daubert*, therefore, is that judges no longer rely solely on acceptance in the scientific community to determine admissibility but must instead evaluate the reliability of the expert testimony themselves. The Court provided a nonexhaustive list of factors to consider (now known as the

Daubert criteria) such as the falsifiability of the underlying theory, known error rates, and peer review, as well as acceptance in the scientific community. This change in criteria allows for the admission of expert testimony based on new but reliable research that has not yet had time to become accepted in the scientific community, but also poses challenges to expert testimony (e.g., latent fingerprint identification) that has been accepted in professional communities but has not been established as reliable.

It should be noted that in the United States, each state has its own rules of evidence and criminal procedure and therefore sets its own criteria for admissibility of expert testimony. Although many state courts, including those in states with large populations like California, Florida, Illinois, Maryland, Michigan, Minnesota, New Jersey, New York, Pennsylvania, and Washington, still rely on some version of the Frye test for evaluating the admissibility of expert testimony, other state courts have adopted rules of evidence that are modeled on those developed for federal courts, including the rules governing the admissibility of expert evidence.

SCIENTIFIC RESEARCH ON EXPERT PSYCHOLOGICAL TESTIMONY

Expert psychological testimony is unique in that it has been subjected to more empirical research than any other form of expert testimony, and much of this research is published in peer-reviewed psychology and law journals. We summarize a sample of this research below.

Is Psychological Expert Testimony Necessary?

In some domains in which expert psychological testimony is offered, questions about whether the testimony is needed have been raised. For example, opponents of expert testimony on the psychology of eyewitness identification argue that the testimony is not needed because existing safeguards against conviction of the innocent are sufficient and because the testimony offered by the expert is common sense. The question of what laypeople know about the psychology of eyewitness identification and the effectiveness of alternative safeguards, such as the presence of counsel at lineups, motions to suppress identifications, cross-examination, and judges' instructions have been thoroughly investigated in the psychological literature (see Cutler, 2009). For example, surveys and trial simulation experiments have examined the knowledge of lawyers, judges, and prospective jurors concerning the factors that influence eyewitness identification and their sensitivity to these factors when making legal judgments. Generally, this research concludes that existing safeguards are not sufficient to protect defendants from wrongful conviction based on mistaken eyewitness identification, underscoring the importance of understanding whether expert testimony assists jurors' evaluations of other evidence.

Does Expert Testimony Influence Jurors' Decisions?

Researchers have examined the effect of expert psychological testimony on juror decisions in child sexual abuse, intimate partner violence, and sexual assault cases, as well as cases that hinge on eyewitness identification. For example, in the context of a trial of a battered woman who had killed her husband, Schuller and Hastings (1996) examined the impact of two forms of expert testimony: One form explained the defendant's behavior in terms of psychological syndromes, whereas the other explained it in terms of the batterer's dominance and coercion and the women's agency and action. Jurors who heard either type of expert testimony gave more lenient verdicts and more defense-favorable evaluations of the case than did participants who heard no expert testimony. There are variables that moderate the influence of expert testimony. Expert testimony that is concretely linked to trial evidence is more influential than testimony that leaves the link implicit (Kovera, Gresham, Borgida, Gray, & Regan, 1997). Expert testimony based on clinical judgment is more influential than is testimony based on actuarial prediction (Krauss & Sales, 2001), and testimony that presents a qualitative description of the degree to which two forensic samples match is more persuasive than testimony that presents the match in quantitative terms (McQuiston-Surrett & Saks, 2009).

Is Expert Testimony on Psychological Topics Appropriate?

Underlying much expert testimony involving forensic psychological assessment is the assumption that the instruments that we use are reliable and valid in forensic settings. A broad-based review of this literature raised questions about the appropriateness of expert testimony about projective tests, assessments of posttraumatic stress syndrome, assessments of other injuries and dysfunction, and measures of psychopathy, as well as those assessments used in custody evaluations, competence assessments, and risk assessment (Skeem, Douglas, & Lilienfeld, 2009). Some argue that predictions of individual offending based on group tendencies are highly unreliable (Cooke & Michie, 2010). Questions also have been raised about whether empirical research on eyewitness identification (Flowe, Finklea, & Ebbesen, 2009) and false confessions (Perez, 2010), most of which relies on laboratory simulations, generalizes to actual cases.

Is Psychological Expert Testimony Objective?

Although expert witnesses are typically retained by one party to a case and are subjected to an adversarial setting, the expert is expected to be objective—an educator, not an advocate. Does the adversarial context in which expert testimony is provided influence expert objectivity? To examine this question empirically, Murrie, Boccaccini, Johnson, and Janke (2008) assessed the level of agreement in Hare Psychopathy Checklist–Revised (PCL-R) scores among 23 pairs of independent forensic psychologists who evaluated the same individual but were retained by the opposing attorneys in a set of sexual offender civil commitment trials. Scores deviated in the direction of the party who retained the expert. The score deviations differed by a margin greater than one would expect based on the instrument's known standard of error and the correlation between scores was lower than published test–retest correlations. Thus, the pattern of results is consistent with the influence of partisan allegiance in forensic evaluations.

Is Unreliable Expert Testimony Admitted?

Did the *Daubert* decision have its intended influence on judges' admissibility decisions? A content analysis of appellate court opinions from nearly 700 cases showed that although judges admitted expert testimony at the same rates in the years before and after Daubert, judges gave greater scrutiny to the proffered expert testimony following *Daubert*, as intended (Groscup, Penrod, Studebaker, Huss, & O'Neil, 2002): Judges included in their opinions more discussion of FRE 702, more discussion of the *Daubert* decision, and less discussion of *Frye*. There was little discussion about the *Daubert* criteria in these opinions, perhaps because judges do not fully understand the *Daubert* criteria. For example, in a national survey of judges, judges indicated that they lacked the scientific training necessary to fulfill their gatekeeping role, and 5% or fewer judges clearly understood key terms such as falsifiability and error rate (Gatowski et al., 2001).

Researchers have also examined judges' abilities to evaluate the reliability of proffered testimony, as required by *Daubert*, by asking judges to evaluate the admissibility of expert testimony proffered in a hostile work environment sexual harassment case (Kovera & McAuliff, 2000). The plaintiff in the case alleged that she was continuously subjected to sexually suggestive material in the workplace and was the target of unwelcome sexual advances by her co-workers. The judges read a description of expert psychological testimony that varied with respect to internal validity. The three internal validity manipulations were the presence versus absence of (a) a control group, (b) a confound, and (c) experimenter bias due to a non-blind confederate. These manipulations did not significantly influence judges' evaluations, suggesting that they were insensitive to these threats to internal validity. In sum, research on admissibility decisions raises questions about the effectiveness of the *Daubert* criteria for regulating the quality of expert testimony.

Are Jurors Sensitive to Variations in the Reliability of Expert Testimony?

Although the *Daubert* decision places the onus on judges to keep junk science out of the courtroom, the decision also recognizes that the jury provides an additional safeguard; even if junk science is admitted into court, the jury can evaluate it and give it the weight it deserves. Given this assumption, McAuliff Kovera, and Nunez (2009) examined whether prospective jurors are able to recognize missing control groups, confounds, and experimenter bias using methods and materials similar to those used in their study with judges. They found jury-eligible community members were sensitive to missing control groups but not to confounds or experimenter bias.

There are other safeguards that may assist jurors in their evaluations of the reliability of expert evidence. The *Daubert* decision specifically named three: instruction on the burden of proof, cross-examination, and the presentation of contrary evidence. It is not clear how instructing jurors to be more cautious without providing them skills to evaluate expert evidence would increase their sensitivity to variations in evidence quality. Although cross-examination and the presentation of contrary evidence via opposing experts allow for the education of jurors about methodological issues, empirical research to date suggests that these safeguards are also ineffective (Kovera, McAuliff, & Hebert, 1999; Levett & Kovera, 2008, 2009).

CURRENT DIRECTIONS

In practice, expert psychological testimony on a wide variety of topics is accepted in hearings and courts, although not without controversy. The judicial system, professional societies, education and training programs, and individual practitioners will need to take steps to ensure that psychology's contribution to the judicial system is of the highest quality with respect to both the underlying science and the ethics of practice. These issues are not unique to psychology but rather are relevant to all areas of expert testimony.

Although expert evidence moves juror verdicts in the direction supported by the testimony, recent advances in our understanding of the effects of expert testimony on fact finders' decisions highlight the inability of legal decision makers to identify and appropriately weight the scientific reliability of expert evidence. Common safeguards intended to improve fact-finder sensitivity to methodological flaws in the evidence appear ineffective. Continued research to identify methods of helping fact finders differentiate between reliable and unreliable expert testimony is needed.

REFERENCES

Cooke, D. J., & Michie, C. (2010). Limitations of diagnostic precision and predictive utility in the individual case: A challenge for forensic practice. *Law and Human Behavior*, *34*, 259–274.

Cutler, B. L. (Ed.). (2009). *Expert testimony on the psychology of eyewitness identification*. New York, NY: Oxford University Press.

Daubert v. Merrell Dow Pharmaceuticals Inc., 113 S.Ct. 2786 (1993).

Federal Rules of Evidence for United States Courts and Magistrates. (1975). St. Paul, MN: West Publishing Company.

Flowe, H. D., Finklea, K. M., & Ebbesen, E. B. (2009). Limitations on expert psychological testimony on eyewitness identification. In B.L. Cutler (Ed.), *Expert testimony on the psychology of eyewitness identification*. New York, NY: Oxford University Press.

Frye v. United States, 54 App. D.C. 46, 293 F. 1013 (1923).

Gatowski, S. I., Dobbin, S. A., Richardson, J. T., Ginsburg, G. P., Merlino, M. L., & Dahir, V. (2001). Asking the gatekeepers: A national survey of judges on judging expert evidence in a post-*Daubert* world. *Law and Human Behavior, 25,* 433–458.

Groscup, J. L., Penrod, S. D., Studebaker, C. A., Huss, M. T., & O'Neil, K. M. (2002). The effects of *Daubert* on the admissibility of expert testimony in state and federal criminal cases. *Psychology. Public Policy, and Law, 8,* 339–372.

Kovera, M. B., Gresham, A. W., Borgida, E., Gray, E., & Regan, P. C. (1997). Does expert testimony inform or influence juror decision-making? A social cognitive analysis. *Journal of Applied Psychology, 82,* 178–191.

Kovera, M. B., & McAuliff, B. D. (2000). The effects of peer review and evidence quality on judge evaluations of psychological science: Are judges effective gatekeepers? *Journal of Applied Psychology, 85,* 574–586.

Kovera, M. B., McAuliff, B. D., & Hebert, K. S. (1999). Reasoning about scientific evidence: Effects of juror gender and evidence quality on juror decisions in a hostile work environment case. *Journal of Applied Psychology, 84,* 362–375.

Krauss, D., & Sales, B. D. (2001). The effects of clinical and scientific expert testimony on juror decision-making in capital sentencing. *Psychology, Public Policy, & Law, 7,* 267–310.

Levett, L. M., & Kovera, M. B. (2008). The effectiveness of educating jurors about unreliable expert evidence using an opposing witness. *Law and Human Behavior, 32,* 363–374.

Levett, L. M., & Kovera, M. B. (2009). Psychological mediators of the effects of opposing expert testimony on juror decisions. *Psychology, Public Policy, and Law, 15,* 124–148.

McAuliff, B. D., Kovera, M. B., & Nunez, G. (2009). Can jurors recognize missing control groups, confounds, and experimenter bias in psychological science? *Law and Human Behavior, 33,* 247–257.

McQuiston-Surrett, D., & Saks, M. J. (2009). The testimony of forensic identification science: What expert witnesses say and what fact finders hear. *Law and Human Behavior, 33,* 436–453.

Murrie, D. C., Boccaccini, M. T., Johnson, J. T., & Janke, C. (2008). Does interrater (dis)agreement on Psychopathy Checklist scores in sexual violent predator trials suggest partisan allegiance in forensic evaluations? *Law and Human Behavior, 32,* 352–362.

Perez, D. A. (2010). The (in)admissibility of false confession expert testimony. *Touro Law Review, 26,* 23–74.

Schuller, R., & Hastings, P. (1996). Trials of battered women who kill: The impact of alternative forms of expert evidence. *Law and Human Behavior, 20,* 167–187.

Skeem, J., Douglas, K. & Lilienfeld, S. (Eds.). (2009). Psychological science in the courtroom: Consensus and controversies. New York, NY: Guilford.

10

Are Forensic Experts Biased by the Side That Retained Them?*

Daniel C. Murrie

Marcus T. Boccaccini

Lucy A. Guarnera

Katrina A. Rufino

Recently, the National Research Council (NRC, 2009) warned that the accuracy and reliability of many popular forensic-science techniques are unknown, that error rates are rarely acknowledged, and that forensic scientists are prone to bias because they are not independent of the parties requesting their services. Emerging research has clearly documented subjectivity and bias even in the forensic-science procedures that courts have tended to consider most reliable, such as analyses of DNA (Dror & Hampikian, 2011) and fingerprints (Dror & Cole, 2010). Thus, the NRC urged further research on the cognitive and contextual biases that influence forensic experts.

The NRC report did not specifically address mental-health experts or forensic psychological evaluations. But psychological evaluations—like other forensic-science procedures—are often admitted as evidence or presented via expert testimony in adversarial legal proceedings. Indeed, evaluations by mental-health experts influence decisions as grave as death sentences (*Barefoot v. Estelle*, 1983) and indefinite civil confinement (*Kansas v. Hendricks*, 1997). Therefore, recent concerns regarding forensic

*This article was published in *Psychological Science*, *24*, 1889–1897 (2013). We have deleted notes and some information about materials, measures, and debriefing of the participants. We have also deleted a section on differences observed among pairs of evaluators, including a table within that section.

science raise questions about whether forensic psychological evaluations might suffer similar problems of unreliability and bias.

How reliable are forensic psychologists and psychiatrists when they are retained as experts in adversarial legal proceedings? For more than a century, courts and legal scholars have lamented apparent bias among medical experts (Bernstein, 2008; Hand, 1901; Mnookin, 2008; Wigmore, 1923). Likewise, practicing judges and attorneys have complained that experts sacrifice objectivity for advocacy (e.g., Krafka, Dunn, Johnson, Cecil, & Miletich, 2002). But little psychological research has investigated what we call *adversarial allegiance* (Murrie et al., 2009), the presumed tendency for experts to reach conclusions that support the party who retained them. Psychology's delay in investigating adversarial allegiance is disappointing, because psychologists are uniquely suited to explore reliability and bias in decision making.

FIELD STUDIES OF RISK INSTRUMENTS SUGGEST, BUT DO NOT PROVE, ADVERSARIAL ALLEGIANCE

Recently, we investigated adversarial allegiance by examining civil commitment proceedings for sex offenders, also known as sexually-violent-predator (SVP) trials. SVP trials provide an ideal context for studying the possibility of adversarial allegiance, because court decisions depend largely on weighing testimony from opposing experts. Twenty states and the federal system have SVP laws, which allow them to identify sexual offenders whom they consider likely to reoffend and confine them indefinitely after their incarceration (*Kansas v. Hendricks*, 1997). SVP proceedings routinely involve forensic psychologists and psychiatrists who are retained by opposing sides, conduct risk assessments of the same offender, and consider the same data, often using the same instruments. So we could study adversarial allegiance in SVP proceedings by comparing the scores that defense-retained and prosecution-retained evaluators assigned to offenders

using popular risk-assessment instruments (Murrie, Boccaccini, Johnson, & Janke, 2008; Murrie et al., 2009).

Scores on risk instruments are an ideal metric to measure expert opinions because (a) experts routinely administer these instruments to inform legal proceedings, and (b) dozens of studies have documented strong inter-rater agreement when clinicians score these instruments in research and practice contexts that are *not* adversarial. For example, Hare's (2003) Psychopathy Checklist–Revised (PCL-R), an instrument that relies on clinical interview and review of records, is widely used in forensic assessments of risk for violence or sexual violence (Skeem, Polaschek, Patrick, & Lilienfeld, 2011). The PCL-R manual reports strong inter-rater agreement (intraclass correlation, or ICC = .87; Hare, 2003). Indeed, most (92%) pairs of scores from trained raters who score the same offender differ by fewer than 2 points (Gacono & Hutton, 1994), even though PCL-R scores can range from 0 to 40.

However, in a small sample of SVP proceedings that featured PCL-R scores from defense-retained and prosecution-retained evaluators, the ICC for opposing evaluators was .42, which indicated that less than half of the variance in PCL-R scores could be attributed to the offenders' true standing on the PCL-R (Murrie et al., 2009). Moreover, the average PCL-R score from prosecution experts was 24, whereas the average score from defense experts was only 18 (Cohen's $d = 0.78$). The PCL-R may be especially vulnerable to this allegiance effect because it requires clinicians to make inferences about an offender's personality and emotions (e.g., lack of guilt or remorse, superficial charm). The adversarial-allegiance effect was smaller ($d = 0.34$) for the Static-99 (Hanson & Thornton, 2000), a highly structured measure scored from file information about criminal history that requires less subjective judgment.

These field studies (Murrie et al., 2008; Murrie et al., 2009) strongly suggest adversarial allegiance, in that prosecution-retained evaluators assigned higher scores and defense-retained evaluators assigned lower scores to the same offenders. But we cannot draw firm conclusions from these field studies alone, because they investigated scores from experts selected by attorneys. Conceivably, attorneys could have chosen specific experts because they perceived the experts *already* had attitudes or scoring tendencies conducive to their case. Or perhaps attorneys consulted many experts, but arranged testimony only from those whose opinions were most supportive of their case. For example, a defense attorney might retain several evaluators to examine a client, but request testimony only from the evaluator who assigned the lowest risk scores. Thus, the apparent allegiance in field studies might reflect selection effects, whether in terms of which expert an attorney selected to perform an evaluation or which findings an attorney selected to present at trial.

Understanding Adversarial Allegiance Requires a True Experiment

Field studies raise an important question that can be answered only with a true experiment. Is apparent allegiance due simply to attorneys choosing evaluators who have preexisting attitudes that favor their side, or to attorneys calling only experts with the most favorable findings to testify in court (selection effects)? Or do evaluators, once retained and promised payment by one side, tend to form opinions that favor that side (allegiance effects)? If an experiment using random assignment failed to find allegiance effects, it would suggest that the apparent allegiance in the field is due primarily to one or both of these selection effects. But if an experiment using random assignment *did* find allegiance effects, it would suggest that being retained and paid by one side in an adversarial system may compromise objectivity among experts.

To answer this question, we recruited more than 100 experienced forensic psychologists and psychiatrists, provided 2 days of in-person training on

risk instruments from established experts, had them meet with an attorney, and then paid them to score risk instruments for up to four offenders. We deceived participants to believe they were performing a large-scale, paid forensic consultation. But unbeknownst to participants, they all received exactly the same four offender files, and each participant was randomly assigned to believe that he or she was working for either the prosecution or the defense.

Method

Participants

We sent recruitment correspondence to a broad group of practicing forensic evaluators, offering "gold standard" training (and continuing-education credits) on the two most commonly used measures in sex-offender risk assessments: the PCL-R and Static-99R (Helmus, Thornton, Hanson, & Babchishin, 2012). This training was offered at no cost to participants who could commit to returning a few weeks later to spend 1 day scoring offenders at a pay rate typical of forensic consultation ($400). We received more than 100 applications from practicing, doctoral-level forensic clinicians.

Of the 118 clinicians who participated in the risk-measure training, 108 returned to score files for the experiment. Five who scored cases did not pass a manipulation check (i.e., they could not identify which side had retained them), and 4 expressed some suspicion that the cover story of scoring cases for a forensic consultation was a sham . . . . So we report results for the 99 participants (49 ostensibly retained by the defense, 50 ostensibly retained by the prosecution) who accepted the manipulation and believed they were scoring cases for one side of an adversarial process.

Participants (60% female, 40% male) came from 15 states. Most (88%) reported having doctoral degrees in psychology (Ph.D. or Psy.D.). Others reported having a medical degree (7%) or another type of doctoral degree (5%). Most (84%) reported that they had experience conducting forensic evaluations, and most (75%) reported that they had experience conducting sex-offender risk assessments. About half (51%) had used the PCL-R in practice, and about half (49%) had used the Static-99R in practice.

Training

The participants attended a single 2-day training. The first 1.5 days (14 hr) involved training on the PCL-R, conducted by an internationally known expert who had coauthored one version of the Psychopathy Checklist and provided many formal PCL-R workshops. The final half-day of training (4 hr) focused on the Static-99R. Our goal was not to train participants to a predetermined level of reliability (a common practice in validity studies) because evaluators in the field are never required to demonstrate a specified level of reliability before accepting cases. Rather, we provided training to ensure that all participants had, at a minimum, completed the type of high-quality workshop that is offered to professionals in the field. Many evaluators cite workshop training as evidence of their qualifications to score risk measures for SVP cases (Rufino, Boccaccini, Hawes, & Murrie, 2012), although it is possible that some evaluators administer these measures after receiving less formal training. Regarding deception at the training stage, participants were informed only that the training and subsequent scoring were funded by an "out-of-state agency" that wanted to ensure that all participants had rigorous training before they scored offender files.

Deception and Experimental Manipulation: Scoring Cases for the Prosecution or Defense

Participants returned about 3 weeks later to score offender files. They were randomly assigned to either a prosecution-allegiance or a defense-allegiance group and were deceived to believe that they were a part of a formal, large-scale forensic consultation paid for by either a public-defender service or a specialized prosecution unit that prosecutes SVP cases. Immediately after arrival, participants met for 10 to 15 min with a confederate (a former SVP attorney) who posed as an attorney for either the public-defender service or the specialized prosecution unit. The same attorney played both roles, but followed a slightly different script (see the Supplemental Material available online) depending on whether the participant had been randomly assigned to the defense or the prosecution.

The attorney addressed the defense-allegiance participants with statements that are typical of many defense attorneys (e.g., "We try to help the court understand that the data show not every sex offender really poses a high risk of reoffending"). Likewise, he addressed participants in the prosecution-allegiance condition with statements that are typical of prosecutors (e.g., "We try to help the court understand that the offenders we bring to trial are a select group whom the data show are more likely than other sex offenders to reoffend"). In both conditions, he asked participants to score the offenders using the two risk instruments. He also hinted at the possibility of future opportunities for paid consultation.

Participants were led to believe that, as a group, they were reviewing and scoring cases from a large cohort. But in truth, all participants scored the same four case files, which we selected to span the range from low risk to high risk. Each set of case materials was authentic (i.e., from an actual SVP case). The files included de-identified, but real, court, criminal, and correctional records.

*****

The four offender files were selected to be representative of SVP cases generally. One sex offender had adult victims, whereas three had child victims. All had been convicted of multiple sexual offenses. After the participants reviewed a case file, they scored the PCL-R and Static-99R.

Measures

Psychopathy Checklist–Revised. Hare's (2003) PCL-R is a 20-item measure of interpersonal, emotional, and behavioral traits, which clinicians score on the basis of an offender's records and a clinical interview. PCL-R items are rated on a scale from 0 to 2, with higher scores reflecting a higher level of the psychopathic trait; these scores are summed to yield a Total score that can range from 0 to 40. Although forensic evaluators usually emphasize PCL-R Total scores in reports or testimony, PCL-R items are divided into two factors: Factor 1 consists of an Interpersonal facet and an Affective facet, and Factor 2 (Social Deviance) consists of an Impulsive Lifestyle facet and an Antisocial Behavior facet.

*****

Static-99R. The Static-99R is an actuarial risk-assessment instrument designed to predict sexual recidivism among sex offenders (Helmus et al., 2012). Composed of 10 items that address an offender's age and prior living arrangements, as well as several aspects of his offense history, the Static-99R is scored on the basis of file review. According to the Static-99 Clearinghouse (n.d.), the Static-99 (and now the Static-99R) is "the most widely used sex offender risk assessment instrument in the world, and is extensively used in the United States, Canada, the United Kingdom, Australia, and many European nations." It is widely accepted in legal proceedings, given its strong empirical relation to important outcomes and strong evidence of validity and reliability.

*****

Clinician attitudes. One potential explanation for any allegiance effects we might observe would be preexisting differences in clinicians' attitudes (i.e., if participants assigned to score files for the prosecution tended to have a harsher perspective on sexual offenders than participants assigned to score files for the defense). So, although we randomly assigned participants to the prosecution and defense conditions, we nevertheless had participants complete two additional measures that allowed us to check whether participants in the two conditions were similar in their attitudes regarding sexual offenders.

We asked participants to complete a five-item questionnaire at the end of the scoring day, to avoid revealing that their attitudes and scoring patterns were the focus of study. The questionnaire asked them to rate the extent to which restrictive policies for sex offenders (e.g., SVP laws) are necessary and reasonable. For example, one item read, "Laws that allow states to civilly commit potentially dangerous sex offenders who have completed their sentences are reasonable strategies to protect people in the community" (1 = *strongly disagree*, 5 = *strongly agree*). Internal consistency for this attitudes measure was .79. We also asked participants (at the end of PCL-R training) to report their best estimate of the typical PCL-R Total score among offenders who have committed sexually violent crimes against (a) adults and (b) children.

*****

RESULTS

Overall, the risk scores assigned by prosecution and defense experts showed a clear pattern of adversarial allegiance. As expected, allegiance effects were stronger for the PCL-R, a measure that requires more subjective clinical judgment, than for the Static-99R, a measure that requires less clinical judgment (see Table 1). For the PCL-R Total score, independent-samples t tests indicated that prosecution-retained evaluators assigned significantly higher scores than defense-retained evaluators for Case 1, $t(94) = 4.15, p < .001$; Case 2, $t(94) = 3.73$, $p < .001$; and Case 3, $t(97) = 2.71, p = .008$; but not Case 4, $t(62) = -0.33, p = .97$. Cohen's d for the three cases with significant effects ranged from 0.55 to 0.85, and were similar in magnitude to effects ($d = 0.63$–0.83) documented in a sample of actual SVP proceedings (Murrie et al., 2009). The

Table 1 Differences Between Risk-Measure Scores From Evaluators Randomly Assigned and Paid to Score Cases for the Prosecution or the Defense

Score and case	Prosecution		Defense		Effect size	
	M	SD	M	SD	Cohen's d	95% confidence interval
PCL-R Total						
Case 1	16.64	3.50	13.41	4.10	0.85***	[0.43, 1.26]
Case 2	26.53	4.32	23.22	4.37	0.76***	[0.35, 1.17]
Case 3	26.40	4.69	24.00	4.14	0.55**	[0.14, 0.94]
Case 4	7.81	4.09	7.84	3.36	−0.01	[−0.32, 0.31]
PCL-R Factor 1 (Interpersonal/Affective)						
Case 1	11.22	2.60	8.95	3.20	0.78***	[0.36, 1.18]
Case 2	8.34	2.72	6.51	2.95	0.65**	[0.23, 1.05]
Case 3	11.91	2.80	11.27	2.52	0.24	[−0.15, 0.63]
Case 4	4.74	3.30	4.60	2.66	0.05	[−0.44, 0.54]
PCL-R Factor 2 (Social Deviance)						
Case 1	3.86	1.68	3.13	1.60	0.44*	[0.04, 0.85]
Case 2	15.61	2.26	14.45	2.19	0.52**	[0.11, 0.93]
Case 3	12.26	2.36	10.65	2.00	0.73***	[0.33, 1.14]
Case 4	2.58	1.45	2.98	1.79	−0.25	[−0.74, 0.25]
Static-99R						
Case 1	4.46	0.85	4.06	1.05	0.42*	[0.01, 0.82]
Case 2	5.56	1.35	5.27	1.05	0.24	[−0.16, 0.64]
Case 3	5.62	1.81	5.29	1.57	0.20	[−0.20, 0.59]
Case 4	1.85	1.21	1.69	1.11	0.14	[−0.35, 0.64]

Note: Evaluators scored cases using the Psychopathy Checklist–Revised (PCL-R; Hare, 2003) and the Static-99R (Helmus, Thornton, Hanson, & Babchishin, 2012). Statistical significance of the difference between conditions was determined using independent-samples t tests (two-tailed). For the four cases, ns were as follows—Case 1: $n = 96$; Case 2: $n = 96$; Case 3: $n = 99$; Case 4: $n = 64$.

*$p ≤ .05$. **$p ≤ .01$. ***$p ≤ .001$.

one case for which the PCL-R Total scores did not show an allegiance effect was one we had selected to be unusually low in psychopathy; this case received unusually low scores both from prosecution-retained ($M = 7.81$) and defense-retained ($M = 7.84$) evaluators.

Adversarial-allegiance effects were evident for both Factor 1 (Interpersonal/Affective) and Factor 2 (Social Deviance) scores from the PCL-R, as detailed in Table 1. In terms of absolute value, Factor 1 effects were larger than Factor 2 effects in two of the three cases with Total score allegiance effects, which is consistent with findings that Factor 1 items tend to require more subjective judgment to score (Rufino, Boccaccini, & Guy, 2011). For Case 3, however, there was a significant effect for Factor 2 scores ($d = 0.73$, $p < .001$), but not Factor 1 scores ($d = 0.24$, $p = 24$). Examination of the Factor 1 facets for Case 3 indicated that there was some evidence for an allegiance effect for Facet 2 (Affective traits) scores, $t(97) = 1.94$, $p = .06$, $d = 0.39$, 95% confidence interval (CI) = [−0.01, 0.79], but not Facet 1 (Interpersonal traits) scores, $t(97) = 0.08$, $p = .94$, $d = 0.01$, 95% CI = [−0.38, 0.41].

For the Static-99R, a more structured measure, prosecution-retained evaluators tended to assign higher scores than defense-retained evaluators in each of the four cases (see Table 1), but the difference was large enough to reach statistical significance for only Case 1 ($d = 0.42$, $p = .05$). The effect sizes across these four cases ($ds = 0.14, 0.20, 0.24$, and 0.42) were similar to, although somewhat smaller than, the effect sizes ($d = 0.29–0.37$) reported across 27 actual SVP cases (Murrie et al., 2009).

*****

Potential Explanations for Allegiance Effects

One possible alternate explanation for our findings is that, despite random assignment, evaluators assigned to score for the prosecution maintained harsher attitudes toward sex offenders or had different types of clinical experience than did those assigned to score for the defense. But we found no evidence for this alternate explanation. Prosecution- and defense-retained evaluators did not differ in their ratings on our five-item measure of support for restrictive sex-offender policies, $t(97) = 0.07$, $p = .95$, $d = 0.02$; their estimate of the typical PCL-R Total score among sex offenders with adult victims, $t(93) = 0.51$, $p = .62$, $d = 0.10$; or their estimate of the typical PCL-R Total score assigned to sex offenders with child victims, $t(93) = 0.25$, $p = .80$, $d = 0.05$. Likewise, prosecution- and defense-retained evaluators did not differ in the percentage who had used the Static-99R in practice (52% vs. 45%), $\div^2(1, N = 99) = 0.50$, $p = .48$, odds ratio = 1.33. Those assigned to score for the prosecution were somewhat more likely (62%) to have used the PCL-R in practice than were those assigned to score for the defense (41%), $\div^2(1, N = 99) = 4.45$, $p = .04$, odds ratio = 2.36, but this is a difference that would actually reduce the likelihood of observing an allegiance effect because participants with more experience tended to assign lower PCL-R scores (reported previously by Guarnera, Murrie, Boccaccini, & Rufino, 2012).

Participants with higher scores on the attitude measures also tended to assign higher scores in some cases, but these effects were similar in size and direction for prosecution- and defense-retained evaluators (Guarnera et al., 2012). We could find only one instance in which an attitude or experience measure might help explain an allegiance effect. Recall that the strongest Static-99R allegiance effect occurred in Case 1 ($d = 0.42$). A two-way analysis of variance on Static-99R scores revealed a statistically significant interaction between condition and prior use of the Static-99R in practice, $F(1, 91) = 4.38$, $p = .04$. Specifically, there was a clear allegiance effect for evaluators who had not used the Static-99R in practice ($d = 0.71$, 95% CI = [0.12, 1.29]), but no evidence of an effect for those who had used the Static-99R in practice ($d = 0.00$, 95% CI = [−0.12, 0.12]). However, there was no evidence of a similar interaction for Static-99R scores from other cases, or for PCL-R scores from any case. In short, we could find no variables that seemed to explain the allegiance effects we observed overall.

DISCUSSION

Results from this study underscore recent concerns about forensic sciences (NRC, 2009)—and raise concerns specific to forensic psychology—by demonstrating that some experts who score ostensibly objective assessment instruments assign scores that are biased toward the side that retained them. In the field, some apparent adversarial allegiance may result from selection effects (i.e., a savvy attorney selects experts who are predisposed to the attorney's perspective or presents input only from experts who favor the attorney's perspective), but our results suggest that even without selection effects, the pull of adversarial proceedings tends to influence opinions by paid forensic experts.

Of course, there was considerable variability in scores even from evaluators assigned to the same side, and certainly not every evaluator produced scores consistent with adversarial allegiance. But the systematic score differences among opposing experts could not be explained by chance, random measurement error, or preexisting differences between the experimental groups.

This evidence of allegiance was particularly striking because our experimental manipulation was less powerful than the forces experts are likely to encounter in most real cases. For example, our participants spent only about 15 min with the retaining attorney, whereas experts in the field may have extensive contact with retaining attorneys over weeks or months. Our participants formed opinions on the basis of files only, and they all reviewed identical files, whereas experts in the field may elicit different information by seeking different collateral sources or interviewing offenders in different ways. Therefore, the pull toward allegiance in this study was relatively weak compared with the pull typical of most cases in the field. Consequently, the large group differences provide compelling evidence for adversarial allegiance. Our study could not identify the mechanisms responsible for the allegiance effect. We do not know whether the effect was more attributable to the initial conversation with an attorney, a sense of team loyalty, the monetary payment, or the promise of future work. We do not know the role of confirmation bias, anchoring, or other potentially important cognitive mechanisms. Of course, the role of each mechanism may have varied by participant, and not all participants demonstrated an allegiance effect. Future research is needed to disentangle the roles of these mechanisms and to identify evaluator characteristics that are associated with adversarial allegiance.

Although this study addressed only one kind of evaluation (i.e., assessment of risk for sexual recidivism), there is little reason to believe that this is the only kind of forensic psychological evaluation or forensic-science procedure vulnerable to allegiance effects. Indeed, the evidence of allegiance effects in the case of structured, ostensibly objective instruments that usually reveal strong interrater agreement leaves us even more concerned about the possibility of allegiance effects in the case of procedures that are less structured or less guided by scoring rules. Many forensic-science procedures rely heavily on subjective judgment (e.g., matching bite marks, hair fibers, or tire treads; NRC, 2009), as do many opinions psychologists offer in court (e.g., assigning diagnoses or assessing emotional injury). Our findings underscore the need for research on the cognitive and procedural biases that may facilitate adversarial allegiance, as well as the need for research on potential interventions to reduce allegiance. Indeed, our findings suggest that there may be opportunities to improve forensic psychological practice, broader forensic-science practice, and even legal policy and procedures in ways that might better promote scientific objectivity and reduce adversarial allegiance.

Funding

This research was supported by the National Science Foundation Law & Social Science Program (Award SES 0961082).

REFERENCES

Barefoot v. Estelle, 463 U.S. 880 (1983).

Bernstein, D. E. (2008). Expert witnesses, adversarial bias, and the (partial) failure of the Daubert Revolution. *Iowa Law Review, 93,* 101–137.

DeMatteo, D., & Edens, J. F. (2006). The role and relevance of the Psychopathy Checklist-Revised in court: A case law survey of U.S. courts (1991–2004). *Psychology, Public Policy, and Law, 12,* 214–241. doi:10.1037/1076–8971.12.2.214

Dror, I. E., & Cole, S. A. (2010). The visit in "blind" justice: Expert perception, judgment, and visual cognition in forensic pattern recognition. *Psychonomic Bulletin & Review, 17,* 161–167. doi:10.3758/PBR.17.2.161

Dror, I. E., & Hampikian, G. (2011). Subjectivity and bias in forensic DNA mixture interpretation. *Science and Justice, 51,* 204–208. doi:10.1016/j.scijus.2011.08.004

Gacono, C., & Hutton, H. (1994). Suggestions for the clinical and forensic use of the Hare Psychopathy Checklist–Revised (PCL-R). *International Journal of Law and Psychiatry, 17,* 303–317.

Guarnera, L. A., Murrie, D. C., Boccaccini, M. T., & Rufino, K. (2012, March). *Do attitudes affect psychopathy scores evaluators assign to sexual offenders in Sexually Violent Predator proceedings?* Paper presented at the annual meeting of the American Psychology-Law Society, San Juan, Puerto Rico.

Hand, L. (1901). Historical and practical considerations regarding expert testimony. *Harvard Law Review, 15,* 40–58.

Hanson, R. K., & Morton-Bourgon, K. E. (2009). The accuracy of recidivism risk assessments for sexual offenders: A meta-analysis. *Psychological Assessment, 21,* 1–21. doi:10.1037/a0014421

Hanson, R. K., & Thornton, D. (2000). Improving risk assessments for sex offenders: A comparison of three actuarial scales. *Law and Human Behavior, 24,* 119–136. doi:10.1023/A:1005482921333

Hare, R. D. (2003). *The Hare Psychopathy Checklist–Revised: Second edition.* Toronto, Ontario, Canada: Multi-Health Systems.

Hawes, S. W., Boccaccini, M. T., & Murrie, D. C. (2013). Psychopathy and the combination of psychopathy and sexual deviance as predictors of sexual recidivism: Meta-analytic findings using the Psychopathy Checklist—Revised. *Psychological Assessment, 25,* 233–243. doi:10.1037/a0030391

Helmus, L., Thornton, D., Hanson, R. K., & Babchishin, K. M. (2012). Improving the predictive accuracy of Static-99 and Static-2002 with older sex offenders: Revised age weights. *Sexual Abuse: Journal of Research and Treatment, 24,* 64–101. doi:10.1177/1079063211409951

Kansas v. Hendricks, 521 U.S. 346 (1997).

Krafka, C., Dunn, M. A., Johnson, M. T., Cecil, J. S., & Miletich, D. (2002). Judge and attorney experiences, practices, and concerns regarding expert testimony in federal civil trials. *Psychology, Public Policy, and Law, 8,* 309–332. doi:10.1037/1076–8971.8.3.309

Leistico, A. R., Salekin, R. T., DeCoster, J., & Rogers, R. (2008). A large-scale meta-analysis relating the Hare measures of psychopathy to antisocial conduct. *Law and Human Behavior, 32,* 28–45. doi:10.1007/s10979–007–9096–6

Mnookin, J. (2008). Expert evidence, partisanship, and epistemic confidence. *Brooklyn Law Review, 73,* 587–611.

Morey, L. C. (1991). *Personality Assessment Inventory: Professional manual.* Odessa, FL: Psychological Assessment Resources.

Murrie, D. C., Boccaccini, M. T., Johnson, J. T., & Janke, C. (2008). Does interrater (dis)agreement on Psychopathy Checklist scores in sexually violent predator trials suggest partisan allegiance in forensic evaluations? *Law and Human Behavior, 32,* 352–362. doi:10.1007/s10979–007–9097–5

Murrie, D. C., Boccaccini, M. T., Turner, D., Meeks, M., Woods, C., & Tussey, C. (2009). Rater (dis)agreement on risk assessment measures in sexually violent predator proceedings: Evidence of adversarial allegiance in forensic evaluation? *Psychology, Public Policy, and Law, 15,* 19–53. doi:10.1037/a0014897

National Research Council, Committee on Identifying the Needs of the Forensic Science Community. (2009). *Strengthening forensic science in the United States: A path forward.* Washington, DC: National Academies Press.

Rufino, K. A., Boccaccini, M. T., & Guy, L. S. (2011). Scoring subjectivity and item performance on measures used to assess violence risk: The PCL-R and HCR-20 as exemplars. *Assessment, 18,* 453–463. doi:10.1177/1073191110378482

Rufino, K. A., Boccaccini, M. T., Hawes, S., & Murrie, D. C. (2012). When experts disagreed, who was correct? A comparison of PCL-R scores from independent raters and opposing forensic experts.

Law and Human Behavior, *36*, 527–531. doi:10.1037/h0093988

Skeem, J., Polaschek, D., Patrick, C., & Lilienfeld, S. (2011). Psychopathic personality: Bridging the gap between scientific evidence and public policy. *Psychological Science in the Public Interest*, *12*, 95–162. doi:10.1177/1529100611426706

Static-99 Clearinghouse. (n.d.). *Static-99/Static-99R*. Retrieved from http://www.static99.org/

Wigmore, J. (1923). *A treatise on the Anglo–American system of evidence in trials at common law: Including the statutes and judicial decisions of all jurisdictions of the United States and Canada.* Boston, MA: Little, Brown.

11

Developmental Reversals in False Memory

A New Look at the Reliability of Children's Evidence*

C. J. Brainerd

Jurors in criminal trials are often troubled by the lack of physical/forensic evidence that bears directly on defendants' guilt. Even in capital trials, where mountains of physical evidence are routinely presented, the evidence on which guilt hinges frequently boils down to what people say they remember about who did what, where, when, and to whom (Brainerd & Reyna, 2005). It is foreseeable, then, that false memory reports can produce false convictions; faulty eyewitness identifications (e.g., Wells, Steblay, & Dysart, 2012) and erroneous confession statements (e.g., Kassin, 2012) are well-known examples.

The role of the science of human memory in this circumstance is to supply core findings and theoretical principles that the law can implement to evaluate the reliability of memory evidence. Some especially useful findings, obviously, are ones that identify witness populations that are at high risk of false memory reports. Many examples could be mentioned—witnesses who were intoxicated during crimes, who were suggestively questioned about crimes, who received anesthesia after crimes, or who were taking prescribed medications. Children have long been a population of special interest because they are typically the sole witnesses or victims in certain types of crimes, some of which occur with considerable frequency (e.g., child abuse and neglect).

For many years, experimentation painted a particular picture of children's susceptibility to false memories that has figured in countless

*This article was published in *Current Directions in Psychological Science*, *22*, 335–341 (2013).

hours of expert scientific testimony and has become accepted wisdom in courtrooms. Recently, however, further experimentation has identified flaws in that picture that challenge accepted wisdom and demand that we take a new look at the reliability of children's memory evidence. These matters are the focus of this article. It will be seen along the way that, to paraphrase Kurt Lewin, a memory theory can be a very practical thing.

SOME BRIEF HISTORY

Exegeses of the history of scientific and legal opinions about child testimony and children's susceptibility to remembering things that did not happen (i.e., false memory) can be found in a number of sources (Brainerd & Reyna, 2005; Ceci & Bruck, 1995; Goodman, 2006). The interval of greatest interest runs from roughly 1980 to the present. Before then, statutory exclusion of evidence provided by children was commonplace, on the grounds that their memories are so error-infected (e.g., because they cannot distinguish reality from fantasy) that they can seriously mislead jurors. However, during the 1970s, statistics on sexual and emotional abuse, gathered in the wake of the 1974 Child Abuse Prevention and Treatment Act, stimulated rethinking of exclusionary statutes. Because children's memories are generally the only evidence that such crimes occurred, they are difficult to prosecute unless children can participate in investigative interviews and provide sworn testimony. Exclusionary statutes faded on a state-by-state basis, but eventually, the Federal Rules of Evidence codified that juries are competent to hear and decide how much weight to give to evidence from child witnesses. This is where research on children's false memory comes in.

Beginning with the earliest research, by Binet (1900), childhood has been seen as a peak period for two broad types of false memory, *spontaneous* and *implanted*, which then decline during adolescence and young adulthood. The

spontaneous type is due to endogenous distortion mechanisms, whereas the implanted type is a consequence of postevent misinformation. The research paradigms that are used to study the two varieties of false memory are outlined in Table 1.

As evidence from children became more broadly admissible, the number of cases in which their memories bore the burden of proof mounted, and developmental research on the paradigms in Table 1 grew apace. The nominal objectives were to test theoretical principles and generate stable empirical patterns that investigators and courts could use to assess the reliability of children's memory reports. (See Ceci & Bruck, 1995, and Poole & Lamb, 1998, for excellent discussions of how theoretical principles and empirical patterns were translated into forensic applications.)

A key outcome of this intensive period of research was a data archive showing declines in implanted false memories (for a review, see Ceci & Bruck, 1993) and in spontaneous false memories (for a review, see Brainerd & Reyna, 2005) as children become adults (that is, e.g., the average 12-year-old has fewer false memories than the average 8-year-old). Obviously, this picture fit snugly with traditional ideas about children's memories, and perhaps more importantly, it offered an explanation of some contemporaneous legal events. Those events consisted of high-profile sexual abuse trials that prompted public clamor that the prosecutions were dubious because defendants were being tried for weird and improbable acts. The prototypes were *California v. Buckey* (1990) and *New Jersey v. Michaels* (1994).

The only evidence that the defendants had committed bizarre acts of sexual abuse came from children's memory reports. Much of that information was secured via highly suggestive questioning, which constitutes misinformation (Table 1) if the acts were not committed. Against a backdrop of research showing developmental declines in false memory, the explanation seemed obvious: The improbable acts were false memories, and false memories are

Table 1   Structure of the Two False Memory Paradigms

Phases	Paradigm	
	Spontaneous	*Implanted*
Encoding	Subjects are exposed to target material, such as word lists, written narratives, video or slide sequences, or live staged events.	Same.
Misinformation	None.	Subjects are exposed to interpolated material that reminds them of things that were present in the target material (true memories) and of conceptually related things that were not (false memories).
Memory test	Subjects respond to recall or recognition tests, where the task is to remember only target material. True memory = remembering target items (e.g., *sofa* or *chair* from a word list). False memory = remembering unpresented items that resemble targets (e.g., *couch* or *seat*).	Test = same. True memory = same. False memory = remembering unpresented items that were suggested during the misinformation phase (e.g., "Remember when you read *couch* and *seat* on the word list?").

something to which children are uniquely prone. It should be added that bizarre false memories do not, by themselves, show that false memory rates are universally higher in children, because misinformation can induce adults to remember being abducted by aliens, participating in cannibalistic rituals, and living previous lives (Brainerd & Reyna, 2005; Loftus & Davis, 2006).

Naturally, the developmental decline pattern was interpreted as demonstrating far lower baseline reliability for what children say they remember than for what adults say they remember. In forensic terms, children's recountings are more apt to be tainted by false memories than those of adults, so that, other things being equal, jurors should weigh adults' versions of events more heavily than children's when child and adult recountings conflict. This principle became a staple of expert testimony, and of late, courts have ruled that it has risen to the level of commonsense knowledge that jurors can apply

without guidance from scientific witnesses (Brainerd & Reyna, 2012).

DEVELOPMENTAL REVERSALS IN FALSE MEMORY

Reyna and I noticed a theoretical anomaly in the developmental decline pattern that challenged this principle. Certain theories of false memory predicted that the pattern could not possibly be as ubiquitous as it then seemed and, indeed, that the opposite would be found when false memories depend on understanding the meaning of events (semantic gist). In particular, fuzzy-trace theory predicted that when false memories depend on such understanding, they would exhibit child-to-adult increases if other factors were held constant (Brainerd & Reyna, 1998). This prediction seemed solid, because it was anchored in classic literature showing developmental improvements in spontaneous connection of meaning among events (for a review, see Schneider & Bjorklund, 1998). That was worrisome for forensic application because (a) false memories from meaning connections are the most common ones in everyday life (Lampinen, Copeland, & Neuschatz, 2001; Reyna & Kiernan, 1994), and (b) they are the most compelling ones to adults (Arndt, 2012).

It took a few years for the first data to appear, but when they did, reversals of the developmental decline pattern were confirmed, repeatedly. First, several experiments were published on an influential connected-meaning illusion from the adult literature—the Deese/Roediger/McDermott (DRM) paradigm (Brainerd, Reyna, & Forrest, 2002; Brainerd, Holliday, & Reyna, 2004; Dewhurst & Robinson, 2004). Subjects study short lists of related words (e.g., *nurse, sick, hospital, ill, medicine, . . .*), all of which are associates of a critical unpresented word (*doctor*). On memory tests, that word is falsely recalled and recognized at reliable levels. All of the experiments found developmental reversals for these false memories—the first three experiments showed that false recognition roughly doubled and false recall roughly quintupled between early childhood and young adulthood (see Fig. 1). It is worth reiterating that although the DRM paradigm is a laboratory task, it preserves a core property of everyday false memories—namely, that they arise from meaning relations.

An extensive literature on developmental reversals has now accumulated, and in a recent review of it (Brainerd, Reyna, & Zember, 2011), evidence of reversals from DRM experiments proved to be substantial: More than 50 such experiments have been published, confirming beyond doubt that this semantic illusion increases with age. The literature contains three other well-established patterns that

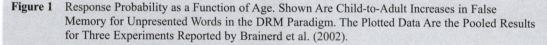

Figure 1   Response Probability as a Function of Age. Shown Are Child-to-Adult Increases in False Memory for Unpresented Words in the DRM Paradigm. The Plotted Data Are the Pooled Results for Three Experiments Reported by Brainerd et al. (2002).

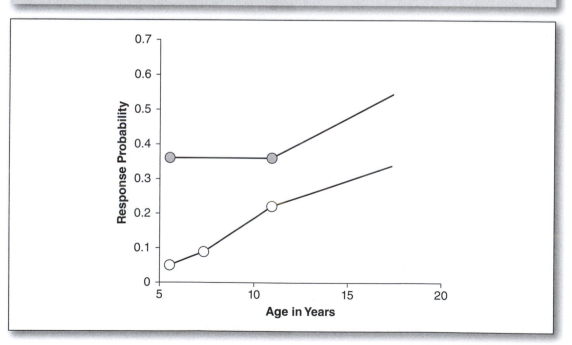

are crucial to forensic application: paradigmatic breadth, ecological validity, and process control.

Paradigmatic Breadth

Because developmental reversals have deep forensic consequences, the first question for most of us is whether they are confined to the 50+ DRM experiments. Actually, their empirical base is quite broad, reversals having been reported with most of the traditional procedures for studying children's false memories. Examples of 10 procedures, with an illustrative developmental reversal study for each, are provided in Table 2. They encompass a wide assortment of memory materials and methods. Across the procedures, the number of published experiments showing developmental reversals is now greater than 80. Their main

Table 2 Paradigms Used in Published Experiments That Detected Developmental Reversals in False Memory, With Illustrative Studies

Paradigm	Methodology
DRM	Subjects study lists of words or pictures that are associates of unpresented items. False memory for unpresented items increases with age. The increase can be greater than the corresponding one for true memories, yielding net reductions in accuracy (Brainerd et al., 2002).
Causal narratives	Subjects study narratives of specific everyday events from which the causes have been omitted. The tendency to falsely remember unpresented causes as having been presented increases with age (Lyons, Ghetti, & Cornoldi, 2010).
Categorized lists	Subjects study lists of words or pictures that are exemplars of familiar categories (e.g., animals, trees). False memory for unpresented exemplars increases with age (Sloutsky & Fisher, 2004).
Emotion terms	Subjects study lists of semantically related words or pictures that vary in emotional valence (e.g., some lists consist of negative items, others of neutral items). Age increases in false memory are greater for emotional items than for neutral items (Brainerd, Holliday, Reyna, Yang, & Toglia, 2010).
Eyewitness identification	Subjects view videos of crimes, in which some characters are perpetrators and others are innocent but conceptually similar bystanders. The tendency to falsely remember innocent bystanders as perpetrators increases with age (Ross et al., 2006).
Group conformity	Subjects participate in staged events or view videos of events. The tendency to falsely remember events that were discussed but not experienced increases with age (Candel, Memon, & Al-Harazi, 2007).
Group play	Subjects participate in group activities that revolve around a stated theme (e.g., a birthday party for Harry Potter characters). The tendency to falsely remember theme-consistent events that did not happen increases with age (Odegard, Cooper, Lampinen, Reyna, & Brainerd, 2009).

(Continued)

Table 2 (Continued)

Paradigm	Methodology
Misinformation	Methodology is described in Table 1. The tendency to falsely remember misinformation as having occurred during the encoding phase increases with age (Connolly & Price, 2006).
Rumor mongering	Subjects participate in staged events or view videos of events. Later, rumors are circulated to them about the acts of certain characters. Subjects' tendency to falsely remember rumored acts as having actually occurred increases with age (Principe, Guiliano, & Root, 2008).
Survival processing	Items are studied under instructions to the think about their usefulness in helping subjects survive in hostile environments in which food and shelter must be obtained and predators must be avoided. False memory for unpresented items increases more with age when study material is processed for survival value than when it is processed for its usefulness for other purposes, such as moving (Otgaar & Smeets, 2010).

commonality is meaning connection: In all instances, the target events that subjects experience are meaningfully related, and the false memories that subjects display preserve those relations.

Ecological Validity

Despite such extensive evidence, every false memory researcher is familiar with the standard objection from forensic quarters: ecological validity. According to that objection, results from laboratory tasks, such as the DRM illusion or categorized lists (exemplars of familiar taxonomic categories), are irrelevant to legal cases because memory evidence is about real-life happenings that are far more complex than list learning. This objection is often offered as though it were a self-evident truth for which no data need to be presented—when data are considered, however, they run rather decidedly in the opposite direction (for many examples, see Banaji & Crowder, 1989).

Still, the objection must be taken seriously, if for no other reason than the history of applied memory research shows that its rhetorical appeal overwhelms disconfirmation by mere facts (Brainerd & Reyna, 2012). Researchers have long addressed this objection by studying analogues of complex real-world memories and demonstrating results similar to those for laboratory tasks (e.g., Ceci & Bruck, 1995; Loftus, 1975). This has been done for developmental reversals in false memory by studying these effects with five forensic memory paradigms: misinformation, eyewitness identification, group conformity, rumor mongering, and narrative memory. It can be seen in Table 2 that when the theoretical conditions for developmental reversals are met, these effects have been detected with all five procedures.

As a final consideration in this vein, consider emotion. A key feature of memory evidence is that witnesses' experiences are emotionally charged; thus, it is crucial to know whether developmental reversals extend to emotional false memories. They do (see Table 2). Developmental reversals in emotional false memories have been reported for both laboratory (e.g., Brainerd, Holliday, Reyna, Yang, & Toglia, 2010) and forensic (e.g., Fernandez-Dols, Carrera, Barchard, & Gacitua, 2008) paradigms. Normally, in legal cases, events are negative and arousing (i.e., crimes are unpleasant but exciting), and thus most developmental reversal studies have focused on that conjunction of emotional attributes (e.g., Fernandez-Dols et al., 2008; Howe, Candel, Otgaar, Malone, & Wimmer, 2010).

Process Control

Beyond demonstrating developmental reversals with a wide range of tasks, an equally fundamental result for legal application is process control of these effects; that is, cause-effect relations between developmental reversals and controlling processes posited in theoretical principles. Process control of false memory is significant because theoretical principles have a broader scope of application than empirical effects. The details of crimes and of what witnesses attempt to remember vary greatly from case to case. For jurors who must decide how much weight to assign to the evidence of different witnesses, theoretical principles that cut through such variability to underlying regularities are immensely useful tools.

So far, good process control has been achieved with the principle that originally predicted developmental reversals—that is, false memories that are rooted in understanding meaning connections among events (e.g., that *dog, cow, horse*, and *sheep* are all farm animals) are apt to increase with age because formation of such connections improves dramatically between childhood and young adulthood. If such improvement is a cause of developmental reversals, it will be possible to shrink or eliminate those effects via two types of manipulations: those that support meaning connection and those that interfere with it. The logic is simple: Support manipulations will shrink developmental reversals by increasing false memory more in younger subjects, whereas interference manipulations will shrink developmental reversals by reducing false memory more in older subjects than in younger subjects. The reason in both instances is that older subjects are more likely to form meaning connections in the first place, so that support manipulations will help them less and interference manipulations will hurt them more.

Developmental DRM studies have confirmed both predictions with various support and interference manipulations. Illustrative data for two support manipulations are plotted in Figure 2. One (gist cuing) encourages subjects to think about semantic relations among words as they study a list; the other (stories) makes those relations

Figure 2 Bias-Corrected False Recognition as a Function of Age. Development Reversals Are Reduced by Instructing Subjects to Think About Semantic Relations Among DRM Words as They Study Lists (a) or by Presenting DRM Words in Stories About Everyday Situations (b). The Data in (a) Are for the 9- and 21-Year-Old Groups in Experiment 2 of Lampinen, Leding, Reed, and Odegard (2006). The Data in (b) Are for the 7- and 11-Year-Old Groups in Howe and Wilkinson (2011). The Bias-Correction Method Was Two-High Threshold.

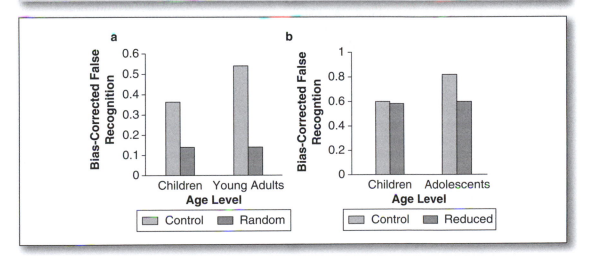

Figure 3 Bias-Corrected False Recognition as a Function of Age. Development Reversals Are Reduced by Presenting Words From Several DRM Lists in Random Order (a) or by Presenting Fewer Words for Each List (b). The Data in (a) Are for the 9- and 21-Year-Old Groups in Experiment 1 of Lampinen, Leding, Reed, and Odegard (2006).

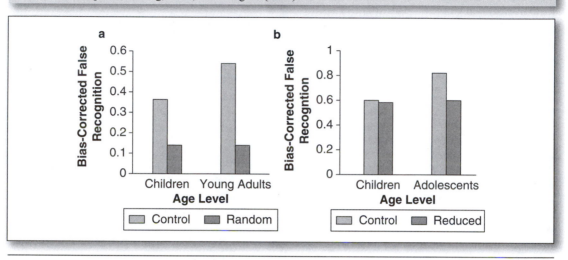

Note: The Data in (b) Are for the 10- and 21-Year-Old Groups in Sugrue and Hayne (2006). The Bias-Correction Method Was Two-High Threshold.

SUMMARY

Developmental research on false memory that began in the 1980s produced fundamental changes in how criminal cases involving children are investigated and tried (e.g., Ceci & Bruck, 1995; Goodman, 2006; Poole & Lamb, 1998). In recent research, developmental reversal effects have challenged the universality of the developmental decline pattern that emerged from this classic work. More changes are in order, now that it is well established that false memory can increase dramatically with age and, hence, that the principle that children's evidence is inherently more infected with false memories than adults' evidence is no longer tenable.

Funding

Preparation of this article was supported by National Institute on Aging Grant 1RC1-AG036915–02.

REFERENCES

Arndt, J. (2012). False recollection: Empirical findings and their theoretical implications. *Psychology of Learning and Motivation, 56*, 81–124.

Banaji, M. R., & Crowder, R. G. (1989). The bankruptcy of everyday memory. *American Psychologist, 44*, 1185–1193.

Binet, A. (1900). *La suggestibilite* [Suggestibility]. Paris, France: Schleicher Freres.

Brainerd, C. J., Holliday, R. E., & Reyna, V. F. (2004). Behavioral measurement of remembering phenomenologies: So simple a child can do it. *Child Development, 75*, 505–522.

Brainerd, C. J., Holliday, R. E., Reyna, V. F., Yang, Y., & Toglia, M. P. (2010). Developmental reversals in false memory: Effects of emotional valence and arousal. *Journal of Experimental Child Psychology, 107*, 137–154.

Brainerd, C. J., & Reyna, V. F. (1998). Fuzzy-trace theory and children's false memories. *Journal of Experimental Child Psychology, 71*, 81–129.

Brainerd, C. J., & Reyna, V. F. (2005). *The science of false memory*. New York, NY: Oxford University Press.

Brainerd, C. J., & Reyna, V. F. (2012). Reliability of children's testimony in the era of developmental reversals. *Developmental Review, 32,* 224–267.

Brainerd, C. J., Reyna, V. F., & Forrest, T. J. (2002). Are young children susceptible to the false-memory illusion? *Child Development, 73,* 1363–1377.

Brainerd, C. J., Reyna, V. F., & Zember, E. (2011). Theoretical and forensic implications of developmental studies of the DRM illusion. *Memory & Cognition, 39,* 365–380.

Candel, I., Memon, A., & Al-Harazi, F. (2007). Peer discussion affects children's memory reports. *Applied Cognitive Psychology, 21,* 1191–1199.

Ceci, S. J., & Bruck, M. (1993). The suggestibility of the child witness: A historical review and synthesis. *Psychological Bulletin, 113,* 403–439.

Ceci, S. J., & Bruck, M. (1995). *Jeopardy in the courtroom: A scientific analysis of children's testimony.* Washington, DC: American Psychological Association.

Connolly, D. A., & Price, H. L. (2006). Children's suggestibility for an instance of a repeated event versus a unique event: The effect of degree of association between variable details. *Journal of Experimental Child Psychology, 93,* 207–223.

Dewhurst, S. A., & Robinson, C. A. (2004). False memories in children: Evidence for a shift from phonological to semantic associations. *Psychological Science, 15,* 782–786.

Fed. R. Evid. P. 601.

Fernandez-Dols, J. M., Carrera, P., Barchard, K. A., & Gacitua, M. (2008). False recognition of facial expressions of emotion: Causes and implications. *Emotion, 8,* 530–539.

Goodman, G. S. (2006). Children's eyewitness memory: A modern history and contemporary commentary. *Journal of Social Issues, 62,* 811–832.

Holliday, R. E., Brainerd, C. J., & Reyna, V. F. (2011). Developmental reversals in false memory: Now you see them, now you don't! *Developmental Psychology, 47,* 442–449.

Howe, M. L., Candel, I., Otgaar, H., Malone, C., & Wimmer, M. C. (2010). Valence and the development of immediate and long-term false memory illusions. *Memory, 18,* 58–75.

Howe, M. L., & Wilkinson, S. (2011). Using story contexts to bias children's true and false memories. *Journal of Experimental Child Psychology, 108,* 75–95.

Kassin, S. M. (2012). Why confessions trump innocence. *American Psychologist, 67,* 431–445.

Lampinen, J. M., Copeland, S. M., & Neuschatz, J. S. (2001). Recollections of things schematic: Room schemas revisited. *Journal of Experimental Psychology: Learning, Memory, and Cognition, 27,* 1211–1222.

Lampinen, J. M., Leding, J. K., Reed, K. B., & Odegard, T. N. (2006). Global gist extraction in children and adults. *Memory, 14,* 952–964.

Loftus, E. F. (1975). Leading questions and the eyewitness report. *Cognitive Psychology, 7,* 560–572.

Loftus, E. F., & Davis, D. (2006). Recovered memories. *Annual Review of Clinical Psychology, 2,* 469–498.

Lyons, K. E., Ghetti, S., & Cornoldi, C. (2010). Age differences in the contribution of recollection and familiarity to false-memory formation: A new paradigm to examine developmental reversals. *Developmental Science, 13,* 355–362.

Odegard, T. N., Cooper, C. M., Lampinen, J. M., Reyna, V. F., & Brainerd, C. J. (2009). Children's eyewitness memory for multiple real-life events. *Child Development, 80,* 1877–1890.

Otgaar, H., & Smeets, T. (2010). Adaptive memory: Survival processing increases both true and false memory in adults and children. *Journal of Experimental Psychology: Learning, Memory, and Cognition, 36,* 1010–1016.

People of the State of California v. Ray Buckey, No. A-750900 (Cal. Super. Ct. L.A. County 1990).

Poole, D. A., & Lamb, M. E. (1998). *Investigative interviews of children.* Washington, DC: American Psychological Association.

Principe, G. F., Guiliano, S., & Root, C. (2008). Rumor mongering and remembering: How rumors originating in children's inferences can affect memory. *Journal of Experimental Child Psychology, 99,* 135–155.

Reyna, V. F., & Kiernan, B. (1994). The development of gist versus verbatim memory in sentence recognition: Effects of lexical familiarity, semantic content, encoding instructions, and retention interval. *Developmental Psychology, 30,* 178–191.

Ross, D. F., Marsil, D. F., Benton, T. R., Hoffman, R., Warren, A. R., Lindsay, R. C. L., & Metzger, R. (2006). Children's susceptibility to misidentifying a familiar bystander from a lineup: When younger is better. *Law and Human Behavior, 30,* 249–257.

Schneider, W., & Bjorklund, D. F. (1998). Memory. In W. Damon, D. Kuhn, & R. S. Siegler (Eds.),

Handbook of child psychology: Cognition, perception, and language (5th ed., Vol. 2, pp. 467–522). New York, NY: Wiley.

Sloutsky, V. M., & Fisher, A. V. (2004). When development and learning decrease memory. *Psychological Science, 15*, 553–558.

State of New Jersey v. Margaret Kelly Michaels, 264 N.J. Super 579, 620–635, 625 A.2d 489 (Super. Ct. App. Div. 1993), aff'd, 136 N.J. 299, 642 A.2d 1372 (1994).

Sugrue, K., & Hayne, H. (2006). False memories produced by children and adults in the DRM paradigm. *Applied Cognitive Psychology, 20*, 625–631.

Wells, G. L., Steblay, N. K., & Dysart, J. E. (2012). Eyewitness identification reforms: Are suggestiveness-induced hits and guesses true hits? *Perspectives on Psychological Science, 7*, 264–271.

12

Future Directions in the Restoration of Competency to Stand Trial*

Patricia A. Zapf

Ronald Roesch

Incompetency to stand trial is a legal concept of jurisprudence that allows defendants who are unable to participate in their own defense to postpone their trial until competency is regained. The U.S. Supreme Court established the current legal standard for determining competency to stand trial in *Dusky v. United States* (1960), and every jurisdiction has adopted or adapted this standard into their competency statutes. The issue of how to deal with incompetent defendants, however, was not addressed in Dusky.

Until the landmark case of *Jackson v. Indiana* (1972), most states allowed the automatic and indefinite confinement of incompetent defendants. This resulted in many defendants being held for lengthy periods of time, often beyond the sentence that might have been imposed had they been convicted. In Jackson, the Supreme Court held that a defendant committed solely on the basis of incompetency "cannot be held more than the reasonable period of time necessary to determine whether there is a substantial probability that he will attain that capacity in the foreseeable future"(p. 738). The Court did not specify restrictions to the length of time a defendant could reasonably be held, nor did it indicate how progress toward the goal of regaining competency could be assessed. Nevertheless, this decision resulted in changes to state laws regarding confinement of incompetent defendants. Many states now place limits on the maximum length of time an incompetent defendant can be held and, if a defendant is determined to be unlikely to ever regain competency, the commitment must be terminated. It is

---

*This article was published in *Current Directions in Psychological Science*, *20*, 43–47 (2011).

worth noting, however, that some states appear to continue to circumvent *Jackson* by allowing long-term and even indefinite confinement of incompetent defendants (Miller, 2003).

Since 1980, a relatively limited amount of research has begun to accumulate with respect to the issue of competency restoration. Although outpatient treatment is possible, most treatment continues to take place in residential forensic facilities (Miller, 2003). The vast majority— around 75%—of incompetent defendants are returned to court as competent within about 6 months (Bennett & Kish, 1990; Golding, Eaves, & Kowaz, 1989; Morris & Parker, 2008; Nicholson & McNulty, 1992). In general, research has examined two types of questions: (a) whether there are certain variables that can predict who will and will not regain competency and (b) whether certain types of treatment programs are more successful than others. We will review the literature on these two questions in the next two sections.

PREDICTION OF RESTORABILITY

As a result of the *Jackson* decision, mental health professionals are often required to predict a defendant's probability of regaining competency. That is, examiners must determine if competency can be restored in a reasonable amount of time. Extrapolating from the work of Meehl (1954), it could be argued that, due to the low base rate of failure to restore competency, evaluators could not predict with any degree of accuracy those defendants who would not regain competency, as those evaluators were likely to automatically assume that competency could be restored. Indeed, in 1980, Roesch and Golding speculated that mental health professionals were limited in their ability to predict which defendants would not be restorable to competence. Research conducted since then has confirmed that the ability of clinicians to predict competency restoration is poor (Carbonell, Heilbrun, & Friedman, 1992; Hubbard, Zapf, & Ronan, 2003; Nicholson, Barnard, Robbins, & Hankins, 1994;

Nicholson & McNulty, 1992). An early study conducted by Cuneo and Brelje (1984) illustrates the problems in predicting restoration. These researchers found a 78% accuracy rate for professionals who were asked to predict whether competency would be restored within 1 year. Although at first glance, this rate may seem impressive, it becomes less so when the high base rate for restoration is taken into consideration (i.e., the fact that most defendants are restored within a 6-month period). The false-positive rate (i.e., the proportion of defendants who are predicted to regain competency but do not) is a more appropriate statistic to evaluate the ability to accurately predict responsiveness to treatment. In the Cuneo and Brelje study, the false-positive rate was 23%. Thus, it appears that clinicians have a difficult time identifying the smaller percentage of incompetent defendants who will not respond to treatment.

Hubbard and Zapf (2003) used logistic regression to investigate the variables related to predictions of restorability in a sample of 89 incompetent defendants and found that current violent charge and previous criminal history were the two most significant predictors of restorability decisions. In attempting to explain this finding, the authors interviewed key players in the forensic system who postulated that this might be the result of political pressure to hold accountable and to take to trial those individuals charged with violent crimes and those with criminal histories. When criminal, diagnostic, and sociodemographic variables were considered individually, defendants predicted to not be restorable were more likely to be older and to have impairment in the ability to understand information about the legal process, whereas those predicted to be restorable were more likely to have less serious diagnoses (i.e., nonpsychotic mental disorders) and more serious, violent criminal histories (Hubbard et al., 2003).

In a statistically well-controlled study on prediction of competence restoration, Mossman (2007) examined the records of 351 inpatient pretrial defendants who underwent competence restoration at a state psychiatric facility in Ohio, to determine whether there were certain variables available to forensic examiners that could predict restoration outcome. The variables of interest included demographic characteristics, diagnoses, symptom patterns, criminal charges, number of prior psychiatric hospitalizations, and cumulative prior length of stay. Mossman found that there were two typical instances in which a defendant might be considered to have a low probability of restoration: first, if the basis for the defendant's incompetence was a longstanding psychotic disorder that had resulted in lengthy periods of hospitalization, and second, if the basis for the defendant's incompetence was an irremediable cognitive disorder, such as mental retardation, that resulted in a limited grasp of the information that an examiner attempted to convey during an evaluation. Each of these scenarios appears to result in a well-below-average chance of successful restoration.

In a similar study, Morris and Parker (2008) examined data from 1,475 admissions for competency restoration in Indiana between 1988 and 2005 to determine the factors associated with successful restoration to competence. These authors reported that 72.3% of the admissions over this time period were restored to competence within 6 months and 83.9% within 1 year. In addition, those with mood disorders were most likely to be restored to competence and were significantly more likely to be restored than were those diagnosed with psychotic disorders. Defendants with mental retardation (either alone or in conjunction with a mental illness) were significantly less likely to be restored than were defendants with any other psychiatric disorder, and those diagnosed with both mental retardation and a mental illness were significantly less likely to be restored than were defendants with mental retardation alone. Regression analyses indicated that females and those with affective disorders were most likely to be successfully restored, whereas older age, mental retardation, and a psychotic diagnosis were significantly related to a decreased chance of restoration.

The available research has provided two important insights for clinicians who are required to make predictions regarding restorability and for lawmakers charged with developing or refining competency statutes. First, the vast majority of defendants are restored to competency within a 6-month period (and even more within 1 year). Second, certain characteristics have been consistently suggestive of a reduced chance of successful restoration: older age, a diagnosis of mental retardation, and a diagnosis of psychotic disorder (especially if it has resulted in lengthy periods of hospitalization). This is important information for evaluators to consider when opining about the chances of a defendant's successful restoration.

The weaknesses in the available research, however, are its primary focus on diagnosis as a psychiatric indicator of successful or unsuccessful restoration and its reduction of competence to a single construct. Information regarding the specific symptoms associated with unsuccessful and successful restoration attempts and the specific competency-related abilities that are impaired and/or remediable would be more useful in this regard. To date, research on competency (and other psycho-legal issues) has focused almost solely on diagnosis as a psychiatric indicator; however, diagnosis per se is far less informative than is information regarding the extent to which specific psychiatric symptoms are associated with competency-related deficits and successful and/or unsuccessful restoration attempts.

Only relatively recently have some investigators begun to focus more on the specific competency-related abilities than on competency as a singular construct (see Jacobs, Ryba, & Zapf, 2008; Viljoen, Zapf, & Roesch, 2003). Moving forward, research that examines both symptom-level impairments and competency-specific deficits will provide a more detailed illustration of the ways in which specific symptoms (regardless of diagnosis) impact various competency-related abilities. This information could provide key insights regarding the types of symptoms and competency-related deficits that have the most significant implications for competency status and successful remediation. Competency restoration programs could then be developed and tailored to individual defendants and their specific symptoms and deficits.

TREATMENT PROGRAMS FOR COMPETENCY RESTORATION[1]

Incompetence is predicated on two components: a mental disorder or cognitive impairment and a deficit in one or more competency-related abilities that occurs as a result of the mental disorder or cognitive impairment. Thus, treatment programs for the restoration of competency have typically targeted both mental disorder/cognitive impairment and competency-related abilities. It is often the case that improvement in the underlying mental disorder or cognitive impairment results in improvement in competency-related deficits. The most common form of treatment for the restoration of competency involves the administration of psychotropic medication.

The majority of incompetent defendants consent to the use of medication. The issue of an incompetent defendant refusing to consent has been tested in a number of court cases (e.g., *Washington v. Harper*, 1990; *Riggins v. Nevada*, 1992). The U.S. Supreme Court held, in *Sell v. United States* (2003), that antipsychotic drugs could be administered against the defendant's wishes for the purpose of restoring competency, but only in rare, limited circumstances. Writing for the majority, Justice Breyer noted that a court "must find that medication is substantially likely to render the defendant competent to stand trial and substantially unlikely to have side effects that will interfere significantly with the defendant's ability to assist counsel in conducting a defense" (p. 167).

Although medication is the most frequent treatment, some jurisdictions have established educational treatment programs designed to increase a defendant's understanding of the legal process or individualized treatment programs that confront the problems that hinder a defendant's ability to participate in his or her defense (competence-related deficits). In addition, some jurisdictions have implemented treatment programs specifically targeted toward those defendants found incompetent to proceed on the basis of mental retardation.

The success of treatment programs for the restoration of competence is variable and dependent upon the type of treatment program and the type of defendant targeted. Anderson and Hewitt (2002) examined treatment programs designed to restore competency in defendants with mental retardation and found that only 18% of their sample was restored. These researchers concluded that "for the most part, competency training for defendants with [mental retardation] might not be that effective" (p. 349). Other researchers and commentators have found similar results and have noted the difficulty in treating a chronic condition such as mental retardation (Appelbaum, 1994; Pinals, 2005; Wall, Krupp, & Guilmette, 2003).

Treatment programs that target defendants with various other types of mental disorders have met with more success, in that larger proportions of the defendants are restored to competency. Siegel and Elwork (1990) evaluated the use of an educational program as part of the competency restoration process by comparing randomly assigned control and experimental groups. The experimental condition included the use of a videotape that described the roles of courtroom personnel and court procedure, as well as group problem-solving sessions in which problems arising from a defendant's actual legal case were presented and discussed. Results showed greater improvement on Competency Assessment Instrument scores for the experimental group and a greater number of staff recommendations of competency to stand trial (45 days after treatment, 43% of the treated group, but only 15% of the controls were considered competent by staff).

Bertman and colleagues (2003) examined the effectiveness of three types of treatment programs for the restoration of competence: standard hospital treatment, legal rights education, and deficit-focused (competency-related, not psychiatric, deficits) remediation. While the individualized treatment programs (both legal rights education and deficit-focused remediation) led to higher scores on posttreatment competency measures than did standard hospital treatment, the authors were unable to tease apart whether this was a result of the individualized attention or simply a result of the greater number of treatment sessions that those in the individualized treatment groups received. Thus, it is not clear that individualized treatment programs that target specific underlying deficits for each defendant are any more effective than educational programs that teach defendants about their legal rights.

What the available research appears to indicate is that successful restoration is related to how well the defendant responds to psychotropic medications administered to alleviate the symptoms of the mental disorder. The addition of an educational component (either general or individualized) appears to offer some benefit for increasing a defendant's legal knowledge; however, to date, there has not been any published research that specifically examines how either the improved symptoms of mental disorder or improved legal knowledge might impact a defendant's specific competency-related abilities or deficits. Once again, it becomes clear that more information regarding the interplay between psychiatric symptoms and competency-related abilities or deficits could provide better direction for the development and personalization of competency restoration programs.

CALL FOR RESEARCH

Recently, Schwalbe and Medalia (2007) have argued for the use of cognitive remediation as an adjunct to competency restoration programs on the basis that there is evidence to suggest that it leads to improved cognitive functioning (e.g., improved attention, reasoning, memory, executive function), which not only improves the success of competency training but also improves the individual competency-related abilities required of a defendant (i.e., the specific prongs

of the Dusky standard). Although they provide no data, Schwalbe and Medalia make a sound, rational argument for the inclusion of a specific treatment component that targets the exact abilities to be restored. This is precisely the type of rationale upon which treatment programs for competency restoration should be developed and tested.

Future research on competency restoration is necessary to further develop and refine effective competency restoration programs for various types of defendants. Focusing on specific cognitive deficits and symptoms of mental disorder and the interplay between these and various competency-related abilities and deficits will provide critical information to increase our understanding of both the construct of competence (and all that it entails) and how we can develop and refine effective interventions for the successful restoration of competency.

Note

1. Our discussion of treatment focuses on adults found incompetent. As Viljoen and Grisso comment (2007), adolescent competence concerns are due infrequently to mental illness but more often to deficits stemming from developmental immaturity and/or mental retardation. As a consequence, neither psychotropic medication nor psychoeducational programs are likely to be effective.

REFERENCES

Anderson, S. D., & Hewitt, J. (2002). The effect of competency restoration training on defendants with mental retardation found not competent to proceed. *Law and Human Behavior*, *26*, 343–351.

Appelbaum, K. L. (1994). Assessment of criminal-justice-related competencies in defendants with mental retardation. *Journal of Psychiatry and Law*, *22*, 311–327.

Bennett, G., & Kish, G. (1990). Incompetency to stand trial: Treatment unaffected by demographic variables. *Journal of Forensic Sciences*, *35*, 403–412.

Bertman, L. J., Thompson, J. W., Jr., Waters, W. F., Estupinan-Kane, L., Martin, J. A., & Russell, L.

(2003). Effect of an individualized treatment protocol on restoration of competency in pretrial forensic inpatients. *Journal of the American Academy of Psychiatry and Law, 31,* 27–35.

Carbonell, J., Heilbrun, K., & Friedman, F. (1992). Predicting who will regain trial competence: Initial promise unfulfilled. *Forensic Reports, 5,* 67–76.

Cuneo, D., & Brelje, T. (1984). Predicting probability of attaining fitness to stand trial. *Psychological Reports, 55,* 35–39.

Dusky v. United States, 362 U.S. 402 (1960).

Golding, S. L., Eaves, D., & Kowaz, A. (1989). The assessment, treatment and community outcome of insanity acquittees: Forensic history and response to treatment. *International Journal of Law and Psychiatry, 12,* 149–179.

Hubbard, K. L., & Zapf, P. A. (2003). The role of demographic, criminal, and psychiatric variables in examiners' predictions of restorability to competency to stand trial. *International Journal of Forensic Mental Health, 2,* 145–155.

Hubbard, K. L., Zapf, P. A., & Ronan, K. A. (2003). Competency restoration: An examination of the differences between defendants predicted restorable and not restorable to competency. *Law and Human Behavior, 27,* 127–139.

Jackson v. Indiana, 406 U.S. 715 (1972).

Jacobs, M. S., Ryba, N. L., & Zapf, P. A. (2008). Competence-related abilities and psychiatric symptoms: An analysis of the underlying structure and correlates of the MacCAT-CA and the BPRS. *Law and Human Behavior, 32,* 64–77.

Meehl, P. E. (1954). *Clinical vs. statistical prediction.* Minneapolis, MN: University of Minnesota Press.

Miller, R. D. (2003). Hospitalization of criminal defendants for evaluation of competence to stand trial or for restoration of competence: Clinical and legal issues. *Behavioral Science and Law, 21,* 369–391.

Morris, D. R., & Parker, G. F. (2008). Jackson's Indiana: State hospital competence restoration in Indiana. *Journal of the American Academy of Psychiatry and Law, 36,* 522–534.

Mossman, D. (2007). Predicting restorability of incompetent criminal defendants. *The Journal of the American Academy of Psychiatry and the Law, 35,* 34–43.

Nicholson, R., Barnard, G., Robbins, L., & Hankins, G. (1994). Predicting treatment outcome for incompetent defendants. *Bulletin of the American Academy of Psychiatry and the Law, 22,* 367–377.

Nicholson, R., & McNulty, J. (1992). Outcome of hospitalization for defendants found incompetent to stand trial. *Behavioral Sciences and the Law, 10,* 371–383.

Pinals, D. (2005). Where two roads met: Restoration of competence to stand trial from a clinical perspective. *New England Journal of Civil and Criminal Confinement, 31,* 81–108.

Riggins v. Nevada, 504 U.S. 127 (1992).

Roesch, R., & Golding, S. L. (1980). *Competency to stand trial.* Urbana, IL: University of Illinois Press.

Schwalbe, E., & Medalia, A. (2007). Cognitive dysfunction and competency restoration: Using cognitive remediation to help restore the unrestorable. *Journal of the American Academy of Psychiatry and Law, 35,* 518–525.

Sell v. United States, 539 U.S. 166 (2003).

Siegel, A. M., & Elwork, A. (1990). Treating incompetence to stand trial. *Law and Human Behavior, 14,* 57–65.

Viljoen, J., & Grisso, T. (2007). Prospects for remediating juveniles' adjudicative incompetence. *Psychology, Public Policy, and Law, 13,* 87–114.

Viljoen, J. L., Zapf, P. A., & Roesch, R. (2003). Diagnosis, current psychiatric symptoms, and the ability to stand trial. *Journal of Forensic Psychology Practice, 3,* 23–37.

Wall, B. W., Krupp, B. H., & Guilmette, T. (2003). Restoration of competency to stand trial: A training program for persons with mental retardation. *Journal of the American Academy of Psychiatry and Law, 31,* 189–210.

Washington v. Harper, 494 U.S. 210 (1990).

13

THE UTILITY OF SCIENTIFIC JURY SELECTION

Still Murky After 30 Years*

JOEL D. LIEBERMAN

In the United States, attorneys have come to use trial consultants in almost all major litigation (Lieberman & Sales, 2007; Strier, 1999). Among the services consultants provide is scientific jury selection (SJS), which involves the use of social science research techniques to identify desirable and undesirable jurors. SJS operates on the assumption that by applying scientific methodology, consultants should be able to predict whether certain types of individuals will be supportive of one side or the other in a trial, with greater accuracy than attorneys who rely on their own experience and intuitive judgments. However, there is considerable debate regarding the effectiveness of SJS. For approximately 30 years, psychologists have attempted to determine the utility of this approach by indirectly testing the effects of background characteristics on verdict decisions through experimental research and

with direct examinations of cases where SJS has been used. In this article, I review the relevant research that provides insight into SJS effectiveness and discuss the problems inherent in determining what effectiveness means in the context of trial outcomes.

JURY SELECTION PROCESS

The jury selection process (known as *voir dire*) allows attorneys to eliminate potentially biased prospective jurors from serving on trials. There are two mechanisms for eliminating jurors: a challenge for cause and a peremptory challenge. A challenge for cause enables an attorney to eliminate a prospective juror when it can be demonstrated that the individual is so biased that they could not render a fair verdict (e.g., as a

---

*This article was published in *Current Directions in Psychological Science*, *20*, 48–52 (2011).

function of their expressed attitudes, behavior, experiences, relationship to a trial participant such as the defendant or a witness) or is unwilling to follow the law. Attorneys are allowed an unlimited number of challenges for cause.

Alternatively, an attorney can use a limited number of peremptory challenges, in which he or she can eliminate a prospective juror without providing any justification. Although there are certain restrictions placed on peremptory challenges, such as eliminating jurors strictly on the basis of race (*Batson v. Kentucky*, 1986), these restrictions are often circumvented. For example, Black Americans continue to be disproportionately excluded as prospective jurors (Baldus, Woodworth, Zuckerman, Weiner, & Broffitt, 2001). Periodically the judge may require an attorney to explain the logic behind excluding a minority juror if there is suspicion that the juror has been inappropriately challenged. In such a situation, it is essential that the attorney provide a race-neutral justification to avoid court sanctions. In experimental research, actual attorneys (as well as law students and college students asked to assume the role of attorneys) made race-neutral justifications for race-based jury selection decisions in the absence of any potential judicially imposed penalties (Sommers & Norton, 2007). Thus, it is not clear if race-based challenges are fully intentional. If race-based exclusions are guided by inherent biases, then an SJS approach should provide more objective selection criteria.

Ultimately, attorneys must use some strategy to guide their decision making during *voir dire*. Attorneys may rely on their own beliefs about the influence of factors such as race, income, occupation, religion, marital status, and appearance. These beliefs may develop based on attorneys' own experiences, lessons learned from other lawyers, or suggestions in trial tactics manuals. Alternatively, attorneys may hire trial consultants to identify jurors who are likely to be sympathetic, hostile, or impartial to the parties involved in the case. It should be noted that trial consultants may assist attorneys in other ways, including the development of case themes, evidence presentation, monitoring the effectiveness of case presentation during the trial, and posttrial interviews of jurors.

SJS TECHNIQUES

A variety of techniques are used to make SJS-based recommendations. One of the primary tools jury consultants use is the community survey, which typically involves measuring the persuasiveness of arguments and evidence to be presented. In addition, respondents are asked about perceptions of case characteristics, litigants, and other trial related issues (e.g., exposure to pretrial publicity), as well as their own backgrounds and activities. This facilitates the development of demographically based profiles of individuals who are most (or least) responsive to specific case themes (Lieberman & Sales, 2007). Consultants may also assist in the development of similar pretrial surveys (albeit without questions regarding evidence persuasiveness) that are given to individuals summoned to the courthouse for the trial. Prospective jurors can then potentially be questioned more thoroughly (depending upon the jurisdiction) and challenged during *voir dire*, if necessary. It should be noted that only some states allow extensive questioning of jurors and, in some jurisdictions, only after an attorney petitions to do so.

Trial consultants also use mock juries and focus groups to assist in SJS. Mock juries can be used to examine how different types of individuals respond to different trial strategies and approaches to information presentation (e.g., several variations of opening or closing arguments). Focus groups are used in a similar manner but may have a less formal structure.

EFFECTIVENESS OF SJS

It is difficult to determine the actual effectiveness of SJS. Although selection consultants have reported high success rates, a number of factors make definitive judgments difficult. The high costs associated with employing a trial consultant make SJS more likely to be used in cases where the clients can also afford premier legal representation. Thus, highly skilled attorneys tend to work on cases involving selection consultants. In addition, when a client has substantial financial resources, those resources will likely be used to improve the quality of other aspects of litigation, such as hiring distinguished expert witnesses. Consequently, it is difficult to separate selection consultant effectiveness from overall legal representation quality.

Finally, it is difficult to determine SJS effectiveness in the absence of a meaningful definition of success. For example, from a defense perspective, it may not be necessary for a verdict to be completely in favor of the defense for the case outcome to be considered a success. A lower amount of monetary damages than might otherwise be rendered could be viewed as a success in civil trials, as could a conviction on lesser charges or a hung jury in criminal cases.

However, psychologists have conducted a variety of research studies that shed some light on the topic of SJS effectiveness. These explorations have involved examining the relationship between demographics or personality factors and verdict inclination, and studying the outcome of both real and simulated trials where SJS is used.

Demographic Factors

The effect of demographic characteristics on verdict inclinations has been investigated for a wide variety of factors, including occupation, age, socioeconomic status, ethnicity/race, and gender. However, these factors typically account for less than 2% of verdict variance when examined independently, and less than 5% when combined together (Diamond, Saks, & Landsman, 1998; Hastie, Penrod, & Pennington, 1983; Visher, 1987). Further, the effects of demographic factors tend to be inconsistent and often context dependent. For example, although gender is an unreliable verdict predictor, it may moderate judgments in cases involving sexual violence (Kovera, Gresham, Borgida, Gray, & Regan, 1997). In addition, the influence of juror race often depends on racial similarity between the juror and the defendant and on the seriousness of the crime. Jurors may also be more punitive toward racially similar defendants in specific situations, such as when the majority of jury members are of a different race and there is strong evidence against the defendant (Kerr, Hymes, Anderson, & Weathers, 1995).

The influence of a variety of personality and attitudinal factors on verdict inclinations has also been examined. Although some general personality traits such as authoritarianism, belief in a just world, and locus of control have some degree of predictive validity, greater verdict variance is accounted for when aspects of a "legal personality" or legal attitudes are measured. Examples of legal attitudes include measures of Legal Authoritarianism (reflecting attitudes toward the rights of the accused and civil liberties; Narby, Cutler, & Moran, 1993) and the Juror Bias Scale (measuring beliefs that a defendant actually committed a crime and perceptions of reasonable doubt or the degree of certainty regarding guilt necessary to render a conviction; Kassin & Wrightsman, 1983). In addition, the Pretrial Juror Attitudes Questionnaire (PJAQ) has recently been developed, which measures factors such as conviction proneness, system confidence, cynicism toward the defense, racial bias, social justice, and innate criminality (Lecci & Myers, 2009). Although Legal Authoritarianism and the Juror Bias Scale typically account for about 15% of verdict variance, there is evidence that the PJAQ can account for about 21% of verdict variance (Lecci & Myers, 2009). However, it should be noted that in most cases a trial judge would not allow the full range of questions on a personality scale to be asked.

Not surprisingly, greater predictive accuracy is often obtained when more specific measures of legal attitudes relevant to trials at hand are used. For example, attitudes toward tort reform and legal claims in civil cases, attitudes toward psychiatrists in insanity cases (e.g., Moran, Cutler, & De Lisa, 1994), or endorsement of myths about battered women in cases where an abused wife was accused of killing her husband (Vidmar & Schuller, 1989) have all been shown to be predictive in relevant cases.

Despite the fact that the trend of focusing on more specific personality and attitudinal measures in jury selection research has led to increased verdict prediction, the amount of verdict variance accounted for remains relatively low. These findings may imply that SJS may not be much more useful than traditional judgments made by attorneys. However, it is premature to base conclusions on studies that have simply looked at background characteristics in isolation and have not evaluated a full-scale SJS approach utilized by professional consultants.

Moreover, there is minimal research directly examining the effectiveness of SJS, and extant studies suffer from a variety of methodological limitations, making it difficult to draw meaningful conclusions. For example, Horowitz (1980) investigated the performance of law students trained in either a traditional jury selection or an SJS approach. Individuals in the SJS group were given results of pretrial survey responses and profiles indicating the desirableness of the prospective jurors. The SJS approach was more successful in cases with a strong relationship between the demographic, personality, and attitudinal factors (e.g., a case involving the sale of illegal drugs). Alternatively, traditional jury selection was superior in cases where there was a weak relationship between these factors (e.g., a murder and a drunk-driving case). Unfortunately, the artificiality of the methodology limits these findings; the law students were not experienced practicing attorneys, and the students in the SJS condition were not professional consultants using the full resources of a consulting firm.

In other research, accuracy rates (i.e., the ability to predict jurors' verdicts) over 70% have been reported or estimated for SJS (e.g., Moran, Cutler, & Loftus, 1990). However, it is unclear how much credibility should be given to these rates because materials used are highly artificial

or because direct comparisons are not made between individuals selected using an SJS method and those selected using a traditional method. In some cases, estimates are based on posttrial interviews in which responses of actual jurors exposed to the trial are compared to individuals excused from jury service. Consequently, it is difficult to draw meaningful conclusions, because important individual differences between the groups may exist and because the different groups were not presented with the same evidence. Similarly, comparisons have been made between cases that trial consultants worked on and cases in which they were not used (e.g., Nietzel , Dillehay, & Himelein, 1987). Other researchers have reported results on the utility of SJS techniques from studies that have used a very small sample of cases (e.g., Frederick, 1984), making it difficult to have faith in these studies' reliability and validity.

The issue of small sample size was addressed to some extent in research by Seltzer (2006). Seltzer reported the relationship between background characteristics and trial-relevant attitudes in cases he had been involved in as a trial consultant. His sample included cases involving the use of 27 telephone surveys and 9 focus groups. The findings indicated that background characteristics were somewhat related to case attitudes. Education, race, and church attendance had predictive value in more than 25% of the cases, while gender, media habits, employment status, and occupation were predictive in 10% to 25% of the cases. Number of children, voter registration status, marital status, and income had low predictive ability across cases. However, these results are difficult to interpret, because the dependent measures were relevant case attitudes rather than case outcome. Further, there was no type of control group examining attorney effectiveness in the absence of trial consultant recommendations.

Thus, higher-quality studies are needed to support the limited evidence that exists regarding SJS effectiveness and the types of cases in which SJS may be most useful (e.g., cases where the relationship between verdicts and demographic factors, attitudes, and personality characteristics is most powerful). It has been argued that SJS may be most beneficial when evidence is equivocal and a slight advantage may impact the outcome of the case (Moran et al., 1994). Consequently, it is important to consider the effect of evidence strength when attempting to determine SJS effectiveness.

Evidence Strength

Despite the emphasis that SJS places on identifying important individual differences among potential jurors, research has indicated that evidence strength is a much better predictor of jury verdicts than are juror characteristics. For example, Visher (1987) interviewed jurors who had served on 38 forcible sexual assault trials. The relationship between demographic charactereristics, case-relevant attitudes (toward "blaming the victim" and being "tough on crime"), attitudes regarding the defendant, victim behavior (e.g., use of alcohol or drugs before the incident), as well as evidence and case characteristics (e.g., physical evidence, eyewitness testimony, use of a weapon) were examined. Juror characteristics accounted for only 2% of verdict variance, while evidence strength accounted for 34% of the variance (8% accounted for by victim and defendant characteristics).

Although these findings imply that SJS should exert a weak influence in cases where the evidence is relatively strong for one side, it is important to remember that such cases are unlikely to go to trial and will often be settled or dismissed. Jurors typically sit on more evenly matched trials. In situations where evidence is relatively balanced, small increases in predictive ability gained from SJS may be highly advantageous (Moran et al., 1994).

CONCLUSION

Attorneys in the United States place considerable emphasis on jury selection. To assist in this process, attorneys have come to widely use selection consultants in major civil litigation as well as in highly publicized criminal trials. Over the past 3 decades, a variety of approaches to evaluate the utility of SJS have been used. However, extant studies have a variety of limitations that prevent clear conclusions from being drawn. For example, demographic and personality factors have been shown to be weak verdict predictors when examined outside the context of full-scale SJS services. In some cases, this is used as evidence that SJS is not an effective tool. However, this conclusion may be premature. Background factors can have greater predictive ability when highly specific attitudinal measures are used and when juror characteristics are examined on a case-by-case basis, rather than when factors are applied across a wide variety of cases. In this vein, SJS allows for enhanced specificity by conducting community surveys in the jurisdiction where a trial will be held and by looking at attitudinal factors specific to the case at hand. SJS should be most effective when such case-relevant attitudes have been measured, when the evidence is equivocal, and when extended *voir dire* is allowed. Several research endeavors have simulated consultant activities. However, these types of studies have not utilized the full scope of resources available to trial consulting firms and have typically not captured the realism of actual trials. There is currently a large gap in the literature regarding true evaluative assessments of SJS. Hopefully, psychologists will narrow this gap as the fields of trial consulting and jury decision making continue to develop.

REFERENCES

Baldus, D. C., Woodworth, G., Zuckerman, D., Weiner, N. A., & Broffitt, B. (2001). The use of peremptory challenges in capital murder trials: A legal and empirical analysis. *University of Pennsylvania Journal of Constitutional Law, 3*, 1–172.

Batson v. Kentucky, 476 U.S. 79 (1986).

Diamond, S. S., Saks, M. J., & Landsman, S. (1998). Juror judgments about liability and damages:

Sources of variability and ways to increase consistency. *DePaul Law Review, 48*, 301–325.

Frederick, J. T. (1984). Social science involvement in voir dire: Preliminary data on the effectiveness of "SJS." *Behavioral Sciences & the Law, 2*, 375–394.

Hastie, R., Penrod, S., & Pennington, N. (1983). *Inside the jury*. Cambridge, MA: Harvard University Press.

Horowitz, I. A. (1980). Juror selection: A comparison of two methods in several criminal cases. *Journal of Applied Social Psychology, 10*, 86–99.

Kassin, S. M., & Wrightsman, L. S. (1983). The construction and validation of a juror bias scale. *Journal of Research in Personality, 17*, 423–442.

Kerr, N. L., Hymes, R. W., Anderson, A. B., & Weathers, J. E. (1995). Defendant–juror similarity and mock juror judgments. *Law and Human Behavior, 19*, 545–567.

Kovera, M. B., Gresham, A. W., Borgida, E., Gray, E., & Regan, P. C. (1997). Does expert testimony inform or influence juror decision-making? A social cognitive analysis. *Journal of Applied Psychology, 82*, 178–191.

Lecci, L. B., & Myers, B. (2009). Predicting guilt judgments and verdict change using a measure of pretrial bias in a videotaped mock trial with deliberating jurors. *Psychology, Crime & Law, 15*, 619–634.

Lieberman, J. D., & Sales, B. D. (2007). *Scientific jury selection*. Washington, DC: American Psychological Association.

Moran, G., Cutler, B. L., & De Lisa, A. (1994). Attitudes toward tort reform, scientific jury selection, and juror bias: Verdict inclination in criminal and civil trials. *Law and Psychology Review, 18*, 309–328.

Moran, G., Cutler, B. L., & Loftus, E. F. (1990). Jury selection in major controlled substance trials: The need for extended voir dire. *Forensic Reports, 3*, 331–348.

Narby, D. J., Cutler, B. L., & Moran, G. (1993). A meta-analysis of the association between authoritarianism and jurors' perceptions of defendant culpability. *Journal of Applied Psychology, 78*, 34–42.

Nietzel, M. T., & Dillehay, R. C., Himelein, M. J. (1987). Effects of voir dire variations in capital trials: A replication and extension. *Behavioral Sciences & the Law, 5*, 467–477.

Seltzer, R. (2006). Scientific jury selection: Does it work? *Journal of Applied Social Psychology, 36*, 2417–2435

Sommers, S. R., & Norton, M. I. (2007). Race-based judgments, race-neutral justifications: Experimental examination of peremptory use and the Batson challenge procedure. *Law and Human Behavior, 31*, 261–273.

Strier, F. (1999). Whither trial consulting? Issues and projections. *Law and Human Behavior, 23*, 93–115.

Vidmar, N.J., & Schuller, R.A. (1989). Juries and expert evidence: Social framework testimony. *Law and Contemporary Problems, 52*, 133–176.

Visher, C. (1987). Juror decision making: The importance of evidence. *Law and Human Behavior, 11*, 1–17.

14

Parental Divorce and Children's Adjustment*

Jennifer E. Lansford

In the United States, between 43% and 50% of first marriages end in divorce (U.S. Census Bureau, 2004), and 50% of American children will experience their parents' divorce (National Center for Health Statistics, 2008). Given the large number of families affected by divorce each year, parents, clinicians, and policymakers alike are concerned with understanding how experiencing parental divorce affects children's adjustment. Indeed, many parents considering divorce ask whether they should stay together for the sake of their children.

Key questions in the research literature have focused on whether divorce per se affects children's adjustment and, if so, why and how. The literature has at times portrayed two extreme positions on whether divorce affects children's adjustment (Cherlin, 1999). The first extreme position holds that the longterm effects of divorce on children are quite debilitating and that children carry a lasting negative burden years after the divorce in terms of mental health and interpersonal relationships (e.g., Glenn, 2001; Popenoe, 1993, 2003; Wallerstein, Lewis, & Blakeslee, 2000). This work has drawn criticism for methodological (e.g., reliance on small samples of clinical populations) and ideological reasons. For example, Coontz (1992) points out that many condemnations of divorce and nontraditional families stem from misguided perceptions of family life in previous decades and that myths about family life in the past reflected reality for only a small subset of middle-class European Americans. At the opposite extreme is the position that divorce has no measurable long-term effects on children (e.g., Harris, 1998). This extreme has been criticized because it appears to conflict with hundreds of empirical studies to the contrary.

Between these two extremes, most researchers have come to the conclusion that divorce has some negative effects on children's adjustment

*This article was published in *Perspectives on Psychological Science*, *4*, 140–152 (2009). We have deleted portions of a general introductory section, portions of sections on genetic effects, and demographic characteristics of children, as well as sections on stigmatization, divorce laws and policies, and child-support policies and enforcement.

but that these effects may be small in magnitude and not universal . . . .

The main purpose of this review is to provide an overview of the nuances represented in the patterns of findings regarding links between parental divorce and children's short-term and long-term adjustment. First, I consider how divorce is related to several different aspects of children's adjustment. Second, I examine the timing of divorce, demographic characteristics, children's adjustment prior to the divorce, and stigmatization as moderators of the links between divorce and children's adjustment. Third, I examine income, interparental conflict, parenting, and parents' well-being as mediators of relations between divorce and children's adjustment. Fourth, I describe the caveats and limitations of the research literature. Finally, I consider the notable policies related to grounds for divorce, child support, and child custody in light of how they might affect children's adjustment to their parents' divorce.

INDICATORS OF CHILDREN'S ADJUSTMENT

Although findings regarding whether and how parental divorce is related to children's adjustment are not always clear in the literature, there is agreement among most researchers that children experiencing parental divorce are at risk for a variety of negative developmental outcomes (see Cherlin, 1999, for a review). However, the magnitude of these effects appears to depend on the indicators of adjustment under consideration, and some studies find no differences on particular outcomes between children whose parents divorce and those whose parents stay together (Ruschena, Prior, Sanson, & Smart, 2005). Externalizing behaviors, internalizing problems, academic achievement, and quality of social relationships are frequently included indicators of adjustment in the divorce literature. Studies that have examined these indicators of adjustment at discrete time points provide some

evidence that children whose parents have divorced have more externalizing and internalizing problems, lower academic achievement, and more problematic social relationships than do children whose parents have not divorced (e.g., Cherlin et al., 1991; Emery, Waldron, Kitzmann, & Aaron, 1999).

Meta-analyses have revealed that divorce has larger effects on relationships with nonresidential fathers and externalizing behaviors than it does on internalizing problems or academic achievement (Amato, 2001; Amato & Keith, 1991b). In the earlier meta-analysis (Amato & Keith, 1991b), divorce was found to have larger effects on academic achievement than on internalizing problems, but in the later meta-analysis (Amato, 2001), divorce was found to have larger effects on internalizing problems than on academic achievement . . . .

A problem with relying on indicators of adjustment measured at a single point in time is that these indicators are likely to look worse if they are assessed in close temporal proximity to the time of the divorce, but they show improvement over time because the short-term effects of divorce tend to look worse than the longterm effects. The examination of developmental trajectories of adjustment has several advantages over the examination of adjustment at discrete points in time. The examination of trajectories makes it possible to track change over time from before the divorce occurs to some period following the divorce. The inclusion of predivorce adjustment in these models is important because of evidence that children whose parents eventually divorce show poorer adjustment prior to the divorce than do children whose parents do not divorce (e.g., Cherlin, Chase-Lansdale, & McRae, 1998; Doherty & Needle, 1991). Links between parental divorce and children's adjustment are often attenuated or eliminated by controlling for predivorce adjustment. For example, Sun and Li (2001) used longitudinal data from a nationally representative sample and found that differences in academic achievement between children whose parents divorced and children whose parents stayed together could be accounted for almost entirely by children's academic achievement and family functioning prior to the divorce.

Although one can control for prior adjustment in analyses predicting subsequent adjustment at a discrete point in time, such analyses do not allow for an examination of how these effects continue to develop over time. Children often have more short-term adjustment difficulties immediately after their parents' divorce, but these difficulties may lessen in severity or disappear following an initial adjustment period (Chase-Lansdale & Hetherington, 1990). Studying trajectories of adjustment that extend from before the parents' divorce to a period well after the divorce will provide a more complete picture of children's longterm adjustment.

To overcome the limitations of cross-sectional approaches, Cherlin et al. (1998) followed a large sample of children born in 1958 in Great Britain prospectively from childhood to the age of 33. Prior to their parents' divorce, individuals whose parents eventually divorced had more internalizing and externalizing problems than did individuals whose parents did not divorce. However, divorce itself also contributed to higher levels of longterm internalizing and externalizing problems into adulthood. It is important to note that their findings suggested that some of the effects of divorce during childhood may not manifest themselves shortly after the divorce and that they may not become apparent until adolescence or adulthood. The gap between groups of individuals whose parents had and had not divorced widened over the course of several years from childhood to adulthood. Cherlin et al. (1998) suggested that parental divorce may curtail educational achievement or disrupt social relationships in ways that are not apparent until children try to enter the labor market, marry, or have children of their own.

In a sample of American children followed from before kindergarten through Grade 10, Malone et al. (2004) used latent change score models to examine trajectories of teacher-rated externalizing behavior over time. Parental divorce was unrelated to girls' externalizing behavior trajectories, regardless of the timing of divorce. Parental divorce was related to boys' externalizing trajectories differently depending on the timing of the divorce. In particular, parental divorce during elementary school was related to an increase in boys' externalizing behaviors that began in the year of the divorce and persisted for years afterward. Parental divorce during middle school was related to an increase in boys' externalizing behaviors in the year of the divorce that declined below baseline levels in the year following the divorce and persisted into subsequent years.

Several studies also address whether parental divorce during childhood relates to long-term effects on adults' own romantic relationships and their relationships with their parents later in life. Intergenerational studies suggest that parental divorce doubles the risk that one's own marriage will end in divorce, in part because individuals whose parents have divorced are less likely to view marriage as a lifelong commitment (Amato & DeBoer, 2001); the risk is exacerbated if both spouses experienced their parents' divorce (Hetherington & Elmore, 2004). There is also evidence that intergenerational transmission of divorce is mediated by interpersonal skill deficits (e.g., communication patterns not conducive to supporting a long-term intimate relationship) that make it more difficult for individuals whose parents have divorced to sustain their own intimate relationships (Amato, 1996). In addition to being at greater risk for difficulties in romantic relationships, adults whose parents divorced have lower quality relationships with their parents (particularly fathers) during adulthood, on average (Lye, 1996). However, these associations depend on the parents' marital quality prior to the divorce, the gender of the parent, and the gender of the adult child (Booth & Amato, 1994; Orbuch, Thornton, & Cancio, 2000).

To summarize, research suggests that children whose parents have divorced have higher levels of externalizing behaviors and internalizing problems, lower academic achievement, and more problems in social relationships than do children whose parents have not divorced. But, the magnitude of these effects is attenuated after controlling for children's adjustment prior to the divorce and other potential confounds. Furthermore, even though children whose parents divorce have worse adjustment on average than do children whose parents stay together, most children whose parents divorce do not have long-term negative outcomes. For example, in their longitudinal study of a representative sample of 17,414 individuals in Great Britain who were followed from ages 7 to 23, Chase-Lansdale, Cherlin, and Kiernan (1995) reported that the likelihood of scoring in the clinical range on the Malaise Inventory, which measures a wide range of adult emotional disorders, was 11% for young adults who had experienced their parents' divorce and 8% for young adults who had not experienced their parents' divorce. Nevertheless, analyses using data from this sample after they were followed to age 33 led Cherlin et al. (1998) to conclude that the adjustment gap between individuals who had and had not experienced parental divorce widened over time and that although part of the effect of parental divorce could be attributed to factors prior to the divorce, experiencing parental divorce during childhood was related to worse mental health when the offspring were in their 20s and 30s.

Hetherington and Kelly (2002) concluded that 25% of individuals whose parents divorce have serious long-term social, emotional, or psychological problems in adulthood in comparison with 10% of individuals whose parents have stayed together; still, this means that 75% of individuals whose parents divorce do not have serious long-term impairment during adulthood. Even studies that do find long-term effects of divorce generally report that the effect sizes are small . . . . Taken together, these findings indicate that the majority of children whose parents divorce do not have long-term adjustment problems, but the risk of externalizing behaviors, internalizing problems, poorer academic achievement, and problematic social relationships is greater for children whose parents divorce than for those whose parents stay together. Different children may manifest adjustment problems in

different ways. Future research should adopt a more person-centered approach to investigate whether, for example, those children whose grades are dropping are the same children whose internalizing or externalizing problems are increasing following their parents' divorce.

MODERATORS OF LINKS BETWEEN DIVORCE AND CHILDREN'S ADJUSTMENT

Despite the research suggesting that divorce is related to children's adjustment, there is considerable evidence that these effects do not operate in the same way for all children. Links between divorce and children's adjustment are moderated by several factors, including children's age at the time of their parents' divorce, children's age at the time of the study, the length of time since the divorce, children's demographic characteristics (gender, race/ethnicity), children's adjustment prior to the divorce, and stigmatization of divorce (by location or historical period).

Children's Age at Divorce, Age at the Time of the Study, and Length of Time Since Divorce

Studies have shown mixed results with respect to how the timing of divorce affects children's adjustment (see Hetherington, Bridges, & Insabella, 1998). Hetherington (1989) suggests that, in comparison with older children, young children may be less capable of realistically assessing the causes and consequences of divorce, may feel more anxious about abandonment, may be more likely to blame themselves, and may be less able to take advantage of resources outside the family to cope with the divorce. All of these factors may contribute to findings that young children experience more problems after their parents divorce than do children who are older when the divorce occurs (Allison & Furstenberg, 1989). Note that this conclusion applies specifically to divorce; other findings suggest that adjusting to parents' remarriage may be harder for adolescents than for younger children (Hetherington, Stanley-Hagan, & Anderson, 1989). It may be that divorce has effects on particular outcomes that are salient during the developmental period during which the divorce occurs . . . .

A methodological problem is that in many studies, children's reported age reflects their age at the time of the study rather than their age at the time of their parents' divorce. Amato (2001) noted this lack of availability of children's age at the time of the divorce as a limitation in his meta-analysis. The most common approach is to study children in a particular developmental stage (e.g., early childhood, middle childhood, adolescence) and compare the adjustment of children whose parents have divorced with the adjustment of children whose parents have not divorced. A drawback of this strategy is that the length of time between the parents' divorce and the time of the assessment will vary considerably across the sample. Lansford et al. (2006) addressed this limitation by using the time of parental divorce as an anchor point and modeling trajectories of adjustment over a period from 1 year prior to the divorce to 3 years after the divorce. This approach makes it possible to compare children at comparable points of time in relation to their parents' divorce. Lansford et al. (2006) also analyzed a matched group of children whose parents did not divorce. Results suggested that parental divorce occurring from kindergarten to Grade 5 exerted more adverse effects on internalizing and externalizing problems than did parental divorce occurring from Grades 6 to 10, whereas parental divorce occurring from Grades 6 to 10 exerted more adverse effects on grades.

Children's Demographic Characteristics

Researchers have attempted to understand how children's demographic characteristics (primarily gender and race) may moderate the link between parental divorce and children's adjustment. Early research findings suggested that parental divorce was related to more adjustment difficulties for boys than girls but that parents' remarriage was related to more adjustment difficulties for girls than for boys (see Hetherington, Cox, & Cox, 1985). However, recent findings have been more mixed; there is no consistent pattern regarding whether divorce has more adverse effects on girls or boys. Some studies report that boys have more adjustment problems following parental divorce than do girls (Morrison & Cherlin, 1995; Shaw, Emery, & Tuer, 1993). Other studies report that girls have more adjustment problems following parental divorce than do boys (Allison & Furstenberg, 1989). Still other studies report no gender differences (e.g., Amato & Cheadle, 2005; Sun & Li, 2002). There is also evidence that the particular outcomes affected by parental divorce may differ by gender. For example, early childbearing has been found to be associated with parental divorce for girls, and more unemployment has been found to be associated with parental divorce for boys (McLanahan, 1999). In their meta-analysis, Amato and Keith (1991b) found no gender differences except that boys whose parents divorced had a harder time adjusting socially than did girls.

*****

Children's Adjustment Prior to the Divorce

Some evidence suggests that children whose parents eventually divorce already have more adjustment problems many years before the divorce (Cherlin et al., 1998). Genetic or other environmental factors may be contributing to these adjustment problems, and the children's adjustment may have appeared to be just as problematic even if the parents had not divorced. Chase-Lansdale et al. (1995) found a steeper increase in adjustment problems after parental divorce for children who were well-adjusted prior to the divorce than for children with predivorce adjustment problems (or for children whose parents did not divorce). However, the long-term adjustment of children with predivorce adjustment problems was worse than it was for children who were better adjusted prior to the divorce (Chase-Lansdale et al., 1995). Controlling for children's adjustment prior to their parents' divorce greatly reduces differences between children whose parents divorce and those whose parents stay together (Cherlin et al., 1991).

Children with positive attributes such as attractiveness, easy temperament, and social competence are also more resilient following their parents' divorce (Hetherington et al., 1989). In part, this may be because children with such attributes are more likely to have strong support networks outside the family (e.g., from teachers or peers) and to evoke positive responses from others. In an epidemiological sample of 648 children who were initially assessed when they were 1–10 years old and assessed again 8 years later, Kasen, Cohen, Brook, and Hartmark (1996) found significant interactions between temperament assessed in the first 10 years of life and family structure in the prediction of subsequent adjustment. In particular, the risk of oppositional defiant disorder was exacerbated for children who had early affective problems and were living with a single mother or in a stepfamily; the authors speculated that the stress of adjusting to new living arrangements may have overwhelmed the coping capacities of these already vulnerable children. On the other hand, Kasen et al. (1996) also found that the risk of overanxiety disorder was reduced for children (especially boys) who were socially immature early in life and were living with a single mother; the authors speculated that needing to play more "adult" roles in a single-parent family may have enhanced the social skills of previously immature children. Thus, children's adjustment can moderate the effects of divorce on subsequent adjustment.

*****

MEDIATORS OF LINKS BETWEEN DIVORCE AND CHILDREN'S ADJUSTMENT

Most researchers no longer simply compare the adjustment of children whose parents have and have not divorced. Instead, researchers have adopted more complex models of how divorce may be related to children's adjustment and now investigate moderators as described previously or analyze their data to understand the mechanisms through which divorce might affect children's adjustment. Several scholars have argued that processes occurring in all types of families are more important than family structure in relation to the well-being of children and adolescents (e.g., Dunn, Deater-Deckard, Pickering, & O'Connor, 1998; Lansford, Ceballo, Abbey, & Stewart, 2001). Taking family process and other mediating variables into account attenuates the association between the experience of parental divorce and children's adjustment (e.g., Amato & Keith, 1991b; Mechanic & Hansell, 1989). It is also important to keep in mind that divorce can be conceptualized more as a process than as a discrete event, with the family processes leading up to and following the divorce being an integral part of the divorce itself.

Income

In a review of five theoretical perspectives on why marital transitions may be related to children's adjustment, Hetherington et al. (1998) found some support for an economic disadvantage perspective suggesting that a drop in household income often accompanies divorce and mediates the link between parents' divorce and children's adjustment. Twenty-eight percent of single mothers and 11% of single fathers live in poverty in comparison with 8% of two-parent families (Grall, 2007). Following their parents' divorce, children most often live with single mothers who do not have the same financial resources they did prior to the divorce, especially if they are not receiving regular child-support payments from nonresidential fathers. This sometimes necessitates a change for the worse in housing, neighborhoods, and schools. These economic hardships and their sequelae can lead to behavioral and emotional problems in children. For example, Guidubaldi, Cleminshaw, Perry, and McLoughlin (1983) surveyed children whose parents had and had not divorced and found differences between them on 27 out of 34 outcomes before controlling for income, but only found 13 differences between them after controlling for income, suggesting that income plays an important role but does not account for all of the effect of divorce on children's adjustment. Furthermore, children's adjustment often worsens rather than improves following remarriage and its accompanying increase in economic resources (Hetherington et al., 1989). Taken together, these findings suggest that income is important, but there is more contributing to children's adjustment problems following divorce than a decrease in household income.

Interparental Conflict

Interparental conflict has received substantial empirical attention. There is consistent evidence that high levels of interparental conflict have negative and long-lasting implications for children's adjustment (Davies & Cummings, 1994; Grych & Fincham, 1990). Amato (1993) and Hetherington et al. (1998) found more support for a parental conflict perspective on why divorce is related to children's adjustment than for any other theoretical perspective that has been proposed to account for this link. Averaging across measures in their review, children in high-conflict, intact families scored .32 standard deviation below children in low-conflict, intact families and .12 standard deviation below children in divorced families on measures of adjustment, suggesting that exposure to high levels of conflict was more detrimental to children than was parental divorce (Hetherington et al., 1998). To illustrate, using data from the National Survey of Families and Households, Vandewater and Lansford (1998) found that when interparental conflict and family structure (married and never divorced vs.

divorced and not remarried) were considered simultaneously after controlling for family demographic covariates and children's prior adjustment, high interparental conflict was related to more externalizing behaviors, internalizing problems, and trouble with peers, but family structure was not significantly related to child outcomes. The finding that children whose parents divorce look worse before the divorce than do comparable children whose parents do not divorce is also consistent with this perspective; worse adjustment prior to the divorce could be accounted for, in part, by exposure to interparental conflict.

If divorce leads to a reduction in children's exposure to interparental conflict, one might expect that their adjustment would improve. Indeed, this issue is at the heart of parents' question of whether they should stay in a conflicted marriage for the sake of the children. In an important longitudinal investigation of this issue, Amato, Loomis, and Booth (1995) found that children's problems decrease when parents in a high-conflict marriage divorce (which encompassed 30%–49% of divorces), whereas children's problems increase when parents in a low-conflict marriage divorce. Booth and Amato (2001) examined correlates of divorce for low-conflict couples and found that factors such as less integration in the community, having fewer friends, not owning a home, and having more positive attitudes toward divorce were related to an increased likelihood of divorce; the authors suggest that because these factors may be less salient to children than conflict between their parents, the divorce may come as more of an unwelcome and unexpected shock, accounting for the more negative effects of divorce on children from low-conflict families than those seen in children from high-conflict families.

*****

Parenting

Another mechanism that has been proposed many times in the literature as an explanation for the links between parental divorce and children's adjustment is the disruption in parenting practices that may occur following divorce. Divorce can make it more difficult for parents to monitor and supervise children effectively (Buchanan, Maccoby, & Dornbusch, 1996; McLanahan & Sandefur, 1994), to discipline consistently (Hetherington, Cox, & Cox, 1979), and to provide warmth and affection (Forehand, Thomas, Wierson, & Brody, 1990; Hetherington & Stanley-Hagan, 1999). After divorce, parent–child conflict often increases, and family cohesion decreases (Short, 2002).

As with studies of children's adjustment showing that children whose parents eventually divorce have significantly more pre-divorce adjustment problems than do children whose parents do not divorce, parents who eventually divorce have been found to have more problematic parenting practices as long as 8–12 years before the divorce than do parents who do not divorce (Amato & Booth, 1996; Shaw et al., 1993). Parenting problems contribute to children's adjustment problems in all types of family structures. Several studies provide evidence that controlling for the quality of parenting attenuates the link between parental divorce and children's adjustment (Amato, 1986; Amato & Gilbreth, 1999; Simons, Whitbeck, Beaman, & Conger, 1994; Tschann, Johnson, & Wallerstein, 1989; Videon, 2002) . . . .

Some studies have investigated whether contact with the noncustodial parent and the quality of this relationship also mediate the link between parental divorce and children's adjustment. In a meta-analysis of 63 studies, Amato and Gilbreth (1999) found that improved child adjustment (academic achievement and fewer externalizing and internalizing problems) was unrelated to frequency of contact with nonresident fathers but was associated with nonresident fathers' payment of child support, authoritative parenting, and feelings of father–child closeness.

Parents' Well-Being

Yet another possible mediator of the link between parental divorce and children's adjustment is parents' well-being. Marital conflict and divorce increase parents' depression, anxiety, and stress, which decrease parents' ability to parent well and may in turn negatively affect children's adjustment. Mothers' history of delinquent behavior has also been found to account for much of the link between parental divorce and children's externalizing behaviors (Emery et al., 1999). These relations are complicated. Through assortative mating, parents with problems such as depression, substance use, or antisocial behavior are at risk of selecting spouses with similar problems (Maes et al., 1998). These parental risk factors increase marital conflict and divorce (Merikangas, 1984). Children may share some of these parental characteristics genetically or through shared environmental experiences.

CAVEATS

Because children cannot be randomly assigned to family structure groups, studies of links between parents' divorce and children's adjustment are necessarily correlational. Despite researchers' attempts to control for potential confounds, it is possible that uncontrolled variables account for associations between divorce and adjustment. Two large bodies of research that present important caveats for understanding links between parental divorce and children's adjustment are studies of children's adjustment in stepfamilies and studies of genetic effects.

Remarriage and Stepfamilies

Much of the literature comparing the adjustment of children whose parents have or have not divorced is complicated by the fact that children are often exposed not only to one marital transition (i.e., their biological parents' divorce) but to multiple marital transitions (e.g., the initial divorce plus subsequent remarriages and divorces). If these multiple transitions are not taken into account, children's adjustment to divorce may be confounded with children's adjustment to remarriage and possibly multiple divorces. The present review focuses on parental divorce rather than stepfamilies, but several excellent reviews provide nuanced information about children's adjustment following their parents' remarriage (e.g., Dunn, 2002; Hetherington & Clingempeel, 1992; Hetherington et al., 1999).

Genetic Effects

Recent research has attempted to estimate the relative contributions of genes and environments in accounting for the likelihood that parents will divorce and the adjustment of their children following the divorce (Neiderhiser, Reiss, & Hetherington, 2007). Lykken (2002) presents evidence that a monozygotic twin has a 250% increase in risk of divorcing if his or her cotwin has divorced. Furthermore, divorce is more concordant between monozygotic than dizygotic twins (McGue & Lykken, 1992). These findings support the role of genetics as a risk factor for divorce, but Jocklin, McGue, and Lykken (1996) further specified the personality mechanisms through which this effect occurs. That is, they found between 30% and 42% of the heritability of divorce to be associated with the heritability of the personality characteristics of positive emotionality, negative emotionality, and less constraint, which were, in turn, associated with divorce (Jocklin et al., 1996).

*****

DIVORCE LAWS AND POLICIES

The questions of whether family structure per se affects children's adjustment and, if so, why and how it does so are important in informing policy because one can adjust policy to influence different proximal mechanisms that may affect children's adjustment. At one level, answers to questions related to whether and how divorce affects children's adjustment also influence how hard it should be for parents to divorce in the first place (e.g., determining if it is better to stay in a conflicted marriage for

the sake of the children). States differ in terms of requirements related to waiting periods, counseling, the length of separation needed prior to divorce, and other factors that affect how hard it is to get a divorce in a given state. Despite shifts in rates immediately after a new policy is implemented, the difficulty of divorcing and rates of divorce are for the most part unrelated after this initial phase (Wolfers, 2003), so policies are unlikely to influence how many parents divorce over the long run.

*****

Child Custody Policies

Child custody policies include several guidelines that determine with whom the child lives following divorce, how time is divided in joint custody situations, and visitation rights. The most frequently applied custody guideline is the "best interests of the child" standard, which takes into account the parents' preferences, the child's preferences, the interactions between parents and children, children's adjustment, and all family members' mental and physical health (see Kelly, 1994). Recently, the approximation rule has been proposed as an alternative to the best interests of the child standard because of concerns that the latter does not provide enough concrete guidance and leaves too many factors to be evaluated at the discretion of individual judges (American Law Institute, 2002). The approximation rule holds that custody should be awarded to each parent to approximate the amount of time each spent in providing care for the children during the marriage. Opinions range from support of the approximation rule as an improvement over the best interests of the child standard (Emery, Otto, & O'Donohue, 2005) to criticisms that the approximation rule would lead to biases against fathers and be less sensitive to the needs of individual families than is the best interests of the child standard (Warshak, 2007). Regardless of the custody standard applied, custody disputes that are handled through mediation rather than litigation have been found to be related to more involvement of the nonresidential parent in the child's life, without increasing interparental conflict (Emery, Laumann Billings, Waldron, Sbarra, & Dillon, 2001; Emery, Sbarra, & Grover, 2005).

A distinction is made between legal custody, which involves making decisions regarding the child, and physical custody, which involves daily living arrangements. The most common arrangement following divorce is for parents to share joint legal custody but for mothers to have sole physical custody. Several studies have investigated whether children's adjustment is related to custody arrangements following their parents' divorce. Using data from a large national sample, Downey and Powell (1995) found few differences between the adjustment of children whose fathers had custody following divorce and those whose mothers had custody. For the few outcomes in which differences did emerge, children appeared somewhat better adjusted in paternal custody families if income was left uncontrolled, but after controlling for income, children appeared somewhat better adjusted in maternal custody families (Downey & Powell, 1995).

Major benefits of joint custody include the access to financial resources and other resources that a second parent can provide and the more frequent and meaningful contact that is possible between both parents and the child (Bender, 1994). The major concerns raised with respect to joint custody are that it may prolong children's exposure to conflict between parents with acrimonious relationships and reduce stability that is needed for children's positive adjustment (Johnston, 1995; Twaite & Luchow, 1996). In a meta-analysis of 33 studies comparing joint physical or legal custody with sole maternal custody, Bauserman (2002) concluded that children in joint custody (either physical or legal) had fewer externalizing and internalizing problems and better academic achievement and social relationships than did children in sole maternal custody. Parents with joint custody reported having less past and current conflict than did parents with sole custody, but the findings regarding better adjustment of children in joint custody held after controlling for interparental conflict. Nevertheless, caution is warranted, because there are a wide array of factors affecting the selection of joint versus sole custody that can plausibly explain differences in adjustment for children in these different custody situations. An additional methodological concern is that only 11 of the 33 studies included in Bauserman's meta-analysis were published—21 were unpublished dissertations, and 1 was another unpublished manuscript. Therefore, the majority of the studies included in the meta-analyses have not passed the rigor of peer review. The finding that joint physical and joint legal custody were equally associated with better child adjustment is consistent with the finding from Amato and Gilbreth's (1999) meta-analysis that there was little relation between children's adjustment and the frequency with which they had contact with their father. Amato and Gilbreth (1999) found that the quality of children's relationship with their father is a more important predictor of children's adjustment than is frequency of contact. If joint physical or legal custody promotes more positive father–child relationships, this might account for the more positive adjustment of children in joint custody reported by Bauserman (2002).

*****

Summary and Conclusions

In this article, I reviewed the research literature on links between parental divorce and children's adjustment. First, I considered evidence regarding how divorce is related to children's externalizing behaviors, internalizing problems, academic achievement, and social relationships. Research suggests that children whose parents have divorced have higher levels of externalizing behaviors and internalizing problems, lower academic achievement, and more problems in social relationships than do children whose parents have not divorced. However, even though children whose parents divorce have worse adjustment on average than do children whose parents do not divorce, most children whose parents divorce do not have longterm negative outcomes.

Second, I examined children's age at the time of the divorce, age at the time of the study, length of time since the divorce, demographic characteristics, children's adjustment prior to the divorce, and stigmatization as moderators of the links between divorce and children's adjustment. There is evidence that, for behavioral outcomes, children who are younger at the time of their parents' divorce may be more at risk than are children who are older at the time of the divorce, but for academic outcomes and social relationships (particularly with romantic partners), adolescents whose parents divorce may be at greater risk than are younger children. The evidence is inconclusive regarding whether girls or boys are more affected by divorce, but there is some evidence that European American children are more negatively affected by divorce than are African American children. Children who have adjustment difficulties prior to divorce are more negatively affected by divorce than are children who are functioning well before the divorce. In cultural and historical contexts in which divorce is stigmatized, children may show worse adjustment following divorce than they do in contexts where divorce is not stigmatized.

Third, I examined income, interparental conflict, parenting, and parents' well-being, as mediators of relations between divorce and children's adjustment. All four of these mediators attenuate the link between parental divorce and children's adjustment difficulties. Interparental conflict has received the most empirical support as an important mediator.

Fourth, I noted the caveats of the research literature. This review focused on the relation between divorce and children's adjustment, but stepfamily formation and subsequent divorces are often part of the experience of children whose biological parents divorce. Recent work using adoption and twin designs demonstrates the importance of both genetics and environments (and their interaction) in predicting the likelihood of divorce and children's adjustment following parental divorce.

Fifth, I considered notable policies related to grounds for divorce, child custody, and child support in light of how they might affect children's adjustment to their parents' divorce. Policies that reduce interparental conflict and provide economic security to children have the potential to benefit children's adjustment. Evaluating whether particular policies are related to children's adjustment following their parents' divorce has the potential to inform future policymaking.

It is important to end this review by emphasizing that not all children experience similar trajectories before or after experiencing their parents' divorce. Thus, trajectories of adjustment that may be typical of many children may not be exhibited by an individual child. Furthermore, what initially appear to be effects of divorce are likely to be a complex combination of parent, child, and contextual factors that precede and follow the divorce in conjunction with the divorce itself.

REFERENCES

Allison, P. D., & Furstenberg, F. F., Jr. (1989). How marital dissolution affects children: Variations by age and sex. *Developmental Psychology*, *25*, 540–549.

Amato, P. R. (1986). Marital conflict, the parent–child relationship, and child self-esteem. *Family Relations*, *35*, 403–410.

Amato, P. R. (1993). Children's adjustment to divorce: Theories, hypotheses, and empirical support. *Journal of Marriage and the Family*, *55*, 23–38.

Amato, P. R. (1996). Explaining the intergenerational transmission of divorce. *Journal of Marriage and the Family*, *58*, 628–640.

Amato, P. R. (2001). Children of divorce in the 1990s: An update of the Amato and Keith (1991) meta-analysis. *Journal of Family Psychology*, *15*, 355–370.

Amato, P. R. (2003). Reconciling divergent perspectives: Judith Wallerstein, quantitative family research, and children of divorce. *Family Relations*, *52*, 332–339.

Amato, P. R., & Afifi, T. D. (2006). Feeling caught between parents: Adult children's relations with parents and subjective well-being. *Journal of Marriage and Family*, *68*, 222–235.

Amato, P. R., & Booth, A. (1996). A prospective study of divorce and parent–child relationships. *Journal of Marriage and the Family, 58,* 356–365.

Amato, P. R., & Cheadle, J. (2005). The long reach of divorce: Divorce and child well-being across three generations. *Journal of Marriage and Family, 67,* 191–206.

Amato, P. R., & DeBoer, D. D. (2001). The transmission of marital instability across generations: Relationship skills or commitment to marriage? *Journal of Marriage and the Family, 63,* 1038–1051.

Amato, P. R., & Gilbreth, J. G. (1999). Nonresident fathers and children's well-being: A meta-analysis. *Journal of Marriage and the Family, 61,* 557–573.

Amato, P. R., & Keith, B. (1991a). Parental divorce and adult wellbeing: A meta-analysis. *Journal of Marriage and the Family, 53,* 43–58.

Amato, P.R., & Keith, B. (1991b). Parental divorce and the well-being of children: A meta-analysis. *Psychological Bulletin, 110,* 26–46.

Amato, P.R., Loomis, L.S., & Booth, A. (1995). Parental divorce, marital conflict, and offspring well-being during early adulthood. *Social Forces, 73,* 895–915.

American Law Institute. (2002). *Principles of the law of family dissolution: Analysis and recommendations.* Newark, NJ: Matthew Bender.

Bauserman, R. (2002). Child adjustment in joint-custody versus sole-custody arrangements: A meta-analytic review. *Journal of Family Psychology, 16,* 91–102.

Bender, W. N. (1994). Joint custody: The option of choice. Journal *of Divorce and Remarriage, 21,* 115–131.

Booth, A., & Amato, P. R. (1994). Parental marital quality, parental divorce, and relations with parents. *Journal of Marriage and the Family, 56,* 21–34.

Booth, A., & Amato, P. R. (2001). Parental predivorce relations and offspring postdivorce well-being. *Journal of Marriage and the Family, 63,* 197–212.

Buchanan, C. M., Maccoby, E. E., & Dornbusch, S. M. (1996). *Adolescents after divorce.* Cambridge, MA: Harvard University Press.

Buehler, C., Krishnakumar, A., Stone, G., Anthony, C., Pemberton, S., Gerard, J., & Barber, B. K. (1998). Interparental conflict styles and youth problem behaviors: A two-sample replication study. *Journal of Marriage and the Family, 60,* 119–132.

Chase-Lansdale, P. L., Cherlin, A. J., & Kiernan, K. K. (1995). The longterm effects of parental divorce on the mental health of young adults: A developmental perspective. *Child Development, 66,* 1614–1634.

Chase-Lansdale, P. L., & Hetherington, E. M. (1990). The impact of divorce on life-span development: Short and long term effects. In P.B. Baltes, D.L. Featherman, & R.M. Lerner (Eds.), *Life-span development and behavior* (pp. 105–150). Hillsdale, NJ: Erlbaum.

Cherlin, A. J. (1998). Marriage and marital dissolution among Black Americans. *Journal of Comparative Family Studies, 29,* 147–158.

Cherlin, A. J. (1999). Going to extremes: Family structure, children's well-being, and social science. *Demography, 36,* 421–428.

Cherlin, A. J., Chase-Lansdale, P. L., & McRae, C. (1998). Effects of parental divorce on mental health throughout the life course. *American Sociological Review, 63,* 239–249.

Cherlin, A. J., Furstenberg, F. F., Chase-Lansdale, P. L., Kiernan, K .E., Robins, P. K., Morrison, D. R., & Teitler, J. O. (1991). Longitudinal studies of effects of divorce on children in Great Britain and the United States. *Science, 252,* 1386–1389.

Coontz, S. (1992). *The way we never were: American families and the nostalgia trap.* New York: Basic Books.

Davies, P. T., & Cummings, E. M. (1994). Marital conflict and child adjustment: An emotional security hypothesis. *Psychological Bulletin, 116,* 387–411.

Doherty, W .J., & Needle, R. H. (1991). Psychological adjustment and substance use among adolescents before and after parental divorce. *Child Development, 62,* 328–337.

D'Onofrio, B. M., Turkheimer, E., Emery, R. E., Maes, H .H., Silberg, J., & Eaves, L .J. (2007). A children of twins study of parental divorce and offspring psychopathology. *Journal of Child Psychology and Psychiatry, 48,* 667–675.

D'Onofrio, B. M., Turkheimer, E., Emery, R. E., Slutske, W. S., Heath, A. C., Madden, P. A., & Martin, N. G. (2005). A genetically informed study of marital instability and its association with offspring psychopathology. *Journal of Abnormal Psychology, 114,* 570–586.

D'Onofrio, B. M., Turkheimer, E., Emery, R. E., Slutske, W. S., Heath, A. C., Madden, P. A., & Martin, N. G. (2006). A genetically informed study of the processes underlying the association between parental marital instability and offspring adjustment. *Developmental Psychology, 42,* 486–499.

Downey, D., & Powell, B. (1995). Do children in single-parent households fare better living with same-sex parents? *Journal of Marriage and the Family, 55,* 55–71.

Dunn, J. (2002). The adjustment of children in step-families: Lessons from community studies. *Child and Adolescent Mental Health, 7,* 154–161.

Dunn, J., Deater-Deckard, K., Pickering, K., & O'Connor, T. G. (1998). Children's adjustment and prosocial behaviour in step-, single-parent, and non-stepfamily settings: Findings from a community study. *Journal of Child Psychology and Psychiatry, 39,* 1083–1095.

Emery, R.E., Laumann-Billings, L., Waldron, M. C., Sbarra, D. A., & Dillon, P. (2001). Child custody mediation and litigation: Custody, contact, and coparenting 12 years after initial dispute resolution. *Journal of Consulting and Clinical Psychology, 69,* 323–332.

Emery, R. E., Otto, R. K., & O'Donohue, W. T. (2005). A critical assessment of child custody evaluations: Limited science and a flawed system. *Psychological Science in the Public Interest, 6,* 1–29.

Emery, R. E., Sbarra, D., & Grover, T. (2005). Divorce mediation: Research and reflections. *Family Court Review, 43,* 22–37.

Emery, R. E., Waldron, M., Kitzmann, K. M., & Aaron, J. (1999). Delinquent behavior, future divorce or nonmarital childbearing, and externalizing behavior among offspring: A 14-year prospective study. *Journal of Family Psychology, 13,* 568–579.

Forehand, R., Thomas, A. M., Wierson, M., & Brody, G. (1990). Role of maternal functioning and parenting skills in adolescent functioning following parental divorce. *Journal of Abnormal Psychology, 99,* 278–283.

Garfinkel, I., Melli, M. S., & Robertson, J. G. (1994). Child support orders: A perspective on reform. *Future of Children, 4,* 84–100.

Glenn, N. (2001). Is the current concern about American marriage warranted? *Virginia Journal of Social Policy and the Law,* 5–47.

Grall, T. S. (2007). *Custodial mothers and fathers and their child support: 2005.* Washington, DC: U.S. Bureau of the Census.

Grounds for Divorce. (n.d.). Retrieved March 1, 2008, from http://www.divorcelawinfo.com/Pages/grounds.html

Grych, J. H., & Fincham, F. D. (1990). Marital conflict and children's adjustment: A cognitive-contextual framework. *Psychological Bulletin, 108,* 267–290.

Guidubaldi, J., Cleminshaw, H. K., Perry, J. D., & McLoughlin, C. S. (1983). The impact of parental divorce on children: Report of the nationwide NASP study. *School Psychology Review, 12,* 300–323.

Hamilton, W. L., Burstein, N. R., & Long, D. (1998). *Using incentives in welfare reform: The New York State Child Assistance Program.* Cambridge, MA: Abt Associates.

Harris, J. R. (1998). *The nurture assumption: Why children turn out the way they do.* New York: Free Press.

Hetherington, E. M. (1989). Coping with family transitions: Winners, losers, and survivors. Child Development, 60, 1–14.

Hetherington, E. M., Bridges, M., & Insabella, G. M. (1998). What matters? What does not? Five perspectives on the association between marital transitions and children's adjustment. American Psychologist, 53, 167–184.

Hetherington, E. M., & Clingempeel, W. G. (1992). Coping with marital transitions: A family systems perspective. Monographs of the Society for Research in Child Development, 57 (2–3, Serial No. 227).

Hetherington, E. M., Cox, M., & Cox, R. (1979). *Stress and coping in divorce: A focus on women.* In J. E. Gullahorn (Ed.), (pp. 95–128). Washington, DC: V. H. Winston & Sons.

Hetherington, E. M., Cox, M., & Cox, R. (1985). Long-term effects of divorce and remarriage on the adjustment of children. *Journal of the American Academy of Child Psychiatry, 24,* 518–530.

Hetherington, E. M., & Elmore, A. M. (2004). The intergenerational transmission of couple instability. In P. L. Chase-Lansdale, K. Kiernan, & R. J. Friedman (Eds.), *Human development across lives and generations: The potential for change* (pp. 171–203). New York: Cambridge University Press.

Hetherington, E. M., Henderson, S. H., Reiss, D., Anderson, E. R., Bridges, M., Chan, R.W., et al. (1999). Adolescent siblings in stepfamilies: Family functioning and adolescent adjustment. 64 *Monographs of the Society for Research in Child Development, 64(*4).

Hetherington, E. M., & Kelly, J. (2002). *For better or worse*. New York: Norton.

Hetherington, E. M., & Stanley-Hagan, M. (1999). The adjustment of children with divorced parents: A risk and resiliency perspective. *Journal of Child Psychology and Psychiatry, 40*, 129–140.

Hetherington, E. M., Stanley-Hagan, M., & Anderson, E. R. (1989). Marital transitions: A child's perspective. *American Psychologist, 44*, 303–312.

Jeynes, W. (2002). *Divorce, family structure, and the academic success of children*. New York: Haworth Press.

Jocklin, V., McGue, M., & Lykken, D. T. (1996). Personality and divorce: A genetic analysis. *Journal of Personality and Social Psychology, 71*, 288–299.

Johnston, J. R. (1995). Research update: Children's adjustment in sole custody compared to joint custody families and principles for custody decision making. *Family and Conciliation Courts Review, 33*, 415–425.

Kasen, S., Cohen, P., Brook, J. S., & Hartmark, C. (1996). A multiple-risk interaction model: Effects of temperament and divorce on psychiatric disorders in children. *Journal of Abnormal Child Psychology, 24*, 121–150.

Katz, S. N. (1994). Historical perspective and current trends in the legal process of divorce. *Future of Children, 4*, 44–62.

Kelly, J. B. (1994). The determination of child custody. *Future of Children, 4*, 121–142.

Lansford, J. E., Ceballo, R., Abbey, A., & Stewart, A. J. (2001). Does family structure matter? A comparison of adoptive, two parent biological, single mother, stepfather, and stepmother households. *Journal of Marriage and the Family, 63*, 840–851.

Lansford, J. E., Malone, P. S., Castellino, D. R., Dodge, K. A., Pettit, G. S., & Bates, J. E. (2006). Trajectories of internalizing, externalizing, and grades for children who have and have not experienced their parents' divorce. *Journal of Family Psychology, 20*, 292–301.

Laosa, L. M. (1988). Ethnicity and single parenting in the United States. In E. M. Hetherington & J. D. Arasteh (Eds.), *Impact of divorce, single parenting, and stepparenting on children* (pp. 23– 49). Hillsdale, NJ: Erlbaum.

Laumann-Billings, L., & Emery, R. E. (2000). Distress among young adults from divorced families. *Journal of Family Psychology, 14*, 671–687.

Lye, D. N. (1996). Adult child–parent relationships. *Annual Review of Sociology, 22*, 79–102.

Lykken, D. T. (2002). How relationships begin and end: A genetic perspective. In A. L. Vangelisti, H. T. Reis, & M. A. Fitzpatrick (Eds.), *Stability and change in relationships* (pp. 83–102). New York: Cambridge University Press.

Maes, H. H. M., Neale, M. C., Kendler, K. S., Hewitt, J. K., Silberg, J. L., Foley, D. L., et al. (1998). Assortative mating for major psychiatric diagnoses in two population-based samples. *Psychological Medicine, 28*, 1389–1401.

Malone, P. S., Lansford, J. E., Castellino, D. R., Berlin, L. J., Dodge, K. A., Bates, J. E., & Pettit, G. S. (2004). Divorce and child behavior problems: Applying latent change score models to life event data. *Structural Equation Modeling, 11*, 401–423.

Martinez, C. R., Jr., & Forgatch, M. S. (2002). Adjusting to change: Linking family structure transitions with parenting and boys' adjustment. *Journal of Family Psychology, 16*, 107–117.

McGue, M., & Lykken, D. T. (1992). Genetic influence on risk of divorce. *Psychological Science, 3*, 368–373.

McLanahan, S. S. (1999). Father absence and the welfare of children. In E. M. Hetherington (Ed.), *Coping with divorce, single parenting, and remarriage: A risk and resiliency perspective* (pp. 117–145). Hillsdale, NJ: Erlbaum.

McLanahan, S., & Sandefur, G. (1994). *Growing up with a single parent*. Cambridge, MA: Harvard University Press.

Mechanic, D., & Hansell, S. (1989). Divorce, family conflict, and adolescents' well-being. *Journal of Health and Social Behavior, 30*, 105–116.

Merikangas, K. R. (1984). Divorce and assortative mating among depressed patients. *American Journal of Psychiatry, 141*, 74–76.

Morrison, D. R., & Cherlin, A. J. (1995). The divorce process and young children's well-being: A prospective analysis. *Journal of Marriage and the Family, 57*, 800–812.

Nakonezny, P. A., Shull, R. D., & Rodgers, J. L. (1995). The effect of no-fault divorce law on the divorce rate across the 50 states and its relation to income, education, and religiosity. *Journal of Marriage and the Family, 57*, 477–488.

National Center for Health Statistics. (2008). Marriage and divorce. Retrieved March 3, 2008, from http://www.cdc.gov/nchs/fastats/ divorce.htm

Neiderhiser, J. M., Reiss, D., & Hetherington, E. M. (2007). The non-shared environment in adolescent development (NEAD) project: A longitudinal family study of twins and siblings from adolescence to young adulthood. *Twin Research and Human Genetics, 10*, 74–83.

O'Connor, T. G., Caspi, A., DeFries, J. C., & Plomin, R. (2000). Are associations between parental divorce and children's adjustment genetically mediated? An adoption study. *Developmental Psychology, 36*, 429–437.

Orbuch, T. L., Thornton, A., & Cancio, J. (2000). The impact of marital quality, divorce, and remarriage on the relationships between parents and their children. *Marriage and Family Review, 29*, 221–246.

Popenoe, D. (1993). American family decline, 1960–1990: A review and appraisal. *Journal of Marriage and the Family, 55*, 527–542.

Popenoe, D. (2003). Can the nuclear family be revived? In M. Coleman & L. Ganong (Eds.), *Points and counterpoints: Controversial relationship and family issues in the 21st century* (pp. 218–221). Los Angeles: Roxbury Publishing.

Reifman, A., Villa, L. C., Amans, J. A., Rethinam, V., & Telesca, T. Y. (2001). Children of divorce in the 1990s: A meta-analysis. *Journal of Divorce and Remarriage, 36*, 27–36.

Roberts, P. G. (1994). Child support orders: Problems with enforcement. *Future of Children, 4*, 101–120.

Ruschena, E., Prior, M., Sanson, A., & Smart, D. (2005). A longitudinal study of adolescent adjustment following family transitions. *Journal of Child Psychology and Psychiatry, 46*, 353–363.

Shaw, D. S., Emery, R. E., & Tuer, M. D. (1993). Parental functioning and children's adjustment in families of divorce: A prospective study. Journal of Abnormal Child Psychology, 21, 119–134.

Short, J. L. (2002). The effects of parental divorce during childhood on college students. *Journal of Divorce and Remarriage, 38*, 143–156.

Simons, R. L., Whitbeck, L. B., Beaman, J., & Conger, R. D. (1994). The impact of mothers'

parenting, involvement by nonresidential fathers, and parental conflict on the adjustment of adolescent children. *Journal of Marriage and the Family, 56*, 356–374.

Sun, Y., & Li, Y. (2001). Marital disruption, parental investment, and children's academic achievement: A prospective analysis. *Journal of Family Issues, 22*, 27–62.

Sun, Y., & Li, Y. (2002). Children's well-being during parents' marital disruption process: A pooled time-series analysis. *Journal of Marriage and Family, 64*, 472–488.

Thomas, A., & Sawhill, I. (2005). For love and money? The impact of family structure on family income. *Future of Children, 15*, 57–74.

Tschann, J. M., Johnson, J. R., & Wallerstein, J. S. (1989). Family processes and children's functioning during divorce. *Journal of Marriage and the Family, 51*, 431–444.

Twaite, J. A., & Luchow, A. K. (1996). Custodial arrangements and parental conflict following divorce: The impact on children's adjustment. *Journal of Psychiatry and Law, 24*, 53–75.

U.S. Census Bureau. (2004). Detailed tables: Number, timing and duration of marriages and divorces, 2004. Washington, DC: Author. Retrieved March 3, 2008, from http://www.census.gov/ population/www/socdemo/marr-div/2004detailed_tables.html

Vandewater, E. A., & Lansford, J. E. (1998). Influences of family structure and parental conflict on children's well-being. *Family Relations, 47*, 323–330.

Videon, T. M. (2002). The effects of parent-adolescent relationships and parental separation on adolescent well-being. *Journal of Marriage and the Family, 64*, 489–503.

Wallerstein, J. S., Lewis, J. M., & Blakeslee, S. (2000). *The unexpected legacy of divorce: A 25 year landmark study*. New York: Hyperion.

Warshak, R. A. (2007). The approximation rule, child development research, and children's best interests after divorce. *Child Development Perspectives, 1*, 119–125.

Wolfers, J. (2003) Did unilateral divorce laws raise divorce rates? A reconciliation and new results. National Bureau of Economic Research Working Paper No. 10014. Retrieved March 1, 2008, from http://www.nber.org/papers/w10014

UNIT 4

CRIMINAL AND DELINQUENT BEHAVIOR

INTRODUCTION AND COMMENTARY

It is difficult to choose only a handful of articles and do justice to this very broad area. Too many topics are left untouched. However, the articles reprinted in this section represent cutting-edge research, including research on crimes that are either neglected or just beginning to be examined in the academic literature.

Violent crimes receive extensive research attention, and forensic psychologists are frequently asked to assess the potential for violence in criminal defendants, offenders, and mentally disordered populations. Skeem and Monahan (2011) offer a concise review of the many instruments designed to predict or assess the probability that a given individual will engage in violent activity. The best of the instruments have proven their worth in that reliability and validity have been sufficiently established. Both actuarial instruments and those based on structured professional judgment have achieved respectable research findings, but clinicians should carefully choose the appropriate instrument for the specific questions that need to be answered. Skeem and Monahan also argue persuasively that, rather than designing still more instruments, it is now time to move on and focus on understanding the causes of violence and preventing its occurrence.

In an important article relevant to the antisocial activity of juveniles, Steinberg (2007) summarizes the recent research on adolescent brain development. Steinberg's work has been heavily cited in both the psychological literature and in opinions of the U.S. Supreme Court, such as rulings that persons who committed their offenses as juveniles should not be given the death penalty and should not be sentenced to mandatory life without parole. As Steinberg emphasizes, adolescents can be mature intellectually but not emotionally. They often take risks without truly understanding the consequences of those risks. Steinberg and other developmental researchers do not maintain that juveniles should not be held responsible for their crimes; rather, they assert that their responsibility is mitigated by their age.

The Steinberg article should be read in tandem with Bonnie and Scott's (2013) article, which also focuses on the teenage brain. Like Steinberg, these authors emphasize that the spate of developmental research in this area must be taken into consideration in making policy decisions regarding juveniles. It is clear that the developing brain is just that—developing. As a general principle, adolescents do not possess the maturity to fully appreciate the consequences of their actions. Nevertheless, Bonnie and Scott warn that this research cannot necessarily be applied to every adolescent; some are more developed than others. We cannot say, the authors assert, that this particular 14-year-old is like all other 14-year-olds or is unlike 17-year-olds. The article reminds us that developmental research is crucial to consider in policy decision making relevant to juveniles but that individual differences may still be taken into account in assessing juveniles for such matters as transferring them to criminal courts.

The next four articles in this section again take us on a different path, focusing on specific crimes. Porter and Gavin (2010) have provided an excellent review of 40 years of research literature on infanticide and neonaticide, with the latter term signifying a killing within 24 hours of the baby's birth (some research uses 48 hours). These are relatively rare criminal behaviors that tend to receive the most attention immediately when they occur, if they are publicized by the media. Occasionally, a high-profile trial will follow. The authors review demographics of the children and the parents, as well as various typologies proposed for parents (typically mothers) who kill. They note that perpetrators should not be regarded as either "monsters" or "psychotic," although a small percentage of these deaths are caused by mothers with severe mental illness. Research has provided a good understanding of who commits these crimes and why, but we need a better understanding of how to prevent them. The authors end by offering suggestions in this regard.

One topic that does receive attention is child sex abuse, and there is a vast literature in this area. In the following article, Babchishin, Hanson, and Hermann (2011) discuss a topic that is sometimes but not always associated with direct abuse. Online sex offenders do not necessarily physically abuse children. As the authors point out, these offenders range from those who are simply curious about child pornography to those who use the Internet to meet with and carry out sexual assaults on underage victims. Are these online offenders, or subgroups of online offenders, different from traditional child sex abusers (referred to as "offline" offenders)? Using a meta-analytic approach, the researchers identified demographic and psychological variables that connected or distinguished the two major groups. Both groups, for example, had greater rates of childhood physical and sexual abuse than did the general population, but online offenders seemed to have greater self-control and greater victim empathy but also displayed greater sexual deviancy (e.g., pedophilic interests). Online offenders were also disproportionately Caucasian males. Babchishin et al. emphasize that research is too new to draw firm conclusions about differences between online and offline offenders, but they note that this is a promising area for future research.

Next, Boudreaux, Lord, and Etter (2000) provide an excellent review of child abduction, from both historical and current perspectives. They note the difficulty of obtaining accurate information on this crime, because research often combines stranger, parental, and other family abductions, and because there are often differences in reporting laws from state to state. For example, some abductions may be reported as sexual assaults. The article reviews victim characteristics, offender characteristics, and offender motives. The authors call for more consistent operational definitions and, importantly, training for children at various ages. Family and caretakers also should be involved in the training, because these adults may not be aware of the warning signs that portend abductions of children of various ages.

In the final article of this section, Elwood (2009) tackles the topic of evaluating sex offenders for possible civil commitment after the expiration of their prison sentences. Elwood takes no stand on the "correctness" of sexually violent person (SVP) statutes: They are legal and we must adapt to them, he emphasizes. However, defining mental disorder as it relates to sex offenders is problematic for the mental health practitioner. Elwood's article was written before the fifth edition of the *Diagnostic and Statistical Manual of Mental Disorders* was released, and there are frequent references to earlier editions of that clinical manual, but this does not significantly affect the substance of his work. He notes that—in addition to assessing mental disorder in sex offenders being considered for civil commitment—the evaluating clinician must define the other key constructs that have been specified by the courts, such as "predisposition" and "serious difficulty controlling one's behavior," and he proposes a model for how this might be accomplished. SVP evaluations are common in both the federal system and in about 20 states, but criteria for conducting them are often lacking, and some clinicians may use inappropriate instruments, not designed for that purpose. Many psychologists express discomfort at making predictions that sex offenders will pose a continuing danger and should qualify as sexual predators for this reason. SVP evaluations represent an area of forensic psychology that is growing, controversial, and demanding of further research.

15

CURRENT DIRECTIONS IN VIOLENCE RISK ASSESSMENT*

JENNIFER L. SKEEM

JOHN MONAHAN

Forensic psychology has become recognized as a specialty practice area and has grown tremendously over recent years as an assessment-focused enterprise. A variety of instruments have been published to help clinicians evaluate legally relevant questions about individuals involved in the civil-, criminal-, or juvenile-justice systems. Many of these instruments improve clinicians' ability to forecast the likelihood that an individual will behave violently. Increasingly, these instruments are being applied in response to statutes and regulations that require specialized assessments to identify "high risk" individuals for detention or "low risk" individuals for release.

In this article, we provide a current snapshot of the violence risk assessment field. After highlighting the contexts in which risk is assessed, we describe a framework for understanding alternative approaches to assessing risk and compare those approaches. We draw attention to modern debates about whether group-based instruments are useful for assessing an individual's risk and whether the risk assessment and risk reduction should be separated.

We wish to be clear about our use of terminology. We endorse the general definition of risk assessment given by Kraemer et al. (1997, p. 340): "The process of using risk factors to estimate the likelihood (i.e., probability) of an outcome occurring in a population." These authors define a risk factor as a correlate that precedes the outcome in time, with no implication that the risk factor and outcome are causally related. Our outcome of focus is physical violence to others.

LEGAL CONTEXT

The populations in which violence risk is assessed vary across many legal contexts. In

*This article was published in *Current Directions in Psychological Science*, *20*, 38–42 (2011).

the criminal- and juvenile-justice systems, risk assessment can be a component of decision making regarding bail, sentencing, and parole. In the mental health system, civil commitment on the ground of "dangerousness," commitment as a sexually violent predator, and the tort liability of clinicians for their patients' violence often turn on issues of risk assessment. Risk assessment for workplace violence and violent terrorism are also becoming increasingly common.

The law regulating the process of violence risk assessment has become much more developed in the United States in recent years. Some cases specify risk factors that may and may not be used to estimate risk (e.g., race is Constitutionally proscribed as a risk factor, whereas gender and age are permitted; Monahan, 2006). Some statutes have come to explicitly require that specific instruments be administered in the risk assessment process. For example, Virginia's Sexually Violent Predator statute not only mandates the use of a specific instrument but also specifies the cutoff score on that instrument that must be achieved to proceed further in the commitment process.

ASSESSMENT APPROACHES

No distinction in the history of risk assessment has been more influential than Paul Meehl's (1954) cleaving the field into "clinical"and "actuarial" (or statistical) approaches. In recent years, however, many instruments that are not adequately characterized by a simple clinical–actuarial dichotomy have been published. The risk assessment process now exists on a continuum of rule-based structure, with completely unstructured (clinical) assessment occupying one pole of the continuum, completely structured (actuarial) assessment occupying the other pole, and several forms of partially structured assessment lying between the two.

The violence risk assessment process might usefully be seen as having the four components shown in Table 1: (a) identifying empirically valid risk factors, (b) determining a method for measuring (or "scoring") these risk factors, (c) establishing a procedure for combining scores on the risk factors, and (d) producing an estimate of violence risk. It is possible to array five current approaches to violence risk assessment according to whether the approach structures (i.e., specifies

Table 1 Violence Risk Assessment Approaches and Their Structured Components

Approach/tool	Structured component of the violence risk assessment process			
	Identify risk factors	Measure risk factors	Combine risk factors	Produce final risk estimate
Clinical judgment				
Standard list of risk factors	X			
HCR-20	X	X		
COVR & LSI-R	X	X	X	
VRAG	X	X	X	X

Note: HCR-20 = Historical Clinical Risk-20; COVR = Classification of Violence Risk; LSI-R = Level of Service Inventory Revised; VRAG = Violence Risk Appraisal Guide.

rules for generating) none, one, two, three, or all four components of this process. Purely clinical risk assessment structures none of the components. The clinician selects, measures, and combines risk factors and produces an estimate of violence risk solely according to his or her clinical experience and judgment.

Performing a violence risk assessment by reference to a standard list of risk factors that have been found to be empirically valid (e.g., age, past violence), such as the lists provided in psychiatric texts, structures one component of the process. Such lists function as memory aids to help clinicians identify which risk factors to attend to in conducting their assessments, but such lists do not further specify a method for measuring these risk factors.

The "structured professional judgment" (SPJ) approach exemplified by the HCR Historical-Clinical-Risk Management-20 (HCR-20; Webster, Douglas, Eaves, & Hart, 1997) structures two components of the process: both the identification and the measurement of risk factors, which may be scored as 0 if absent, 1 if possibly present, or 2 if definitely present. Structured professional judgment instruments do not go further to structure how the individual risk factors are to be combined in clinical practice. As Webster et al. (1997, p. 22) have stated, "it makes little sense to sum the number of risk factors present in a given case... [I]t is both possible and reasonable for an assessor to conclude that an assessee is at high risk for violence based on the presence of a single risk factor."

Approaches to risk assessment that structure three components of the process are illustrated by the Classification of Violence Risk (COVR; Monahan et al., 2001) and the Level of Service Inventory (LSI; Andrews, Bonta, & Wormith, 2004). These instruments structure the identification, measurement, and combination of risk factors (via a classification-tree design or summing scores). But those who developed the instruments do not recommend that the final risk assessment reflect only the combined scores on the assessed risk factors. Given the possibility that rare factors influence the likelihood of violence in a particular

case—and that, precisely because such factors rarely occur, they will never appear on an actuarial instrument—a professional review of the risk estimate is advised (while realizing that clinicians may overidentify "rare" factors). However, little is known about how often or how much clinicians modify actuarial risk estimates or about the justifications they provide for such modifications.

The best-known forensic instrument that structures all four of the components of the violence risk assessment process is the Violence Risk Appraisal Guide (VRAG; Quinsey, Harris, Rice, & Cormier, 2006). This instrument not only structures the identification, measurement, and combination of risk factors; it also specifies that once an individual's violence risk has been actuarially characterized, the risk assessment process is complete. As Quinsey et al. have stated, "What we are advising is not the addition of actuarial methods to existing practice, but rather the replacement of existing practice with actuarial methods" (p. 197).

Does One Approach Predict Better Than Another?

Of these five approaches, the unstructured ("clinical") one has the least empirical support. In the last major study of this approach, Lidz, Mulvey, and Gardner (1993) concluded that clinical judgment has been undervalued in previous research. Not only did the clinicians pick out a statistically more violent group, but the violence that the predicted group committed was more serious than the acts of the comparison group. Nonetheless, the low sensitivity and specificity of these judgments show that clinicians are relatively inaccurate predictors of violence. (p. 1010)

We know of no research that systematically compares the predictive utility of strategies that structure none, one, two, three, or all four components of the process. However, relevant data on approaches that structure two or more components are available. Recent debates about whether it is more appropriate to structure clinical judgment (e.g., HCR-20) or replace it altogether (e.g., VRAG) has prompted a number of "horse race" studies that compare the predictive efficiency of leading instruments.

Taken together, these studies provide little evidence that one validated instrument predicts violence significantly better than another. In a recent meta-analysis of 28 studies that controlled well for methodological variation, Yang, Wong, and Coid (2010) found that the predictive efficiencies of nine risk assessment instruments (including the HCR-20, LSI-R, and VRAG) were essentially "interchangeable," with estimates of accuracy falling within a narrow band (Area Under the Curve = .65 to .71). Although most of these studies used total scores on the HCR-20 rather than structured clinical judgments (low/medium/high risk), there is some evidence that those judgments both predict violence and add incremental predictive utility to scores derived by actuarially combining items (see Heilbrun, Douglas, & Yasuhara, 2009). But this latter claim is contested (Hanson & Morton-Bourgon, 2009).

Why might well-validated instruments perform equally in predicting violence? One persuasive explanation is that they tap—albeit in different ways—"common factors"or shared dimensions of risk, despite their varied items and formats. In an innovative demonstration, Kroner, Mills, and Morgan (2005) printed the items of four well-validated instruments (e.g., LSI-R, VRAG) on strips of paper, placed the strips in a coffee can, shook the can, and then randomly selected items to create four new tools. The authors found that the "coffee can instruments" predicted violent and nonviolent offenses as well as the original instruments did. Factor analyses suggested that the instruments tap four overlapping dimensions: criminal history, an irresponsible lifestyle, psychopathy and criminal attitudes, and substance-abuse-related problems. Despite surface variation, well-validated instruments may generally tap "along-standing pattern of dysfunctional and aggressive

interpersonal interactions and antisocial and unstable lifestyle that are common to many perpetrators of violence" (Yang et al., 2010).

The strongest risk factors for violence seem to be shared not only among risk assessment instruments but also across key groups. In particular, an increasing body of research suggests that only a small proportion of violence committed by people with major mental illness—perhaps as little as 10%—is directly caused by symptoms (see Skeem, Manchak, & Peterson, 2011). Most people with mental illness have the same leading risk factors for violence as their healthy counterparts do.

Are Empirically Based Instruments Useful for Individuals?

One issue that has generated controversy is the argument of Hart, Michie, and Cooke (2007) that the margins of error surrounding individual risk assessments of violence are so wide as to make such predictions "virtually meaningless" (p. 263). Cooke and Michie (2010) concluded, "it is clear that predictions of future offending cannot be achieved, with any degree of confidence, in the individual case" (p. 259).

This position has been vigorously contested. For example, Hanson and Howard (2010) demonstrate that the wide margin of error for individual risk assessments is a function of having only two possible outcomes (violent/not violent) and therefore conveys nothing about the predictive utility of a risk assessment tool. Because all violence risk assessment approaches, not just actuarials, yield some estimate of the likelihood that a dichotomous outcome will occur, none are immune from Hart et al.'s (2007) argument. Instead, their argument "if true,... would be a serious challenge to the applicability of any empirically-based risk procedure to any individual for anything" (Hanson & Howard, 2010, p. 277).

Our view is that group data theoretically can be, and in many areas empirically are, highly informative when making decisions about individual cases. Consider two examples from other forms of risk assessment. In the insurance industry, "until an individual insured is treated as a member of a group, it is impossible to know his expected loss, because for practical purposes that concept is a statistical one based on group probabilities. Without relying on such probabilities, it would be impossible to set a price for insurance coverage at all" (Abraham, 1986, p. 79). In weather forecasting, a wealth of data is available on given events occurring under specified conditions. Therefore, when meteorologists "predict a 70 percent chance of rain, there is measurable precipitation just about 70 percent of the time" (National Research Council, 1989, p. 46). Finally, consider the revolver analogy of Grove and Meehl (1996, pp. 305–306):

Suppose you are a political opponent held in custody by a mad dictator. Two revolvers are put on the table and you are informed that one of them has five live rounds with one empty chamber, the other has five empty chambers and one live cartridge, and you are required to play Russian roulette. If you live, you will go free. Which revolver would you choose? Unless you have a death wish, you would choose the one with the five empty chambers. Why? Because you would know that the odds are five to one that you will survive if you pick that revolver, whereas the odds are five to one you will be dead if you choose the other one. Would you seriously think, "Well, it doesn't make any difference what the odds are. Inasmuch as I'm only going to do this once, there is no aggregate involved, so I might as well pick either one of these two revolvers; it doesn't matter which"?

Although the probabilities associated with risk assessment clearly will never be as certain as those associated with the number of bullets in a six-chamber revolver, we find compelling Grove and Meehl's point that group data can powerfully inform individual assessments of risk.

Should Risk Assessment and Reduction Be Separated?

In the United States, correctional agencies that manage a staggering number of youth and adults are increasingly endorsing structured risk assessment approaches, as well as programs that aim to reduce reoffending by targeting risk factors like anger, poor self control, and antisocial attitudes. In this context, companies have begun marketing complex (and poorly validated) assessment systems that explicitly include purported treatment-relevant variables in their risk estimates and ostensibly serve the risk reduction enterprise better than do simple actuarial tools. Theoretically, treatment-relevant variables are risk factors that can be changed and are causally linked with violence.

This has sparked debate about whether the pursuits of risk assessment and risk reduction should be separated or integrated. Baird (2009) favors separation, arguing that the addition of treatment-relevant variables to otherwise parsimonious risk equations that emphasize past (mis) behavior will dilute their predictive utility. Andrews (2009) challenges Baird's data and reasoning, arguing that some treatment-relevant variables are risk factors and should be integrated in risk estimates. He argues that efficient prediction can be achieved by statistically selecting and combining a few highly predictive risk factors but that tools that sample risk domains more broadly and include treatment-relevant risk factors can be equally predictive.

Given a pool of instruments that are well validated for the groups to which an individual belongs, our view is that the choice among them should be driven by the ultimate purpose of the evaluation. If the ultimate purpose is to characterize an individual's likelihood of future violence relative to other people, then choose the most efficient instrument available. This is appropriate for a single event decision in which there is no real opportunity to modify the risk estimate based on future behavior (see Heilbrun, 1997). If the ultimate purpose is to manage or reduce an individual's risk, then value may be added by choosing an instrument that includes treatment-relevant risk factors. (Although an integrated instrument would be most parsimonious, we can easily envision a two-stage process in which a risk assessment step was followed by an independent risk management step.) This choice is appropriate for ongoing decisions in which the risk estimate can be modified to reflect ebbs and flows in an individual's risk over time. Beyond focusing risk reduction efforts, these instruments could provide incentive for changing behavior (a parole board cannot advise an inmate to undo his past commission of an assault but can advise him to develop employment skills).

This view comes with three important caveats. First, techniques that include treatment-relevant risk factors will add no value to simpler approaches unless the risk assessment is followed by a period of control over the individual during which those factors are translated into an individual supervision and treatment plan (rather than simply filed away) and systematically targeted with appropriate services (rather than ignored in resource allocation). Second, treatment-relevant variables can and do appear in statistically derived risk assessment instruments (see Monahan et al., 2001); an instrument's degree of structure cannot be equated with its relevance to risk reduction. Third, even well-validated instruments offer little direct validity data for the treatment-relevant variables they include. It is not enough to demonstrate that a variable is a risk factor for violence; here, it must further be shown that the variable reduces violence risk when successfully changed by treatment (i.e., is a causal risk factor; Kraemer et al., 1997). This is a crucial issue to address in future research if tools continue to be sold on the promise of informing risk reduction.

FUTURE DIRECTIONS

The violence risk assessment field may be reaching a point of diminishing returns in instrument development. We might speculate that incremental advances could be made by exploring novel assessment methods, including implicit measures (Nock et al., 2010) or simple heuristics (Goldstein & Gigerenzer, 2009). But specific structured techniques seem to account for very little of the variance in predictive accuracy. If we are approaching a ceiling in this domain, there clearly are miles to go on the risk reduction front. We hope that forensic psychology shifts more of its attention from predicting violence to understanding its causes and preventing its (re)occurrence.

REFERENCES

Abraham, K. (1986). *Distributing risk: Insurance, legal theory, and public policy*. New Haven, CT: Yale University Press.

Andrews, D. (2009, September). The Level of Service Assessments: A question of confusion, selectivity, and misrepresentation of evidence in Baird (2009). Paper presented at the meeting of the International Community Corrections Association, Orlando, Florida. Available online at http://www.iccaweb.org/documents/D.Andrews_Service.Assessments.pdf

Andrews, D., Bonta, J., & Wormith, J. (2004). Manual for the Level of Service/Case Management Inventory (LS/CMI). Toronto, Ontario, Canada: Multi-Health Systems.

Baird, C. (2009). A *question of evidence: A critique of risk assessment models used in the justice system*. Madison WI: National Council on Crime & Delinquency. Available electronically at http://www.nccd-crc.org/nccd/pubs/2009_a_question_evidence.pdf

Cooke, D., & Michie, C. (2010). Limitations of diagnostic precision and predictive utility in the individual case: A challenge for forensic practice. *Law and Human Behavior, 34*, 259–274.

Goldstein, D., & Gigerenzer, G. (2009). Fast and frugal forecasting. *International Journal of Forecasting, 25*, 760–772.

Grove, W. M., & Meehl, P. E. (1996). Comparative efficiency of informal (subjective, impressionistic) and formal (mechanical, algorithmic) prediction procedures: The clinical-statistical controversy. *Psychology, Public Policy, and Law, 2*, 293–323.

Hanson, R. K., & Howard, P. (2010). Individual confidence intervals do not inform decision-makers about the accuracy of risk assessment evaluations. *Law and Human Behavior, 34*, 275–281.

Hanson, R. K., & Morton-Bourgon, K. E. (2009). The accuracy of recidivism risk assessments for sexual offenders: A meta-analysis. *Psychological Assessment, 21*, 1–21.

Hart, S. D., Michie, C., & Cooke, D. J. (2007). Precision of actuarial risk assessment instruments: Evaluating the 'margins of error' of group versus individual predictions of violence. *British Journal of Psychiatry, 190* (Suppl.), 60–65.

Heilbrun, K. (1997). Prediction versus management models relevant to risk assessment: The importance of legal decision-making context. *Law and Human Behavior, 21*, 347–359.

Heilbrun, K., Douglas, K. S, & Yasuhara, K. (2009). Controversies in violence risk assessment. In J. L. Skeem, K. S. Douglas, & S. O. Lilienfeld (Eds.), *Psychological science in the courtroom: Controversies and consensus* (pp. 333–356). New York, NY: Guilford.

Kraemer, H., Kazdin, A., Offord, D., Kessler, R., Jensen, P., & Kupfer, D. (1997). Coming to terms with the terms of risk. *Archives of General Psychiatry, 54*, 337–343.

Kroner, D., Mills, J., & Morgan, B. (2005). A coffee can, factor analysis, and prediction of antisocial behavior: The structure of criminal risk. *International Journal of Law & Psychiatry, 28*, 360–374.

Lidz, C., Mulvey, E., & Gardner, W. (1993). The accuracy of predictions of violence to others. *JAMA: The Journal of the American Medical Association, 269*, 1007–1011.

Meehl, P. (1954). *Clinical versus statistical prediction: A theoretical analysis and a review of the evidence.* Minneapolis, MN: University of Minnesota.

Monahan, J. (2006). A jurisprudence of risk assessment: Forecasting harm among prisoners, predators, and patients. *Virginia Law Review, 92*, 391–435.

Monahan, J., Steadman, H., Silver, E., Appelbaum, P., Robbins, P., Mulvey, E., et al. (2001). *Rethinking risk assessment: The MacArthur Study of Mental Disorder and Violence.* New York, NY: Oxford University Press.

National Research Council. (1989). *Improving risk communication.* Washington, DC: National Academy Press.

Nock, M. K., Park, J. M., Finn, C. T., Deliberto, T. L., Dour, H. J., & Banaji, M. R. (2010). Measuring the suicidal mind: Implicit cognition predicts suicidal behavior. *Psychological Science, 21*, 511–517.

Quinsey, V. L., Harris, G. T., Rice, M. E., & Cormier, C. A. (2006). *Violent offenders: Appraising and managing risk* (2nd ed.). Washington, DC: American Psychological Association.

Skeem, J., Manchak, S., & Peterson, J. (2011). Correctional policy for offenders with mental disorder: Creating a new paradigm for recidivism reduction. *Law and Human Behavior, 35*, 110–126.

Webster, C., Douglas, K., Eaves, D., & Hart, S. (1997). *HCR-20: Assessing Risk for Violence* (Version 2). Vancouver, British Columbia, Canada: Simon Fraser University.

Yang, M., Wong, S. C. P., & Coid, J. W. (2010). The efficacy of violence prediction: A meta-analytic comparison of nine risk assessment tools. *Psychological Bulletin, 136*, 740–767.

16

RISK TAKING IN ADOLESCENCE

*New Perspectives From Brain
and Behavioral Science**

LAURENCE STEINBERG

Adolescents and college-age individuals take more risk than children or adults do, as indicated by statistics on automobile crashes, binge drinking, contraceptive use, and crime; but trying to understand why risk taking is more common during adolescence than during other periods of development has challenged psychologists for decades (Steinberg, 2004). Numerous theories to account for adolescents' greater involvement in risky behavior have been advanced, but few have withstood empirical scrutiny (but see Reyna & Farley, 2006, for a discussion of some promising approaches).

FALSE LEADS IN RISK-TAKING RESEARCH

Systematic research does not support the stereotype of adolescents as irrational individuals who believe they are invulnerable and who are unaware, inattentive to, or unconcerned about the potential harms of risky behavior. In fact, the logical-reasoning abilities of 15-year-olds are comparable to those of adults, adolescents are no worse than adults at perceiving risk or estimating their vulnerability to it (Reyna & Farley, 2006), and increasing the salience of the risks associated with making a potentially dangerous decision has comparable effects on adolescents and adults (Millstein & Halpern-Felsher, 2002). Most studies find few age differences in individuals' evaluations of the risks inherent in a wide range of dangerous behaviors, in judgments about the seriousness of the consequences that might result from risky behavior, or in the ways that the relative costs and benefits of risky activities are evaluated (Beyth-Marom, Austin, Fischoff, Palmgren, & Jacobs-Quadrel, 1993).

Because adolescents and adults reason about risk in similar ways, many researchers have posited

*This article was published in *Current Directions in Psychological Science, 16*, 55–59 (2007).

that age differences in actual risk taking are due to differences in the information that adolescents and adults use when making decisions. Attempts to reduce adolescent risk taking through interventions designed to alter knowledge, attitudes, or beliefs have proven remarkably disappointing, however (Steinberg, 2004). Efforts to provide adolescents with information about the risks of substance use, reckless driving, and unprotected sex typically result in improvements in young people's thinking about these phenomena but seldom change their actual behavior. Generally speaking, reductions in adolescents' health-compromising behavior are more strongly linked to changes in the contexts in which those risks are taken (e.g., increases in the price of cigarettes, enforcement of graduated licensing programs, more vigorously implemented policies to interdict drugs, or condom distribution programs) than to changes in what adolescents know or believe.

The failure to account for age differences in risk taking through studies of reasoning and knowledge stymied researchers for some time. Health educators, however, have been undaunted, and they have continued to design and offer interventions qof unproven effectiveness, such as Drug Abuse Resistance Education (DARE), driver's education, or abstinence-only sex education.

A NEW PERSPECTIVE ON RISK TAKING

In recent years, owing to advances in the developmental neuroscience of adolescence and the recognition that the conventional decision-making framework may not be the best way to think about adolescent risk taking, a new perspective on the subject has emerged (Steinberg, 2004). This new view begins from the premise that risk taking in the real world is the product of both logical reasoning and psychosocial factors. However, unlike logical-reasoning abilities, which appear to be more or less fully developed by age 15, psychosocial capacities that improve decision making and moderate risk taking—such as impulse control, emotion regulation, delay of gratification, and resistance to peer influence—continue to mature well into young adulthood (Steinberg, 2004; see Fig. 1). Accordingly, psychosocial immaturity in these respects during adolescence may undermine what otherwise might be competent decision making. The conclusion drawn by many researchers, that adolescents are as competent decision makers as adults are, may hold true only under conditions where the influence of psychosocial factors is minimized.

Evidence for Developmental Neuroscience

Advances in developmental neuroscience provide support for this new way of thinking about adolescent decision making. It appears that heightened risk taking in adolescence is the product of an interaction between two brain networks. The first is a socioemotional network that is especially sensitive to social and emotional stimuli, that is particularly important for reward processing, and this is remodeled in early adolescence by hormonal changes in puberty. It is localized in limbic paralimbic areas of the brain, an interior region that includes the amygdala, ventral striatum, orbitofrontal cortex, medial prefrontal cortex, and superior temporal sulcus. The second network is a cognitive-control network that subserves executive functions such as planning, thinking ahead, and self-regulation, and that matures gradually over the course of adolescence and young adulthood largely independently of puberty (Steinberg, 2004). The cognitive-control network mainly consists of outer regions of the brain, including the lateral prefrontal and parietal cortices and those parts of the anterior cingulate cortex to which they are connected.

In many respects, risk taking is the product of a competition between the socioemotional and cognitive-control networks (Drevets & Raichle, 1998), and adolescence is a period in which the former abruptly becomes more assertive (i.e., at

Figure 1 Hypothetical Graph of Development of Logical Reasoning Abilities Versus Psychosocial Maturation. Although Logical Reasoning Abilities Reach Adult Levels by Age 16, Psychosocial Capacities, Such as Impulse Control, Future Orientation, or Resistance to Peer Influence, Continue to Develop Into Young Adulthood.

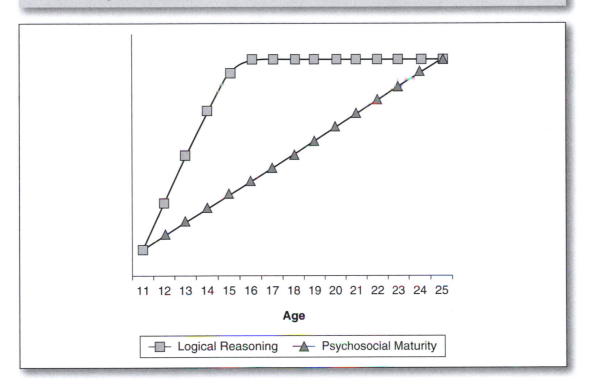

puberty) while the latter gains strength only gradually, over a longer period of time. The socioemotional network is not in a state of constantly high activation during adolescence, though. Indeed, when the socioemotional network is not highly activated (for example, when individuals are not emotionally excited or are alone), the cognitive-control network is strong enough to impose regulatory control over impulsive and risky behavior, even in early adolescence. In the presence of peers or under conditions of emotional arousal, however, the socioemotional network becomes sufficiently activated to diminish the regulatory effectiveness of the cognitive-control network. Over the course of adolescence, the cognitive-control network matures, so that by adulthood, even

under conditions of heightened arousal in the socioemotional network, inclinations toward risk taking can be modulated.

It is important to note that mechanisms underlying the processing of emotional information, social information, and reward are closely interconnected. Among adolescents, the regions that are activated during exposure to social and emotional stimuli overlap considerably with regions also shown to be sensitive to variations in reward magnitude (cf. Galvan, et al., 2005; Nelson, Leibenluft, McClure, & Pine, 2005). This finding may be relevant to understanding why so much adolescent risk taking—like drinking, reckless driving, or delinquency—occurs in groups (Steinberg, 2004). Risk taking may be heightened in adolescence because teenagers spend so much time with their peers, and the mere presence of peers makes the rewarding aspects of risky situations more salient by activating the same circuitry that is activated by exposure to nonsocial rewards when individuals are alone.

The competitive interaction between the socioemotional and cognitive-control networks has been implicated in a wide range of decision-making contexts, including drug use, social-decision processing, moral judgments, and the valuation of alternative rewards/costs (e.g., Chambers, Taylor, & Potenza, 2003). In all of these contexts, risk taking is associated with relatively greater activation of the socioemotional network. For example, individuals' preference for smaller immediate rewards over larger delayed rewards is associated with relatively increased activation of the ventral striatum, orbitofrontal cortex, and medial prefrontal cortex—all regions linked to the socioemotional network—presumably because immediate rewards are especially emotionally arousing (consider the difference between how you might feel if a crisp $100 bill were held in front of you versus being told that you will receive $150 in 2 months). In contrast, regions implicated in cognitive control are engaged equivalently across decision conditions (McClure, Laibson, Loewenstein, & Cohen, 2004). Similarly, studies show that increased activity in regions of the socioemotional network is associated with the selection of comparatively risky (but potentially highly rewarding) choices over more conservative ones (Ernst et al., 2005).

Evidence From Behavioral Science

Three lines of behavioral evidence are consistent with this account. First, studies of susceptibility to antisocial peer influence show that vulnerability to peer pressure increases between preadolescence and mid-adolescence, peaks in mid-adolescence—presumably when the imbalance between the sensitivity to socioemotional arousal (which has increased at puberty) and

capacity for cognitive control (which is still immature) is greatest—and gradually declines thereafter (Steinberg, 2004). Second, as noted earlier, studies of decision making generally show no age differences in risk processing between older adolescents and adults when decision making is assessed under conditions likely associated with relatively lower activation of brain systems responsible for emotion, reward, and social processing (e.g., the presentation of hypothetical decision-making dilemmas to individuals tested alone under conditions of low emotional arousal; Millstein, & Halpern-Felsher, 2002). Third, the presence of peers increases risk taking substantially among teenagers, moderately among college-age individuals, and not at all among adults, consistent with the notion that the development of the cognitive-control network is gradual and extends beyond the teen years. In one of our lab's studies, for instance, the presence of peers more than doubled the number of risks teenagers took in a video driving game and increased risk taking by 50% among college undergraduates but had no effect at all among adults (Gardner & Steinberg, 2005). In adolescence, then, not only is more merrier—it is also riskier.

What Changes During Adolescence?

Studies of rodents indicate an especially significant increase in reward salience (i.e., how much attention individuals pay to the magnitude of potential rewards) around the time of puberty (Spear, 2000), consistent with human studies showing that increases in sensation seeking occur relatively early in adolescence and are correlated with pubertal maturation but not chronological age (Steinberg, 2004). Given behavioral findings indicating relatively greater reward salience among adolescents than adults in decision-making tasks, there is reason to speculate that, when presented with risky situations that have both potential rewards and potential costs, adolescents may be more sensitive than adults to variation in rewards but comparably sensitive (or perhaps even less sensitive) to variation in costs (Ernst et al., 2005).

It thus appears that the brain system that regulates the processing of rewards, social information, and emotions is becoming more sensitive and more easily aroused around the time of puberty. What about its sibling, the cognitive-control system? Regions making up the cognitive-control network, especially prefrontal regions, continue to exhibit gradual changes in structure and function during adolescence and early adulthood (Casey, Tottenham, Liston, & Durston, 2005). Much publicity has been given to the finding that synaptic pruning (the selective elimination of seldom-used synapses) and myelination (the development of the fatty sheaths that "insulate" neuronal circuitry)—both of which increase the efficiency of information processing—continue to occur in the prefrontal cortex well into the early 20s. But frontal regions also become more integrated with other brain regions during adolescence and early adulthood, leading to gradual improvements in many aspects of cognitive control such as response inhibition; this integration may be an even more important change than changes within the frontal region itself. Imaging studies using tasks in which individuals are asked to inhibit a "prepotent" response–like trying to look away from, rather than toward, a point of light—have shown that adolescents tend to recruit the cognitive-control network less broadly than do adults, perhaps overtaxing the capacity of the more limited number of regions they activate (Luna et al., 2001).

In essence, one of the reasons the cognitive-control system of adults is more effective than that of adolescents is that adults' brains distribute its regulatory responsibilities across a wider network of linked components. This lack of cross-talk across brain regions in adolescence results not only in individuals acting on gut feelings without fully thinking (the stereotypic portrayal of teenagers) but also in thinking too much when gut feelings ought to be attended to (which teenagers also do from

time to time). In one recent study, when asked whether some obviously dangerous activities (e.g., setting one's hair on fire) were "good ideas,"adolescents took significantly longer than adults to respond to the questions and activated a less narrowly distributed set of cognitive-control regions (Baird, Fugelsang, & Bennett, 2005). This was not the case when the queried activities were not dangerous ones, however (e.g., eating salad).

The fact that maturation of the socioemotional network appears to be driven by puberty, whereas the maturation of the cognitive-control network does not, raises interesting questions about the impact—at the individual and at the societal levels— of early pubertal maturation on risk-taking. We know that there is wide variability among individuals in the timing of puberty, due to both genetic and environmental factors. We also know that there has been a significant drop in the age of pubertal maturation over the past 200 years. To the extent that the temporal disjunction between the maturation of the socioemotional system and that of the cognitive-control system contributes to adolescent risk taking, we would expect to see higher rates of risk taking among early maturers and a drop over time in the age of initial experimentation with risky behaviors such as sexual intercourse or drug use. There is evidence for both of these patterns (Collins & Steinberg, 2006; Johnson & Gerstein, 1998).

IMPLICATIONS FOR PREVENTION

What does this mean for the prevention of unhealthy risk taking in adolescence? Given extant research suggesting that it is not the way adolescents think or what they don't know or understand that is the problem, a more profitable strategy than attempting to change how adolescents view risky activities might be to focus on limiting opportunities for immature judgment to have harmful consequences. More than 90% of all American high-school students have had sex, drug, and driver education in their schools, yet large proportions of them still have unsafe sex, binge drink, smoke cigarettes, and drive recklessly (often more than one of these at the same time; Steinberg, 2004). Strategies such as raising the price of cigarettes, more vigilantly enforcing laws governing the sale of alcohol, expanding adolescents' access to mental-health and contraceptive services, and raising the driving age would likely be more effective in limiting adolescent smoking, substance abuse, pregnancy, and automobile fatalities than strategies aimed at making adolescents wiser, less impulsive, or less shortsighted. Some things just take time to develop, and, like it or not, mature judgment is probably one of them.

The research reviewed here suggests that heightened risk taking during adolescence is likely to be normative, biologically driven, and, to some extent, inevitable. There is probably very little that can or ought to be done to either attenuate or delay the shift in reward sensitivity that takes place at puberty. It may be possible to accelerate the maturation of self-regulatory competence, but no research has examined whether this is possible. In light of studies showing familial influences on psychosocial maturity in adolescence, understanding how contextual factors influence the development of self-regulation and knowing the neural underpinnings of these processes should be a high priority for those interested in the well-being of young people.

REFERENCES

Baird, A., Fugelsang, J., & Bennett, C. (2005, April). "What were you thinking?": An fMRI study of adolescent decision making. Poster presented at the annual meeting of the Cognitive Neuroscience Society, New York.

Beyth-Marom, R., Austin, L., Fischoff, B., Palmgren, C., & JacobsQuadrel, M. (1993). Perceived consequences of risky behaviors: Adults and adolescents. *Developmental Psychology, 29*, 549–563.

Casey, B. J., Tottenham, N., Liston, C., & Durston, S. (2005). Imaging the developing brain: What have we learned about cognitive development? *Trends in Cognitive Science, 9*, 104–110.

Chambers, R. A., Taylor, J. R., & Potenza, M. N. (2003). Developmental neurocircuitry of motivation in adolescence: A critical period of addiction vulnerability. *American Journal of Psychiatry, 160*, 1041–1052.

Collins, W. A., & Steinberg, L. (2006). Adolescent development in interpersonal context. In W. Damon & R. Lerner (Series Eds.) & N. Eisenberg (Vol. Ed.), *Handbook of Child Psychology: Social, emotional, and personality development* (Vol. 3, pp. 1003–1067). New York: Wiley.

Drevets, W. C., & Raichle, M. E. (1998). Reciprocal suppression of regional cerebral blood flow during emotional versus higher cognitive processes: Implications for interactions between emotion and cognition. *Cognition and Emotion, 12*, 353–385.

Ernst, M., Jazbec, S., McClure, E. B., Monk, C. S., Blair, R. J. R., Leibenluft, E., & Pine, D. S. (2005). Amygdala and nucleus accumbens activation in response to receipt and omission of gains in adults and adolescents. *Neuroimage, 25*, 1279–1291.

Galvan, A., Hare, T., Davidson, M., Spicer, J., Glover, G., & Casey, B. J. (2005). The role of ventral frontostriatal circuitry in reward-based learning in humans. *Journal of Neuroscience, 25*, 8650–8656.

Gardner, M., & Steinberg, L. (2005). Peer influence on risk-taking, risk preference, and risky decision-making in adolescence and adulthood: An experimental study. *Developmental Psychology, 41*, 625–635.

Johnson, R., & Gerstein, D. (1998). Initiation of use of alcohol, cigarettes, marijuana, cocaine, and other substances in US birth cohorts since 1919. *American Journal of Public Health, 88*, 27–33.

Luna, B., Thulborn, K. R., Munoz, D. P., Merriam, E. P., Garver, K. E., Minshew, N. J., et al. (2001). Maturation of widely distributed brain function subserves cognitive development. *Neuroimage, 13*, 786–793.

McClure, S. M., Laibson, D. I., Loewenstein, G., & Cohen, J. D. (2004). Separate neural systems value immediate and delayed monetary rewards. *Science, 306*, 503–507.

Millstein, S. G., & Halpern-Felsher, B. L. (2002). Perceptions of risk and vulnerability. *Journal of Adolescent Health, 31S*, 10–27.

Nelson, E., Leibenluft, E., McClure, E., & Pine, D. (2005). The social re-orientation of adolescence: A neuroscience perspective on the process and its relation to psychopathology. *Psychological Medicine, 35*, 163–174.

Reyna, V., & Farley, F. (2006). Risk and rationality in adolescent decision-making: Implications for theory, practice, and public policy. *Psychological Science in the Public Interest*, *7*, 1–44.

Spear, P. (2000). The adolescent brain and age-related behavioral manifestations. *Neuroscience and Biobehavioral Reviews*, *24*, 417–463.

Steinberg, L. (2004). Risk-taking in adolescence: What changes, and why? *Annals of the New York Academy of Sciences*, *1021*, 51–58.

17

THE TEENAGE BRAIN

Adolescent Brain Research and the Law*

Richard J. Bonnie

Elizabeth S. Scott

In recent years, policymakers, the media, and the public have shown a great deal of interest in the expanding body of knowledge on adolescent brain development—an interest that reflects an expectation that accumulating knowledge about the structure and functioning of the developing teenage brain can usefully inform law and public policy (Wallis, 2004). In this article, we examine the relevance of developmental neuroscience to legal policies dealing with adolescents and discuss several applications. Specifically, we explain how developmental understanding of teenage risk taking and criminal activity can contribute to legal policies that protect adolescents during this distinct developmental period and that also promote the public interest. We emphasize, however, that current knowledge does not provide a scientific basis for evaluating the "maturity" of adolescents on an individual basis for legal purposes.

ADOLESCENCE IN AMERICAN LAW

Although adolescence is recognized by developmentalists as a distinct stage separate from childhood and adulthood, the law typically does not adopt rules applicable specifically to adolescents. Instead, on various issues, lawmakers have tended to draw binary age boundaries between "minors," who are presumed to be vulnerable, dependent, and incompetent to make decisions, and adults, who are viewed as autonomous, responsible, and entitled to exercise legal rights and privileges (Scott, 2000). Although adolescents become legal adults for most purposes at 18 years of age (the "age of majority"), the threshold for defining adult status is not uniform. For example, driving privileges are extended to adolescents in many states at 16 years of age and the right to purchase alcohol at 21 years of age; in most

*This article was published in *Current Directions in Psychological Science*, *22*, 158–161 (2013).

states, youths 14 years of age (or even younger) can be tried as adults when charged with serious crimes. The statutory age for making health decisions (especially reproductive decisions and treatment of behavioral health disorders) has been set at 14 years in many states. Policies setting these age boundaries are based on many considerations, depending on the issue—administrative convenience, parental rights, child welfare, economic impact, and the public interest—as well as assumptions, often rooted primarily in conventional wisdom, about whether youths at a given age are sufficiently mature, as a class, to be treated as adults for the particular statutory purpose.

On most issues, the threshold of adult status is relatively settled and is not highly controversial; this may explain why brain science has not played much of a role (Woolard & Scott, 2009). In general, research indicating that substantial structural and functional changes in the brain occur during adolescence has reinforced a background supposition favoring protective policies until teenagers reach 18 years of age. This approach has been generally satisfactory, except to some youth advocates who favor extending adult rights and privileges to younger adolescents and who, therefore, are generally hostile to neuroscience input in the policy arena (Steinberg, 2009).

LINKING NEUROSCIENCE EVIDENCE TO YOUTHFUL RISK TAKING

Developmental neuroscience research that can be linked to youthful risk taking and offending is in a relatively early stage, and currently its relevance to the key policy issues is indirect. Nonetheless, the existing research on the timing of developments in brain structure and function is consistent with and supplements the larger body of behavioral research; this new research provides the basis for understanding why many adolescents become involved in risky activity and desist as they

mature into adulthood (Casey, Getz, & Galvan, 2008; Steinberg, 2009).

It seems likely that asymmetries in the timing of development of different brain regions contribute to risk taking and immature judgment in adolescence. The research indicates that the prefrontal cortex matures gradually; maturation extends over the course of adolescence and into early adulthood. This region controls the brain's executive functions— advanced cognitive processes employed in planning, controlling impulses, and weighing the consequences of decisions before acting. Maturation in the connections between the prefrontal cortex and other regions of the brain also occurs gradually, resulting in improvement over time in impulse control and emotional regulation. In contrast, changes in the limbic system around puberty result in increases in emotional arousal and in reward and sensation seeking (including sensitivity to social stimuli; Chein, Albert, O'Brien, Uckert, & Steinberg, 2011; Steinberg, Cauffman, Woolard, Graham, & Banich, 2009). This gap between early increases in sensation seeking and later development of emotional and behavioral controls has been described by one scientist as "starting the engines without a skilled driver" (Dahl, 2001, p. 8), and it may shed light on much teenage risk taking and criminal activity. In short, the hypothesis, which is based on neurobiological research, is that teenagers are attracted to novel and risky activities, including criminal activity, particularly with peers, at a time when they lack the judgment to exercise self-control and to consider the future consequences of their behavior.

NEUROSCIENCE, TEEN ALCOHOL USE, DRIVING, AND PUBLIC POLICY

Developmental research, accompanied by pertinent brain research, is playing an increasingly important role in shaping policies relating to adolescent risk taking—drug and alcohol use, the extension of driving privileges, and juvenile justice. Adolescent tendencies to experiment with intoxicating substances (at increasingly younger ages) and to get high (typically in groups) are paradigmatic examples of sensation seeking and risk taking. Moreover, age of onset and intensity of adolescent drinking are strongly predictive of problem drinking and alcohol use disorders in adulthood, and this trajectory may be attributable in part to the vulnerability of the adolescent brain. Extensive use of alcohol in adolescence may also have effects that increase the risk of severe and long-lasting addiction (Wong, Mill, & Fernandes, 2011; Yucel, Lubman, Solowij, & Brewer, 2007). (Similar accounts have been given for teenage use of tobacco, marijuana, and other drugs.) These findings argue for maintaining the 21-year-old drinking age and for intensifying efforts to prevent early onset of alcohol use (Bonnie & O'Connell, 2007).

Policymakers have paid increasing attention in recent years to the lethal mixture of teen driving at night accompanied by peers and alcohol. The result has been developmentally informed "graduated licensing" legislation that lengthens the process of obtaining a license and controls the circumstances under which teens are permitted to drive, gradually increasing their exposure to higher risk conditions (such as nighttime driving and driving with teen passengers). A recent National Research Council (NRC) report (NRC, 2007) noted in support of graduated licensing that adolescent capacity to exercise executive functions is "still under construction" during the initial years of driving and can be "overwhelmed by strong emotion, multitasking, sleep deprivation, and substance abuse" (p. 18). The report explained that deficits in judgment, impulse control, planning, and attention are magnified by extra passengers, music, cell phones, and other sources of stimulation or distraction (NRC, 2007). Some policy analysts have suggested that graduated licensing restrictions should apply to all initial license applicants younger than 21 years of age (Masten, Foss, & Marshall, 2011).

NEUROSCIENCE AND JUVENILE JUSTICE POLICY

Neuroscience has played an increasingly prominent role in juvenile crime policy because questions about whether and when adolescent offenders should be punished as adults have been hotly contested. In this section, we offer a brief historical review that clarifies this emerging role, and then we identify specific questions on which this research potentially can inform legal policy.

During most of the 20th century, the law assumed that juvenile crime was a product of immaturity and that young offenders should be dealt with in a separate justice system with a primary goal of rehabilitation. However, in the 1980s and 1990s, partly in response to increasing rates of violent juvenile crime, a wave of punitive law reforms swept the country. Supporters of tougher policies rejected altogether the idea that juveniles were different from adults in any way that was relevant to criminal responsibility or punishment (Scott & Steinberg, 2008). Legislatures enacted harsh laws that greatly expanded the category of youths subject to criminal court jurisdiction. Use of confinement also increased in the juvenile system.

In the past decade, enthusiasm for harsh punishment of juveniles has waned somewhat, and lawmakers once again appear to accept the relevance of developmental differences to justice policy. This change is attributable to declining crime rates, convincing evidence that incarcerating juveniles increases recidivism, and concerns that imposing harsh adult sentences on teenagers violates basic principles of fairness. Increasingly, lawmakers and the public accept the idea that juvenile offenders should usually be subject to developmentally appropriate dispositions within the juvenile justice system and that those who are transferred to criminal court should receive more lenient sentences than their adult counterparts. In a new wave of law reform, legislatures and courts have moderated the tough laws adopted in the 1990s, keeping more adolescents in juvenile court and reducing the emphasis on long incarceration. The contemporary view, however, is not simply a revival of the traditional rehabilitative model based on naïve characterizations of juvenile offenders as children. Increasingly, policymakers have turned to developmental science, particularly neuroscience, to inform justice policy through a more sophisticated understanding of how dimensions of adolescent development affect juveniles' criminal activity as well as their response to justice-system interventions (Scott, 2013).

Adolescent brain research has the potential to influence juvenile crime policy in two important ways. First, to the extent that neuroscience research provides evidence that immature brain functioning influences decision making and risk taking implicated in criminal behavior, it is relevant to the question of whether adolescents are less culpable than adults and deserve less punishment for similar offenses. Behavioral research has found that adolescents differ from adults in their greater propensity for risk taking and susceptibility to peer influence and their reduced capacity for self-regulation and for attending to future consequences. These characteristics diminish adolescents' responsibility to the extent that their decisions to offend are likely to be rooted in transient developmental processes rather than antisocial values or deficiencies in character (Scott & Steinberg, 2003; Steinberg & Scott, 2003). This argument for diminished responsibility is reinforced and strengthened to the extent that these well-demonstrated developmental characteristics are explained by normal and predictable neurobiological processes. This research can offer a powerful challenge to laws that classify juveniles charged with crimes as adults. Second, studies of changing brain structure and function over the course of adolescence reinforce arguments based on behavioral research that most adolescent crime is a product of the developmental influences described earlier, and thus most teenagers will "mature out" of their criminal tendencies. Generally, this perspective supports policies that keep youths in the juvenile justice system, where interventions can be tailored to promote healthy development and to reduce reoffending.

THE PERSUASIVE IMPACT OF ADOLESCENT BRAIN RESEARCH

Adolescent brain research has captured the attention of lawmakers in recent years and has been cited by courts, legislatures, and other officials to justify support for laws and policies that deal more leniently with adolescent offenders than with adults. For reasons that are not clear, this research seems to carry greater weight as "hard science" than the large body of behavioral research that it largely confirms.

Three recent Supreme Court opinions invoked developmental research in finding harsh adult sentences for juveniles to be unconstitutional under the Eighth Amendment prohibition of "cruel and unusual punishment." In each of these opinions, the court emphasized the reduced culpability of juveniles because of their developmental immaturity, pointing to adolescents' diminished decision-making capacity, their vulnerability to external pressures (including peer pressure), and their unformed characters. In *Roper v. Simmons* (2005), the court rejected the death penalty as a disproportionate sentence for a crime, relying heavily on behavioral research. Both *Graham v. Florida* (2010) and *Miller v. Alabama* (2012) also pointed to brain science in striking down sentences of life without parole for juveniles. This research provided evidence of "fundamental differences between juvenile and adolescent minds" in "parts of the brain involved in behavioral control" (*Miller v. Alabama*, p. 2464).

This invocation of developmental neuroscience evidence by our nation's highest court is a powerful signal of the potential importance of this research for legal regulation of juvenile crime. Moreover, the message that immature brain functioning contributes to teenage offending, making young offenders less culpable than adults and more likely to reform, has resonated with politicians, the media, and the public in recent years. Across the country, neuroscience research indicating that teenage brains differ from those of adults has been offered in support of a broad range of policies dealing more leniently with young offenders. For example, the

Washington State Legislature in 2005 cited developmental brain research in abolishing mandatory minimum sentences for juveniles, as did Governor Bill Owens of Colorado in explaining his support for abolishing the application of a harsh sentencing statute to juveniles. In combination, behavioral and neurobiological research on adolescence have played an important role in advancing policies that recognize the immaturity of young offenders in responding to juvenile crime.

THE LIMITS OF NEUROSCIENCE

A recent study published in *Science* suggests that neuroscience evidence that does no more than describe the biological underpinning of a behavioral diagnosis (psychopathy in this study) can have an influence (whether legitimate or not) on judges making decisions in individual criminal cases (Aspinwall, Brown, & Tabery, 2012). Not surprisingly, prosecutors and attorneys for juveniles increasingly seek to introduce neuroscience evidence in criminal trials—to demonstrate that the brain functioning of a particular juvenile facing criminal charges was or was not sufficiently mature to hold the youth responsible for his or her offense. This has largely been unsuccessful, often because courts have found it to be irrelevant to the legal issue at hand—such as whether the youth lacked criminal intent (Maroney, 2009). However, the use of this research is also highly problematic on scientific grounds. So far, neuroscience research provides group data showing a developmental trajectory in brain structure and function during adolescence and into adulthood; however, the research does not currently allow us to move from that group data to measuring the neurobiological maturity of an individual adolescent because there is too much variability within age groups and across development (Dosenbach et al., 2010). Indeed, we do not currently have accurate behavioral measures of maturity. At some point, neuroscience and accompanying behavioral studies may provide age norms against which an individual adolescent's brain development and functioning can be measured. However, today an expert who offers an opinion that a particular 14-year-old defendant has a mature or immature brain as compared with other 14-year-olds (or "has the maturity of a 17-year-old") is exceeding the limits of science. Currently, the only legitimate use of adolescent brain research in individual cases is to provide decision makers with general descriptions of brain maturation.

It is difficult to predict the extent to which developmental neuroscience research will inform legal policy and practice in the future. Legal policy toward adolescents will always be based on many considerations, of which developmental maturity is only one. Currently, the research is important primarily in domains of public policy relating to adolescent risk taking, particularly in juvenile justice policy, where it is invoked to support rehabilitative programs in juvenile courts and to challenge policies that subject juvenile offenders to the same punishment as their adult counterparts.

REFERENCES

Aspinwall, L. G., Brown, T. R., & Tabery, J. (2012). The double-edged sword: Does biomechanism increase or decrease judges' sentencing of psychopaths? *Science, 337,* 846–849.

Bonnie, R. J., & O'Connell, M. E. (2007). *Reducing underage drinking: A collective responsibility.* Washington, DC: National Academies Press.

Casey, B. J., Getz, S., & Galvan, A. (2008). The adolescent brain. *Developmental Review, 28,* 62–77.

Chein, J., Albert, D., O'Brien, L., Uckert, K., & Steinberg, L. (2011). Peers increase adolescent risk taking by enhancing activity in the brain's reward circuitry. *Developmental Science, 14,* F1–F10.

Dahl, R. (2001). Affect regulation, brain development, and behavioral/emotional health in adolescence. *CNS Spectrum, 6,* 1–12.

Dosenbach, N. U. F., Nardos, B., Cohen, A., Fair, D., Power, J., Church, J., . . . Schlagger, B., (2010). Prediction of individual brain maturity using fMRI. *Science, 329,* 1358–1361.

Graham v. Florida, 130 S. Ct. 2011 (2010).

Maroney, T. A. (2009). The false promise of adolescent brain science in juvenile justice. *Notre Dame Law Review, 85,* 89–176.

Masten, S. V., Foss, R. D., & Marshall, S. W. (2011). Graduated driver licensing and fatal crashes involving 16- to 19-year-old drivers. *Journal of the American Medical Association, 306,* 1098–1103.

Miller v. Alabama, 132 S. Ct. 2455 (2012).

National Research Council. (2007). *Preventing teen motor crashes: Contributions from the Behavioral and Social Sciences: Workshop Report.* Washington, DC: National Academies Press.

Roper v. Simmons, 125 S. Ct. 1183 (2005).

Scott, E. S. (2000). The legal construction of adolescence. *Hofstra Law Review, 29*(2), 547–598.

Scott, E. S. (2013). *Miller v. Alabama* and the future of juvenile crime regulation. *Law and Inequality: A Journal of Theory and Practice, 31* (2).

Scott, E. S., & Steinberg, L. (2003). Blaming youth. *Texas Law Review, 81,* 799–845.

Scott, E. S., & Steinberg, L. (2008). *Rethinking juvenile justice.* Cambridge, MA: Harvard University Press.

Steinberg, L. (2009). Should the science of adolescent brain development inform public policy? *American Psychologist, 64,* 739– 750.

Steinberg, L., Cauffman, E., Woolard, J., Graham S., & Banich, M. (2009). Are adolescents less mature than adults? Minors' access to abortion, the death penalty, and the alleged APA "flip-flop." *American Psychologist, 64,* 583–594.

Steinberg, L., & Scott, E. (2003). Less guilty by reason of adolescence: Developmental immaturity, diminished responsibility and the juvenile death penalty. *American Psychologist, 58,* 1009–1018.

Wallis, C. (2004, May 10). What makes teens tick? Inside the adolescent brain. *Time, 163,* 56–62, 65.

Wong, C. C. Y., Mill, J., & Fernandes, C. (2011). Drugs and addiction: An introduction to epigenetics. *Addiction, 106,* 480–489.

Woolard, J., & Scott, E. (2009). The legal regulation of adolescence. In R. Lerner & L. Steinberg (Eds.), *Handbook of adolescent psychology* (3rd ed., Vol. 2, pp. 345–371). New York, NY: Wiley.

Yucel, M., Lubman, D. I., Solowij, N., & Brewer, W. J. (2007). Understanding drug addiction: A neuropsychological perspective. *Australian and New Zealand Journal of Psychiatry, 41,* 958–968.

18

Infanticide and Neonaticide

A Review of 40 Years of Research Literature on Incidence and Causes*

Theresa Porter

Helen Gavin

Infanticide and Neonaticide Incidence

Infanticide is the killing of young children, whereas neonaticide is the killing of the infant within the first 24 hours after birth. Both should be distinguished from the more general term of filicide, which is the killing by a parent of any child of their own.

The killing of infants and newborns is one of the most common forms of murder by women. Unwanted babies, particularly the female or handicapped ones, were left to the elements in ancient times, possibly with the hope that they would be taken in by passersby to be raised as slaves, perhaps with the awareness that they would die from exposure or the attentions of wild animals. In the 20th and 21st centuries, the murder of infants and children remains a significant problem. In the last 30 years, while child deaths due to diseases, accidents, and congenital defects have decreased (Finkelhor & Ormrod, 2001), the incidence of homicide for children younger than the age of 1 year has increased in some areas (Finkelhor, 1997) and is currently estimated to be 8.0 per 100,000 in the United States. In Canada, however, the incidence is estimated to be less than 3.0 per 100,000 (Hatters-Friedman, Horwitz, & Resnick, 2005).

*This article was published in *Trauma, Violence, & Abuse*, *11*(3), 99–112 (2010). Due to the length of the original article, we deleted a brief introductory section, a section on legal issues, tables, and portions of most major sections. We also deleted anecdotes and illustrations. We recommend that readers access the original article for a comprehensive literature review of this important topic.

The majority of the murders of infants and newborns are by the biological mother. The U.S. Department of Health and Human Services estimates that, of the 2,000 children killed annually in the United States, 1,100 are killed by the biological mother (Kohm & Liverman, 2002). In 1999, in a single U.S. state, more than 50 infants were abandoned in dumpsters (McKee, 2006). Furthermore, approximately 31,000 newborns are abandoned in U.S. hospitals annually (McKee, 2006). Two separate studies of the infanticide rate in England, Scotland, and Wales found that infants less than 1-year old are at 4 times greater risk of being murdered than any other age group, with the 1st day of life being the highest risk. For Scotland, the rate of infant murder was 43 per million, compared to the rate of 29 per million for young adults during the same study period (Marks & Kumar, 1993, 1996). In Germany, there is a three times higher homicide risk for infants born to eastern German women than those born to western German women (Spiegel, 2008).

Examining the incidence statistics is difficult, as this is a crime that it is either unrecorded or recorded with other offences. Most countries do not have a government agency mandated to track infant deaths and when tracking does occur, it is often as part of an aggregate with other types of death (Kohm & Liverman, 2002). However, seven incidence studies between 1994 and 2006 suggest that the rate of infanticide/neonaticide in industrialized countries (England, Scotland, Wales, United States, Canada, New Zealand) ranges from 2.4 per 100,000 to 7.0 per 100,000 . . . .

Government statistics on child homicide can be confusing. First, they are only an accounting of known homicides and it is likely that infants are the class of homicide victims least identified due to the ease of hiding the corpse. . . . Furthermore, the cause of death of an infant may be difficult to establish and may be falsely attributed to sudden infant death syndrome (SIDS). …Furthermore, several studies have indicated that, despite the medical examiner reporting grounds for homicide in an infant's death, the police may not make a report and the local courts may not prosecute the case (McKee, 2006).

The way sources aggregate information may also be problematic. The Bureau of Justice Statistics website has a page listing Homicide Trends in the United States, but it combines deaths by parents with deaths by stepparents, thereby distorting the information. In the United States, stepfathers do have a high murder rate, but when one compares biological parents, mothers kill their children at a higher rate than fathers (Kohm & Liverman, 2002).

*****

CHARACTERISTICS OF NEONATICIDAL WOMEN VERSUS INFANTICIDAL WOMEN

In 1970, Resnick published his groundbreaking study of neonaticide. He performed a literature review of documented newborn murders from the mid-18th century until 1968 in 13 different languages and found that women who kill their newborns were substantively different from women who kill their infants or toddlers. His work has been supported in numerous other international studies that show that women who murder newborns tend to be younger than 25 years old, emotionally immature, unmarried, often living with their parents, unemployed, or attending school . . . . They do not seek prenatal care and are often no longer involved with the baby's father. For example, Emerick, Foster, and Campbell (1986) in their study of infant homicides in Oregon found that the infant deaths were associated with lack of prenatal care and non-hospital birthing.

Resnick (1970) and several other studies have confirmed that the majority of neonaticidal women are not mentally ill at the time of the murder and maternal suicide after neonaticide is rare. Hatters-Friedman, Heneghan, and Rosenthal (2007), in their review of 81 women who either denied or concealed their pregnancies, found that none had psychotic denial and a psychiatry consult was only requested on four of the women. In 2001, Meyer and Oberman reviewed 37 cases of neonaticide and found that most of the perpetrators did not have a major mental illness. In D'Orban's British study, she found that the majority of the neonaticidal women were not suffering from psychosis or depression. Haapasalo and Peta¨ja¨ (1999), in their Finnish study of 15 neonaticides, proposed that mental illness was not a relevant variable, with less than 30% of the women claiming any psychological issues. Similarly, the Finnish sample of Putkonen, Collander, Weizmann-Henelius, and Eronen (2007) of 14 psychiatrically evaluated cases found only four cases with psychotic symptoms.

The majority of infants killed in the 1st day are born out of a hospital, usually at the woman's home (Paulozzi & Sells, 2002), although there are recorded cases of neonaticides in birthing units (Mendlowicz, da Silva, Gekker, de Moreas, Rapaport, & Jean-Louis, 2000, cited in Hatters-Friedman & Resnick, 2009). Newborns who are the second child of a woman under age 19 are at an increased risk of homicide (Overpeck cited in Spinelli, 2003). The hallmark example of neonaticide is that the newborn is unwanted and so the woman, after concealing the pregnancy for 9 months, gives birth alone, and then kills the newborn via non-weapon methods such as suffocation, strangulation, or drowning (Meyer & Oberman, 2001).

Women who murder infants who are older than 1 day are significantly different to women who murder newborns. They tend to be older than 25, use weapon as well as non-weapon methods of murder, are often married, and well educated (Resnick, 1970; . . . .

These women tend to premeditate their murders (Logan, 1995, in Dalley, 1997) and may murder the infant as retaliation against another person, during an episode of abuse, or to remove an unwanted child (D'Orban, 1979).

Mental Illness and Infanticide

*****

A subset of women who murder their infants do have a definitive mental illness that can be shown to have strongly influenced their behaviors. For example, in the study by Kauppi, Kumpulainen, Vanamo, Merikanto, and Karkola (2008) of 10 Scandinavian women who murdered infants, 6 had psychotic symptoms, and in the study by Lewis and Bunce (2003) of 55 filicidal women, 52.7% were psychotic. In the study by Krisher, Stone, Sevecke, and Steinmeyer (2007) of 57 infanticidal women, 24% were initially found incompetent to stand trial due to mental illness.

However, as with neonaticides, a large number of infanticide cases do not involve a severe mental illness that precluded the woman from being aware of the wrongfulness of her actions (Hatters-Friedman & Resnick, 2009) . . . .

Other factors besides severe mental illness are involved in infanticide. For example, Spinelli (2003) reports that women who drop out of school are eight times more likely to murder their infant than women who had a college education, even when age is controlled. Furthermore, research has found that infanticide is associated with the woman's anger. Krischer, Stone, Sevecke, and Steinmeyer (2007) in a cluster analysis of 57 infanticidal and neonaticidal women found that infanticide was associated with the woman's anger as well as her youth. Two separate studies reported women in their samples, who were not designated as mentally ill admitted to having fantasies of harming their infants (Jennings, Ross, Popper, & Elmore, 1999; Levitzky & Cooper, 2000). Jennings et al. (1999) compared clinically depressed and non-depressed mothers and found that 7% of the non-depressed women admitted to having thoughts of harming their offspring. Levitzky and Cooper (2000) questioned 23 women with infants experiencing colic syndrome and found that 70% reported explicit fantasies and thoughts of aggression toward the infant, but only 26% said the thoughts solely occurred during a colic episode. There are also no major distinctions in other factors, for example, personality test results for women who murdered their children do not significantly differ from those of women who murder adults (McKee, Shea, Mogy, & Holden, 2001).

Often, infanticide is attributed to a woman being in a postpartum state of extreme hormonal fluctuation. However, there have been surprisingly few studies in this area and those that exist largely show that hormone changes do not have a significant impact on a woman's mental health, despite longstanding assumptions to the contrary (Wisner & Stowe, 1997) . . . . To date, there has not been a definitive study that showed conclusively that the hormonal changes associated with childbirth cause clinical-level mood changes.

The terms "baby blues," "postpartum depression," and "postpartum psychosis" are often used as if synonymous, despite their significant differences. The "blues" are the most common, occurring in between 25% and 85% of women. These mild symptoms of crying and irritability begin within a few days of childbirth and end by the 2nd week (Dobson & Sales, 2000).

Depression, a clinical diagnosis that meets the *Diagnostic and Statistical Manual of Mental Disorders* (Fourth Edition, Text Revision; DSM-IV-TR) standards, affects between 7% and 19% of women and generally lasts up to a few months (Campbell & Cohn, 1991). Despite being temporally associated with childbirth, multiple studies have shown that this is not a form of mental illness specific to postpartum women . . . .

Psychosis occurs in postpartum women at a rate of less than 1 case per 1,000 births (Terp & Mortensen, 1998) and generally requires an inpatient hospitalization to stabilize the symptoms of hallucinations and delusions. Its onset appears to be within 2 weeks to 2 months of childbirth and to be related to an underlying predisposition to mania and bipolar disorder rather than being caused by childbirth or hormone changes (Hay, 2009). For example, Kendell, Chalmers, and Platz (1987) examined records in more than 54,000 births over a 12-year period, looking for psychiatric admissions within 90 days postpartum. They found 120 cases, most within the initial 30 days and with those who had a history of bipolar disorder being at highest risk. Similarly, Sit, Rothschild, and Wisner (2006), in their review of research

from 1966 to 2005, found that the start of puerperal psychosis began within the first 4 weeks postpartum and was associated with bipolar disorder. C. Dean and Kendell (1981) compared the hospitalization lengths for postpartum and non-postpartum women with mania and found no difference in type of treatment or hospitalization length . . . .

Long-term follow-up studies indicate that most women who have an episode of psychosis in the 2 to 3 months after giving birth will go on to have more episodes, regardless of future childbearing (Lewis & Bunce, 2003; Valdimarsdottir, Hultman, Harlow, Cnattingius, & Sparen, 2009) . . . .

Psychosis-related infanticide is extremely rare as the underlying illness itself is rare (Hatters-Friedman et al., 2005). Furthermore, infanticides related to psychosis tend to involve desired children rather than unwanted ones and immediate confessions rather than attempts to hide culpability (Lewis & Bunce, 2003). Psychotic infanticidal women are less likely to have prior involvement in CPS than non-psychotic infanticidal women.

Malingering of mental illness can arise in infanticide cases, as with other types of homicide. A review of Brazilian neonaticide cases over 95 years found an increase in the number of claimed amnesia cases after the enactment of a 1940 infanticide statute that emphasized the role of mental illness as a mitigating factor (Mendlowicz, Rapaport, Mecler, Golshan, & Moraes, 2002). This strongly suggests that many of these women were malingering an untestable symptom to avoid being held accountable for their actions.

In summary, while some women experience minor emotional disruptions following childbirth, psychosis and clinical levels of depression related to giving birth are rare. In both cases, however, the research to date indicates that these symptoms of mental illness are not unique forms caused by hormonal changes but rather are manifestations of preexisting mental illnesses. The majority of infanticides and neonaticides are not related to the woman's mental illness.

Language About the Victims

The perpetrators of infanticide often use language in a manner that deflects their responsibility and distances them from the event. Stanton and Simpson (2006) noted that, during interviews with women who had murdered their children, the women made statements such as "when my baby died," rather than "when I killed my baby." A similar manner of using language to diffuse the woman's responsibility is seen in many articles on infanticide. While studies may use the term "mother" to discuss the murderer of the infant, the infant is often termed "victim." In English, language is generally used in a dichotomous way, with either opposites or matched pairs, black/white, salt/pepper. It is usual to hear or read pairings of "mother/child" or "mother/infant," "victim/perpetrator" or "victim/murderer." The pair "mother" with "victim" suggests a reluctance to view women as murderers.

Several commentators have suggested that infanticide is caused by the woman's feeling "trapped" or "stressed" due to child care. However, parenting is not generally seen as such a stressful burden that homicide is a foreseeable outgrowth. Rather, in neonaticide and infanticide, the women have negative attitudes toward their infants and "do not wish to spend their physical emotional and social energy raising them" (Palermo, 2002, p. 141). . . .

Infanticidal and Neonaticidal Means

Due to their small size and inability to defend themselves, the murder of an infant does not require either strength or skill. Therefore, smothering, strangling, suffocating, and drowning are all common methods of infanticide, although many other means are used including starving burning, stabbing or cutting shooting, exposure, gross assault, gassing, scalding, poisoning, and defenestration . . . . Finkelhor and Ormrod (2001) suggest that women are more likely to use their hands

as a weapon and less likely to use firearms, compared to men, but Lewis, Baranoski, Buchanan and Benedek (1998; in Palermo, 2002) indicated that up to 25% of women who murdered their children use weapons.

Gender of Murdered Infants/Neonates

While infanticide of females appears to be higher than infanticide of males in India and China (Sahni et al., 2008), many studies report a higher rate of infanticide of male than female infants in industrialized western nations (see Table 5). Lester (1991) proposes that this discrepancy is related to the higher murder rate of males in general. The problem with this argument is that the majority of murders of adult men are perpetrated by other men (Fox & Zawitz, 2007; U.S. Dept of Justice, 2006). It does not necessarily follow that, while most adult male murders are perpetrated by other males, infant male murders would be perpetrated by females. Women commit the majority of all infant murders, so why are they killing more male infants?

Marleau, Dube, and LeVeille (2004) suggest that more males than females are born and therefore a higher infanticide rate is simply an artefact of the higher availability of male infants. While the ratio of male to female live births is slowly moving toward 1:1 in industrialized nations, currently approximately 1–2% more boys are born than girls. Marleau et al. reported that, in their sample of 420 infanticide cases, 58.3% of the murdered infants were male. Beyer et al. (2008), Bropokman and Nolan (2006), Crimmins et al. (1997), and Hodgins and Dube (1995) all report a similar 5–6% higher rate of infanticide of males. Even accounting for the differences in live births, about 6% more male infants were murdered than female infants in industrialized nations. One possible explanation is that a male infant is more "other" to a woman than a female infant. Is the male infant somehow symbolic of the woman's male sex partner? At this point, the issue is unclear and will require more research.

Denial/Concealment

*****

One of the hallmark factors in neonaticide compared to infanticide is the secrecy of the pregnancy and subsequent birth. As noted above, women who commit neonaticide are markedly different from women who commit infanticide. Neonaticidal women tend to be younger, emotionally immature, and do not desire to become a parent at the time of the homicide. Many of these women manage to conceal their pregnancies from their parents and others for the entire 9 months, although, according to Beyer et al. (2008), at least one other person was aware of the pregnancy in 83% of the cases.

The issue of whether the woman was aware of her pregnancy would be a relevant factor in a neonaticide trial. Given the multiple signs and symptoms of pregnancy, especially by the end of the 9th month, including very specific location of weight gain, amenorrhea, and fetal movement, it seems unlikely that most women could remain passively oblivious to pregnancy, without other factors contributing to the lack of awareness (Vallone & Hoffman, 2003). According to Beyer et al. (2008), in their sample of 40 neonaticidal women, over half had a history of previous pregnancies, giving them a clear frame of reference for their physical signs and precluding any logical claims that they were unaware of their pregnancies. Beyer et al. (2008) further notes that in the majority of cases the women went through labor and then murdered the infant within close proximity to others, without disturbing anyone, let alone calling for help. This behavior suggests intentional concealment. If a woman found herself experiencing labor and giving birth, somehow without ever having known she was pregnant, an expected reaction would be to call for help. Even if she mistakenly believed the baby was stillborn, calling for help would still be the expected behavior, not placing the infant in the trash as is done in these cases.

Is it ever possible to be totally unaware of a pregnancy until the point of labor? The research by Wessel, Endrika, and Buscher (2002), based on a Berlin population study, found that 1 in 2,455 cases reach labor without the woman being aware that she was pregnant. While it does occur, it is clearly rare. Furthermore, the women in this study were not accused of neonaticides and so their claims of obliviousness lack secondary gain.

Several studies use the term "denial"rather than concealment to discuss the unwanted pregnancy that results in neonaticides. They suggest that the woman denies her pregnant state to herself. Dulit (2000) posits that there are three types of "denial"seen in neonaticides cases. The first seems to be less a form of denial and more a simple desire: I hope I'm not pregnant. The second involves deliberate deception of others and seems best described by concealment. The third, "true"denial, is a function of actively pushing the facts away: "I can't think about this now."To deny something first requires an acknowledgment that the reality exists and then requires active inattention (Kohm & Liverman, 2002). Therefore, these are not cases of chronic mentally ill women who deny their pregnancies due to mental disturbance. Rather, these women are cognitively aware of their pregnancies but their behaviors and emotions do not match that awareness (Lee, Li, Kwong, & So, 2006). The woman makes a decision not to alter her behaviors (get a gynecological exam, pregnancy test, abortion, prenatal care), not to form any maternal prenatal attachments, and, ultimately, to murder the newborn infant.

Beier et al. (2006), after reviewing both forensic and obstetric cases of denial and concealment of pregnancy, found that these groups were identical and devised the term "pregnancy negation."They suggest that pregnancy negation might be viewed as a type of conversion or adjustment disorder; however, pregnancy negation lacks the egodystonic factor necessary to be a type of conversion disorder and does not fit the time frame necessary for an adjustment disorder.

Recidivism

*****

What is the likelihood that a woman who murders her infant will go on to commit another act of violence toward an infant in the future? At this point, there are very limited data available on that topic. A group of 47 Argentine infanticidal women were followed for 237 days following discharge from prison and 11% engaged in maladaptive behavior during the follow-up period. However, as the follow-up period was less than 1 year and recidivism rates are usually reported in 5-year, 10-year, and 15-year periods, it remains unclear whether infanticidal women go on to commit more acts of violence.

Stanton and Simpson (2006), in their interviews of mentally incompetent infanticidal women, noted that these women did not express concerns about living with their illness upon release and did not reference valuing professional psychological help during their hospital stays. This suggests that these women underestimated their risk for relapse and therefore risk to others in the future.

For infanticides and neonaticides unrelated to maternal psychosis, the above cases indicate that the risk for recidivism clearly exists and should not be underestimated or based on the woman's lack of prior criminal arrests. The majority of women who kill their children had no prior arrest history (McKee, 2006), but as the cases of Hoyte, Noe, Folbigg, and Courjault show, a lack of previous arrests does not mean a lack of criminal or violent behavior.

TYPOLOGIES

Resnick (1970) was the first to suggest that typologies could be developed to describe and categorize infanticidal events and introduced the concept of neonaticide as a separate category. Although the expression "typology" may not be completely relevant here, as such terminology and classification had not been established at this point, Resnick has still described classifications that could illustrate distinctions in the motivations for killing. These include

- killings for "altruistic" reasons;
- killing by an acutely psychotic woman;
- killing of an unwanted infant;
- accidental killing via severe child abuse;
- killing for revenge against another; and
- neonaticides.

For Resnick, altruistic reasons for killing a child could include ending the child's real or imagined suffering. For example, a mother who plans to kill herself may feel that her child would suffer if left behind in the world and so kills the child too.

From Resnick's initial list, multiple other categorization forms have been designed, of varying length, comprehensiveness, and utility . . . .

Both Resnick's and D'Oban's typologies have been validated internationally and remain the best known, although McKee's typology appears to be highly useful for forensic purposes.

There are problems with the current typologies, stemming from the subjectivity of the terms. As Mugavin (2005) points out, most typologies include a discussion of "violent" and "non-violent" methods to murder the infant. For example, he cites Resnick who compared infanticidal methods used by men to those used by women. The methods men used are described as "more active" while the methods women used are described as "passive." Is it possible to classify murder as non-violent or passive? It is unlikely that the experience of being slowly drowned or smothered seems non-violent to the victim.

"Altruism" as a descriptor of motivation for infanticide is also problematic. As Harder (1967; in Stanton, 2002) suggests, the idea that the murder of an infant was somehow altruistic probably comes from the continual myth that women are always loving mothers, even during murder. This view represents a social perspective rather than scientific objectivity and could, according to Lewis and Bunce (2003), have ramifications in court proceedings. Scott's terminology, "result of stimulus arising from victim" is also problematic, as it seems to imply that the infant was somehow culpable of his or her own murder.

Furthermore, as with any typology system, there is the problem of overlap; cases that are complex and do not fit neatly into any single category. For example, the American press recently published a story of a chronic schizophrenic woman who murdered her infant, following a fight with the baby's father. Should this be classified as due to mental illness or for revenge? For forensic purposes, a more functional classification system might be

*****

CONCLUSION

At this point, research has given a fairly accurate understanding of who commits infanticide, why and by what means:

- Neonaticide is generally committed by women who often conceal the pregnancy, give birth away from a hospital and then suffocate, strangle or drown the unwanted newborn before hiding the corpse. Neonaticidal women generally do not have an incapacitating mental illness.
- Infanticides are generally committed by more mature women who use a variety of violent methods, may premeditate the crime, and engage in infanticide for reasons ranging from retaliation against another adult to child abuse or neglect to removal of an unwanted child.
- A subset of infanticides are committed by women during a psychotic episode. These women are likely to have significant psychiatric problems for the remainder of their life, regardless of their childbearing, as psychosis is not the result of maternal hormone fluctuations.

While this produces a greater understanding of the causes of neonaticide and infanticide, there is still a lack a strong conceptualization as to how to prevent these crimes from occurring. For those infanticide cases related to the woman's psychosis, it may be useful to educate gynecologists, obstetricians, and birthing unit staff regarding this issue and for them to educate partners and parents of women giving birth. Open conversations with women regarding their and their family's history of mental illness would assist in identifying some women with predispositions to psychosis. Public service messages by the media on this topic would also be useful to educate the public of warning signs and symptoms. For neonaticide, because the perpetrators largely avoid any obstetric contact, another avenue of education would be needed. Social networking sites are becoming a common communication venue for women younger than 30 years and could be useful in increasing awareness about concealed pregnancies and neonaticide risks among young people. School personnel could be educated regarding the signs of concealed pregnancy. It is also important that the courts and policy makers focus on the problems of chivalric justice as well as the possibility of serial or repeat neonaticide/infanticide.

REFERENCES

Adshead, G., Brooke, D., Samuels, M., Jenner, S., & Southall, D. (2000). Maternal behaviors associated with smothering: A preliminary descriptive study. *Child Abuse & Neglect, 24,* 1175–1183.

American Psychiatric Association (2000): *Diagnostic and Statistical Manual of Mental Disorders, Fourth Edition, Text Revision.* Washington, DC, American Psychiatric Association.

Angier, D. (2005). Fountain mom gets 25 years for killing newborn. 7/23/05 *News Herald.* Retrieved September 25, 2009, from http://www.newsherald.com/articles/class-76048-killing-bodycopy justified.html

Begley, S., & Underwood, A. (1998, August 17). Death of the innocents. *Newsweek.* Retrieved September 3, 2009, from http://www./archive/5473-newsweek/august-1998.html

Beier, K., Wille, R., & Wessel, J. (2006). Denial of pregnancy as a reproductive dysfunction: a proposal for international classification systems. Journal of Psychosomatic Research, 61, 723–730.

Bennet, M., Jr., Hall, J., Frazier, L., Jr., Patel, N., Barker, L., & Shaw, K. (2006). Homicide of children aged 0–4 years,2003–04: Results from the National Violent Death Reporting System. *Injury Prevention, 12,* ii39–ii43.

Beyer, K., McAuliffe-Mack, S., & Shelton, J. (2008). Investigative analysis of neonaticide: An exploratory study. *Criminal Justice and Behavior, 35,* 525–535.

Bourget, D., & Gagne, P. (2005). Paternal filicide in Québec. *Journal American Academy Psychiatry Law, 33,* 354–360.

Bourget, D., Grace, J., & Whitehurst, L. (2007). A review of maternal and paternal filicide. *Journal American Academy Psychiatry Law, 35,* 74–82.

Bropokman, F., & Nolan, J. (2006, July). The dark figure of infanticide in England and Wales: Complexities of diagnosis. *Journal of Interpersonal Violence, 21,* 869–888.

Busch, F. (1997). A mother on trial. Retrieved September 25, 2009, from www.nytimes.com/books/97/09/14/reviews/970914.14buscht. html

Campbell, S., & Cohn, J. (1991). Prevalence and correlates of postpartum depression in first time mothers. *Journal of Abnormal Psychology, 100,* 594–599.

The Canadian Press. (2008). The Canadian press: Woman who put newborn in firepit gets conditional sentence 2/8/08. *CBC News 2008.* Retrieved September 25, 2009, from http://www.cbc.ca/ canada/new-brunswick/story/2008/02/08/morrow-trial.html

Cooper, P., Campbell, E., Day, A., Kennerly, H., & Bond, A. (1988). Nonpsychotic psychiatric disorder after childbirth; a prospective study of prevalence, incidence, course and nature. *British Journal of Psychiatry, 152,* 799–806.

Cox, J. L., Murray, D., & Chapman, G. (1993). A controlled study of the onset, duration and prevalence of postnatal depression. *British Journal of Psychiatry, 163,* 27–31.

Crimmins, S., Langley, S., Brownstein, H., & Spunt, B. (1997, February). Convicted women who have killed children: A self psychology perspective. *Journal of Interpersonal Violence, 12,* 49–69.

Crittenden, P., & Craig, S. (1990). Developmental trends in the nature of child homicide. *Journal Interpersonal Violence, 5,* 202–216.

Cummings, P., Theis, M., Mueller, B., & Rivara, F. (1994). Infant injury death in Washington State, 1981 through 1990. *Archives of Pediatrics & Adolescent Medicine, 148,* 1021–1026.

D'Orban, P. T. (1979). Women who kill their children. *The British Journal of Psychiatry, 134,* 560–571.

Dalley, M. (1997/2000). The killing of Canadian children by a parent(s) or guardian(s): Characteristics and trends 1990–1993. Royal Canadian Mounted Police January 1997 & 2000 Missing Children's Registry & National Police Services. Retrieved September 25, 2009, from http://www.rcmp-grc. gc.ca/omc-ned/ resear-recher/kill-tuer-eng.pdf

Dean, C., & Kendell, R. E. (1981, August). The symptomatology of puerperal illnesses. British Journal of *Psychiatry, 139,* 28–33.

Dean, P. (2004). Child homicide and infanticide in New Zealand. *International Journal of Law and Psychiatry, 27,* 339–348.

Dobson, V., & Sales, B. (2000). The science of infanticide and mental illness. *Psychology, Public Policy and Law, 6,* 1098–1112.

Drescher-Burke, K., Krall, J., & Penick, A. (2004). *Discarded infants and neonaticides: A review of the literature.* Berkeley, CA: National Abandoned Infants Assistance Resource Center, University of California at Berkeley.

Dulit, E. (2000). Girls who deny a pregnancy. Girls who kill the neonate. *Adolescent Psychiatry, 25,* 219–235.

Emerick, S. J., Foster, L. R., & Campbell, D. T. (1986, April). Risk factors for traumatic infant death in Oregon 1973–1982. *Pediatrics, 77,* 518–522.

Finkelhor, D. (1997). The homicides of children and youth: a developmental perspective. In G. K. Kantor & J. L. Jasinski (Eds.), *Out of the darkness: Contemporary perspectives on family violence,* pp. 17–34. Thousand Oaks, CA: SAGE.

Finkelhor, D., & Ormrod, R. (2001). Homicides of children and youth. U.S. Department of Justice Office of Justice Programs Office of Juvenile Justice and Delinquency Prevention 10/2001. Retrieved September 25, 2009, from http://www.nexthorizon.unh.edu/ccrc/ pdf/jvq/CV34.pdf

Fox, J., & Zawitz, M. (2007). US Department of Justice, Bureau of Justice Statistics Web Site. Retrieved July 28, 2009, from http:// www.ojp.usdoj.gov/bjs/homicide/homtrnd.htm

Fox News. (2007). Baby-drops introduced in germany as infanticide cases spike. 3/27/07. Retrieved September 25, 2009, from http://www.foxnews.com/story/0,2933,261588,00.html

Glendinning, L. Inside the mind of a killer mother. *The Age.* October 25, 2003. Retrieved September 3, 2009, from http://www.theage.com.au/articles/2003/10/24/1066974316572.html

Guileyardo, J., Prahlow, J., & Bernard, J. (1999). Filicide and filicide classification. *The American*

Journal of Forensic Medicine and Pathology, 20, 286–292.

Haapasalo, J., & & Petäjä, S (1999). Mothers who killed or attempted to kill their child: Life circumstances, childhood abuse, and types of killing. *Violence and Victims, 14,* 219–239.

Harder, T. (1967). The psychopathology of infanticide. *Acta Psychiatr Scand, 43,* 196–245.

Harris, B. (1994). Biological and hormonal aspects of postpartum depressed mood. *British Journal of Psychiatry, 164,* 288–292.

Hatters-Friedman, S., Heneghan, A., & Rosenthal, M. (2007, March-April). Characteristics of women who deny or conceal pregnancy. *Psychosomatics, 48,* 117–122.

Hatters-Friedman, S., Horwitz, S., & Resnick, P. (2005). Child murder by mothers: A critical analysis of the current state of knowledge and a research agenda. *American Journal Psychiatry, 162,* 1578–1587.

Hatters-Friedman, S., & Resnick, P. (2009). Neonaticide: Phenomenology and considerations for prevention. *International Journal of Law and Psychiatry, 32,* 43–47.

Hay, P. (2009). Post-partum psychosis: Which women are at highest risk. PLoS Medicine, 6, e1000027.

Herman-Giddens, M. E., Smith, M. J., Mittal, M. Carlson, J., & Butts, J. (2003). Newborns killed or left to die by a parent. *JAMA, 289,* 1425–1429.

Hodgins, S., & Dube, M. (1995). Parents who kill their children: A cohort study. Retrieved September 3, 2009, from http://homicideworkinggroup.cos.ucf.edu/include/documents/hrwg95.pdf#page1/4151

Hundley, W. (2008). The Dallas morning news, 11/8/08 Deana Schlosser, plano mom who cut off baby's arms, moving to output care. Retrieved September 3, 2009, from http://www.dallasnews.com/sharedcontent/dws/dn/latestnews/stories/110808dnmetschlosser.18ca635cc.html

Jason, J., Carpenter, M., & Tyler, C. (1983). Underrecording of infant homicide in the United States. *Am J Public Health, 73,* 195–197.

Jennings, K., Ross, S., Popper, S., & Elmore, M. (1999). Thoughts of harming infants in depressed and nondepressed mothers. Journal of Affective Disorders, 54, 21–28.

Kauppi, A., Kumpulainen, K., Vanamo, T., Merikanto, J., & Karkola, K. (2008). Maternal depression and filicide: Case study of ten mothers. *Archives of Women's Mental Health, 11,* 201–206.

Kendell, R., Chalmers, J., & Platz, C. (1987). Epidemiology of puerperal psychosis. *British Journal of Psychiatry, 150,* 662–673.

Kohm, L., & Liverman, T. (2002). Prom mom killers: the impact of blame shift and distorted statistics on punishment for neonaticides. *William and Mary Journal of Women and the Law, 9,* 43–71.

Krischer, M., Stone, M., Sevecke, K., & Steinmeyer, E. (2007). Motives for maternal filicide: results from a study with female forensic patients. *International Journal of Law and Psychiatry, 30,* 191–200.

Kumar, C., McIvor, R., Davies, T., Brown, N., Papadopoulos, A., Wieck, A., & . . . Marks, M. (2003). Estrogen administration does not reduce the rate of recurrence of affective psychosis after childbirth. *The Journal of Clinical Psychiatry, 64,* 112–118.

Kumar, R., & Robson, K. (1984). A prospective study of emotional disorders in childbearing women. *The British Journal of Psychiatry, 144,* 35–47.

La Nacion, 2005. Condenaron a Tejerina a 14 anos de prision. June 10, 2005. Retrieved September 24, 2009, from http://www.lanacion.com.ar/nota.asp?nota_id1/4711765

Lambie, I. (2001). Mothers who kill: The crime of infanticide. *International Journal of Law and Psychiatry, 24,* 71–80.

Lee, A. C. W., Li, C. H., Kwong, N. S., & So, K. T. (2006). Neonaticide, newborn abandonment, and denial of pregnancy—Newborn victimisation associated with unwanted motherhood. *Hong Kong Medical Journal, 12,* 61–64.

Lester, D. (1991). Murdering babies. A cross-national study. *Social Psychiatry and Psychiatric Epidemiology, 26,* 83–85.

Levene, S., & Bacon, C. J. (2004). Sudden unexpected death and covert homicide in infancy. *Archives of Disease in Childhood, 89,* 443–447.

Levitzky, S., & Cooper, R. (2000). Infant colic syndrome: Maternal fantasies of aggression and infanticide. *Clinical Pediatrics, 39,* 395–399.

Lewis, C. F., Baranoski, M., Buchanan, J., & Benedek, E. (1998). Factors associated with weapon use in maternal filicide. *Journal of Forensic Sciences, 43,* 613–618.

Lewis, C. F., & Bunce, S. C. (2003). Filicidal mothers and the impact of psychosis on maternal filicide. *J Am Acad Psychiatry Law, 31,* 459–470.

Logan, M. (1995). Mothers who murder: A comparative study of filicide and neonaticide. *RCMP Gazette, 57,* 2–10.

Marks, M., & Kumar, R. (1993). Infanticide in England and Wales. *Medical Science and the Law, 33,* 320–339.

Marks, M., & Kumar, R. (1996). Infanticide in Scotland. *Medical Science and the Law, 36,* 299–305.

Marleau, J., Dube, M., & LeVeille, S. (2004). Neonaticidal mothers: Are more boys killed? *Medicine, Science and the Law, 44*, 311–316.

McKee, G. (2006). *Why mothers kill: A forensic psychologist's casebook*. UK: Oxford University.

McKee, G., Shea, S., Mogy, R., & Holden, C. (2001). MMPI 2 profiles of filicide, mariticidal and homicidal women. *Journal of Clinical Psychology, 57*, 367–374.

Mendlowicz, M., Rapaport, M., Mecler, K., Golshan, S., & Moraes, T. (1998). Case controls study on the socio-demographic characteristics of 53 neonaticidal mothers. *International Journal of Law and Psychiatry, 21*, 209–219.

Mendlowicz MV, da Silva, Filho JF, Gekker M, de Moraes TM, Rapaport MH, Jean-Louis F. (2000). Mothers murdering their newborns in the hospital. *Gen Hosp Psychiatry, 22*(1), 53–5.

Mendlowicz, M., Rappaport, M., Fontenelle, L., Jean-Louis, G., & De Moraes, T. (2002, March). Amnesia and neonaticides. *American Journal of Psychiatry, 159*, 111–113.

Meyer, C., & Oberman, M. (2001). *Mothers who kill their children: understanding the acts of moms from Susan Smith to the "prom mom."* New York: NYU press.

Mugavin, M. (2005). A metasynthesis of filicide classification systems: psychosocial and psychodynamic issues in women who kill their children. *Journal of Forensic Nursing, 1*, 65–72.

Mulryan, N., Gibbons, P., & O'Connors, I. (2002). Infanticide and child murder—Admissions to the Central Mental Hospital 1850–2000. *Ir J Psych Med, 19*, 8–12.

O'Hara, M., Schlechte, J., Lewis, D., & Varner, M. (1991, February). Controlled prospective study of postpartum mood disorders: Psychological, environmental and hormonal variables. *Journal of Abnormal Psychology, 100*, 63–73.

Overpeck, M., Brenner, R., Trumble, A., Trifiletti, L., & Berendes, H. (1998, October). Risk factors for infant homicide in the United States. *New England Journal of Medicine, 339*, 1211–1216.

Palermo, G. (2002). Murderous parents. *International Journal of Offender Therapy and Comparative Criminology, 46*, 123–143.

Paulozzi, M., & Sells, M. (2002, March 8). Variations in homicide risk during Infancy: US 1989–1998. *CDC Morbidity and Mortality Weekly Report, 51*, 187–189.

Putkonen, H., Collander, J., Weizmann-Henelius, G., & Eronen, M. (2007). Legal outcomes of all suspected neonaticides in Finland 1980–2000. *International Journal of Law and Psychiatry, 30*, 248–254.

Rapaport, E. (2006). Mad women and desperate girls: Infanticide and child murder in law and myth. *33 Fordham Urb. L.J.* 527 (2005–2006).

Reich, T., & Winokur, G. (1970, July). Postpartum psychosis in patients with manic depressive disease. The *Journal of Nervous and Mental Disease, 151*, 60–68.

Resnick, P. (1970, April). Murder of the newborn: A psychiatric review of neonaticide. Am *J Psychiatry, 126*, 1414–1420.

Resnick, P., & Hatters-Friedman, S. (2003, August). Book review: Spinelli's infanticide. *Psychiatric Services, 54*, 1172.

Robling, S., Paykel, E., Dunn, V., Abbott, R., & Katona, C. (2000). Long-term outcome of severe puerperal psychiatric illness: A 23 year follow-up study. *Psychological Medicine, 30*, 1263–1271.

Rouge-Maillart, C., Jousset, N., Gaudin, A., Bouju, B., & Penneau, M. (2005). Women who kill their children. The American Journal of Forensic *Medicine and Pathology, 26*, 320–326.

Sahni, M., Verma, N., Narula, R., Varghese, R., Sreenivas, V., & Puliyel, J. M. (2008). Missing girls in India: Infanticide, feticide and made-to-order pregnancies? Insights from hospital-based sex-ratio-at-birth over the last century. PLoS ONE, 3:e2224. Published online May 21, 2008.

Saunders, E. (1989). Neonaticides following "secret"pregnancies: seven case reports. *Public Health Reports, 104*, 368–372.

Schipoliansky, C., & Childs, D. (2009). When parents kill their kids (the case of the frozen babies). *ABC News*. June 18, 2009. Retrieved September 3, 2009, http://abcnews.go.com/Health/MindMood News/story?id1/47864712&page1/41

Schmidt, P., Grab, H., & Madea, B. (1996). Child homicides in Cologne (1985–1994). *Forensic Science International, 79*, 131–144.

Scott, P. D. (1973). Parents who kill their children. *Medicine, Science and the Law, 13*, 120–126.

Siegel, C., Graves, P., Maloney, K., Norris, J., Calogne, B., & Lezotte, D. (1996). Mortality from intentional and unintentional injury among infants of young mothers in Colorado 1986–1992. *Archives of Pediatrics & Adolescent Medicine, 150*, 1077–1083.

Silverman, R., & Kennedy, L. (1988, Summer). Women who kill their children. *Violence & Victims, 3*, 113–127.

Sit, D., Rothschild, A. J., & Wisner, K. L. (2006). A review of postpartum psychosis. *Journal of Women's Health, 15*, 352–368.

Spiegel. (2008, February 25). German politician blames communism for child killings. Retrieved September 3, 2009, from http://www. spiegel.de/international/germany/0,1518,537577,00.html

Spinelli, M. (2001). A systematic investigation of 16 cases of neonaticide. *Am J Psychiatry, 158,* 811–813.

Spinelli, M. (2003). *Infanticide: Psychosocial and legal perspectives on mothers who kill.* Washington, DC: American Psychiatric Publishing Inc.

Stangle, H. (2008). Murderous Madonna: Femininity, violence, and the myth of postpartum mental disorder in cases of maternal infanticide and filicide. *William & Mary Law Review, 50,* 699.

Stanton, J., & Simpson, A. (2002). Filicide: a review. *International Journal of Law and Psychiatry, 25,* 1–14.

Stanton, J., & Simpson, A. (2006). The aftermath: Aspects of recovery described by perpetrators of maternal filicide committed in the context of severe mental illness. *Behavioral Sciences and the Law, 24,* 103–112.

Taguchi, H. (2007). Maternal filicide in Japan: Analyses of 96 cases and future directions for prevention. *Psychiatria et Neurology Japonica, 109,* 110–127.

Terp, I., & Mortensen, P. (1998). Postpartum psychosis: clinical diagnoses and relative risk of admission after parturition. *The British Journal of Psychiatry, 172,* 521–526.

Tracey, S. (2008). Tears, fury follow infanticide verdict Guelph Mercury. September 12, 2008. Retrieved September 3, 2009, from http://www.canadiancrc.com/Newspaper_Articles/Guelph_Mercury_Tears_fury_follow_infanticide_verdict_12SEP08.aspx

Troutman, B., & Cutrona, C. (1990). Nonpsychotic postpartum depression among adolescent mothers. *Journal of Abnormal Psychology, 99,* 467–474.

Tschinkel, S., Harris, M., Lenoury, J., & &Healy, D. (2007). Postpartum psychosis: two cohorts compared 1875–1924 and 1994–2005. *Psychological Medicine, 37,* 529–536.

U.S. Dept of Justice, Bureau of Justice Statistics. (2006). Homicide trends in the U.S. Retrieved July 27, 2009, from http://www.ojp.usdoj.gov/bjs/homicide/gender.htm

Valdimarsdottir, U., Hultman, C., Harlow, B., Cnattingius, S., & Sparen, P. (2009). Psychotic illness in first time mothers with no previous psychiatric hospitalizations: A population based study. *PLoS Medicine.* February 10, 2009. Retrieved May 28, 2009, from http://www.plosmedicine.org/article/info%3Adoi%2F10.1371%2Fjournal.pmed.1000013

Vallone, D. C. & Hoffman, L. M. (2003) Preventing the Tragedy of Neonaticide Holistic Nursing Practice: September/October 17 Issue 5 223–230.

Van Gent, E., & Verhoeven, W. (1992). Bipolar illness, lithium prophylaxis and pregnancy. *Pharmacopsychiatry, 25,* 187–191.

Vanamo, T., Kauppi, A., Karkola, K., Merikanto, J., & Räsänen, E. (2001). Intra-familial child homicide in Finland 1970–1994: incidence, causes of death and demographic characteristics. *Forensic Science International, 117,* 199–204.

Verkerk, G., Denollet, J., Van Heck, G., Van Son, M., & Pop, V. (2005). Personality factors as determinants of depression in postpartum women: A prospective 1 year follow-up study. *Psychosomatic Medicine, 67,* 632–637.

Videbech, P., & Gouliaev, G. (1995). First admission with puerperal psychosis: 7–14 years of follow-up. *Acta Psychiatrica Scandinavica, 91,* 167–173.

Wessel, J., Endrika, J., & Buscher, U. (2002). Frequency of denial of pregnancy: results and epidemiological significance of a 1-year prospective study in Berlin. *Acta Obstetricia et Gynecologica Scandinavica, 81,* 1021–1027.

Whalley, L., Roberts, D., Wentzel, J., & Wright, A. (1982). Genetic factors in puerperal affective psychoses. *Acta Psychiatrica Scandinavica, 65,* 180–188.

Wilczynski, A. (1997). Mad or bad? Child killers, gender and the courts. *British Journal of Criminology, 37,* 419–436.

Wilczynski, A., & Morris, A. (1993). Parents who kill their children. Criminal Law Review, 31, in Rapaport, E. (2006). Mad women and desperate girls: Infanticide and child murder in law and myth. *Fordham Urban Law Journal, 33,* 527.

Wisner, K., & Stowe, Z. (1997). Psychobiology of postpartum mood disorders. *Seminars in Reproductive Medicine, 15,* 77–89.

19

THE CHARACTERISTICS OF ONLINE SEX OFFENDERS

*A Meta-Analysis**

KELLY M. BABCHISHIN

R. KARL HANSON

CHANTAL A. HERMANN

INTRODUCTION

As with any new technology, the Internet provides new opportunities for sexual exploitation. The Internet is a largely unregulated environment in which it is possible to collect and distribute child pornography as well as to lure potential victims. The number of sexual offenders who have used the Internet in their crimes (online offenders) has increased considerably in the past 5 years (Motivans & Kyckelhahn, 2007; Wolak, Finkelhor, & Mitchell, 2009). Although they remain a small proportion of identified sex offenders, there is increasing concern about how to manage, assess, and treat online offenders. One fundamental question is how different are online offenders from typical (offline) sex offenders?

Several typologies of online offenders have been suggested in the literature. For example, online offenders have been categorized as those who (a) access child pornography out of curiosity or impulse, without specific sexual interest in children; (b) access child pornography to satisfy sexual fantasies, but do not commit contact sex offenses; (c) create and distribute child pornography solely for financial gain; and, lastly, (d) use the Internet to facilitate contact sex offenses (Krone, 2004; Lanning, 2001). Thus, it is possible that online offenders, or subgroups of online offenders, are truly a distinct type of sexual offender.

*This article was published in *Sexual Abuse: A Journal of Research and Treatment, 23*, 92–123 (2011). We have removed Tables 1 and 5 and the two appendices as well as sections of the methodology.

In contrast, it is plausible that the same basic factors involved in the onset and maintenance of offline sexual offending are also involved in online sexual offending, with the exception that online offenders use the Internet to offend. Akin to the advent of photographs or home videos, the Internet may simply be another technology that allows sexual offenders easier access to child pornography and potential victims. Routine activity theory posits that predatory criminal behavior (i.e., involving damage to a person or property) requires motivated offenders, suitable targets, as well as a lack of supervision (L. E. Cohen & Felson, 1979). Applying this theory to online offenders, the largely unregulated Internet market supplies suitable targets and the lack of supervision needed for motivated offenders to download or distribute child pornography and commit contact sexual offenses (e.g., child luring). It is possible that the opportunity provided by the Internet would lead some individuals to succumb to temptations that they would have otherwise effectively controlled.

Empirical evidence supports both similarities and differences between online and offline offenders. Seto, Hanson, and Babchishin (2011) found that approximately half of online offenders admitted to committing a contact sexual offense and 12.2% had an official history of contact sexual offenses. In addition, Seto, Cantor, and Blanchard (2006) found a large proportion of online offenders displayed pedophilic interests. Taken together, these findings suggest that at least some online offenders may have similar characteristics to offline offenders. In contrast, studies have also found differences between online and offline offenders . . . .

There are two important questions to ask with regards to the typologies of online sexual offenders: (a) Are sexual offenders with online crimes different from offenders with offline crimes? (b) Are online-only offenders different from offline-only offenders? As mentioned earlier, some online offenders are expected to have an official prior contact offense (12.2%) or report a prior contact offense (approximately 55.1%; Seto et al., 2011). It is also possible that offline offenders have

online offences. Although initially we hoped to have an online-only group, a mixed group, and an offline-only group, the data from most of the available studies were not presented in a way to allow for such comparisons. Consequently, the current review compared offenders with any online offenses (referred to as online offenders) with offenders identified by offline offences (referred to as offline offenders). All results should therefore be interpreted as comparisons between mixed offenders. The online groups would be expected to have a significant proportion of offenders with offline offenses and the offline group would be expected to contain offenders with online offences. As a result, any observed differences would likely be smaller than those obtained had we been able to compare pure groups of online-only and offline-only sexual offenders.

In this article, we report a meta-analysis addressing the degree that online offenders differ from offline offenders, and from the general population. To date, the literature is mostly descriptive in nature (e.g., age, marital status) and tends to only report information concerning a single sample of online offenders. Nevertheless, aggregating these findings will provide information on some of the key characteristics of online offenders. Several of the factors reviewed have been linked to sexual recidivism (e.g., age, marital status, sexual deviancy) and, therefore, can offer some direction to professionals as to how to assess and treat online offenders (Hanson & Morton-Bourgon, 2005).

METHOD

Selection of Studies

Computer searches of Digital Dissertations, National Criminal Justice Reference System (NCJRS), PsychINFO, PubMed, Scholar Portal, and the Web of Science were conducted using the following key terms: Internet offend*, Internet child molest*, child abuse imag*, imag* of child abuse, online offend*, child porn*, web, cyber, and character*, trait, feature, and attribut*. Additional articles were found through reference lists of the collected articles, review articles in this area, contacts with researchers in the field of online offenders, and requests posted in July 2009 to an e-mail list of members of the Association for the Treatment of Sexual Abusers.

To be included in the current meta-analysis, the study had to include an identifiable sample of online offenders. Recent samples (post 2000) of child pornography offenders were included because it was presumed that a majority of these offenders would have used the Internet and other computer technology in their offenses. The study had to report on at least one of the characteristics of online offenders targeted by this review, which included any demographic or psychological variables. At the end of coding, only variables with three or more studies were meta-analyzed. The study also needed to include sufficient statistical information to calculate an effect size (Cohen's *d*). Studies without comparison groups of offline offenders were included if an appropriate normative group could be found to make the necessary comparisons.

*****

Online offenders. In most samples, online offenders were identified by their convictions ($k=16$) or their arrests and/or charges ($k = 8$). Two samples were identified using self-reports and one sample was identified using both conviction as well as self-report information. The total sample sizes for online offenders ranged from 26 to 870 participants (median $=100$; $N=$ 4,844). All online offender samples consisted of adults. Child pornography offenders were included in all samples of online offenders; about half of the samples also included child luring offenders. The proportion of the offenders committing different types of online offenses was difficult to determine from the information given in the reports. Of the 27 samples, 9 samples had information on prior nonsexual offense history, representing 1,150 online offenders. Of these, approximately 136 online

offenders had at least one prior nonsexual offense (11.8%; 95% confidence interval [CI] = 6.0% to 17.5 %). Seven samples examined offenders who were in or had received treatment and five samples had at least some participants who had received treatment. The treatment status of the remaining samples was unknown ($k = 15$).

*****

Offline offenders. Nine studies compared offline and online offenders. In most samples, offline offenders were identified by their convictions ($k = 7$) and two samples were identified using self-reports. The total sample size for offline offenders ranged from 25 to 526 participants (median = 104; $N = 1,342$). All offline offender samples consisted of adults, most of whom had sexual offended against children ($k = 7$; 2 samples were predominantly child molesters but included some offenders with adult victims). Treatment status was unknown for four samples. Of the samples who included treatment status, most offline offenders either had received or were in treatment ($k = 3$) and two sample had at least some offenders who had received treatment.

*****

RESULTS

Online Offenders Compared With Offline Offenders

Meta-analytic summaries were only conducted for variables reported in at least three studies, resulting in nine comparisons between offline and online offenders. In terms of demographic variables, online offenders were less likely to be of a racial minority ($d = 0.87$) than offline offenders (see Table 2; note that the *d* values were calculated such that positive values indicate more deviant characteristics among the offline offenders compared with the online offenders). Approximately 8.2% of online offenders were classified as a racial minority compared with 35.4% of the offline offenders (see Table 3). Online offenders were younger than offline offenders (38.6 vs. 43.6). This difference was only significant, however, in the fixed-effect analysis.

Offline offenders reported more physical abuse compared to online offenders (40.8% vs. 24.4%). This difference was only significant, however, in the fixed-effect analysis, not the random-effects analysis. Rates of childhood

Table 2 Meta-Analysis of the Characteristics of Online Offenders Compared With Offline Offenders

	Random		*Fixed*				
	d	*95% CI*	*d*	*95% CI*	*Q*	*N*	*k*
Demographic variables							
Racial minority	0.865	0.581 to 1.149	0.865	0.581 to 1.149	0.04	762	3
Younger	−0.281	−0.565 to 0.003	−0.238	−0.337 to −0.139	25.75**	1,667	6
Developmental history							
Any childhood physical abuse	0.286	−0.027 to 0.598	0.228	0.007 to 0.449	3.15	666	3
Any childhood sexual abuse	0.129	−0.174 to 0.431	0.083	−0.132 to 0.298	3.35	666	3
Psychological variables							
Cognitive distortions	0.404	−0.083 to 0.891	0.657	0.541 to 0.774	16.84**	1,291	4
Emotional identification with children	0.128	−0.229 to 0.486	0.282	0.170 to 0.393	11.60*	1,344	4
Loneliness	−0.137	−0.410 to 0.136	−0.013	−0.118 to 0.092	10.73*	1,650	4
Low impression management	−0.383	−0.687 to −0.079	−0.249	−0.364 to −0.134	4.78	1,244	3
Low self-esteem	−0.047	−0.396 to 0.302	−0.052	−0.161 to 0.056	9.78*	1,509	3
Low victim empathy	0.561	0.327 to 0.795	0.603	0.486 to 0.720	3.23	1,249	3
Sexual deviancy	−0.565	−0.787 to −0.342	−0.565	−0.787 to −0.342	0.68	435	3

Note: CI = confidence interval; *k* = number of studies. The offline offender group was the referent group; positive values indicate more deviant characteristics among the offline offenders compared with the online offenders.

*p < .05. **p < .001.

sexual abuse were not significantly different between offline and online offenders.

In terms of psychological variables, offline offenders had lower rates of victim empathy than online offenders ($d = 0.56$). Offline offenders were also found to have less sexual deviancy compared with online offenders ($d = -0.57$). Sexual deviancy was measured using penile plethysmography, the Sexual Fantasy Questionnaire (Wilson, 1978; Girl and Boy items), and the sexual deviancy item of the STABLE-2007 (Hanson, Harris, Scott, &

Helmus, 2007). In addition, offline offenders were found to display more cognitive distortions ($d = 0.66$) and slightly more emotional identification with children ($d = 0.28$) than the online offenders. These differences, however, were only statistically significant in the fixed-effect analyses, not the random-effects analyses.

On average, the online offenders reported less socially desirable responding than the offline offenders ($d = -0.38$). Two of the three studies used the 1998 version of Paulhus's Impression Management Scale (IMS; Paulhus, 1998), whereas

Table 3 Descriptives of Online Offenders, Offline Offenders, and Normative Groups

	Online Sexual Offenders			Offline Sexual Offenders			Normative Groups
	N	M	95% CI	N	M	95% CI	Median Value of Comparison
Demographic variables							
Age (in years)	1,845	38.6	37.3–40.0	840	43.6	40.7–46.4	46.6
Currently not married (%)	2,490	69.6	63.3–75.8	—	—	—	44.8
Never married (%)	2,164	50.4	38.0–62.8	—	—	—	30.9
Racial minority (%)	2,014	8.16	5.32–1 1.0	496	35.4	28.1–42.7	21.6
Incomplete high school degree (%)	1,630	10.6	6.63–14.5	—	—	—	12.0
Unemployed (%)	700	14.7	8.38–21.1	—	—	—	5.82
Developmental history							
Any childhood physical abuse (%)	277	24.4	10.6–38.2	422	40.8	23.2–58.5	8.36
Any childhood sexual abuse (%)	1,027	21.1	14.8–27.4	422	33.5	21.6–45.4	8.49
Any substance abuse (%)	911	16.0	11.7–20.2	—	—	—	13.0

Note: CI = confidence interval; M = average. Random-effects meta-analysis was used to aggregate averages and proportions for online and offline offenders. Psychological variables are not reported because studies used different scales, resulting in noncomparable numbers.

the third study used a German translation of the 1991 version of the IMS (Paulhus, 1991). There were no significant differences between the groups in terms of loneliness or self-esteem.

Online Offenders Compared With Normative Groups

The offender characteristics that were compared with population values are displayed in Table 4. Online offenders reported significantly more physical ($d = 0.66$) and sexual abuse ($d = 0.58$) than males in the general population (note that the d values were calculated such that positive values indicate more deviant characteristics among the online offenders compared with the normative groups). Not only were online offenders more likely than offline offenders to be young and Caucasian, they were also younger than the general population ($d = 0.37$; 38.6 years vs. 46.6 years) and less likely to be a racial minority ($d = -0.42$; 8.2% vs. 21.6%). Compared with the general male population, online offenders were more likely to have never been married ($d = 0.49$; 50.4% vs. 30.9%) and to be unmarried at the time of assessment ($d = 0.62$, 69.6% vs. 44.8%). Online offenders were also more likely to be unemployed ($d = 0.67$; 14.7% vs. 5.8%). Of the studies that reported when these data were collected (9 of 11), unemployment status was mostly coded at the time of arrest/investigation ($n = 5$), prior to arrest ($n = 1$), prior to incarceration ($n = 1$), or during pretreatment assessments in community treatment centers ($n = 2$). Online offenders were also found to have more substance abuse than the normative groups, but this differences was only significant in the fixed-effect analysis ($d = 0.17$, 16% vs. 13%). There was no difference between online offenders and the normative groups on education.

DISCUSSION

The current study is the first to provide a quantitative review of the emerging research on the characteristics of online offenders. Although the available research is still rather limited, some broad conclusions are possible. In terms of demographic features, online offenders tend to be Caucasian males who are younger than the general population. Although they were not different than the general population in terms of education, they were twice as likely to be unemployed. Both online and offline offenders reported significantly more physical and sexual abuse than males in the general population. In comparison with offline offenders, online offenders had greater victim empathy, greater sexual deviancy, and lower impression management. In addition, offline offenders tended to be older than online offenders as well as have greater emotional identification with children and more cognitive distortions. These differences, however, were only significant in the fixed-effect analyses. Lastly, there were no significant differences between offline and online offenders in terms of loneliness or self-esteem.

The finding that youth and unemployment are risk factors for online sexual offending is consistent with typical crime patterns (Andrews & Bonta, 2006). Although being of a racial minority is a well-established risk factor for violent crime (Sampson & Lauritsen, 1997), there has been relatively little research on the association between race and sexual crime. The observation of a relative high proportion of offenders of a racial minority among offline offenders was unexpected. Whether this pattern continues to be present in other current samples of offline offenders has yet to be determined.

One possible explanation for the predominance of Caucasian online sex offenders is the distribution of Internet use in the general population. There is little evidence to support this explanation, however, as the racial distribution of Internet users closely resemble the distribution in the general population. In the United States, for example, approximately 76% of adult Internet users surveyed are Caucasian ($N= 2,258$; Rainie, 2010), which is similar to the proportion of Caucasian in the general U.S. population (78%; Census, 2001).

Table 4 Meta-Analysis of the Characteristics of Online Offenders Compared With Normative Groups

	Random		Fixed			N	
	d	*95% CI*	*d*	*95% CI*	*Q*	*(Thousands)*	*k*
Demographic variables							
Incomplete high school degree	−0.012	−0.308 to 0.284	−0.094	−0.196 to 0.007	30.75**	2289.3	6
Never married	0.487	0.258 to 0.716	0.424	0.371 to 0.477	118.96**	12702.2	9
Not currently married	0.619	0.445 to 0.793	0.563	0.512 to 0.615	97.38**	36273.9	12
Racial minority	−0.424	−0.604 to −0.243	−0.394	−0.482 to −0.305	38.92**	887708.6	14
Unemployed	0.674	0.456 to 0.892	0.747	0.620 to 0.874	24.21*	242766.0	11
Younger	0.371	0.281 to 0.460	0.394	0.346 to 0.442	35.92*	446218.5	15
Developmental history							
Any childhood physical abuse	0.663	0.075 to 1.250	0.552	0.371 to 0.734	25.09**	8.3	4
Any childhood sexual abuse	0.580	0.322 to 0.837	0.475	0.374 to 0.576	15.34*	26.1	5
Any substance abuse[a]	0.158	−0.032 to 0.349	0.170	0.063 to 0.278	4.67	137.1	3

Note: CI = confidence interval; k = number of studies. Online offenders was the referent group; positive values indicate more deviant characteristics among the online offenders than the normative group. Therefore normative sample included rates of general population for any substance abuse and rates of offender substance abuse at index.

[a]Normative sample included rates of general population for any substance abuse and rates of offender substance abuse at index.

*$p < .05$. **$p < .001$

The high rates of physical and sexual abuse among both online and offline offenders is consistent with the common observation that offenders often report negative family backgrounds, with sex offenders displaying higher rates of sexual abuse than nonsex offenders (Jespersen, Lalumiere, & Seto, 2009; Whitaker et al., 2008). The lack of appropriately nurturing and directive family environments creates conditions under which diverse behavioral problems can develop. In males, these behavioral problems are often expressed as externalizing disorders as well as increased risk of sexual misconducts (e.g., Jespersen et al., 2009; Kaufman & Widom, 1999; Widom, & Ames, 1994).

The current study also found that online offenders possessed significantly more sexually deviant interests than offline offenders. This finding was based on different measures and only three studies. There could be some bias in the comparisons between the online and offline offenders, however, because an interest in viewing child pornography would have influenced the assessments of sexual deviancy. Nevertheless, the variability in the finding was small, indicating consistency in the results of the three studies. Given the strong association between pedophilia and child molestation, the relatively low rates of sexual deviance among the offline offenders invites explanation. One explanation is that police only proceed with child pornography cases in cases where the children portrayed are obviously physically immature. In contrast, many men charged with child molestation would have offended against victims whose physical form approximated that of young adults. As such, police activities may have bias our samples by selectively charging online offenders who are more likely to have pedophilic interests.

In addition, a plausible hypothesis for the low rates of hands-on sexual offenses despite high rates of sexual deviancy among online offenders is that online-only offenders may have greater self-control and less impulsivity than offline offenders. Gottfredson and Hirschi's general theory of crime (1990) postulates that self-control reduces the attractiveness of both crime and opportunities to commit crime. Researchers have found that low self-control and, more generally, impulsivity are related to and even predicts general criminality (Andrews & Bonta, 2006; Caspi, Henry, McGee, & Moffitt, 1995; Pratt & Cullen, 2000) . . . .

It is also possible that some online offenders do not act on their sexual deviant interests because of an avoidance of emotional closeness in sexual relationships. Namely individuals differ in the amount of closeness they prefer in intimate relationships (Schmitt, Shackelford, & Buss, 2001). For example, men tend to seek more short-term relationships (lacking emotional depth and commitment) than women (Buss & Schmitt, 1993). In addition, individuals with inaccessible parents in childhood tend to avoid closeness in future relationships (see Popovic, 2005, for review). Generalizing these finding to online offenders, it is possible that online offenders avoid emotional closeness in sexual relationships, in fact reducing sexual relationships to pictures in order to avoid people. If this hypothesis is true, online-only offenders would be less likely to be in a romantic relationship than offline offenders. A related explanation is that online offenders have a larger proportion of deviant sexual interest compared to offline offenders and, consequently, would be less interested than offline offenders in romantic relationships with consenting adults.

The current study found that online offenders were less likely to be married than males in the general population, but there were insufficient studies to compare the marital status of online offenders with offline offenders. However, Webb, Craissati, & Keen (2007) found that online offenders were more likely to have *never* been married (57%) than offline offenders (41%), $d = 0.35$, 95% CI = 0.02 to 0.69). In contrast, Elliott et al. (2009) found the opposite pattern, although not significant, whereas online offenders were more likely to be involved in a romantic relationship (23%) than the offline offenders (20%; $d = -0.16$, 95% CI = -0.02 to 0.34).

If online-only offenders are truly avoiding emotional closeness, it would also be expected that there would be an association between viewing child pornography and other forms of impersonal sexual paraphilias, such as exhibitionism and voyeurism. Currently, there is little research exploring differences in noncontact sexual offenses between offline and online offenders. Coward et al. (2009) found that online offenders tended to report more noncontact sexual offenses (13.3%) than offline offenders (8.3%), although this trend was not significant ($d = 0.32$, 95% CI = -0.08 to 0.72). In the pornography collections of online offenders sampled in Seto and Eke (2008), materials specifically representing voyeuristic interest (e.g., stories, surreptitious videos) were present in 27% of offenders and were suggestive of a specific sexual interest in 6% (e.g., high level of organization, large proportion of voyeuristic materials relative to other pornographic materials). In contrast, Galbreath, Berlin, and Sawyer (2002) found that only a minority of online offenders had paraphilic diagnoses of voyeurism (8%) and exhibitionism (3%). Currently, there is insufficient research to conclude whether online and offline offenders differ in their preference for closeness in relationships. Clearly, more research must be conducted to better understand whether emotional avoidance is a possible explanation for why some online offenders do not have contact sexual offenses despite possessing deviant sexual interested in children.

Relatively few differences on other psychological variables were identified in this review. Low victim empathy and high cognitive distortions among the offline offenders could potentially facilitate contact with victims by reducing psychological barriers to offending. As well, it is possible that offline offenders develop distorted thinking as postoffense justifications for their deviant behavior. In either case, online offenders tend to have fewer cognitive distortions, less emotional identification with children, and greater victim empathy than offline offenders. Despite sexual deviancy, most of these online offenders are not expected to have committed a contact sexual offense (Seto et al., in press), suggesting some inhibitory mechanisms are present.

It was difficult to determine whether the relatively low impression management found among the online offenders was a strength or weakness. The Impression Management scale of the Balanced Inventory of Desirable Responding is intended to measure the degree to which individuals present themselves in an unduly optimistic light (Paulhus, 1998). On the surface, this sounds undesirable. Research has found, however, that offenders who admit to the minor transgressions included in this scale are *more* likely (not less likely) to recidivate (Tan & Grace, 2008). It may be that the differences found are because of the high levels of social desirability presented by the comparison groups of (largely) child molesters. The research on social desirability is not advanced enough, however, to identify what "normal" levels of social desirability for child molesters would be.

Overall, the rate of prior criminal involvement was low among the online sexual offenders. Although there were insufficient studies for direct comparison between the online and offline offenders, only 12% of the online offenders had prior offenses for nonsexual crimes. Even if the rates of prior sexual offenses are included (12.2%, see Seto et al, 2011), the rate of prior criminal involvement is substantially less than in samples of child molesters. For example, 59% of U.S. offenders who victimized children had previously served sentences and one in four had a prior history of violence (Greenfeld, 1996).

One unique aspect of the current study is that it compared online and offline offenders with normative populations. This approach has several advantages. Given the early stage of research on online offenders, many of the studies did not include a comparison group. Consequently, appreciating the findings of these single sample studies requires comparisons with normative samples. Furthermore, we attempted to ground the observations in nonarbitrary metrics, such as percentages (see Blanton & Jaccard, 2006).

The value of this approach can be seen in the analysis of childhood sexual abuse. Given that there were no significant differences between the online and offline offenders, it would be easy for readers looking only at the *d* values to assume that this variable was not important. However, comparisons of the absolute rates for the sexual offender groups (21% and 34%) against the rates for the male population (9%) suggests that childhood sexual abuse is a relevant variable for understanding sexual misconduct in adults.

Appropriate norms are required, of course, for valid comparisons. Currently, there are well-documented norms for many demographic variables, but relatively few normative studies for psychological variables. Although the collection of norms may, in itself, have little intrinsic interest, they enable single group studies to be analyzed, and facilitate knowledge accumulation.

Limitations

Approximately 1 in 8 online offenders is expected to have an official history of contact sexual offenses and approximately half are expected to report past contact sexual offenses (Seto et al., 2011). The current study, however, only examined online offenders as one group, and did not separate online-only offenders from online offenders with prior contact sexual offenses. Such a comparison could not be completed because most studies did not report the results for pure groups of online offenders and offline offenders. It is quite likely the differences between online-only offenders (without any history of sexual offenses) and offline offenders would be larger if those with prior contact sexual offenses were excluded. Further refining online offender grouping would also allow for the examination of whether there is a substantial difference between online-only offenders and offenders with both online and offline offenses.

Implications

The observation that online offenders are disproportionately Caucasian males has implications for law enforcement, as well as for understanding the victims involved. Most of the victims depicted in child pornography are Caucasian (Wolak, Finkelhor, & Mitchell, 2005b), despite the relatively advanced efforts to police this type of material in Europe and North America. The tendency for men to prefer sexual partners of the same race will drive demand for depictions of sexual abuse of children sharing the same racial profile. A change in the racial distribution of the child pornography victims portrayed on the Internet will likely signal an expansion of this deviant market into more racially diverse segments of the male population.

Research in this field is too new to conclude whether online offenders are truly distinct from offline offenders. Nevertheless, the available results suggest two lines of promising inquiry for future research and clinical evaluations. One line of inquiry would explore the inhibitors and self-control mechanisms that limit the extent to which online offenders act on their deviant interests. Another line of inquiry would explore the extent to which the emotional distance inherent in pornography use is a core feature of the sexual preference of online offenders. Given the rate at which offenders are entering the criminal justice system, the information needed to test these hypotheses should be available in the not-too-distant future.

REFERENCES

References marked with an asterisk indicate studies included in the meta-analysis. The name of the setting is given at the end of the reference when studies that correspond to a single setting cannot be identified by the name of the first author.

*Abondo, M., Bouvet, R., & Le Gueut, M. (2009, May). *Le telechargement de fich-iers pedopornographiques signetil line psychopathologie? A propos d'une etude d'expertises psychiatriques en France* [Does downloading child pornography indicate a psychopathology? Results from a study of psychiatric expertise in France]. Paper presented at the Cinquieme congres international francophone sur l'agression sexuelle [5th International Francophone Conference on Sexual Aggression], Montreal, Quebec, Canada.

Andrews, D. A., & Bonta, J. (2006). *The psychology of criminal conduct* (4th ed.). Cincinnati, OH: Anderson.

*Arros, P., Aury, L., Bonnet, M., Carrier, S., Decastiau, A., Diloisy, C, . . . Rougerie, P. (2005). *Population: Situation matrimoniale* [Population: Marital Status]. Retrieved from http://www.msee.fr/fr/themes/document.asp?reg_id=8&ref_id=9181

*Australian Bureau of Statistics. (2009). *Australian labour market statistics: Labour force by sex* (Catalogue No. 6202). Retrieved from http://www.ausstats.abs.gov.au/ausstats/meisubs.nsf/0/CD8FD05B4533132ECA2575ED001DAF71/$File/6202003.xls

*Baartz, D. (2008). *Australians, the Internet and technology-enabled child sex abuse. A statistical*

profile. Canberra, Australia: Australian Federal Police.

*Bates, A., & Metcalf, C. (2007). A psychometric comparison of Internet and non-Internet sex offenders from a community treatment sample. *Journal of Sexual Aggression, 13,* 11–20. doi:10.1080/13552600701365654

Beckett, R. C. (1987). *The Children and Sex Questionnaire.* Unpublished manuscript.

Beckett, R. C, & Fisher, D. (1994, November). *Assessing victim empathy: A new measure.* Paper presented at the 13th Annual Conference of the Association for the Treatment of Sexual Abusers, San Francisco, CA.

Bilsky, W., & Hosser, D. (1998). Social support and loneliness: Psychometric comparison of two scales based on a nationwide representative survey. *Zeitschrift fur Differentielle und Diagnostische Psychologie, 19,* 130–144.

Blanchard, R., Kolla, N. J., Cantor, J. M, Klassen, P. E., Dickey, R., Kuban, M. E., & Blak, T. (2007). IQ, handedness, and pedophilia in adult male patients stratified by referral source. *Sexual Abuse: A Journal of Research and Treatment, 19,* 285–309. doi:10.1007/slll94–007–9049–0

Blanton, H., & Jaccard, J. (2006). Arbitrary metrics in psychology. *The American Psychologist, 61,* 27–41. doi:10.1037/0003–066X.61.1.27

*Bourke, M. L., & Hernandez, A. E. (2009). The "Butner Study" redux: A report of the incidence of hands-on child victimization by child pornography offenders. *Journal of Family Violence, 24,* 183–191. doi: 10.1007/sl0896–008–9219-y

Bumby, K. M. (1996). Assessing the cognitive distortions of child molesters and rapists: Development and validation of the MOLEST and RAPE scales. *Sexual Abuse: A Journal of Research and Treatment, 8,* 37–54.

*Buschman, J., & Bogaerts, S. (2009). Polygraph testing Internet offenders. In D. Wilcox (Ed.), *The use of polygraph in assessing, treating, and supervising sex offenders: A practitioner's guide* (pp. 111–126). Chichester, England: Wiley-Blackwell. [Buschman]

*Buschman, J., Bogaerts, S., Foulger, S., Wilcox, D., Sosnowski, D., & Cushman, B. (2009). Sexual history disclosure polygraph examinations with cybercrime offences. A first Dutch explorative study. *International Journal of Offender Therapy and Comparative Criminology.* Advance online publication. doi: 10.1177/0306624X09334942 [Buschman]

Buss, D. M., & Schmitt, D. P. (1993). Sexual strategy theory: An evolutionary perspective on human mating. *Psychological Review, 100,* 204–232.

Caspi, A., Henry, B., McGee, R. O., & Moffitt, T. E. (1995). Temperamental origins of child and adolescent behavior problems: From age three to fifteen. *Child Development, 66,* 55–68.

*Chevalier, F., Macario-Rat, I., & Mansuy, A. (2008). Une photographie du marche du travail en 2007: Resultats de l'enquete emploi [A snapshot of the job market in 2007: Results from an employment survey] (Rep. No. 1206). Retrieved from http://www.insee.fr/fr/themes/document.asp?ref_id=ipl206

Cohen, J. (1988). *Statistical power analysis for the behavioral sciences* (2nd ed.). Hillsdale, NJ: Lawrence Erlbaum.

Cohen, L. E., & Felson, M. (1979). Social change and crime rate trends: A routine activity approach. *American Sociological Review, 44,* 588–608.

*Coward, A. I., Gabriel, A. M., Schuler, A., & Prentky, R. A. (2009, March). *Child Internet victimization: Project development and preliminary results.* Poster presented at the American Psychology-Law Society Conference, San Antonia, TX.

*Eke, A., & Seto, M. C. (2009). [Ontario Sex Offender Registry sample independent of police case sample reported by Seto and Eke (2008)]. Unpublished raw data.

*Elliott, I. A., Beech, A. R., Mandeville-Norden, R., & Hayes, E. (2009). Psychological profiles of Internet sex offenders: Comparisons with contact sexual offenders. *Sexual Abuse: A Journal of Research and Treatment, 21,* 76–92. doi: 10.1177/1079063208326929 [U.K. Probation Service]

*Endrass, J., Urbaniak, E, Hammermeister, L. C, Benz, C, Elbert, T., Laubacher, A., & Rossegger, A. (2009). The consumption of Internet child pornography and violent sex offending. *BMC Psychiatry, 9,* 1–7. doi:10.1186/1471 244X-9–43 [Switzerland]

*Faust, E., Renaud, C, & Bickart, W. (2009, October). *Predictors of re-offense among a sample offederally convicted child pornography offenders.* Paper presented at the 28th Annual Conference for the Association of the Treatment of Sexual Abusers, Dallas, TX.

Fleiss, J. L. (1994). Measures of effect size for categorical data. In H. Cooper & L. V. Hedges (Eds.),

The handbook of research synthesis (pp. 245–260). New York, NY: Russell Sage Foundation.

Fleiss, J. L., Levin, B., & Paik, M. C. (2003). *Statistical methods for rates and proportions* (3rd ed.). Hoboken, NJ: Wiley.

*Fortin, F., & Roy, J. (2007). Cyberpedophilie: profiles d'amateur de pedopornographie. [Cyberpedophilia: Profils of users of child pornography]. In M. St-Yves & M. Tanguay (Eds.), *Psychologie des entrevues d'enquete: De la recherche a la pratique* [From research to practice: The psychology of investigative interviews] (pp. 465–502). Montreal, Quebec, Canada: Editions Yvon Blais.

*Frei, A., Erenay, N., Dittmann, V., & Graf, M. (2005). Paedophilia and the Internet: A study of 33 convicted offenders in the Canton of Lucerne. *Swiss Medical Weekly, 135,* 488–494. Retrieved from http://www.smw.ch/docs/pdf200x/2005/33/smw-11095.pdffSwitzerland]

*Galbreath, N. W, Berlin, F. S., & Sawyer, D. (2002). Paraphilias and the Internet. In A. Cooper (Ed.), *Sex and the Internet: A guidebook for clinicians* (pp. 187–205). Philadelphia, PA: Branner-Routledge.

*Goodwin, R. D., Hoven, C. W., Murison, R., & Hotopf, M. (2003). Association between child physical abuse and gastrointestinal disorders and migraine in adulthood. *American Journal of Public Health, 93,* 1065–1067. Retrieved from http://ajph.aphapublications.org/cgi/ reprint/93/7/1065

*Gorey, K. M., & Leslie, D. R. (1997). Lhe prevalence of child sexual abuse: Integrative review adjustment for potential response and measurement biases. *Child Abuse & Neglect, 21,* 391–398. doi:10.1016/S0145–2134(96)00180–9

Gottfredson, M., & Hirschi, T. (1990). *General theory of crime.* Palo Alto, CA: Stanford University Press.

Greenfeld, L. A. (1996). *Child victimizers: Violent offenders and their victims* (NCJ-153258). Retrieved from http://bjs.ojp.usdoj.gov/content/pub/pdf/cvvoatv.pdf

Hanson, R. K, Harris, A. J. R., Scott, L-L., & Helmus, L. (2007). *Assessing the risk of sexual offenders on community supervision: The Dynamic Supervision Project* (User Report 2007–05). Ottawa, Ontario: Public Safety Canada.

Hanson, R. K, & Morton-Bourgon, K. E. (2004). *Predictors of sexual recidivism: An updated meta-analysis* (User Report 2004–02). Ottawa, Ontario: Public Safety Canada.

Hanson, R. K., & Morton-Bourgon, K. E. (2005). The characteristics of persistent sexual offenders: A meta-analysis of recidivism studies. *Journal of Consulting and Clinical Psychology, 73,* 1154–1163. doi:10.1037/0022–006X.73.6.1154

Hasselblad, V., & Hedges, L. V. (1995). Meta-analysis of screening and diagnostic tests. *Psychological Bulletin, 117,* 167–178.

Hedges, L. V. (1994). Fixed effect models. In H. Cooper & L. V. Hedges (Eds.), *The handbook of research synthesis* (pp. 285–299). New York, NY: Russell Sage Foundation.

Hedges, L. V., & Vevea, J. L. (1998). Fixed- and random-effects models in meta-analysis. *Psychological Methods, 3,* 486–504.

*Howitt, D., & Sheldon, K. (2007). The role of cognitive distortions in paedophilic offending: Internet and contact offenders compared. *Psychology, Crime, & Law, 13,* 469–486. doi:10.1080/106831 60601060564 [Sheldon]

*Institut National de la Statistique et des Etudes Economiques [National Institute of Statistic and Economic Studies]. (2007). Population totale par sexe, age et etat matrimonial au 1 er Janvier: Evaluation proviso ire prenant en compte les resultats des derniers recensements (Tableau 6) [Total population by sex, age, and marital status]. Retrieved from http://www.insee.fr/rr/themes/detail.asp?ref_id=irsd2006&page=irweb/sd2006/dd/sd2006_population.htm

Jespersen, A. F., Lalumiere, M. L., & Seto, M. C. (2009). Sexual abuse history among adult sex offenders and non-sex offenders: A meta-analysis. *Child Abuse & Neglect, 33,* 179–192. doi:10.1016/j.chiabu.2008.07.004

*Jung, S., & Gulamhusein, A. (2007, November). *The excuses of Internet child pornography users.* Poster presented at the 26th Annual Conference of the Association for the Treatment of Sexual Abusers, San Diego, CA. [Edmonton]

Kaufman, J. G., & Widom, C. S. (1999). Childhood victimization, running away, and delinquency. *Journal of Research in Crime and Delinquency, 36,* 347–370. doi:10.im/0022427S99036 00400\

*Kreider, R. (2005). *Number, timing, and duration of marriages and divorces: 2001.* Retrieved from http://www.census.gov/prod/2005pubs/p70–97 .pdf

Krone, T. (2004). Typology of online child pornography offending. *Trends and Issues in Crime and Criminal Justice, 279,* 1–6. Retrieved from http://

aic.gov.au/documents/4/F/8/%7B4F8B4249–7BEE-4F57-B9ED-993479D9196D% 7Dtandi 279.pdf

Lanning, K. V. (2001). *Child molesters: A behavioral analysis* (4th ed.). Retrieved from http:// www .missingkids.com/en_US/publications/NC70.pdf

*Laulik, S., Allam, J., & Sheridan, L. (2007). An investigation into maladaptive personality functioning in Internet sex offenders. *Psychology, Crime, & Law, 13,* 523–535. doi:10.1080/10683160 701340577

*Luckett Clark, S., & Weismantle, L. (2003). *Employment status: 2000* (Rep. No. C2KBR-18). Retrieved from http://www.census.gov/ prod/2003pubs/c2kbr-18.pdf

*Matsuzawa, Y. K. (2009). *MMPI-2 characteristics of Internet sex offenders* (Unpublished doctoral dissertation). Pepperdine University, Malibu, CA.

*MacMillian, H. L., Fleming, J. E., Trocme, N., Boyle, M. H, Wong, M., Racine, Y. A., . . . Offord, D. R. (1997). Prevalence of child physical abuse and sexual abuse in the community. *Journal of the American Medical Association, 278,* 131–135. Retrieved from http://jama. ama-assn.org/cgi/reprint/278/2/131

*May-Chahal, C, & Cawson, P. (2005). Measuring child maltreatment in the United Kingdom: A study of the prevalence of child abuse and neglect. *Child Abuse & Neglect, 29,* 969–984. doi:org/1 0.1016/j .chiabu.2004.05.009

*McLaughlin, J. F. (2000). *Cyber child sex offender typology.* Retrieved from http://www.ci.keene. nh.us/police/Typology.html

*Middleton, D., Mandeville-Norden, R., & Hayes, E. (2009). Does treatment work with Internet sex offenders? Emerging findings from the Internet Sex Offender Treatment Programme (i-SOTP). *Journal of Sexual Aggression, 15,* 5–19. doi:10.1080/13552600802673444 [U.K. Probation Service]

Motivans, M., & Kyckelhahn, T. (2007). *Federal prosecution of child sex exploitation offenders, 2006* (Rep. No. NCJ219412). Retrieved from http://bjs.ojp.usdoj.gov/index,cfm?ty=pbdetail &iid=886

Musch, J., Brockhaus, R., & Broder, A. (2002). Ein Inventar zur Erfassung von zwei Faktoren sozialer Erwunschtheit [An inventory to measure two factors of social desirability]. *Diag-nostica, 48,* 121–129.

*National Center for Education Statistics, Department of Education. (2001). *Dropout rates in the United States: 2000* (NCES No. 2002–114). Retrieved from http://nces.ed.gov/ pubs2002/2002114.pdf

*Neutze, J., Seto, M. C, Schaefer, G. A., Mundt, I. A., & Beier, K. M. (2009). *Predictors of child pornography offenses and child sexual abuse in a community sample ofpedophiles and hebephiles.* Unpublished manuscript. Institute of Sexology and Sexual Medicine, Berlin, Germany.

*O'Brien, M. & Webster, S. D. (2007). The construction and preliminary validation of the Internet Behaviours and Attitudes Questionnaire (TBAQ). *Sexual Abuse: A Journal of Research and Treatment, 19,* 237–256. doi:10.1007/slll94–007–9057–0 [sample 1 = O'Brien; sample 2 = U.K. Probation Service]

*Office Federal de la Statistique [Federal Office of Statistics]. (2005). *Recensement federal de la population 2000: Structure de la population, langue principale et religion* [Population survey 2000: Structure of the population, language, and religion]. Retrieved from http:// www.bfs.admin. ch/bfs/portal/fr/index/themen/01/22/publ.Document .69602.pdf

*Office Federal de la Statistique [Federal Office of Statistics]. (2009). *Etat et structure de la population—Indicateurs: Population residante permanente selon l'age et le sexe* [Structure of the population: Permanent residence by age and sex]. Retrieved from http://www.bfs.admin.ch/bfs/portal/fr/index/themen/01/02/blank/key/alter/nach_ geschl echt.html

*Office of National Statistics. (2004). *Focus on statistics: Ethnicity & identity.* Retrieved from http:// www.statistics.gov.uk/cci/nugget.asp?id=455

*Office ofNational Statistics. (2005). *Mid-2005 marital status population estimates: England and Wales.* Retrieved from http://www.statistics.gov .uk/STATBASE/ssdataset.asp?vlnk=9535

*Office of National Statistics. (2008a). *Mid-2007 population estimates for UK, England & Wales, Scotland, & Northern Ireland.* Retrieved from http://www.statistics.gov.uk/statbase/product. asp?vlnk=l 5106

*Office ofNational Statistics. (2008b). *Statistical bulletin: Labour market statistics.* Retrieved from http://www.statistics.gov.uk/pdfdir/lmsuk0609 .pdf

Overton, R. C. (1998). A comparison of fixed-effects and mixed (random-effects) models for meta-analysis tests of moderator variable effects. *Psychological Methods, 3,* 354–379.

Paulhus, D. L. (1991). Measurement and control of response bias. In J. P. Robinson, P. R. Shaver, & L. S. Wrightsman (Eds.), *Measures of personality and social psychological attitudes* (pp. 17–59). New York, NY: Academic Press.

Paulhus, D. L. (1998). *Manual for the Balanced Inventory of Desirable Responding: Version 7.* Buffalo, NY: Multi-Health Systems.

Popovic, M. (2005). Intimacy and its relevance in human functioning. *Sexual and Relationship Therapy, 20,* 31–49.

Pratt, T. C, & Cullen, F. T. (2000). The empirical status of Gottfredson and Hirschi's general theory of crime: A meta-analysis. *Criminology, 38,* 931–964.

Rainie, L. (2010). *Internet, broadband, and cell phone statistics. Pew Internet & American Life Project.* Retrieved from http://www.pewinternet.org/Static-Pages/Trend-DataAVhos-Online.aspx

Russell, D., Peplau, L. A., & Cutrona, C. A. (1980). The revised UCLA Loneliness Scale: Concurrent and discriminant validity evidence. *Journal of Personality and Social Psychology, 39,* 472–480.

Sampson, R. J., & Lauritsen, J. L. (1997). Racial and ethnic disparities in crime and criminal justice in the United States. *Crime and Justice, 21,* 311–374. doi: 10.1086/449253

Sanchez-Meca, J., Marin-Martinez, F., & Chacon-Moscoso, S. (2003). Effect sized indices for dichotomized outcomes in meta-analysis: Metric in meta-analysis. *Psychological Methods, 8,* 448–467. doi:10.1037/1082–989X.8.4.448

Schaefer, G. A., & Feelgood, S. (2006, September). *Validation of a new scale for measuring victim empathy in pedophiles: the Empathy for Children Scale (ECS).* Paper presented at the 9th International Conference of the International Association for the Treatment of Sexual Offenders (IATSO), Hamburg, Germany.

Schmidt, F. L., Oh, I., & Hayes, T. L. (2009). Fixed-versus random-effects models in meta-analysis: Model properties and an empirical comparison of differences in results. *British Journal of Mathematical and Statistical Psychology, 62,* 97–128. doi:10.1348/000711007X255327

Schmitt, D. P., Shackelford, T. K., & Buss, D. M. (2001). Are men really more "oriented" toward short-term mating than women? A critical review of theory and research. *Psychology, Evolution & Gender, 3,* 211–239. doi: 10.1080/14616660110119331

Seto, M. C. (2008). Pedophilia: Psychopathology and theory. In D. R. Laws & W. T. O'Donohue (Eds.), *Sexual deviance: Theory, assessment, and treatment* (2nd ed., pp. 164–182). New York, NY: Guilford Press.

*Seto, M. C, Cantor, J. M., & Blanchard, R. (2006). Child pornography offenses are a valid diagnostic indicator of pedophilia. *Journal of Abnormal Psychology, 115,* 610–615. doi:10.1037/0021–843X.115.3.610 [CAMH]

*Seto, M. C, & Eke, A. W. (2008, October). *Predicting new offenses committed by child pornography offenders.* Paper presented at the 27th Annual Conference of the Association for the Treatment of Sexual Abusers, Atlanta, GA. [Seto]

Seto, M. C, Hanson, R. K., & Babchishin, K. M. (2011). Contact sexual offending by men arrested for child pornography offenses. *Sexual Abuse: A Journal of Research and Treatment 23,* 124–145

*Seto, M.C., Reeves, L., & Jung, S. (in press). Motives for child pornography offending: Explanations given by offenders. *Journal of Sexual Aggression,* [sample 1 = Seto; sample 2 = Edmonton]

*Sheldon, K., & Howitt, D. (2007). *Sex offenders and the Internet.* Chichester, England: Wiley. [Sheldon]

*Sheldon, K., & Howitt, D. (2008). Sexual fantasy in paedophile offenders: Can any model explain satisfactorily new findings from a study of Internet and contact sexual offenders? *Legal and Criminological Psychology, 13,* 137–158. doi:10.1348/135532506X173045 [Sheldon]

*Statistics Canada. (2003a). *Census 2001: Profiles Quebec.* Retrieved from http://wwwl2.statcan.ca/ english/censusO 1 /products/standard/prprofile/prprofile.cfm?G=24

*Statistics Canada. (2003b). *Profile of labour force activity, class of worker, occupation, industry, place of work, mode of transportation, language of work and unpaid work for Canada: Census 2001.* (Rep. No. 95F0490XCB2001001). Retrieved from http://wwwl2.statcan.ca/ english/census01/products/standard/profiles/Retrieve-Profile.cfm?Temporal=2001&PID=56 178&APATH=1&RL=6&IPS=95F0490XCB2001001

*StatisticsCanada. (2004). *Legal marital status, age-groups, and sex for population Jor Canada: 2001 Ce«ms* (Rep.No.95F0407XCB2001009). Retrieved from http://wwwl2.statcan.gc.ca/english/censusOl/Products/standard/themes/DataProducts.cfm?S=l &T=3 8&ALEVEL=2&FREE=0

*Statistics Canada. (2007a). *Census 2006: Canada, provinces, territories, census metropolitan areas and census.* Retrieved from http://www12.statcan.ca/english/census06/data/topics/ListProducts.cfm?Temporal=2006&APATH=3&THEME=66&FREE=0&GRP=l

*Statistics Canada. (2007b). *Census 2006: Labour market activity, industry, occupation, education, language of work, place of work and mode of transportation; Quebec.* Retrieved from http://www12.statcan.ca/english/census06/data/profiles/release/

*Statistics Canada. (2008a). *Labour force survey: Table 4, thousands of dropouts and dropout rate, by sex, Canada, 1990–1991 to 2004–2005 school year averages.* (Rep.No. 81–004-XIE). Retrieved from http://www.statcan.gc.ca/pub/81–004-x/2005004/8984-eng.htm#table1

*Statistics Canada. (2008b). *Visible minority groups, generation status, age groups, and sex for the population 15 years and over of Canada: 2006 Census* (Catalogue No. 97–562-XCB2006010). Retrieved from http://www12.statcan.ca.proxy.bib.uottawa.ca/english/cen-sus06/data/topics/ListProducts.cfm?Temporal=2006&APATH=3&THEME=80&FREE=0 &SUB=802&GRP=1

*Statistics Netherlands. (2005). *The Dutch national census 2001: 40 Excel tables.* Retrieved from http://www.cbs.nl/enGB/menu/themas/dossiers/volkstellingen/publicaties/artikelen/archief/2005/2005-virtual-dutch-census-art.htm

*Statistics New Zealand. (2005). *2001 Census: Ethnic groups* (Catalogue No. 02.324.0001). Retrieved from http://www.stats.govt.nz/Census/2001-census-data/2001-census-ethnic-groups .aspx

*Substance Abuse and Mental Health Services Administration Office of Applied Studies. (2008). *Results from the 2007 national survey on drug use and health: National findings.* Retrieved from http://oas.samhsa.gov/nsduh/2k7nsduh/2k7Results.pdf

*Sullivan, C. (2007). *Internet trades of child pornography: Profiling research—update.* Retrieved from http://www.dia.govt.nz/Pubfomis.nsf7URL/Profilingupdate3 .pdf7$file/Profilingupdate3 .pdf

*Swiss Federal Statistical Office. (2005). *Key findings of the Swiss labour force survey: 2004 in brief* (Rep. No. 51099). Retrieved from http://www.bfs.admin.ch/bfs/portal/en/index/themen/03/22/publ.Docum ent.51099.pdf

Tan, L., & Grace, R. C. (2008). Social desirability and sexual offenders. *Sexual Abuse: A Journal of Research and Treatment, 20,* 61–87. doi:10.1177/1079063208314820

Thornton, D. (1989). *Self-Esteem Scale.* Unpublished manuscript.

*Tomak, S., Weschler, F. S., Ghahramanlou-Holloway, Virden, T, & Nademin, M. E. (2009). An empirical study of the personality characteristics of Internet sex offenders. *Journal of Sexual Aggression, 15,* 139–149. doi:10.1080/13552600902823063

*U.S. Census Bureau. (2001a). *Census 2000: Sex by age total population.* Retrieved from http:// factfmder.census.gov/servlet/DTTable?_bm=y&-geoJd=01000US&-ds_name=DEC_2000 _SF 1 _U&-mt_name=DEC_2000_SF 1 _U_PCT012

*U.S. Census Bureau. (2001b). *Male population by age, race and Hispanic or Latino origin for the United States: 2000* (Rep. No. PHC-T-9). Retrieved from http://www.census.gov/ population/www/cen2000/briefs/phc-t9/tables/tab02 .pdf

*Webb, L., Craissati, J., & Keen, S. (2007). Characteristics of Internet child pornography offenders: A comparison with child molesters. *Sexual Abuse: A Journal of Research and Treatment, 19,* 449–465. doi: 10.1007/sl 1194–007–9063–2

Whitaker, D. J., Brenda, L., Hanson, R. K., Baker, C. K., McMahon, P. M., Ryan, G., . . . Rice, D. D. (2008). Risk factors for the perpetration of child sexual abuse: A review and meta-analysis. *Child Abused Neglect, 32,* 529–548. doi:10.1016/j.chiabu.2007.08.005

Widom, C. S., & Ames, M. A., (1994). Criminal consequences of childhood sexual victimization. *Child Abuse & Neglect, 18,* 303–318.

Wilson, G. D. (1978). *The secrets of sexual fantasy.* London, England: Dent.

Wilson, R. J. (1999). Emotional congruence in sexual offenders against children. *Sexual Abuse: A Journal of Research and Treatment, 11,* 33–47.

*Wolak, J., Finkelhor, D., & Mitchell, K. J. (2005a). *Child-pornography possessors arrested in Internet-related crimes: Findings from the National Juvenile Online Victimization Study* (NCJ No. 210701). Retrieved from http://www.missingkids.com/en_US/publications/NC144.pdf

Wolak, J., Finkelhor, D., & Mitchell, K. J. (2005b). The varieties of child pornography production. In E. Quayle & M. Taylor (Eds.), *Viewing child pornography on the Internet: Understanding the offense, managing the offender, and helping the victims* (pp. 31–48). Dorset, England: Russell House.

*Wolak, J., Finkelhor, D., & Mitchell, K. (2009). *Trends in arrests of "online predators"*. Retrieved from http://www.unh.edu/news/NJOV2.pdf

*Wood, J. M., Seto, M. C, Flynn, S., Wilson-Cotton, S., & Dedmon, P. (2009, October). *Is it "just" pictures? The use of polygraph with Internet offenders who deny abusive sexual contact*. Poster presented at the 28th Annual Conference of the Association of the Treatment of Sexual Abusers, Dallas, TX.

20

CHILD ABDUCTION

An Overview of Current and Historical Perspectives*

MONIQUE C. BOUDREAUX

WAYNE D. LORD

STEPHEN E. ETTER

Intensive nationwide media coverage of child abductions by strangers has served to focus child safety training programs on issues such as "stranger danger," leaving children vulnerable to other more common forms of abduction (Finkelhor, Hotaling, & Sedlak, 1990). The National Incidence Studies of Missing, Abducted, Runaway, and Thrownaway Children (NISMART) report that incidence rates of children abducted by a family member range from 163,200 to 354,100 annually, whereas nonfamily child abductions range from 3,200 to 4,600 cases annually, with 62% of nonfamily child abductions perpetrated by strangers (Finkelhor et al., 1990).

Parents and children are justifiably concerned about the possibility of abduction (Stickler, 1996). Providing parents and caregivers with accurate information on child abduction and teaching children appropriate abduction prevention skills could aid in reducing their fears as well as save lives. Research shows that although some methodologies are more effective than others, children are able to learn and maintain abduction prevention strategies over time (Holcombe, Wolery, & Katzenmeyer, 1995; Miltenberger & Olsen, 1996; Yarmey, 1988). Yarmey found that children who had been *streetproofed* (e.g., eyewitness-type cognitive training on reporting suspicious incidents, remembering license plates, streets, and safety measures specifically related to child abduction) had more reliably complete recall than nonstreetproofed children. With training, they became more aware

*This article was published in *Child Maltreatment, 5,* 63–71 (2000).

of their surroundings and appeared better able to recognize questionable or dangerous situations.

The quality of abduction prevention materials and training methods must be carefully examined. Roberts, Alexander, and Fanurik (1990) assessed the training of authors and publishers who prepared sexual abuse and abduction prevention materials used in classroom settings. Only 51% ($n = 17$) had related professional experience such as psychology, sociology, or law enforcement. Only 35% ($n = 11$) had degrees in a related academic discipline. In addition, 36% ($n = 12$) claimed that they did no reliability/validity testing of their materials. Fifty-seven percent ($n = 19$) stated that they did informal evaluations, presenting their materials either to a group of professional experts or to a group of children. Only 6% ($n = 2$) performed extensive research relating to the materials. Prevention training programs should accurately depict the potential dangers children face. Before reliable and valid preventive measures/educational programs can be developed, the topic of child abduction must be more thoroughly assessed. Universal definitions must be formulated, and incidence rates, victim and offender characteristics, and offender motives should be examined. Child victimization offense patterns vary within different victim and offender subgroups, and using a generalized curriculum reduces the effectiveness of child safety training programs (Boudreaux, Lord, & Dutra, 1999; Kaufman et al., 1998).

It is difficult to glean accurate information on child abduction for several reasons. First, a number of highly publicized stranger abduction cases in the early 1980s resulted in a social climate of heightened concern and emotion regarding the safety of children. This yielded overestimated initial incidence rates of child abduction (Best & Thibodeau, 1997; Finkelhor et al., 1990). Second, early statistics combined many different types of child abduction (e.g., family and nonfamily abductions) and age groups of children (e.g., preteen and teenaged children), impeding researchers' abilities to identify specific critical issues and draw clear conclusions regarding the dynamics of an abduction. Third, many child abductions are not reported to law enforcement agencies such as the Federal Bureau of Investigation (FBI) or child assistance agencies such as the National Center for Missing and Exploited Children (NCMEC). Finally, data collection has been hindered by variations in state laws (e.g., definitions) and the use of different data collection methods. Locating child abduction case files within law enforcement agencies can be particularly cumbersome because abductions may be filed under other crime categories (e.g., homicide and sexual assault) (Finkelhor et al., 1990).

OPERATIONAL DEFINITIONS

Defining *child abduction* is problematic for two basic reasons: (a) There is no single accepted definition of child abduction (i.e., the legal definitions of the terms *child* and *abduction* can vary from jurisdiction to jurisdiction), and (b) there are different forms of child abduction, each with inconsistent terms, which if not specifically defined, can cause confusion (e.g., *parental abduction, family abduction, stereotypical abduction, missing children,* and *kidnapped children*). These issues, combined with the investigative difficulties that arise when the victim is not available or unable to provide useful information about the crime, can increase confusion.

Legal definitions of child abduction can widely differ from coercive movement or detention of a person for a short time or duration to long-term confinement. In California, moving a person 22 feet can be interpreted as abduction (Finkelhor, Hotaling, & Sedlak, 1992). In one California case, an offender who took a girl a few feet away to a car and sexually assaulted her faced additional charges of kidnapping. The Supreme Court has stated that it is "not a matter of how much distance, it is the fact of the movement" (cited in Forst & Blomquist, 1991, p. 135). Forst and Blomquist stated that California's ruling follows the *any movement rule* where any movement, even in the context of another crime, is considered kidnapping. Other courts follow the *incidental rule* where movement or confinement in the context of another crime is considered incidental. In these jurisdictions, the offender is charged only with the "original" crime.

Historically, federal law addressing abduction was greatly affected by the 1932 Lindbergh kidnapping (Forst & Blomquist, 1991). Initially, this law excluded the prosecution of parents and allowed the death penalty in certain cases. The death penalty would not be imposed, however, if the victim was released unharmed. Interstate transport was presumed after 7 days. This eventually was changed to 24 hours (Forst & Blomquist, 1991). Currently, federal law states that the victim must be taken and/or confined and held for ransom, reward, or otherwise either willingly (e.g., by ruse, lure, or trick) or by force. Federal law continues, in most cases, to exclude cases of parental abduction.

It is FBI policy, however, that any reported or suspected child abduction or mysterious disappearance of a child will receive an immediate and aggressive response. The immediate response may be either a full investigation based on the assumption that a violation of the federal kidnapping statute has occurred or a preliminary inquiry to determine whether the federal kidnapping statute has been violated.

Law enforcement agencies are required to intervene when a parent has violated a custody agreement, communicate with other jurisdictions in parental abduction cases, and arrest parents who abduct their children (most states consider parental abduction a felony) (Forst & Blomquist, 1991). The Parental Kidnapping Prevention Act (PKPA) of 1980 requires authorities of every state to enforce existing orders made by any state court exercising proper jurisdiction and prevents modification of such orders by other than the state with original jurisdiction. It also authorizes the use of the federal Unlawful Flight to Avoid Prosecution (UFAP) warrant, which will elicit investigative resources from the FBI and the Federal Parent Locator Service (FPLS) in family abductions.

Legal definitions differ from public stereotypes of child abduction. Finkelhor et al. (1992) states that the main element of both constructs is "the coerced, unauthorized movement of a child, the detention of a child, or the luring of a child for the purposes of committing another crime" (p. 228). The public view of stranger abduction has yielded what Finkelhor et al. (1990) term *stereotypical abduction.* This definition of abduction, perpetrated by a stranger, includes any one of the following: (a) The child is held overnight, (b) is transported a distance of 50 miles or more from the point of abduction, (c) is killed, (d) is ransomed, or (e) the perpetrator shows an intent to keep the child permanently. Although the NISMART legal definition of nonfamily abduction includes many short-term, short-distance offenses committed by strangers and acquaintances (3,200 to 4,600 cases annually), the stereotypical kidnapping subset only includes the "most serious" stranger abduction cases (200 to 300 cases annually) (Finkelhor et al., 1990). The stereotypical abduction definition has no legal bearing on the case. However, cases that fulfill these criteria are more often covered by the media.

In addition, the definition of child abduction varies in the literature (Lanning, 1995). Some definitions focus on the relationship between the offender and victim (e.g., extrafamilial, intrafamilial, parental, nonfamily, and stranger abduction). Other definitions are derived from the motivation of the offender (e.g., ransom, sexual assault, etc.). Researchers frequently disagree on the specific terms of these definitions. Attempting to assess these various operational definitions via scientific/statistical analyses does not allow researchers to draw clear conclusions regarding the dynamics of child abduction.

Defining the seemingly simple term *child* is equally complicated (Lanning, 1994). Lanning (1995) states that although scenarios involving a sadistic pedophile who abducts, molests, and tortures to death a 12-year-old boy and a sexually motivated serial killer who has sex with and strangles a 17-year-old prostitute are both considered child abductions, their dynamics and the ensuing investigations are drastically different. Whereas legal definitions can vary depending on the state and statute, Lanning (1994) reports that teenaged children (13 to 17) are a particularly challenging group to classify from both legal and societal perspectives. Although still considered children according to federal law (birth to age 18), their more adultlike appearance and behavior can affect their treatment within the legal system (Forst & Blomquist, 1991; Lanning, 1994).

Recent research has shown the importance of assessing the victimization of children from a developmental perspective (Boudreaux et al., 1999; Cloud, 1996; Crittenden & Craig, 1990; Finkelhor, 1995, 1997; Hanfland, Keppel, & Weis, 1997). The dynamics of victimization such as abduction and homicide change as children age. Breaking down the child victim population into more distinct age groups is critical to the understanding of key crime characteristics and for predicting possible future criminal activity by the offender.

VICTIM CHARACTERISTICS

Generally, female children are at higher risk of abduction than males (Boudreaux et al., 1999; Cloud, 1996; Elliott, Browne, & Kilcoyne, 1995; Finkelhor et al., 1990; Hanfland et al., 1997). However, victimology changes as the age of the victim changes (Boudreaux et al., 1999; Cloud, 1996; Hanfland et al.,1997). In a study of 550 child abduction victims, Boudreaux et al. (1997) found that although females (70%) were at higher risk of abduction than males (30%), younger victims were more often male (birth to 3 years). Females from preschool through high school (aged 3 to 18 years) were at least 3 times more likely to be abducted than males. In cases in which children were abducted and subsequently murdered, Hanfland et al. (1997) reported that teenage girls (ages 13 to 17) were at highest risk, followed by younger girls (ages 1 to 12), younger boys, and teenage boys. NISMART also found that in general, older children (ages 14 to 17) were at higher risk for becoming victims of abduction and homicide

(Finkelhor et al., 1990). Recent analyses of NISMART data, however, indicate that in the stereotypical nonfamily abductions in which the child was killed, Caucasian, preteen children were the more likely victims (Asdigian, Finkelhor, & Hotaling, 1995).

Male and female children are equally likely to be abducted by their parents (Forehand, Long, & Zogg, 1989). These abductions are typically highly emotional, meant to hurt or obtain revenge against the other parent; the victim's gender is inconsequential. The greatest percentage of children abducted by parents are ages 3 to 5 years. The breakdown of victims by age include those younger than age 3 (5%), 3 to 5 years (34%), 6 to 8 years (22%), 9 to 11 years (26%), and 12 and older (13%) (Forehand et al., 1989).

NISMART reported that teenagers were at higher risk of abduction by nonfamily members; girls in particular were identified as the highest risk victims (Finkelhor et al., 1990). Hanfland et al. (1997) found that children who were abducted and then killed were more likely to be females victimized by strangers. Cloud (1996) reported similar findings, with males more likely to be victimized by family members and females by acquaintances and strangers.

Victim gender and other physical characteristics (e.g., race, hair color, physical development, and age) appear to be selection criteria for offenders abducting a victim to meet particular sexual fantasies/needs (Elliott et al., 1995; Finkelhor et al., 1990; Ressler, Burgess, & Douglas, 1988). Elliott et al. (1995) interviewed child sex offenders (convicted of hands-on assaults against children younger than age 18) who described how they selected and maintained their victims. Although abduction was not specifically addressed in this study, it appeared that many of these offenders abducted their victims via lures, tricks, or physical force. For most offenders (72%), gender of the victim was a selection criterion. Fifty-eight percent targeted females and 14% targeted males (28% selected both genders). In contrast to these findings, Hanfland et al. (1997) stated that offenders do not frequently select specific victims based on clearly defined criteria. Clearly, additional research is required to assess the importance of victim characteristics to offenders.

Child abduction victims are primarily Caucasian (72%), with fewer African American (18%) and other minority victims (10%) (Boudreaux et al., 1999). The overall racial distribution of this victim population is reflective of the demographic composition of American society as measured by the U.S. census (U.S. Department of Commerce, 1992) and does not appear to be an effect of the abduction phenomenon (child census data: Caucasian, 75%; African American, 15%; and other minorities, 10%). However, Boudreaux et al. (1997) found that victim race varied by victim age, with Caucasian victims older than African Americans and other minorities. Young African American children (birth through age 5) were at greater risk of abduction than young Caucasian children. Further analyses of racial differences within and between child age groups are needed.

OFFENDER CHARACTERISTICS

In general, child abductors are familiar with their victims (60%; $n = 284$) (Cloud, 1996). Hanfland et al. (1997) reported a lower overall level of victim-offender familiarity (48%). However, the victim-offender relationship changes with victim age, with family members more often the abductors of younger children (infants, toddlers, and preschoolers) and acquaintances and strangers more common offenders of school-age children (Boudreaux et al., 1999).

Most child abductors are parents or primary caregivers (Finkelhor et al., 1990; McGuire, 1994). Family abduction (child taken by a family member) 1988 incidence rate estimates ranged from 163,200 to 354,100 cases (Finkelhor et al., 1990). McGuire found that 90% of all child abduction cases in Los Angeles were perpetrated by the child's parent. Parental abduction also appears to be correlated with a history of family violence (American Prosecutors Research Institute, 1995). Forst and Blomquist (1991)

found that most cases were related to custody battles. They reported that in 50% of such cases, the location of the child was known; however, retrieving the child from the offending parent was the issue. Plass (1998) reported that 61% of family abduction cases derived from the NISMART sample involved children held in a known location. Cole and Bradford (1992) found that although the incidence rate for abduction in custody cases was relatively low (abduction rate was 4%), 80% of the parental offenders in their Canadian sample ($n = 489$ cases over 6 years in Ottawa Family Court) were male. Hegar and Greif (1991) concurred, stating that fathers were more likely to abduct their children during custody disputes (55%; $n = 205$). Finkelhor et al. (1990) also found that three out of four perpetrators were male in family abduction cases.

On the other hand, nonfamily (e.g., friends, acquaintances, and strangers) abductions appear to occur less frequently (Finkelhor et al., 1990). NISMART estimated that in 1988 there were 3,200 to 4,600 nonfamily abductions that met one of the legal definitions of abduction. Sixty-two percent of these cases involved stranger offenders (Finkelhor et al., 1990). The NCMEC, however, processed 1,648 non-family abduction cases from April 1984 to December 1994 (Lanning & Burgess, 1995). Forst and Blomquist (1991) found that stranger abductions represented less than 1% of all missing children. As with family abductors, nonfamily child abductors were typically male (Boudreaux et al., 1999; Finkelhor et al., 1990; Hanfland et al., 1997).

Child abductors, generally male (87%; $n = 430$) and Caucasian (71%; $n = 352$), usually victimized children from within their own race (Boudreaux et al., 1999). Although offenders were more often Caucasian, the racial distribution of the offender sample was not representative of the racial frequency within the U.S. population (U.S. Department of Commerce, 1992), with fewer Caucasian and more African American offenders (20%) than would be expected (adult census data: Caucasian, 80%; African American, 12%; and other minorities, 8%).

Behavioral patterns of child abductors appeared to vary based on factors such as the offender's gender, motivation for the abduction, and relationship to the victim. Boudreaux et al. (1999) found that female offenders rarely committed sex or profit (e.g., drug, robbery, or extortion) abductions but often abducted for emotion-based reasons (51%)—for example, child abuse fatalities resulting in parents claiming abduction (false allegation), revenge, retribution, and rage-based crimes. Female abductors were also motivated by maternal desire (44%) such as abduction with the intent of keeping the child. Male offenders, on the other hand, abducted primarily for sex (60%), followed by emotion (27%), and profit (13%) . In addition, intrafamilial and extrafamilial sex offenders were found to use different modus operandi (MO) behavioral strategies to obtain and retain their victims (Kaufman et al., 1998). Many of these offenders abducted their victims via lures, tricks, or physical force. Intrafamilial offenders were more likely to give gifts to victims, whereas extrafamilial offenders were more likely to use alcohol and drugs to gain victim compliance.

Behavioral patterns of abductors also differed from those of nonabductors (Lanning & Burgess, 1995). Abductors (defined as individuals who in 50% or more of their offenses used different locations for the initial encounter and the assault) had little contact with children outside their offenses, more often used weapons and restraints, and more often victimized strangers than did nonabducting sex offenders (Lanning & Burgess). Abductors, however, were not more likely to physically injure their victims. These offenders did not appear to display more aggression than nonabductors (Prentky et al., 1991). Lanning and Burgess believed that abduction serves as a method of victim control. They suggested that abductors, in general, may be less able to manipulate (e.g., lure or con) their victims without the use of force (e.g., weapons and restraints) due to lower social skills and lack of familiarity with children.

MOTIVATION

Although nonfamily abductions occur less frequently, they typically occur for the following reasons: (a) desire to possess a child (these cases occur less frequently and involve primarily infants), (b) sexual gratification, (c) financial gain (extortion, etc.), (d) retribution (e.g., revenge or collecting on an unpaid debt), and (e) desire to kill (this alone is reported to motivate and gratify some offenders) (Forst & Blomquist, 1991; Lanning, 1995). However, as discussed by Lanning, the interpretation of offender motivations and behaviors is complicated and may not be clear to law enforcement or forensic professionals.

Maternal Desire

Offender motivation has not been sufficiently addressed in existing abduction research. For example, nonfamily members stealing infants with no financial motive is a relatively rare event. Typically, the motive in these cases is the desire to have a child or to fill a void in the offender's life (Ankrom & Lent, 1995). Based on interviews with offenders, it was determined that abductions were typically well planned by offenders, who felt pressure to have a child and often feigned pregnancy. These offenders developed a fantasy, devised a plan to access a child, abducted the child, and settled back into life, providing some explanation for the presence of the new child to friends and family (Ankrom & Lent, 1995). This type of abduction, termed *infant abduction* by those in law enforcement, has occurred more frequently in recent years (Burgess & Lanning, 1995). The NCMEC identified 119 cases of infant abduction (all victims were younger than 6 months of age) from 1983 to 1992. Forty-eight of these cases occurred in 1983 to 1987, and 71 occurred during 1988 to 1992 (Burgess & Lanning, 1995).

In the Burgess and Lanning (1995) study, infant abductors were almost always female (112 of 119) and were racially mixed (43% Caucasian, 38% African American, 15% Latino, and 4% unknown). However, this offender racial distribution was not reflective of the national demographic pattern, with African Americans and other minorities over-represented (U.S. Department of Commerce, 1992). These offenders did not appear to target a particular gender of victim (male victims, 52%; females, 48%) but searched for a child that matched their particular racial requirements (theirs or the purported father's).

Fortunately, more than 90% of these victims were recovered, most within 25 miles of the abduction site. The offenders typically abducted their victims from hospitals (68%) and were often determined to have visited multiple hospitals/nurseries prior to the abduction, casing the facility much like a bank robber does when selecting a bank to rob. They usually lived near the abduction site. A smaller proportion (25%) of victims were abducted from their homes: Home abductions, however, were often more likely to include violence, with the offender prepared to physically confront the victim's parents (Burgess & Lanning, 1995).

Sexual Gratification

With the increased societal awareness of reported child sexual abuse, sexual gratification as a motive for child abduction has received more attention in the literature. NISMART found that two thirds of nonfamily abductions involved sexual assault (Finkelhor et al., 1990). Hazelwood, Dietz, and Warren (1992) also found that 60% ($n = 18$) of the incarcerated sexual sadists in their study held their victims (both children and adults) captive for more than 24 hours. However, when victims are not recovered alive, determining if sexual assault occurred can be difficult, particularly if the remains are decomposed or if sexual acts occurred that may not leave physical evidence (e.g., touching) (Lanning, 1995).

In child abduction/homicide cases, sexual gratification is the most common motive (Cloud, 1996; Hanfland et al., 1997). Boudreaux et al.

(1999) found that females, particularly Caucasian females, were more often victims than males. In addition, sex offenses occurred most often in older school-age children by nonfamily male offenders. The prevalence of older females as victims of sexual abduction may reflect ease of victim access. Older children are typically more mobile and independent and as they are granted more freedom to conduct their activities, they are less likely to receive continual adult supervision. Young children are more likely to be under their parent's constant care and supervision.

Profit

Although kidnapping laws were initially formed to address the problem of abducting a child for financial gain (e.g., ransom), this form of abduction is less common in society today (Cloud, 1996; Finkelhor et al., 1990). Boudreaux et al. (1999) found that profit-based abductions (e.g., extortion, robbery, or drug related) more often involved older victims (high school) and male minority offenders and victims. Finkelhor (1995) would classify this as an example of developmental targeting. As children age, they begin to acquire more valuable possessions and money and are at higher risk of profit-based victimization.

Retribution

Parental abduction offense characteristics have been addressed, to some extent, in the literature (Forehand et al., 1989; Plass, 1998). The motive for parental abduction typically involves a divorce/custody dispute in which parents take the child for revenge or because one parent believes that the other parent is abusing the child (Forst & Blomquist, 1991). Forehand et al. stated that the primary reason for abduction given by offending parents involves the personal safety of either the child or themselves. These offending parents provide additional justifications including: (a) a belief that the child has been neglected/abused, (b) the desire to be a full-time parent, (c) the desire to punish the other parent, and (d) to stop divorce proceedings. In 47% of parental abduction cases, the abducting parent makes contact with the other parent either to state facts about safety and intention, to influence the parental relationship (e.g., initiate reconciliation or withdrawal of impending divorce proceedings), or to rationalize the crime (Forehand et al., 1989).

According to Hegar and Greif (1991), most parents whose children were abducted by the other parent believed their children were abducted primarily for revenge purposes. Seventy-seven percent of the respondents stated that they believed the child was taken to hurt or punish them. In addition, most reported that they had been worried about the possibility of abduction before it occurred and half stated that the abducting parent had actually threatened to abduct. One must cautiously interpret these findings, however, considering that they result from self-report measures wherein the respondents may have presented a biased version of the actual events.

Homicide

Abductions resulting in homicide occur far less frequently than the abductions of children who are eventually returned home alive (Finkelhor et al., 1990; Lanning, 1995). NISMART estimates that between 43 and 147 nonfamily abductions result in homicide annually (Finkelhor et al., 1990). In addition, Finkelhor et al. (1992) found that 5% ($n = 70$) of 1,400 identified nonfamily child abduction cases involved homicide. Elliott et al. (1995) found that 8% ($n = 7$) of 91 child sex offenders murdered or attempted to murder their victims during or after the assault. Although it is difficult to assess a perpetrator's intent, research has indicated that a number of abductors kill their victims because of a predisposition to do so (Hanfland et al., 1997). Abduction outcomes need to be carefully documented and analyzed as it is still unclear exactly how many and under which circumstances children are returned home unharmed.

RISK FACTORS FOR ABDUCTION

Offenders select their victims for a variety of reasons. Child sex offenders, for example, more often selected female victims than males (Conte, Wolf, & Smith, 1989; Elliott et al., 1995). When asked to provide reasons for victim selection, 42% of the offenders in the Elliott et al. study stated that the child's attractiveness ("being pretty") was important, as was the way the child dressed (27%). The child's physical size and age were also important (18%) as some offenders believed that younger children were less likely to report the crime (Conte et al., 1989). The child's behavior was also important for some offenders. Forty-nine percent of offenders stated they wanted children who appeared to lack confidence or had low self-esteem, and 13% searched for innocent or trusting children (Elliott et al., 1995).

In addition, most of these offenders (84%) reported repeatedly using the same techniques to obtain their victims (Elliott et al., 1995). Lanning and Burgess (1995) stated that although abduction is part of the offender's MO, various methods (e.g., levels of force and type of attainment) of abduction are used by different offenders. Many offenders claimed to search for lone victims in locations where children often congregate such as schools, shopping centers, arcades, and playgrounds. Some offenders devised ways to become welcome in the child's home. Most offenders coerced, bribed, or eased the child into the sexual contact rather than employing immediate physical force (19%) (Elliott et al., 1995). Kaufman et al. (1998) concurred, reporting that most sexual offenders used approaches with the intent to desensitize their victims to sexual contact. By slowly easing the child into sexual contact, the offender is able to constantly reassess the potential risk of discovery while establishing a caring prosocial persona, thus deterring detection by others (Kaufman et al., 1998). Kaufman et al. also found that adolescent offenders were more likely to use various MO strategies (e.g., gift giving, giving and taking away of benefits, and use of pornography, threats, and weapons) than adult offenders, possibly indicating their need to do more to obtain and retain control over their victims.

The significance of the crime location and the time of occurrence may signify particular spatial and temporal constraints on the offender (Rossmo, 1993). Offenders may commit criminal acts by choosing victims from more familiar areas where the offender feels safe and where offender efforts are minimized (Rossmo, 1993). The offender's behavior can thus be predicted by using the nearness or least-effort principle (Rossmo, 1993). Factors such as distance (both objective and perceived), time, money, the offender's mode of transportation, and if urban, the layout of the city (e.g., traffic patterns) all affect the offender's choices and resulting behavior. Offenders may perceive distance based on: (a) the attractiveness of origins and destinations, (b) number and types of barriers present, (c) familiarity with routes, (d) physical distance, or (e) attractiveness of routes (Rossmo, 1993). Capone and Nichols (1976) concurred, stating that crime distance is often a function of the distribution of opportunities and their different levels of attractiveness to offenders.

Ultimately, the availability and location of the victim plays a key role in the determination of where and when offenses occur. For example, in homicide cases, the site where the murder occurred, although important in identifying spatial behavior patterns, may be less meaningful than the disposal site (Ressler et al., 1988). The offender may be forced to kill a victim in a certain location but may be able to choose the site of remains disposal. Thus, although few studies examine potential victim risk factors, the earlier described research does indicate the appearance of patterns in offender behavior.

CONCLUSION

The primary focus of child abduction research has been an attempt to determine accurate incidence and prevalence rates. However, existing abduction literature fails to address who, exactly, is being abducted (e.g., age and gender of victim) and under what circumstances; neither does the literature specifically address abduction outcome.

For example, how many children are abducted and then killed? How many children are returned to their homes alive? Case resolution must be examined so that investigative resources may be appropriately allocated. Child abduction-homicide cases must be assessed separately but should ultimately be compared with cases in which the victim is returned unharmed. Through this process, researchers and law enforcement professionals will be able to identify which victims, given particular offender and offense characteristics, may be at higher risk of homicide.

In addition, recent child abduction and homicide research findings have identified the critical nature of victim age in determining specific offense patterns (Boudreaux et al., 1999; Crittenden & Craig, 1990; Finkelhor, 1995, 1997; Lanning, 1994). Developmental victimology, as termed by Finkelhor (1997), has significant practical application in child abduction investigations. As children grow up and face the physical, social, and emotional changes that come with increasing age, crime patterns change. These patterned changes can provide investigators with more effective means of predicting offender, offense, and remains disposal characteristics. At the onset of an abduction investigation, the only information consistently known is the victim's age, gender, and race. Providing law enforcement and forensic professionals with sound child abduction typologies based on factors such as victim age, gender, and offense motive could improve investigative resource management and search efforts. Future child victimization research (e.g., child abuse, neglect, abduction, and homicide) should be conducted from a developmental perspective to take advantage of the age and circumstance-related patterns characteristic of various victim age groups (Finkelhor, 1995, 1997).

Future child abduction research should also delineate clear and consistent operational definitions and attempt to deconstruct generalized child abduction findings. Few large-scale nationally representative studies exist that examine specific child abduction patterns (Boudreaux et al., 1999; Hanfland et al., 1997). Future research efforts should attempt to expand on these findings.

Child abduction victim, offender, and offense patterns should also be used in the formation of more scientifically sound child safety training programs. Teaching children how to protect themselves against attacks by strangers (i.e., stranger danger) should be only one aspect of a well-rounded program that identifies the various threats children face. Research findings clearly indicate that although most abductions are committed by familiar offenders (Cloud, 1996; Finkelhor et al., 1990; Kaufman et al., 1998), offender patterns change with victim age, with younger children at higher risk of abduction by family and older children more vulnerable to nonfamily abductions (Boudreaux et al., 1999; Finkelhor, 1997). In addition, intrafamilial and extrafamilial offenders have been found to use different modus operandi behavioral strategies to obtain and retain their victims (Kaufman et al., 1998). These findings illustrate the need to create tailor-made abduction prevention education programs by child age group, teaching children how to combat the varied MO strategies of particular offenders. Kaufman et al. point out the importance of involving family and other caregivers in the educational process as offenders may victimize children using methods not detectable by parents.

The dynamics of crimes against children are different from those committed against adults (Finkelhor, 1997). Law enforcement agencies should create specially trained teams to handle cases involving crimes against children. Academicians and law enforcement professionals must coordinate their efforts. Research must continue to identify and assess the special dynamics of crimes against children, examining in detail the valuable data law enforcement provides. Law enforcement professionals should improve the way in which abduction cases are reported and filed. Although abductions may be perpetrated in conjunction with other crimes (e.g., homicide and sexual assault), case files should be cross-referenced as abductions and should be reported to national clearinghouses such as the NCMEC or the Violent Criminal Apprehension Program (ViCAP). In addition, law enforcement agencies must use relevant research findings in the training of investigative professionals

for implementation in investigations of crimes against children. It is only through collaborative multidisciplinary efforts that child abduction investigations can be more effective, increasing the likelihood of the offender's identification, arrest, and prosecution, as well as the victim's safe return.

REFERENCES

American Prosecutors Research Institute. (1995). Surveys on family violence and FBI aid. *National Center for Prosecution of Child Abuse Update, 8*(5/6).

Ankrom, L. G., & Lent, C. J. (1995). Cradle robbers. *FBI Law Enforcement Bulletin, 64*(9), 12–17.

Asdigian, N. L., Finkelhor, D., & Hotaling, G. (1995). Varieties of nonfamily abduction of children, and adolescents. *Criminal Justice and Behavior, 22,* 215–232.

Best, J., & Thibodeau, T. M. (1997). Measuring the scope of social problems: Apparent inconsistencies across estimates of family abductions. *Justice Quarterly, 14,* 719–737.

Boudreaux, M. C., Lord, W. D., & Dutra, R. L. (1999). Child abduction: Age-based analyses of offender, victim, and offense characteristics in 550 cases of alleged child disappearance. *Journal of Forensic Sciences, 44,* 539–553.

Burgess, A. W., & Lanning, K. V. (Eds.). (1995). *An analysis of infant abductions.* Alexandria, VA: National Center for Missing and Exploited Children.

Capone, D. L., & Nichols, W. W. (1976). Urban structure and criminal mobility. *American Behavioral Scientist, 20,* 199–213.

Cloud, M. Y. (1996). Abducted and murdered children: Behavioral based analyses of victims, offenders and remains disposal methodologies. *Dissertation Abstracts International, 57*(5), 3397.

Cole, W. A., & Bradford, J. M. (1992). Abduction during custody and access disputes. *Canadian Journal of Psychiatry, 37,* 264–266.

Conte, J. R., Wolf, S., & Smith, T. (1989). What sexual offenders tell us about prevention strategies. *Child Abuse and Neglect, 13,* 293–301.

Crittenden, P. M., & Craig, S. E. (1990). Developmental trends in the nature of child homicide. *Journal of Interpersonal Violence, 5,* 202–216.

Elliott, M., Browne, K., & Kilcoyne, J. (1995). Child sexual abuse prevention: What offenders tell us. *Child Abuse and Neglect, 19,* 579–594.

Finkelhor, D. (1995). The victimization of children: A developmental perspective. *American Journal of Orthopsychiatry, 65,* 177–193.

Finkelhor, D. (1997). The homicides of children and youth: A developmental perspective. In G. Kaufman Kantor & J. Jasinski (Eds.), *Out of the darkness: Contemporary perspectives on family violence* (pp. 17–34). Thousand Oaks, CA: SAGE.

Finkelhor, D., Hotaling, G., & Sedlak, A. J. (1990). *Missing, abducted, runaway, and thrownaway children in America.* Washington, DC: U.S. Department of Justice.

Finkelhor, D., Hotaling, G., & Sedlak, A. J. (1992) The abduction of children by strangers and non-family members. *Journal of Interpersonal Violence, 7,* 226–243.

Forehand, R., Long, N., & Zogg, C. (1989). Parental child abduction: The problems and possible solution. In B. B. Lahey & A. E. Kazdin (Eds.), *Advances in clinical child psychology* (Vol. 12, pp. 113–137). New York: Plenum.

Forst, M. L., & Blomquist, M. E. (1991). *Missing children: Rhetoric and reality.* Lexington, MA: Lexington Books.

Hanfland, K. A., Keppel, R. D., & Weis, J. G. (1997). *Case management for missing children homicide investigation.* Olympia, WA: Attorney General of Washington.

Hazelwood, R. R., Dietz, P. E., & Warren, J. (1992). The criminal sexual sadist. *FBI Law Enforcement Bulletin, 61*(2), 12–20.

Hegar, R.L., & Greif, G. L. (1991). Abduction of children by their parents: A survey of the problem. *Social Work, 36,* 421–426.

Holcombe, A., Wolery, M., & Katzenmeyer, J. (1995). Teaching preschoolers to avoid abduction by strangers: Evaluation of maintenance strategies. *Journal of Child and Family Studies, 4,* 177–191.

Kaufman, K. L., Holmberg, J. K., Orts, K. A., McCrady, F. E., Rotzien, A. L . . . Hilliker, D. R. (1998). Factors influencing sexual offenders' modus operandi: An examination of victim-offender relatedness and age. *Child Maltreatment, 3,* 349–361.

Lanning, K. V. (1994). Sexual homicide of children. *APSAC Advisor, 7*(4), 40–44.

Lanning, K. V., (1995). Investigative analysis and summary of teaching points. In K. V. Lanning & A. W. Burgess (Eds.), *Child molesters who abduct: Summaryof the case in point series* (pp. 17–36). Alexander, VA: National Center for Missing and Exploited Children.

Lanning, K. V. & Burgess, A. W. (Eds.). (1995). *Child molesters who abduct: Summary of the case point series.* Alexander, VA: National Center for Missing and Exploited Children.

McGuire, J. (`994). Re-painting the Golden Gate Bridge: Coordination of services for abducted children reunited with their families. *Child and Adolescent Social Work Journal, 11,* 149–164.

Miltenberger, R. G., & Olsen, L. A. (1996). Abduction prevention training: A review of findings and issues for future research. *Education and Treatment of Children, 19,* 69–82.

Plass, P. S. (1998). A typology of family abduction events. *Child Maltreatment, 3,* 244–250.

Prentky, R. A., Knight, R. A., Burgess, A. W., Ressler, R., Campbell, J., & Lanning, K. V. (1991). Child molesters who abduct. *Violence and Victims, 6,* 213–224.

Ressler, R. K., Burgess, A. W., & Douglas, J. E. (1988). *Sexual homicide: Patterns and motives.* Lexington, MA: Lexington Books.

Roberts, M. S., Alexander, K., & Fanurik, D. (1990). Evaluation of commercially available materials to prevent child sexual abuse and abduction. *American Psychologist, 46,* 782–783.

Rossmo, D. K. (1993, August). Multivariate spatial profiles as a tool in crime investigation. Paper presented at the Workshop of Crime Analysis Through Computer Mapping, Chicago.

Stickler, G. B. (1996). Worries of parents and their children. *Clinical Pediatrics, 35*(2), 84–90.

U.S. Department of Commerce. (1992). *United States general population charactics. 1990 census of population.* Washington, DC: Government Printing Office.

Yarmey, A. D. (1988). Streetproofing and bystanders' memory for a child abduction In M. M. Gruneberg, P. E. Morris, & R. N. Sykes (Eds.), *Practical aspects of memory: Current research and issues, Vol. 1: Memory of everyday life* (pp. 112–116). New York: John Wiley.

21

Mental Disorder, Predisposition, Prediction, and Ability to Control

Evaluating Sex Offenders for Civil Commitment*

Richard W. Elwood

Since 1990, 20 U.S. states have enacted laws to involuntarily commit certain sex offenders as sexually violent persons (SVPs). These statutes, modeled after one another, typically define a SVP as a convicted sex offender who has a mental condition or condition that predisposes them to commit sexually violent offenses and who poses a specified risk to reoffend because of serious difficulty controlling behavior (for review of most current state statutes, see Miller, Amenta, & Conroy, 2005). The U.S. Supreme Court has upheld SVP laws but only when they couple the likelihood to reoffend with a predisposing mental disorder (*Kansas v. Crane*, 2002; *Kansas v. Hendricks*, 1997). SVP laws remain controversial and have been criticized on both scientific and legal grounds (Janus, 2006; Prentky, Janus, Barbaree, Schwartz, & Kafka, 2006; Zander, 2005).

Part of the ongoing controversy reflects disagreement over the meaning of four key constructs: mental disorder, predisposition, prediction, and serious difficulty controlling behavior . . . .

---

*This article was published in *Sexual Abuse: A Journal of Research and Treatment*, 2, 395–411 (2009). We have removed some portions of the introductory section, as well as portions of sections referring to the consequences of differing interpretations of various components of sexually violent person statutes.

This article reviews alternative meanings of these key constructs and evaluates them through clinical and epidemiologic perspectives. In the absence of psychiatric or legal definitions, I consider how they are used in common language or in medical or scientific literature. Definitions are derived by consensus, not science, and are justified by their utility, not proven by data. I propose operational definitions of mental disorder, predisposition, prediction, and serious difficulty controlling behavior to help mitigate the controversy over commitment and clarify the scientific basis and legal requirements of SVP assessments.

*****

MENTAL DISORDERS

DSM-IV-TR defines mental disorder "as a clinically significant behavioral or psychological syndrome or pattern [that is] associated with present distress or disability or with a significantly increased risk of suffering, death, pain, disability, or an important loss of freedom" (American Psychiatric Association, 2000, p. xxxi). The introduction to *DSM-IV-TR* reveals the difficulty defining psychiatric terms in lay language. The editors reject the distinction between mental and physical disorders based on an archaic mind/body dualism. They stress that *DSM-IV-TR* does not classify people but the disorders that people *have*. They refer to "an individual *with* Schizophrenia" rather than "a Schizophrenic." However, defining a mental disorder as something a person *has* may suggest a physical abnormality and imply the very mind/body dualism the editors reject. I am a mature White male. Those attributes describe what I *am* better than longevity, Caucasian ethnicity, and xy genotype describe what I *have*.

The most common mental disorders used to fulfill the legal requirements of civil commitment are the paraphilias and personality disorders (Becker, Stinson, Tromp, & Messer, 2003;

Elwood, Doren, & Thornton, 2008; Levenson, 2004). Paraphilias are defined by recurring, intense sexual fantasies, urges or behaviors that occur for at least 6 months and involve nonhuman objects, suffering or humiliation of oneself or one's partner, or children or other nonconsenting persons, which cause significant distress or impair social, occupational, or another important area of functioning. Among the paraphilias are pedophilia, exhibitionism, sexual sadism, and a separate category, paraphilia not otherwise specified. Personality disorders involve pervasive, abnormal experience and behavior by early adulthood, manifested in cognition, emotion, social, or impulse control, across a broad range of personal and social situations that lead to distress or impaired social, occupational, or other functioning. Both the paraphilias and personality disorders are diagnosed largely from behavior. Therein lies the debate: Do mental disorder diagnoses just *describe* patterns of behavior or must they *explain* them?

Different Interpretations of Mental Disorder

Miller et al. (2005) imply that mental disorders must be validated by a biological basis. They note that no neuropsychological deficit or other "definable entity" has been identified that causes paraphilias or personality disorder. They ask whether pedophilia reflects an "underlying pathology" or is merely a description of signs and symptoms. Decades before, Szasz (1960) took the argument even further, claiming that mental illness is a myth because the thoughts, feelings, and behavior that constitute mental activities are not biological processes.

In their seminal article, Robins and Guze (1970) proposed an ambitious program to validate psychiatric diagnoses by clinical description, outcome, exclusionary criteria, family concordance, and laboratory tests that they hoped would eventually establish their biological etiologies. Writing 25 years later, Andreasen (1995) admitted that no laboratory tests or biological markers for mental disorders had yet been discovered. More recently, Kupfer, First, and Regier (2002) acknowledged that no laboratory marker had yet been found that could identify *DSM-IV-TR* syndromes. They suggest the high comorbidity among mental disorders undermines the claims of distinct biological etiologies. Recent treatment outcome studies also challenge a strictly biologic model of mental disorders. For example, DeRubeis et al. (2005) found that cognitive behavior therapy improved moderate to severe major depression as well as the antidepressant paroxetine. Goldapple et al. (2004) found that both cognitive behavior therapy and paroxetine produced distinct metabolic changes in the limbic and cortical regions of the brain.

*****

Consequences of Different Interpretations of Mental Disorder

The competing interpretations of mental disorders present a choice between (a) accepting *descriptive* diagnoses based on observed signs and symptoms and (b) insisting on *explanatory* diagnoses validated by biological etiologies. Insisting that mental disorders have a known biological etiology basis would invalidate paraphilias and personality disorders and deny the two mental conditions that are most often used to fulfill SVP statutes. Denying those disorders would essentially preclude SVP commitment by current statutes. However, most other mental disorders (including schizophrenia) also lack a clear biological etiology and would likewise have to be abandoned, which Szasz (1960) has long advocated. However, like any interpretation, it is useful only to the extent that it is accepted. Quite the contrary, psychiatrists and psychologists still offer, and patients still seek, mental health treatment, and courts recognize mental disorders in judicial proceedings. Moreover, most *medical diseases are also* descriptive and *cannot be linked to a biological mechanism*. For example, the cause of breast

cancer cannot be determined in 95% of cases (Madigan, Ziegler, Benichou, Byrne, & Hoover, 1995). Abandoning the diagnosis of mental and physical disorders because we cannot identify biological causes is not tenable, let alone useful.

Conclusion

*****

I conclude that the most useful interpretation of mental disorder in civil commitment is ...: *a syndrome (a pattern of behavior and symptoms) that can be reliably diagnosed and has a predictable course,* whether or not that pattern corresponds to any physical abnormality. Recent studies have found that evaluators can reliably diagnose paraphilias (Doren & Elwood, 2009; Packard & Levenson, 2006) and personality disorders (Zanarini et al., 2000). This position is consistent with the continuing evolution of diagnostics through *DSM-III* and its successors. Accepting diagnoses defined by observed behavior and symptoms overcomes the objection to using disorders in SVP cases that have not been shown to have a biological cause. However, descriptive diagnoses beg the question: How can mental disorders diagnosed only by signs and symptoms *predispose* someone to commit a sexual offense?

PREDISPOSE

"Predispose" is not defined by *DSM-IV-TR* or state SVP statutes (Frances, Sreenivasan, & Weinberger, 2008). It is defined in common language and medicine as "to render susceptible" (Merriam-Webster Online, 2009; Stedman's online medical dictionary, 2009) and in law "to dispose or incline in advance" (Merriam-Webster's Dictionary of Law, 2001). The Supreme Court did not define "predispose" in SVP cases but implied that it "makes the person likely to . . ." or "creates a likelihood of such conduct in the future" (*Kansas v. Hendricks*,

1997). The Wisconsin Supreme Court ruled that the state's SVP statute requires a disorder "that *specifically causes* [italics added] that person to be prone to commit sexually violent acts in the future" (*State v. Post*, 1995).

Different Interpretations of Predispose

One way to interpret "predispose" is to link it to an internal cause or process, similar to linking mental disorders to biological etiologies. Miller et al. (2005) imply that position by asking how the paraphilias or personality disorders can predispose someone to commit a sex offense without a "definable entity" that can *cause* those disorders. Doren (2002a) takes a similar view, suggesting that SVP laws typically take "predispose" to mean the effect of a mental condition to cause "an internal drive toward repeating sexual crimes" (p. 99). He contends that predisposition to commit sex offenses is given by the definitions of pedophilia and sexual sadism but must be inferred from behavior for other paraphilias or the personality disorders.

Another way to define "predisposition" is to equate it with "risk factor." For example, the lifetime incidence of breast cancer is far higher among women than men. Thus, female gender "specifically causes" women "to be prone" to develop the disease. Indeed, e*pidemiologists define "cause" as any prior event or condition that increases the incidence of an outcome* (Green, Freedman, & Gordis, 2008). In this way, we can say that their gender predisposes women to breast cancer, without having to invoke estrogen or genetics. Likewise, we can say that being diagnosed with pedophilia predisposes men (makes them more likely) to molest children.

*****

Conclusion

I propose the most useful definition of "predispose" in civil commitment is the *effect of a mental disorder to increase the incidence of sexual recidivism*. In this view, "predisposition" is equivalent to "risk factor" and can be established by a statistical association, without having to invoke a causal mechanism. We need not know *how* a factor increases risk; we need only know that it does. Linking predisposition to a descriptive mental disorder is not circular reasoning. It simply recognizes that a pattern of past behavior predicts future behavior. "Predispose" is used this way throughout the medical literature. A Medline search (PubMed, n.d.) reveals hundreds of studies whose titles claim that hypertension *predisposes* people to strokes, obesity *predisposes* them to diabetes, and psychosocial factors *predispose* women to depression. Many of those claims reflect multiple risk factors not single etiologies. Some make no causal claim whatsoever. Defining predispose this way does not diminish the search for biological causal mechanisms; it just means that using the term *predispose* does not depend on them.

The strength of associations can be assessed by accepted epidemiological statistics, such as relative risk or odds ratio (Clayton & McKeigue, 2001; Green et al., 2008), to eliminate conditions that contribute only a trivial increase in risk. Of course, a clinical assessment is required to establish that a predisposing condition applies to an individual person. The U.S. courts acknowledge that epidemiology cannot prove causation in a specific case but generally accept that epidemiological data can establish that a condition "more likely than not" caused the outcome (Green et al., 2008).

PREDICT

Prediction is arguably the critical component in SVP assessment because SVP laws were specifically enacted to evaluate the risk of sexual offenses and intervene to prevent them. Predict means "to declare or indicate in advance; especially to foretell on the basis of observation, experience, or scientific reason" (Merriam-Webster Online, 2009).

Different Interpretations of Predict

Most psychologists who evaluate the risk of sexual recidivism use actuarial scales (Jackson & Hess, 2007), in much the same way that actuaries assess risk in business or health care. SVP risk estimates predict the probability of sexual recidivism. They are based on the proportion of sex offenders with the same actuarial scores who are known to have reoffended over designated spans of time. However, some critics contend that although actuarial scales estimate recidivism in groups of sex offenders, they cannot estimate the risk of individual members of those groups.

Doren (2002b) narrowly defines prediction as declaring with certainty that an event either will or will not occur, that is, it has a probability of 0% or 100%. He distinguishes prediction from risk assessment, which he means estimates of all probabilities in between. Doren's (2002b) narrow view of prediction may be useful, even preferable, in SVP assessment, but it has little utility if it is not shared. In fact, Doren's definition has not been widely accepted. A Medline search (PubMed) of "predict" finds countless titles referring to *predicting* the probability of violence, suicide, depression, heart disease, and numerous other events and conditions. Other leading figures in sex offender assessment regularly refer to "predicting sexual recidivism" and "predictive accuracy" (Hanson & Morton-Bourgon, 2004; Quinsey, Rice, & Harris, 1995; Thornton, 2006). Clearly, prediction commonly refers to a statement of either the occurrence of an event *or* an estimate of its probability.

Some forensic examiners argue that risk assessment in SVP is not prediction because the event or outcome (sexual recidivism) is usually unknown. Indeed, the purpose of SVP laws is to empower the state to intervene to prevent such an event. However, this claim too is based on a narrow interpretation of prediction. The task facing SVP evaluators is to estimate the probability that a sex offender will reoffend, given (i.e., conditional on) certain other events, such as release from custody and having opportunity. Conditional probability, the probability of an event A, given the occurrence of another event B, or $P(A|B)$, is well established in probability theory. Predicting the probability of certain events includes predicting conditional probabilities of those events given other events. We can meaningfully predict the probability that a subject would reoffend *were* he released subject by discovering the proportion of similar subjects who *were* released under comparable circumstances.

The contention that actuarial scales cannot predict the risk of individuals is based on two separate arguments. First, some critics of SVP laws argue that because individuals within a group do not share the same risk, actuarial predictions cannot predict the recidivism of any member of the group (Berlin, Galbreath, Geary, & McGlone, 2003; Hart, Michie, & Cooke, 2007; La Fond, 2005). For example, Hart et al. (2007) argue that it is difficult to establish relative risk "with a high degree of certainty" from actuarial risk scales (p. s64). This argument challenges not only sexual recidivism risk assessment but actuarial science itself.

However, an alternative conclusion is that actuarial data *can* predict an individual's recidivism risk but cannot predict it *perfectly*. Members of a group clearly do *not* pose equal risk; if they did, the actuarial scales used to assess them would have far higher predictive accuracy. The ability of actuarial scales to predict sexual recidivism better than chance is well established (Bengtson & Långström, 2007; Hanson & MortonBourgon, 2007; Harris & Rice, 2007; Knight & Thornton, 2007). Mean area under the curve values for the Static-99 are typically around .70, which are considered low to moderate (Streiner & Cairney, 2007). Nonetheless, a legitimate question is whether the prediction is *good enough* for a specific application, such as fulfilling the risk threshold under an SVP statute.

Actuarial predictions do not assume that each member of a group shares the overall or average risk; they assume that the average group risk provides the *best* estimate of the risk of any in that group, "best" being the estimate with the least error averaged over repeated predictions ("best" can also be determined by the social costs of false positive and false negative errors). Of course, the accuracy of prediction based on group means is improved by defining more specific groups. The best prediction of the height of an adult male in the United States is the average height of adult men, about 5 ft 9 in. Knowing only that a particular male plays in the NBA, the best prediction of his height is 6 ft 7 in. tall, the average of National Basketball Association players (National Basketball Association, 2006).

Secondly, I have also seen forensic examiners inform the court that actuarial risk estimates only *compare* an individual offender to others with the same score but do not predict (or estimate) an individual's risk. This interpretation may reflect at least in part Doren's view (Doren, 2002a) that risk assessment is not prediction. If so, we could merely substitute "risk estimate" for "prediction" and apply it to individuals. However, the reluctance to specify the risk of a certain individual seems to imply a broader principle that group risks or probabilities do not apply to individuals or single events. This is an esoteric interpretation of prediction. In common practice, weather forecasters do not just compare current weather conditions to those on previous days when it rained; they predict the probability of rain *today*. National Football League referees do not just say that 50% of previous coin tosses turned up heads; they confidently predict that the coin toss at the *next* Super Bowl has a 50/50 chance of turning up heads. Physicians do not just cite proportions of study subjects who had a certain outcome; they predict the risk or likelihood that their patient will have that outcome. Predicting the likelihood of specific events is ubiquitous and useful, if uncertain.

Conclusion

I propose that the most useful definition of prediction in civil commitment is *the estimated probability of an event or outcome from 0% to 100%, which may be conditional on specified conditions*. This definition is consistent with its use in common language, statistics, medicine, psychiatry, and actuarial science. Thus defined, prediction is essentially synonymous with risk assessment. It does not require certainty, but it must be *accurate enough* to be useful or to meet relevant legal standards. Ultimately, courts require that SVP evaluators render an opinion on the risk of a specific person (*State v. Seibert*, 2008). If evaluators cannot speak to an individual's risk, their testimony is irrelevant.

SERIOUS DIFFICULTY CONTROLLING BEHAVIOR

In the *Crane* decision, the U.S. Supreme Court ruled that to commit an SVP, the state must "demonstrate a serious difficulty in controlling behavior [that] distinguish[es] that kind of a person from a dangerous but typical criminal recidivist convicted in an ordinary criminal case" (*Kansas v. Crane*, 2002). The *Crane* Court did not provide a it was necessary to *separately* find serious difficulty controlling clear standard for "inability to control behavior" nor did it define "typical recidivist." Not surprisingly, states soon split over how to satisfy the *Crane* ruling. State courts disagreed on whether behavior (Dries, 2006) and over the need to instruct juries to consider such difficulty.

Different Legal Approaches to "Serious Difficulty Controlling Behavior"

Courts in Washington, Wisconsin, and Florida have ruled that serious difficulty controlling behavior is presumed by a mental disorder combined with a high recidivism risk and need not be specifically determined (Wisconsin Office of Public Defender, n.d.). For example, the Wisconsin Supreme Court ruled that a mental disorder and a high probability of reoffending "necessarily and implicitly includes proof [of] serious difficulty controlling behavior" (*State v. Laxton*,

2002). That ruling extends the Supreme Court's opinion in *Crane* that "pedophilia is a mental disorder that by definition includes . . . lack of control" (*Kansas v. Crane*, 2002). One might surmise that these opinions relieve evaluators from having to determine serious difficulty controlling behavior, at least in cases of pedophilia. However, despite the Wisconsin Supreme Court's "implicit proof" ruling (*State v. Laxton*, 2002), the Wisconsin Criminal Jury Instruction Committee added "serious difficulty in controlling behavior" to the definition of mental disorder in responding to *Crane* (Practice Pointers, 2002). If juries must determine whether a mental condition causes difficulty controlling behavior, evaluators must presumably render an opinion on it. Moreover, even if difficulty controlling behavior can be presumed by pedophilia and some other paraphilias, it is not implied by the definition of APD. Presumably, evaluators must distinguish SVPs diagnosed solely with APD from many "typical recidivists" who are also diagnosed with APD (Moran, 1999).

Courts in other states have ruled that a specific determination of serious difficulty controlling behavior *is* required (Wisconsin Office of Public Defender, n.d.) and that juries must be explicitly instructed accordingly. These rulings thereby impose a third requirement to commit sex offenders (beyond predisposing mental disorder and high risk to reoffend).

*****

The U.S. Board of Prisons recently devised guidelines to help evaluators determine "serious difficulty in refraining from sexually violent conduct or child molestation if released" (Civil Commitment, 2008). The guidelines include repeatedly offending against to the same victim, denying or minimizing offenses, offending while on supervision, and the admitting of an inability to control behavior. Whereas some of these variables are associated with sexual recidivism, none has been shown to *specifically* impair behavioral or volitional control. Moreover, the ability to control one's behavior is not dichotomous. Kansas argued before

the *Crane* Court that "the overwhelming weight of mental health authority would view virtually any person's behavior as falling along a continuum of volitional control" (*Kansas v. Crane*, 2002).

*****

Conclusion

States disagree over how to interpret and apply "difficulty controlling behavior" that is required by the *Crane* decision. Some state courts have ruled that difficulty controlling behavior is presumed by a mental condition and high risk to reoffend whereas other courts have ruled that it must be determined separately. Serious difficulty controlling behavior has been related to volitional impairment but both are hypothetical constructs that are inferred from behavior.

I conclude that the most useful interpretation of serious difficulty controlling behavior is to consider it in the context of two opinions in *Crane*: (a) that serious difficulty controlling behavior distinguishes SVPs from typical criminal recidivists and (b) that pedophilia, by definition, includes serious difficulty controlling behavior. I take the first opinion to set a broad legal standard and the second to provide a clarifying example. On that basis, I propose that serious difficulty controlling behavior be (a) presumed by pedophilia and sexual sadism, likely in some other paraphilias, and (b) determined in cases of personality disorders by whether subjects can be distinguished from usual criminal recidivists.

Discussion

The debate over civil commitment of SVPs in the United States and the practice of risk assessment are both hampered by disagreements over how to define and interpret four fundamental psychological and legal constructs: mental disorder, predisposition, prediction, and serious difficulty controlling behavior. As a result, the controversy over civil commitment at times appears to be more over semantics than substance. This review explored various meanings of those constructs and proposed interpretations based on their utility and common use and informed by clinical, diagnostic, and epidemiologic research.

I propose the following operational definitions as the most useful interpretations in SVP assessments: (a) *mental disorder*, a pattern of behavioral signs and symptoms that can be reliably diagnosed and has a predictable course, whether or not it corresponds to a physical abnormality; (b) *predispose*, the effect of mental disorder to significantly increase the incidence of sexual recidivism, without having to invoke a biological etiology; (c) *prediction*, a statement of the probability of a future event or condition from 0% to 100%, conditional on specified circumstances, and which does not require certainty; and (d) *serious difficulty controlling behavior*, the lack of control associated with a mental disorder that is presumed in pedophilia and sexual sadism, likely in some other paraphilias, and can be determined in personality disorders where SVPs can be distinguished from typical, criminal recidivists.

Definitions are not proven by facts but accepted by consensus. I did not elect these definitions to favor civil commitment. Rather, I contend that they are consistent with their broad use throughout medicine and psychiatry and reflect accepted methods in statistics, epidemiology, and actuarial science. These definitions will not, nor should not, resolve the controversy over SVP commitment but they may help alleviate the semantic arguments between and among its critics and proponents. Hopefully, these proposed definitions will also help evaluators conduct forensic assessments of sexual recidivism that meet scientific, ethical, and legal standards.

REFERENCES

American Psychiatric Association. (1980). *Diagnostic and statistical manual of mental disorders* (3rd ed.). Washington, DC: Author.

American Psychiatric Association. (1994). *Diagnostic and statistical manual of mental disorders* (4th ed.). Washington, DC: Author.

American Psychiatric Association. (2000). *Diagnostic and statistical manual of mental disorders* (text revision). Washington, DC: Author.

Andreasen, N. C. (1995). The validation of psychiatric diagnosis: New models and approaches. *American Journal of Psychiatry, 152*, 161–162.

Becker, J. V., Stinson, J., Tromp, S., & Messer, G. (2003). Characteristics of individuals petitioned for civil commitment. *International Journal of Offender Therapy and Comparative Criminology, 47*, 185–195.

Bengtson, S., & Långström, N. (2007). Unguided clinical and actuarial assessment of re-offending risk: A direct comparison with sex offenders in Denmark. *Sexual Abuse: A Journal of Research and Treatment, 19*, 135–153.

Berlin, F. S., Galbreath, N. W., Geary, B., & McGlone, G. (2003). The use of actuarials at civil commitment hearings to predict the likelihood of future sexual violence. *Sexual Abuse: A Journal of Research and Treatment, 15*, 377–382.

Civil commitment of a sexually violent person, 28 C.F.R. § 549.95. (2008). Retrieved July 16, 2009, from http://ecfr.gpoaccess.gov/cgi/t/text/text-idx ?c=ecfr&sid=2c026685cdda5d6e3c3 ffde8d761c 54b&rgn=div8&view=text&node=28:2.0.3.3.21. 8.43.6&idno=28

Clayton, D., & McKeigue, P. (2001). Epidemiological methods for studying genes and environmental factors in complex diseases. *Lancet, 358*, 1356–1360.

Cooke, D. J., & Michie, C. (2009). Limitations of diagnostic precision and predictive utility in the individual case: A challenge for forensic practice. *Law and Human Behavior*. Prepublished March 11, doi: 10.1007/s10979–009–9176-x

DeRubeis, R. J., Hollon, S. D., Amsterdam, J. D., Shelton, R. C., Young, P. R., Salomon, R. et al. (2005). Cognitive therapy vs. medications in the treatment of moderate to severe depression. *Archives of General Psychiatry. 62*, 409–416.

Doren, D. M. (2002a). *Evaluating sex offenders: A manual for civil commitments and beyond.* Thousand Oaks, CA: Sage.

Doren, D. M. (2002b). The use of actuarial risk assessment. In B. K. Schwartz (Ed.), *The sex offender: Vol. 4. Current treatment modalities and system issues* (pp. 6–1–6–9). Kingston, NJ: Civic Research Institute.

Doren, D. M., & Elwood, R. W. (2009). The diagnostic reliability of sexual sadism. *Sexual Abuse: A Journal of Research and Treatment, 21*, 251–261.

Dries, S. C. (2006). Sexual predators and federal habeas corpus: Has the great writ gone AWOL? *Suffolk University Law Review, 39*, 672–697.

Elwood, R. W., Doren, D. M., & Thornton, D. (2008). Diagnostic and risk profiles of men detained under Wisconsin's sexually violent person law. *International Journal of Offender Therapy and Comparative Criminology*. Prepublished December 4, doi: 10.1177/0306624X08327305.

Frances, A., Sreenivasan, S., & Weinberger, L. E. (2008). Defining mental disorder when it really counts: DSM-IV-TR and SVP/SDP statutes. *Journal of the American Academy of Psychiatry and the Law, 36*, 375–384.

Goldapple, K., Segal, Z., Garson, C., Lau, M., Bieling, P., Kennedy, S., et al. (2004). Modulation of cortical-limbic pathways in major depression. *Archives of General Psychiatry, 61*, 34–41.

Green, M. D., Freedman, M., & Gordis, L. (2008). *Reference guide on epidemiology*. Washington, DC: Federal Judicial Center. Retrieved February 17, 2009, from http://www.fjc.gov/ public/pdf. nsf/lookup/sciman06.pdf/$file/sciman06.pdf

Hanson, R. K., & Morton-Bourgon, K. E. (2004). *Predictors of sexual recidivism: An updated meta-analysis*. Ottawa, Ontario: Public Safety of Canada. Retrieved February 17, 2009, from http://www.publicsafety.gc.ca/res/cor/rep/_ fl/2004–02-pred-se-eng.pdf

Hanson. R. K., & Morton-Bourgon, K. E. (2007). *The accuracy of recidivism risk assessments for sexual offenders: A meta-analysis*. Ottawa, Ontario: Public Safety of Canada. Retrieved February 17, 2009, from http://www.publicsafety.gc.ca/res/ cor/rep/_fl/crp2007–01-en.pdf

Harris, G. T., & Rice, M. E. (2007). Characterizing the value of actuarial violence risk assessments. *Criminal Justice & Behavior, 34*, 1638–1658.

Hart, S. D., Michie, C., & Cooke, D. J. (2007). Precision of actuarial risk assessment instruments: Evaluating the "margins of error' of group vs. individual predictions of violence. *British Journal of Psychiatry, 190* (Suppl. 49), s60-s65.

Hill, A. B. (1965). The environment and disease: Association or causation? *Proceedings of the Royal Society of Medicine, 58*, 295–300.

Jackson, R. L., & Hess, D. T. (2007). Evaluation for civil commitment of sex offenders: A survey of experts. *Sexual Abuse: A Journal of Research and Treatment, 19*, 425–448.

Janus, E. S. (2006). *Failure to protect: America's sexual predator laws and the rise of the preventive state*. Ithaca, NY: Cornell University Press.

Kansas v. Crane, 534 U. S. (2002). Retrieved February 23, 2009, from the World Wide Web site: http://www .oyez.org/cases/2000–2009/2001/ 2001_00_957/

Kansas v. Hendricks, 521 U. S. (1997). Retrieved February 23, 2009, from the World Wide Web site: http://www.oyez.org/cases/1990–1999/ 1996/1996_95_1649/

Kessler, R. C., Berglund, P., Demler, O., Jin, R., Merikangas, K. R., & Walters, E. E. (2005). Lifetime prevalence and age-of-onset distributions of *DSM-IV* disorders in the National Comorbidity Survey Replication. *Archives of General Psychiatry, 62*, 593–602,

Kessler, R. C., McGonagle, K. A., Zhao, S., Nelson, C. B., Hughes, M., Eshleman, S., et al. (1994). Lifetime and 12-month prevalence of DSM-III-R psychiatric disorders in the United States: Results from the National Comorbidity Survey. *Archives of General Psychiatry, 51*, 8–19.

Knight, R. A., & Thornton, D. (2007). *Evaluating and improving risk assessment schemes for sexual recidivism: A long-term follow-up of convicted sexual offenders*. Research report submitted to the U.S. Department of Justice. Retrieved April 28, 2008, from the World Wide Web site: http:// www.ncjrs.gov/pdffiles1/nij/grants/217618.pdf

Kupfer, D. A., First, M. B., & Regier, D. A. (Eds.). (2002). *A research agenda for DSM-V*. Washington, D.C.: American Psychiatric Association. Retrieved February 19, 2009, from http://www .appi.org/pdf/kupfer_2292.pdf

La Fond, J. Q. (2005). *Preventing sexual violence: How society should cope with sex offenders*. Washington, DC: American Psychological Association.

Långström, N., Sjöstedt, G., & Grann, M. (2004). Psychiatric disorders and recidivism in sexual offenders. *Sexual Abuse: A Journal of Research and Treatment, 16*, 139–150.

Levenson, J. S. (2004). Sexual predator civil commitment: A comparison of selected and released offenders. *International Journal of Offender Therapy, and Comparative Criminology, 48*, 638–648.

Madigan, M. P., Ziegler, R. G., Benichou, J., Byrne, C., & Hoover, R. N. (1995). Proportion of breast cancer cases in the United States explained by well-established risk factors. *Journal of the National Cancer Institute, 87*, 1681–1685.

Mayes, R., & Horwitz, A. V. (2005). *DSM-III* and the revolution in the classification of mental illness. *Journal of the History of the Behavioral Sciences, 41*, 249–267.

Meehl, P. E. (1973). *Psychodiagnosis: Selected papers*. New York: Norton.

Merriam-Webster's Dictionary of Law. (2001). Springfield, MA: Merriam-Webster. Retrieved March 9, 2009, from http://research.lawyers.com/glossary/

Merriam-Webster Online. (2009). Springfield, MA: Merriam-Webster. Retrieved February 25, 2009, from http://www.merriam-webster.com/dictionary.htm

Miller, H. A., Amenta, A. E., & Conroy, M. A. (2005). Sexually violent predator evaluations: Empirical evidence, strategies for professionals, and research directions. *Law and Human Behavior, 29*, 29–83.

Montaldi, D. F. (2007). The logic of sexually violent predator status in the United States of America. *Sexual Offender Treatment, 2*(1), 1–28. Retrieved July 17, 2009, from http://www .sexual-offender-treatment.org/index.php?id=57&type=123

Moran, P. (1999). The epidemiology of antisocial personality disorder. *Social Psychiatry and Psychiatric Epidemiology, 34*, 231–242.

National Basketball Association. (2006). *2006–07 Player survey: Height.* Retrieved May 29, 2009, from http://www.nba.com/news/survey_height_2006.html

Packard, R., & Levenson, J. (2006). Revisiting the reliability of diagnostic decisions in sex offender civil commitment. *Sex Offender Treatment, 1*(3). Retrieved October 20, 2008, from http://www .sexual-offender-treatment.org/50.html

Practice Pointers: Chapter 980. (2002, April). *Wisconsin Defender, 10, 4.*

Prentky, R. A., Janus, E., Barbaree, H., Schwartz, B. K., & Kafka, M. P. (2006). Sexually violent predators in the courtroom: Science on trial. *Psychology, Public Policy, and Law, 12*, 357–393.

PubMed (n.d.). National Center for Biotechnology Information (NCBI). Retrieved http://www .ncbi .nlm.nih.gov/sites/entrez

Quinsey, V. L., Rice, M. E., & Harris, G. T. (1995). Actuarial prediction of sexual recidivism. *Journal of Interpersonal Violence, 10*, 85–105.

Regier, D. A., Boyd, J. H., Burke, J. D. Jr., Rae, D. S., Myers, J. K., Kramer, M., Robins, L. N., George, L. K., Karno, M., and Locke, B. Z. (1988). One-month prevalence of mental disorders in the United States: Based on five Epidemiologic Catchment Area sites. *Archives of General Psychiatry, 45*, 977–986.

Robins, E., & Guze, S. B. (1970). Establishment of diagnostic validity in psychiatric illness: Its application to schizophrenia. *American Journal of Psychiatry, 126*, 983–987.

Rothman, K. J., & Greenland, S. (2005). Causation and causal inference in epidemiology. *American Journal of Public Health, 95* (Suppl. 1), S144-S150.

Rounsaville, B. J., Alarcón, R. D., Andrews, G., Jackson, J. S., Kendell, R. E., & Kendler, K. (2002). Basic nomenclature issues for *DSM-V.* In D. A. Kupfer, M. B. First, & D. A. Regier (Eds.), *A research agenda for DSM-V* (pp. 1–29). Washington, D.C.: American Psychiatric ssociation. Retrieved February 19, 2009, from http://www .appi.org/pdf/kupfer_2292.pdf

Seling v. Young, 531 U. S. (2001). Retrieved March 6, 2009, from http://www.oyez.org/cases/2000–2009/2000/2000_99_1185/

State v. Laxton, WI 82, 254 Wis. 2d 185, 647 N.W.2d 784 (2002).

State v. Post, 197 Wis.2d 279, 307 (1995). Retrieved February 19, 2009, from http://www.wicourts.gov/sc/opinion/DisplayDocument.html?content=html&seqNo=16944

State v. Seibert, 308 Wis. 2d 395 (Wis. Ct. App 2008).

Stedman's Online Medical Dictionary. (2009). Philadelphia, PA: Lippincott Williams & Wilkins. Retrieved February 24, 2009, from http://www .stedmans.com/section.cfm/45

Streiner, D. J., & Cairney, J. C. (2007). What's under the ROC? An introduction to receiver operating characteristics curves. *Canadian Journal of Psychiatry, 52*, 121–128.

Thornton, D. (2006). Age and sexual recidivism: A variable connection. *Sexual Abuse: A Journal of Research and Treatment, 18*, 123–135.

Szasz, T. S. (1960). The myth of mental illness. *American Psychologist, 15*, 113–118.

Wilson M. (1993). DSM-III and the transformation of American psychiatry: A history. *American Journal of Psychiatry, 150*, 399–410.

Wisconsin Office of Public Defender (n.d.). *Sexually violent persons commitment.* Retrieved 16, 2009, from http://www.wisspd.org/html/980case/ch980/ch980.asp#IVE___Jury_ Instructions

Woodruff, R. A., Goodwin, D. W., & Guze, S. B. (1974). *Psychiatric diagnosis.* New York: Oxford University Press.

Zanarini, M. C., Skodol, A. E., Bender, D., Dolan, R., Sanislow, C., Schaefer, E., et al. (2000). The Collaborative Longitudinal Personality Disorders Study: Reliability of axis I and II diagnoses. *Journal of Personality Disorders, 14*, 291–299.

Zander, T. K. (2005). Civil commitment without psychosis: The law's reliance on the weakest links in psychodiagnosis. *Journal of Sexual Offender Civil Commitment: Science and the Law, 1,* 17–82.

UNIT 5

VICTIMOLOGY AND VICTIM SERVICES

INTRODUCTION AND COMMENTARY

Services to victims of crimes, assessment of victims and survivors, and research focusing on victims have only recently been recognized as important components of forensic psychology. Yet many psychologists are more likely to come into contact with victims—who often prefer to be called survivors—than with offenders. Forensic psychologists evaluate crime victims, testify about the effects of their experience in both criminal and civil courts, and train law enforcement officers on effective approaches to interviewing them. In the civil context, persons who have been subjected to discrimination in the workplace, including sexual or gender harassment, may be assessed for the psychological effects of this discrimination, such as possible posttraumatic stress disorder.

The first article in this section is about a population that is increasingly at risk of victimization and exploitation. Although financial exploitation is a major concern, many older adults are also physically abused both in their homes and in out-of-home care facilities. The article by Pinsker, McFarland, and Pachana (2010) focuses on financial exploitation but is highly relevant across all forms of victimization. The authors note that there is currently no widely accepted clinical model for determining who is likely to be exploited. They propose that certain protective factors (e.g., social intelligence, particular personality traits, social skills) are less likely to render an older person vulnerable to exploitation. Interestingly, they suggest that persons who rank high on the personality factor of agreeableness may be more disposed to being taken advantage of by others. The authors suggest a number of ways their model may be used to assess older individuals and provide ideas for future research.

Hate crimes are a major concern in society, including hate crimes that occur on college and university campuses. Is a campus that encourages and promotes diversity more or less likely to have high rates of hate crime? The article by Stotzer and Hossellman (2012) gives careful attention to this question. The answer may be obvious, but the authors draw on research and statistics to support it. Basically, colleges that take proactive approaches to increasing minority enrollments in their recruitment strategies have significantly lower rates of reported hate crimes than do colleges that do not take this inclusive approach. The authors speculate that as greater numbers of minority populations are found on campus, diversity becomes commonplace and the campus climate is affected in a positive manner. These findings are particularly relevant in light of court decisions and laws in some states that are inimical to affirmative action programs in colleges and universities.

Next, Ball and her fellow researchers (2012) tackle the topic of dating violence among middle school and high school students. Specifically, Ball et al. report on a preliminary evaluation of a preventive program geared toward at-risk youths. The youths were considered at risk because they experienced or witnessed violence in their own family backgrounds. It is important to recognize that this is a preliminary report, the study did not include a control group, and the number of youth participants was low. Nevertheless, the description of the program is worth our attention, and the preliminary results provide reason for optimism as well as concern. The support-group sessions produced positive changes in relationship skills, particularly among youths who were at the highest risks for violence. However, dating violence, reported by the youths themselves, did not change significantly for most of them. Ball et al. discuss possible explanations and emphasize that violence prevention programs directed at youths require continuing evaluation and fine-tuning to achieve successful results.

The next article also deals with violence between partners, this time adult intimate partners. Research on intimate partner violence has exploded in recent years. This article reports on a qualitative study that, interestingly, focuses on the professionals who work with victims, rather than on the perpetrators or recipients of assault. Cattaneo and Chapman (2011) interviewed a very small group of practitioners (16), but this small group provided some insight into the challenge of working with victims on an ongoing basis. The article addresses the gap between research and practice: Do practitioners follow recommendations found in the research literature? One major "gap" was in the use of risk assessment instruments, which only two practitioners used despite the literature's recommending them, at least to some extent. Literature also finds that victims are good at assessing their risk of future danger, but the practitioners in this sample believed strongly that victims minimize their risk. The authors are frank in acknowledging the limitations of this research but note also that its results suggest options for more work with larger samples of professionals. Gaps between research and practice are important to identify, and articles such as this make a valuable contribution.

22

Exploitation in Older Adults

Social Vulnerability and Personal Competence Factors*

Donna M. Pinsker

Ken McFarland

Nancy A. Pachana

A common stereotype surrounding older adults is one of frailty, submissiveness, and isolation. Older people also tend to be seen as lucrative and easy targets for acts of financial exploitation. Though old age itself does not necessarily predispose an individual to being exploited, certain factors arising from age-related physical, cognitive, and social circumstances can contribute to greater vulnerability (Kurrle, Sadler, & Cameron, 1992; Smith, 1999). As a result, healthcare professionals are often called upon to determine whether an older person is at undue risk of abuse and exploitation.

A number of general risk factors associated with abuse and exploitation in later life have been identified and include extreme dependence, frailty, social isolation, severe physical illness, and cognitive impairment (Choi, Kulick, & Mayer, 1999; Podnieks, 1992; Wilber & Reynolds, 1996). Several authors have also offered comprehensive theoretical frameworks for understanding elder mistreatment and financial exploitation. Wilber and Reynolds began the process by providing a unifying definition of financial abuse and a framework to assist social service providers with verifying suspected cases of abuse. The National Research Council (2003) provided a complex transactional model of elder abuse in which characteristics of the individual and perpetrator are conceptualized within a broader sociocultural

*This article was published in *Journal of Applied Gerontology*, *29*, 740–761 (2010). We have removed some of the introductory section, scenarios, and portions of sections on social intelligence and social skills, as well as a brief concluding section.

213

context. Building on this model, Rabiner, Brown, and O'Keefe (2004; Rabiner, O'Keeffe, & Brown, 2004) provided recommendations for the development, implementation, and evaluation of strategies and policy responses to reduce the risk of exploitation occurring among older adults. The development and refinement of comprehensive theoretical frameworks has contributed to a better understanding of elder abuse and the individual, contextual, and social factors that influence the etiology of abuse and exploitation of older people.

Nevertheless, there is currently no widely accepted or validated clinical framework to assist clinicians with identifying individuals on an *a priori* basis who may be at heightened risk of financial exploitation. The aims of the present article are (a) to introduce an overarching clinical framework of vulnerability to financial exploitation in older people, and (b) to highlight potential markers of such forms of vulnerability to assist clinicians involved in geriatric assessments. In pursuit of these aims, the term *social vulnerability* is used, and defined as the *degree of susceptibility to exploitation*.

SOCIAL VULNERABILITY IN OLDER ADULTS: DEVELOPMENT OF A CLINICAL CONCEPTUAL FRAMEWORK

In devising a clinical assessment framework of social vulnerability for older adults, an earlier clinical model proposed by Greenspan and colleagues (Greenspan, Loughlin, & Black, 2001) in relation to younger adults with developmental disorders provides a useful starting point. Greenspan et al. argue that a central aspect of social vulnerability, and one which is generally overlooked, is a tendency toward credulity and gullibility. Credulity is a propensity to believe things that are unproven or unlikely to be true, whereas gullibility is a susceptibility to being manipulated or deceived, either repeatedly or despite obvious warning signs (Greenspan, 2005; Greenspan et al., 2001). Although the two terms are related, *credulity* pertains to a state of mind or

belief (i.e., cognition), whereas *gullibility* involves some tangible outcome. For example, an individual might accept a sales pitch from a stranger for unnecessary or overpriced home repairs (credulity) and willingly hand over large sums of money prior to completion of the work (gullibility).

*****

The personal competence factors in the model cover four broad domains: everyday intelligence, communication, physical competence, and motivation/personality . . . .

*****

According to Greenspan et al.'s (2001) model, physical limitations can also contribute to exploitation, even when not severely disabling. Deficits in auditory acuity, for example, may result in individuals missing important verbal cues, thereby making them easier to deceive and manipulate . . . .

*****

Greenspan et al.'s (2001) framework provides a useful, holistic clinical model for predicting exploitive susceptibility given certain personal competence factors and environmental conditions. As noted earlier, however, the intended scope of the model was limited to explaining social vulnerability in younger adults with developmental disorders. To this extent, if applied to older adults, use of the model in its current form may (a) overlook aspects of functioning specific to older people, (b) result in inappropriate attributions of factors and their interactions as they relate to older people, and (c) ignore the sequencing of events and impact of lifelong experience. The present work aims to not only introduce a similar framework for describing, explaining, and assessing social vulnerability in older adults but to also overcome difficulties of simply applying Greenspan's conceptualization directly to older people. As an initial conceptualization, the present article focused specifically on the personal competence components of Greenspan's model as they relate to older adults.

PROPOSED FRAMEWORK FOR EXPLAINING SOCIAL VULNERABILITY IN OLDER ADULTS

Using the personal competence components of Greenspan's model as a starting point, a proposed framework for conceptualizing social vulnerability in older people is depicted in Figure 1. As evident in the framework, social vulnerability is depicted as the "hub" of a wheel arrangement, surrounded by "spokes" of personal competence, and with no inference of causal direction. The personal competence domains in the proposed framework for older people are conceptually similar to those of Greenspan's model. There are, however, several departures from the original model, which will now be described.

First, to enhance the relevance of Greenspan's model to older adults, and in particular, older people with dementia, "online" cognitive processes (e.g., memory and executive functions) are included in the current framework as a separate component of personal competence, distinct from general intelligence. A progressive decline in cognitive processes, particularly memory and executive functions, typifies a number of dementia syndromes, Alzheimer's disease being the most prevalent (American Psychiatric Association, 2000).

In circumstances involving exploitation, memory deficits could limit one's ability to retrieve relevant information to make an informed judgment (e.g., recalling that the person has a history of deceptive behavior) or to accurately appraise a given statement or situation. Similarly, deficits in planning, problem-solving, and other executive-type processes could restrict the rapid formulation of strategies to escape or avoid exploitive situations. Thus, in addition to intellectual functioning, the proposed framework for older adults includes a separate domain of personal competence labeled *cognitive functioning*.

In a second modification to Greenspan et al.'s model, the domain of everyday intelligence (practical and social) has been reconceptualized

in the current framework. As implied in Greenspan's model, research in intellectual abilities has suggested that competencies in education, career, and personal life extend beyond academic intelligence, as measured by traditional intelligence (IQ) tests such as the Wechsler Adult Intelligence Scale (Wechsler, 1997), and also rely on social and emotional processes (Bar-On, 2001; Gardner, 1993; Marlowe, 1986; Sevdalis, Petrides, & Harvey, 2007; Sternberg, 1985, 1988; Sternberg et al., 2000). As noted earlier, Greenspan et al. (2001) regarded social intelligence as instrumental in avoiding exploitive social interactions. To highlight the potential importance of effective social reasoning in a model of social vulnerability for older adults, social intelligence features as a separate domain of personal competence in the current framework.

In addition, though Greenspan et al. (2001) acknowledged that there are different conceptual domains of intelligence, only practical and social intelligence are accommodated in their model; academic intelligence is not explicitly mentioned. When applied to older adults, use of the model in its current form may overlook some aspects of IQ, such as verbal comprehension and arithmetic abilities, which could also aid with avoiding exploitation. As a reconceptualization, in the proposed framework for older adults, everyday intelligence has been labeled general intellectual functioning, and academic and practical intelligence are subsumed . . . .

In other modifications to Greenspan's model, the communication component has been labeled *social skill* in the current framework to more clearly distinguish between cognitive (i.e., social intelligence) and behavioral aspects of social behavior. Finally, credulity is conceptualized somewhat differently in the present framework. As noted earlier, Greenspan et al. conceptualized credulity as a social intelligence processing deficit (input) that contributes to a gullible act (outcome). Particularly in older adults, however, credulity could also be conceptualized as an outcome, resulting from dysfunction in other domains such as cognitive functioning. For example, it could be speculated that an unquestioning belief in what

Figure 1 Proposed Framework for Conceptualizing Relationships Between Personal Competence Factors and Social Vulnerability in Older Adults

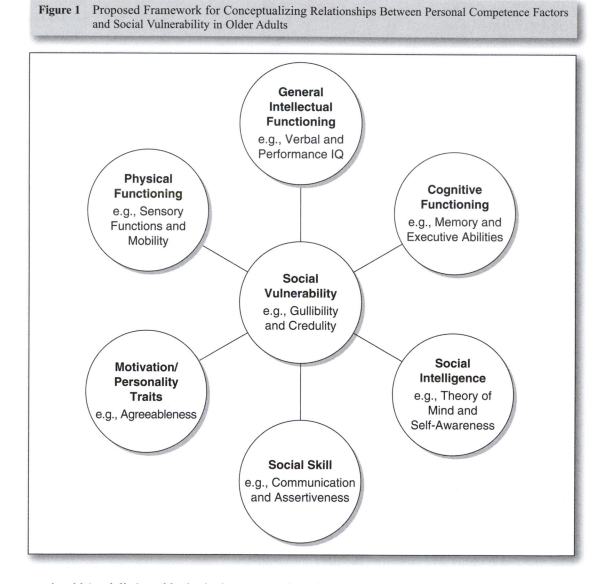

one is told (credulity) could arise in the context of severe memory impairment, and therefore, limited ability to access prior knowledge (Spaan, Raaijmakers, & Jonker, 2005). In this instance, credulity can be seen as an outcome of underlying memory deficits in much the same way that gullibility can be seen as an outcome of deficits in personal competence. Accordingly, credulity and gullibility are both conceptualized in the current framework as outcomes, or indicators of social vulnerability, and located at the hub of the wheel arrangement.

Having presented a framework for understanding social vulnerability and its correlates in older people, the potential impact of deficits in each of the personal competence domains on social vulnerability will now be considered in more detail.

CORRELATES OF SOCIAL VULNERABILITY IN OLDER ADULTS ACCORDING TO THE PROPOSED PERSONAL COMPETENCE FRAMEWORK

According to the proposed model, avoiding exploitation may require a complex array of intellectual and cognitive abilities to detect subtle nuances of deception and to rapidly formulate strategies to escape exploitive situations (Pinsker, Stone, Pachana, & Greenspan, 2006). Thus, significant changes in intellectual and cognitive functioning could trigger important questions pertaining to social vulnerability.

Intellectual Dysfunction and Social Vulnerability

Older adults with dementia and diminished intellectual functioning could experience progressive difficulties with making or communicating informed, rational decisions in situations involving deceit or manipulation. With regard to academic intelligence, diminished verbal reasoning skills, for example, could compromise one's ability to comprehend oral or written material presented by a would-be exploiter and to solve problems of a logical or social nature using language-based reasoning. Impairments in visuospatial reasoning could also impact on an array of abilities relevant to avoiding exploitation such as performing arithmetic calculations, operating electronic devices (e.g., automated teller machines and point- of-sale terminals), completing paperwork such as check slips, and reading and understanding financial statements and graphs (Tversky, 2005). Though more empirical evidence is needed to support this contention, deficits in verbal or visuospatial intelligence could affect negatively in potentially exploitive situations (Rotter, 1980). Therefore, it could be reasonably argued that clinical evaluation of such forms of vulnerability should involve a detailed assessment of intellectual functioning, as measured by standardized IQ tests.

With regard to practical intelligence, and as noted by Greenspan et al. (2001), limited understanding of physical, mechanical, or technical objects and processes in everyday settings could also contribute to exploitation. For example, an individual with limited knowledge of human physiological processes might be more readily coerced into purchasing expensive "miracle cures" for which there is little or no scientific evidence. At present, clinical assessment of practical intelligence in the context of exploitation poses a challenge, as there are few, if any, standardized instruments that specifically target this construct. However, qualitative information pertaining to dysfunction in this domain could be acquired though clinical interviews with the older person and family members.

Cognitive Dysfunction and Social Vulnerability

According to the framework, disruption to online cognitive processes such as memory and executive control, as distinct from intellectual functioning, could also contribute to exploitation in later life. As noted earlier, cognitive deficits that arise early in the course of Alzheimer's disease include impairments in episodic memory, access to semantic knowledge (Spaan et al., 2005), and executive functioning (Backman, Jones, Berger, Laukka, & Small, 2005; Baudic et al., 2006). Executive functions pertain to a complex array of processes involved in higher order reasoning (Baddeley, 1986, 1992; Chan, Shum, Toulopoulou, & Chen, 2008; Lezak, Howieson, & Loring, 2004; Miller & Cummings, 2007; Stuss & Benson, 1986). There is currently no single, universally accepted model to explain the entire range of these abilities. However, most authors converge on the idea that the executive suite of processes includes attention, planning, problem solving, initiation, sequencing, regulation, resistance to interference or distraction, response inhibition, abstraction, cognitive flexibility, speech production, and the temporary storage and manipulation of information (see Chan et al., 2008 for a review).

In the context of social vulnerability, disruption to memory processes could restrict the ability to encode and retrieve information relevant to evaluating false claims, for example, exploitive individuals who "remind" the victim of previous financial agreements that have not been honored. . . .

*****

. . . .With regard to clinical assessment, deficits in memory processes involved in encoding, consolidation, and retrieval may be intricately linked with exploitive susceptibility. A comprehensive memory assessment would, therefore, be indicated when assessing such forms of vulnerability. Individuals with moderate to severe impairment who are deemed to be at risk of exploitation could be referred for more extensive evaluations. Interventions that could assist the individual in everyday situations of vulnerability (e.g., when confronted by a persuasive door-to-door salesperson) include procedural memory training and compensatory strategies (Acevedo & Loewenstein, 2007).

Similarly, detailed assessment of executive functioning and an evaluation of the potential impact of impaired functioning on discerning and managing exploitive situations would be highly pertinent to addressing clinical questions of social vulnerability. Such cases support the need for rehabilitation specialists to carefully assess various aspects of executive functioning purported to underlie diminished planning and problem solving in vulnerable situations (e.g., through role plays) and to use the findings to guide appropriate education programs. According to the proposed framework, deficits in social intelligence and social skill could also have an impact on social vulnerability. These relationships will now be considered.

Social Dysfunction and Social Vulnerability

Appropriate interpersonal conduct is central to successful social interaction, and a probable correlate of social vulnerability, as accomplished social abilities could aid in detecting and avoiding exploitation. As noted earlier, there are facets of social functioning that are less related to observable behaviors (social skills) and more related to unobservable cognitive processes (social intelligence). The two social components of personal competence are discussed separately in the following section.

Social Intelligence and Social Vulnerability

Acts of exploitation typically involve manipulation, coercion, or deception in a social context. To avoid exploitation, an individual's chances are likely to improve considerably if he or she is able to discern the motives and intentions of others in order to predict their behavior. This ability has been termed *theory of mind* (ToM; for example, Baron-Cohen, 1989; Perner & Wimmer, 1985; Premack & Woodruff, 1978) and is thought to represent one among a number of social intelligence abilities. Though empirical research is needed to support a link between impaired ToM and social vulnerability, limitations in the ability to detect deceitful or dishonorable intentions in others could be expected to bestow a distinct disadvantage in situations involving exploitation.

*****

To the extent that deficits in self-awareness and ToM are linked with social vulnerability, clinical interventions to improve self-awareness could potentially reduce the risk of older adults falling victim to exploitation. A number of interventions for improving self-awareness have emerged from the literature on acquired brain injury (see Lucas & Fleming, 2005, for a review) that could prove potentially useful in cognitively impaired older people. For example, restorative or facilitatory techniques could be employed, which include education of the older person, behavioral therapy, and direct feedback from the therapist regarding task performance (e.g., problem solving based on exploitive scenarios). For individuals with severe impairments in self-awareness, which are unlikely to be amendable to restorative interventions, external compensation strategies may be required (e.g., intervention by a family member when the older person is confronted by a door-to-door vendor).

Social Skill and Social Vulnerability

Studies investigating the relationship between social skills and vulnerability to exploitation in later life are similarly lacking. However, deficits in social skills (e.g., communication and assertiveness) could also impinge on a person's ability to terminate exploitive interactions. A person with diminished verbal communication skills may have difficulty communicating his or her needs, even to alert family members, carers, or authorities to potentially exploitive incidences (Nerenberg, 2008). In this case, the clinician would need to evaluate the degree to which the person is able to comprehend information and communicate an appropriate choice.

*****

Various performance-based measures are available to assist the clinician with assessing social skills. Among these instruments are the Social Problem Solving Battery (Bellack, Morrison, Wixted, & Mueser, 1990) and Assessment of Interpersonal Problem Solving Skills (Donahoe et al., 1990; see Mueser & Bellack, 1998, for a comprehensive review of assessment methods). Where diminished social skills are likely to contribute to exploitation, clinicians could incorporate social skills training into the rehabilitation program. Identifying and enlisting the older person's social support network or community-based support systems, such as a visiting social service worker, may also be critical for optimizing the safety of older people.

In summary, because social intelligence and social skill may have unique but overlapping influences on social vulnerability, clinical assessments would ideally target both constructs to elucidate the potential impact of specific social impairments on everyday functioning. Appropriate cognitive and/or social skills training interventions could then be implemented to address specific ability deficits. Moreover, a greater awareness of the dangers confronting vulnerable older adults could be promoted through wider implementation of community education programs.

Motivation and Personality Traits, and Social Vulnerability

According to the proposed conceptual framework for older adults, and the conceptualization of Greenspan et al. (2001), motivation and personality characteristics could also contribute to greater social vulnerability. As noted earlier, the motivation/personality domain includes goals/needs, efficacy beliefs, and attention/affect. Coercive situations can present a considerable challenge for cognitively impaired older people both in attentional and affective terms. Personal needs arising from factors such as social isolation and loneliness could contribute to an older person complying with the demands of exploitive individuals to gain companionship (Dong, Simon, Gorbien, Percak, & Golden, 2007). Furthermore, cognitive and functional decline could lead to low self-efficacy and a dependency on others.

With regard to personality traits, a number of researchers in the area of individual differences have supported a 5-factor taxonomy of personality-based on the "Big Five" dimensions of Extroversion, Openness To Experience, Conscientiousness, Agreeableness, and Neuroticism (e.g., Goldberg, 1990, 1993; John, Angleitner, & Ostendorf, 1988; Koole, Jager, van den Berg, Vlek, & Hofstee, 2001; McCrae & John, 1992). Among the Big Five trait factors, Agreeableness may be particularly relevant to exploitation. Graziano and Eisenberg (1997) contended that individuals high on the Agreeableness trait factor are more disposed to cooperate with others than individuals low on Agreeableness. Koole et al. have shown that highly agreeable individuals are more responsive to feedback and are more willing to cooperate with other people in situations involving social dilemmas. Highly agreeable individuals may, therefore, be more inclined to willingly comply with other's requests than individuals low on Agreeableness, potentially placing them at greater risk of exploitation.

Clinical assessment of personality traits such as agreeableness, in addition to an assessment of the older person's needs and level of self-efficacy in relation to potentially exploitive situations, could provide important insights into particular aspects of personality and motivation that could lead to vulnerable behaviors. Personal needs, for example, loneliness, could be targeted with educational and social activity group interventions and community home-visiting schemes. To the extent that the older person is considered excessively agreeable, appropriate interventions could target compensatory defenses against this natural, and possibly unavoidable, tendency. In dealings with door-to-door vendors in particular, the family should be educated to remain watchful for potential situations of exploitation and intervene where necessary.

Physical Functioning and Social Vulnerability

According to Greenspan et al. (2001) and the framework proposed here, physical limitations could also contribute to social vulnerability. Diminished auditory and visual acuity, conditions that are comparatively common in old age, can result in an affected person missing important verbal and visual cues in exploitive situations (Quinn & Tomita, 1997). Alternatively, physical disability can limit an older person's means to perform or obtain a service in relation to financial matters and thereby result in less informed decision making (Quinn & Tomita, 1997). In older adults for whom clinical questions of social vulnerability arise, assessment of the person's physical functioning and the impact of physical and sensory impairments on promoting exploitive susceptibility should be weighed carefully in the

evaluation process. Interventions to enhance sensory function (e.g., auditory and visual aids) and physiotherapeutic training to improve mobility could be used to improve functional independence and better equip individuals to detect and avoid exploitive interactions.

In summary, this section has highlighted that dysfunction in one or more of the personal competence domains depicted in the proposed framework could contribute to exploitation but in different ways. Whereas more research is needed in this area, a systematic assessment of functioning in each domain of the framework could provide a more holistic assessment approach and inform the design and implementation of more appropriate rehabilitation and education programs to target vulnerability in older people. In the following section, methods currently used in clinical assessments of older adults are examined.

Assessment of Social Vulnerability

At present, clinical determinations of social vulnerability are largely based on the person's presentation at a clinical interview and performance on standardized neuropsychological tests. Neuropsychological assessment in geriatric populations typically focuses on measures of general cognitive status, memory, and "frontal" executive functions as purported correlates of social vulnerability (i.e., the domain of cognitive functioning in the proposed framework). Performance on cognitive measures is then used to infer everyday functional status (Spooner & Pachana, 2006). Whereas memory deficit and executive dysfunction could certainly promote social vulnerability, other potentially important dimensions of personal competence are often neglected in routine assessments.

Furthermore, neuropsychological tests may be sensitive to pathology in certain regions of the brain, but these measures are relatively insensitive to degeneration in other brain regions such as the ventromedial and orbitofrontal cortex (Gregory et al., 2002; Gregory, Serra-Mestres, & Hodges, 1999; Rahman,

Sahakian, Hodges, Rogers, & Robbins, 1999). From a neuroanatomical perspective, functions mediated by these areas are thought to play a pivotal role in high-level personal decision making, self-regulation, and social intelligence (Stuss et al., 2002). Similar neural substrates are likely to be involved in detecting exploitive interactions in social contexts. To date, however, social measures are not routinely administered in clinical assessments of older adults. According to the proposed framework, a recommended approach to assessment is to conceptualize such forms of vulnerability within a broader framework of personal competence that includes aspects of personality, physical functioning, and social abilities, as well as general cognitive functioning.

In addition to neuropsychological assessment, various elder abuse screening instruments have been developed that target symptoms of exploitation in a broader context of abuse (i.e., hub of the wheel in Figure 1). Instruments currently available for such purposes include the Elder Abuse Suspicion Index (EASI; Yaffe, Wolfson, Lithwick, & Weiss, 2006), the Indicators of Abuse Screen (IOA; Reis & Nahmiash, 1998), the Elder Assessment Instrument (EAI; Fulmer, 1984; Fulmer, Paveza, Abraham, & Fairchild, 2000; Fulmer & Whetle, 1986), and the Vulnerability to Abuse Screening Scale (VASS; Schofield & Mishra, 2003, see Fulmer et al., 2004, for a comprehensive discussion on existing elder abuse screening instruments).

The development of elder abuse screening instruments has assisted medical practitioners and social service providers with identifying older people in abusive relationships. It should be noted, however, that these instruments primarily target symptoms of abuse on a post hoc basis, and more predictive measures are needed. Furthermore, these instruments focus predominantly on symptoms of physical and psychological abuse and neglect. Financial exploitation, which represents a salient issue for many older people, has been somewhat neglected. Of the screening instruments that do include a financial component, only a few items are devoted to financial exploitation (e.g., EAI, VASS). Moreover, a tendency toward credulity and gullibility is a potentially important precipitant of exploitation (Greenspan et al., 2001). Nevertheless, these attributes are not directly addressed by any of the aforementioned screening instruments.

A simple approach to assessing credulity, gullibility, and social vulnerability more generally in older adults (i.e., hub of the wheel in Figure 1) would be in the form of a rating scale, analogous to a measure of adaptive behavior (e.g., Adaptive Behavior Assessment Scale; Harrison & Oakland, 2000), or what Greenspan et al. (2001) termed *practical intelligence*. An initial attempt to develop a standardized scale to assess such forms of vulnerability has been described previously (Pinsker et al., 2006). However, additional factor validation is needed to more firmly establish convergent and discriminant evidence for the efficacy of such a scale. Further refinement and development of similar instruments targeting constructs such as credulity and gullibility could offer promise in the future for detecting older people who may be most vulnerable to exploitation. Inception of a standardized scale would also enable empirical investigation of the relationships between personal competence domains and markers of vulnerability in everyday life.

CLINICAL APPLICATION AND FUTURE DIRECTIONS

There have been significant gaps in the conceptualization of social vulnerability and its assessment in research and applied settings. From an applied perspective, clinicians and health professionals working with older adults could use the framework proposed here to guide the assessment process, to aid with the interpretation of test results, and to inform the design and implementation of interventions for potentially vulnerable people. By ascertaining the person's level of functioning in each of the personal competence domains, intervention strategies could more directly target the areas of cognitive and social dysfunction that purportedly contribute to credulous and gullible acts in everyday life.

It would be recommended that professionals working with older people (a) assess functioning in each of the competence domains and consider how dysfunction might potentially contribute to exploitation without making strong assumptions about causality, (b) evaluate interactions between domains and their potential impact on social vulnerability, and (c) provide rehabilitation to the older person and educate him or her, and his or her family members, about the potential exploitive situations an older person might face, thus alerting them to future situations of potential exploitation and suggesting proactive strategies to more effectively manage these situations if they arise.

From a research perspective, given that there has been little prior work in the area of social vulnerability and related constructs such as *credulity* and *gullibility* in cognitively impaired older adults, a number of empirical questions could be pursued. Such questions could include the following: (a) Are cognitively impaired older people especially vulnerable to exploitation compared to neurologically healthy individuals? (b) Are particular domains of personal competence (e.g., specific cognitive functions) more predictive of social vulnerability than others? (c) Can improved interventions be developed to diminish the risk of exploitation? (d) Is there an optimal model of adaptive behavior for older people that strikes a balance between too much credulity and gullibility (extreme trust) and too little credulity and gullibility (extreme suspiciousness)? Whereas the aforementioned questions are by no means exhaustive, systematic investigations along these lines is recommended for future study.

Further research is also needed to examine cultural differences in social vulnerability. At present, generalizability of the conceptual framework to different populations of older people may be limited by cultural differences in perceptions of abuse and exploitation. Beliefs regarding reciprocity, helping behavior, family inheritance, and future beneficiaries could all influence perceptions of social vulnerability and exploitation. For example, sharing family resources might be an entrenched value in some cultures, whereas other cultures might support a belief that an older person's financial resources should be used solely by that person. Therefore, future research is needed to ascertain the nature and patterns of financial exploitation in different ethnic groups, cultural differences in perceptions of social vulnerability, and the extent to which cultural norms promote, or protect against, exploitation of older people.

*****

Funding

This research was supported by a University of Queensland Research Development Grant awarded to Valerie E. Stone, PhD, and Nancy A. Pachana, PhD, School of Psychology, The University of Queensland.

References

Acevedo, A., & Loewenstein, D. A. (2007). Nonpharmacological cognitive interventions in aging and dementia. *Journal of Geriatric Psychiatry and Neurology, 20*, 239–249.

American Psychiatric Association. (2000). *Diagnostic and statistical manual of mental disorders* (4th ed.). Washington, DC: Author.

Bach, L. J., & David, A. S. (2006). Self-awareness after acquired and traumatic brain injury. *Neuropsychological Rehabilitation, 16*, 397–414.

Backman, L., Jones, S., Berger, A. K., Laukka, E. J., & Small, B. J. (2005). Cognitive impairment in preclinical Alzheimer's disease: A meta-analysis. *Neuropsychology, 19*, 520–531.

Baddeley, A. D. (1986). *Working memory.* Oxford, UK: Oxford University Press.

Baddeley, A. D. (1992). Working memory. *Science, 31*, 556–559.

Bar-On, R. (2001). Emotional intelligence and self-actualization. In J. Ciarrochi, J. Forgas, & J. D. Mayer (Eds.), *Emotional intelligence in everyday life: A scientific inquiry* (pp. 82–97). New York: Psychology Press.

Baron-Cohen, S. (1989). The autistic child's theory of mind: A case of specific developmental delay. *Journal of Child Psychology and Psychiatry, 30,* 285–287.

Baudic, S., Dalla Barba, G., Thibaudet, M. C., Smagghe, A., Remy, P., & Traykov, L. (2006). Executive function deficits in early Alzheimer's disease and their relations with episodic memory. *Archives of Clinical Neuropsychology, 21,* 15–21.

Bellack, A., Morrison, R., Wixted, J., & Mueser, K. (1990). An analysis of social competence in schizophrenia. *British Journal of Psychiatry, 156,* 809–818.

Blunt, P. A. (1996). Financial exploitation: The best kept secret of elder abuse. *Aging, 367,* 62–65.

Chan, R. C. K., Shum, D., Toulopoulou, T., & Chen, E. Y. H. (2008). Assessment of executive functions: Review of instruments and identification of critical issues. *Archives of Clinical Neuropsychology, 23,* 201–216.

Choi, N., Kulick, D., & Mayer, J. (1999). Financial exploitation of elders: Analysis of risk factors based on county adult protective services data. *Journal of Elder Abuse and Neglect, 10,* 39–62.

Donahoe, C. P., Carter, M. J., Bloem, W. J., Hirsch, G. L., Laasi, N., & Wallace, C. J. (1990). Assessment of interpersonal problem-solving skills. *Psychiatry, 53,* 329–339.

Dong, X. Q., & Simon, M. A. (2008). Is greater social support a protective factor against elder mistreatment? *Gerontology, 54,* 381–388.

Dong, X. Q., Simon, M. A., Gorbien, M., Percak, J., & Golden, R. (2007). Loneliness in Chinese older adults: A risk factor for elder mistreatment. *Journal of the American Geriatrics Society, 11,* 1831–1835.

Fulmer, T. (1984). Elder abuse assessment tool. *Dimensions of Critical Care Nursing, 3,* 216–220.

Fulmer, T. (1991). Elder maltreatment: Progress in community detection and intervention. *Family and Community Health, 14,* 26–34.

Fulmer, T., Paveza, G., Abraham, I., & Fairchild, S. (2000). Elder neglect assessment in the emergency department. *Journal of Emergency Nursing, 26,* 436–443.

Fulmer, T., & Whetle, T. (1986). Elder abuse screening and intervention. *Nurse Practitioner, 11,* 33–38.

Gallup, G. G. (1998). Self-awareness and the evolution of social intelligence. *Behavioural Processes, 42,* 239–247.

Gallup, G. G., Anderson, J. R., & Platek, S. M. (2003). Self-awareness, social intelligence, and schizophrenia. In A. S. Turner & T. Kircher (Eds.), *The self in neuroscience and psychiatry* (pp. 147–+165). Cambridge, UK: Cambridge University Press.

Gardner, H. (1993). *Multiple intelligences: The theory in practice.* New York: Basic Books.

Goldberg, L. R. (1990). An alternative "description of personality": The Big-Five factor structure. *Journal of Personality and Social Psychology, 59,* 1216–1229.

Goldberg, L. R. (1993). The structure of phenotypic personality traits. *American Psychologist, 48,* 26–34.

Graziano, W. G., & Eisenberg, N. H. (1997). Agreeableness: A dimension of personality. In R. Hogan, J. Johnson, & S. Briggs (Eds.), *Handbook of personality psychology* (pp. 795–824). San Diego, CA: Academic Press.

Greenspan, S. (2005). Credulity and gullibility among service providers: An attempt to understand why snake oil sells. In J. W. Jacobson, R. M. Foxx, & J. A. Mulick (Eds.), *Controversial therapies for developmental disabilities: Fad, fashion, science in professional practice* (pp. 129–138). Mahwah, NJ: Lawrence Erlbaum.

Greenspan, S., Loughlin, G., & Black, R. S. (2001). Credulity and gullibility in people with developmental disorders: A framework for future research. *International Review of Research in Mental Retardation, 24,* 101–135.

Gregory, C., Lough, S., Stone, V. E., Erzinclioglu, S., Martin, L., Baron-Cohen, S., et al. (2002). Theory of mind in patients with frontal variant frontotemporal dementia and Alzheimer's disease: Theoretical and practical implications. *Brain, 125,* 752–764.

Gregory, C., Serra-Mestres, J., & Hodges, J. R. (1999). Early diagnosis of the frontal variant of frontotemporal dementia: How sensitive are standard neuroimaging and neuropsychologic tests? *Neuropsychiatry, Neuropsychology, and Behavioral Neurology, 45,* 128–135.

Harrison, P. L., & Oakland, T. (2000). *Adaptive behavior assessment system manual.* Orlando, FL: Harcourt Brace.

Jacoby, L. L. (1999). Deceiving the elderly: Effects of accessibility bias in cued-recall performance. *Cognitive Neuropsychology, 16,* 417–436.

John, O. P., Angleitner, A., & Ostendorf, F. (1988). The lexical approach to personality: A historical review of trait taxonomic research. *European Journal of Personality, 2,* 171–203.

Keenan, J. P., Gallup, G. G., & Falk, D. (2003). *The face in the mirror.* New York: HarperCollins.

Koole, S. L., Jager, W., van den Berg, A., Vlek, C. A. J., & Hofstee, W. K. B. (2001). On the social nature of personality: Effects of extraversion, agreeableness, and feedback about collective resource use on cooperation in a resource dilemma. *Personality and Social Psychology Bulletin, 27*, 289–301.

Kurrle, S., Sadler, P., & Cameron, I. (1992). Patterns of elder abuse. *Medical Journal of Australia, 157*, 673–676.

Lewis, T. (2001). Fifty ways to exploit your grandmother: The status of financial abuse of the elderly in Minnesota. *William Mitchell Law Review, 28*, 911–954. Lezak, M. D., Howieson, D. B., & Loring, D. W. (Eds.). (2004). *Neuropsychologicalassessment* (4th ed.). New York: Oxford University Press.

Lucas, S. E., & Fleming, J. M. (2005). Interventions for improving self-awareness following acquired brain injury. *Australian Occupational Therapy Journal, 52*, 160–170.

Marlowe, H. A. (1986). Social intelligence: Evidence for multidimensionality and construct independence. *Journal of Educational Psychology, 78*(1), 52–58.

McCrae, R. R., & John, O. P. (1992). An introduction to the five-factor model and its applications. *Journal of Personality, 60*, 175–215.

Miller, B. L., & Cummings, J. L. (Eds.). (2007). *The human frontal lobes: Functions and disorders.* New York: Guilford.

Mueser, K. T., & Bellack, A. S. (1998). Social skills and social functioning. In N. Tarrier (Ed.), *Handbook of social functioning in schizophrenia* (pp. 79–96). Boston: Allyn & Bacon.

National Research Council. (2003). A theoretical model of elder mistreatment. In R. J. Bonnie & R. B. Wallace (Eds.), *Elder mistreatment: Abuse, neglect, and exploitation in an Aging America* (pp. 60–70). Washington, DC: National Academies Press.

Nerenberg, L. (2008). *Elder abuse prevention: Emerging trends and promising strategies.* New York: Springer.

Perner, J., & Wimmer, H. (1985). "John thinks that Mary thinks that . . .": Attribution of second-order false beliefs by 5- to 10-year-old children. *Journal of Experimental Child Psychology, 39*, 437–471.

Pinsker, D. M., Stone, V. E., Pachana, N. A., & Greenspan, S. (2006). Social Vulnerability Scale for Older Adults: A validation study. *Clinical Psychologist, 10*, 109–119. Podnieks, E. (1992). National Survey on Abuse of the Elderly in Canada. *Journal of Elder Abuse and Neglect, 4*, 5–58.

Premack, D., & Woodruff, G. (1978). Chimpanzee problem-solving: A test for comprehension. *Science, 202*, 532–535.

Quinn, M. J., & Tomita, S. K. (1997). *Elder abuse and neglect: Causes, diagnosis, and intervention strategies* (2nd ed.). New York: Springer.

Rabiner, D. J., Brown, D., & O'Keeffe, J. (2004). Financial exploitation of older persons: Policy issues and recommendations for addressing them. *Journal of Elder Abuse and Neglect, 16*, 67–84.

Rabiner, D. J., O'Keeffe, J., & Brown, A. (2004). A conceptual framework of financial exploitation of older persons. *Journal of Elder Abuse and Neglect, 16*, 53–73.

Rahman, S., Sahakian, B. J., Hodges, J. R., Rogers, R. D., & Robbins, T. W. (1999). Specific cognitive deficits in early frontal variant frontotemporal dementia. *Brain, 122*, 1469–1493.

Reis, M., & Nahmiash, D. (1998). Validation of the Indicators of Abuse (IOA) screen. *The Gerontologist, 38*, 471–480.

Rotter, J. B. (1980). Interpersonal trust, trustworthiness, and gullibility. *American Psychologist, 35*, 1–7.

Schofield, M., & Mishra, G. (2003). Validity of a self-report screening scale for elder abuse: Women's Health Australia study. *The Gerontologist, 43*, 110–120.

Segrin, C., & Givertz, M. (2003). Methods of social skills training and development. In J. O. Greene & B. R. Burleson (Eds.), *Handbook of communication and social interaction skills* (pp. 135–176). Mahwah, NJ: Lawrence Erlbaum.

Sevdalis, N., Petrides, K. V., & Harvey, N. (2007). Predicting and experiencing decision-related emotions: Does trait emotional intelligence matter? *Personality and Individual Differences, 42*, 1347–1358.

Smith, R. (1999). *Fraud and financial abuse of older persons.* Canberra, ACT, Australia: Australian Institute of Criminology.

Spaan, P. E. J., Raaijmakers, J. G. W., & Jonker, C. (2005). Early assessment of dementia: The contribution of different memory components. *Neuropsychology, 19*, 629–640.

Spooner, D., & Pachana, N. (2006). Ecological validity in neuropsychological assessment: A case for greater consideration in research with neurologically intact populations. *Archives of Clinical Neuropsychology, 21*, 327–337.

Sternberg, R. J. (1985). *Beyond IQ: A triarchic theory of human intelligence.* New York: Cambridge University Press.

Sternberg, R. J. (1988). *The triarchic mind: A new theory of human intelligence.* New York: Viking.

Sternberg, R. J., Forsythe, G. B., Hedlund, J., Horvath, J. A., Wagner, R. K., Williams, W. M., et al. (2000). *Practical intelligence in everyday life.* New York: Cambridge University Press.

Stone, V. E., Baron-Cohen, S., & Knight, R. T. (1998). Frontal lobe contributions to theory of mind. *Journal of Cognitive Neuroscience, 10*, 640–656.

Stuss, D., Alexander, M. P., Floden, D., Binns, M. A., McIntosh, A. R., Rajah, M. N., et al. (2002). Fractionation and localization of distinct frontal lobe processes: Evidence from focal lesions in humans. In D. Stuss & R. T. Knight (Eds.), *Principles of frontal lobe function* (pp. 392–407). Oxford, UK: Oxford University Press.

Stuss, D., & Benson, D. F. (1986). *The frontal lobes.* New York: Raven Press.

Tversky, B. (2005). Visuospatial reasoning. In K. J. Holyoak & R. G. Morrison (Eds.), *Cambridge handbook of thinking and reasoning* (pp. 209–240). New York: Cambridge University Press.

Wechsler, D. (1997). *Wechsler adult intelligence scale- III/Wechsler memory scalethird edition technical manual.* San Antonio, TX: The Psychological Corporation.

Wilber, K. H., & Reynolds, S. L. (1996). Introducing a framework for defining financial abuse of the elderly. *Journal of Elder Abuse and Neglect, 8*, 61–80.

Wolf, R., & Pillemer, K. (1989). *Helping elderly victims.* New York: Columbia University Press.

Yaffe, M. J., Wolfson, C., Lithwick, M., & Weiss, D. (2006, October). *The Elder Abuse Suspicion Index: A method to improve identification of elder abuse by doctors.* Paper presented at the North American Primary Care Research Group Annual Meeting, Tucson, AZ.

23

HATE CRIMES ON CAMPUS

Racial/Ethnic Diversity and Campus Safety*

REBECCA L. STOTZER

EMILY HOSSELLMAN

*B*rown v. *Board of Education* marked an important turning point in the history of education in the United States. Rejecting the *Plessy* standard of "separate but equal," the *Brown* decision highlighted the importance of diversity in educational outcomes, but the scope and extent of diversity's impact as a policy strategy is still poorly understood. Some have even suggested that increasing diversity is not an exclusively positive experience for universities and colleges and that the increased focus on diversity can increase racial tensions, create self-segregation, and generate feelings of racial hostility (U.S. Department of Justice, 2000) if other structural features are not in place to create a truly inclusive environment (Hurtado, 1992). Taking into account these two possible outcomes—increased levels of racial harmony and understanding, or increased levels of racial hostility and aggression—this study examines the relationship between student and faculty racial/ethnic diversity in colleges and universities on the overall reported racial/ethnic hate crimes on campus. More specifically, this study examined whether or not increased presence of Blacks and Latinos (who are often perceived as "historically disadvantaged" in higher education) and Asian students (who are perceived as the "model minority"), as well as the percent of minority faculty, on campus would increase or decrease the number of reported hate crimes.

THE GOALS OF DIVERSITY IN HIGHER EDUCATION

Despite the ongoing legal debate, higher education has and continues to become increasingly diverse. Although diversity can be defined in

---

*This article was published in *Journal of Interpersonal Violence*, *27*, 644–661 (2012). We have deleted parts of the literature review and methodology, along with short passages from the discussion section.

many ways, reflecting "the presence of different points of view and ways of making meaning, which generally flow from the influence of different cultural and religious heritages" (Schneider, 1996, p. 5), given the history of racial/ ethnic challenges throughout the United States, the presence of racial/ethnic minorities on campus has become an issue that has received a high level of scrutiny. With the minority populations increasing in the United States, colleges and universities will be serving increasing numbers of students of color. The National Center for Educational Statistics (NCES) projects that current trends regarding increased enrollment of minority students will continue over the next 10 years. According to their most recent annual report, college enrollment will increase 4% for White students between 2007 and 2018, 26% for Black students, 38% for Hispanic students, 29% for Asian or Pacific Islander students, 32% for American Indian or Alaskan Native students, and 14% for nonresident aliens (Hussar & Bailey, 2009). Thus, whether through purposeful enrollment through mechanisms like affirmative action, or through the natural increase in college applications as minorities make strides toward equality in U.S. society over all, institutions of higher education will see increased enrollments of minority students.

For the past several decades, most universities and colleges have prioritized the inclusion of a diverse student body, with a particular focus on racial/ethnic diversity. This goal has been met with substantial legal challenge in the last decade. Courts at all levels are struggling with whether or not diversity is a compelling interest of the state, and thus, higher education. In particular, there is a question as to whether or not there are "academic freedoms" possessed by institutions of higher education in determining the composition of their student body that are in conflict with individual freedoms protected by the constitution and the Equal Protection Clause of the Fourteenth Amendment (Grossett, 2001; Notes, 1996). Courts have been split, but the dominant message sent from such cases as *Regents of the University of California v. Bakke*,

Grutter v. Bollinger, and *Gratz v. Bollinger* is that admissions policies must be narrowly tailored. However, the inability of the courts to present a clear reasoning for or against promoting diversity in the university community stems from a lack of information provided to the courts regarding the benefits and costs related to ensuring a diverse campus . . . .

*****

Existing research regarding racial perceptions and college students primarily focuses on individual outcomes for students. Antonio et al. (2004) looked at the effects of racial diversity on complex thinking of college students in small group settings and found a correlation between open-mindedness and the amount of racial diversity in a student's social group. Gurin (1999) found that students with increased exposure to diversity in college went on to have increased involvement in community organizations as adults. Gurin et al. (Gurin, Dey, Hurtado, & Gurin, 2002) found a positive relationship between students' social and classroom experiences with diverse peers and a variety of educational outcomes. Gottfredson et al. (2008) similarly found a positive correlation between diversity and educational outcomes and recommended that institutions of higher learning encourage informal interactions between students of diverse background as well as enrollment in classes that deal with diversity. Chang, Astin, and Kim (2004) found that both generic interactions in the classroom with a diverse group of students, as well as more intimate interactions such as dining with, dating, and studying with a diverse group of students, resulted in higher intellectual ability, better social ability, and higher rates of civic interests.

RACE RELATIONS ON CAMPUS

In one of the few works on strategies an institution can employ to improve racial/ethnic interaction on campus, Hurtado, Milem, Clayton-Pederson, and Allen (1999) describe a host of factors included in campus climate, such as institutional history of inclusion/exclusion, psychological climate (e.g. perceptions of racial tensions), behavioral dimension (e.g. social interactions across races), and structural diversity (diverse students, faculty, and staff). This multidimensional model of campus climate was validated in later research (Hutchinson, Raymond, & Black, 2008), suggesting that there are many features beyond just the presence of a numerically diverse campus community that will affect the overall impact of diversity.

There are two basic perspectives as to what may happen when the number of racial minority students increases. The first perspective is that a rise in minority representation in the student body would result in a negative or violent reaction from the majority students. The campus climate would be tenser, and "under conditions of increasing cultural diversity . . . the differences between groups become salient on an everyday basis. For the first time, many students must learn to deal with classmates and roommates who are *different*" (U.S. Department of Justice, 2000). This tension is evident in studies that ask students about their perceptions of campus climate, with minority studies reporting more experiences of bias than nonminority students (e.g., Rankin, 2003), and although these experiences are less frequently overt forms of bias, more subtle forms of bias are evident even in the classroom (Boysen, Vogel, Cope, & Hubbard, 2009). In fact, some argue that the more "mixed" a campus is, the higher the potential for campus ethnoviolence (Fenske & Gordon, 1998; Marcus, 1994).

There are many ways that students, faculty, and staff can experience institutional and interpersonal discrimination and violence, and hate crimes are a growing concern for campus safety. The Federal Bureau of Investigation defines hate crimes as those "crimes that manifest evidence of prejudice based on race, religion, sexual orientation, or ethnicity" (FBI, 2009) . . . .

In the famous typology of hate crime perpetrators, Levin and McDevitt (1993) found that the majority of hate crime perpetrators were not members of organized hate groups such as the Ku Klux Klan or Neo-Nazis. Rather, they found that most perpetrators engaged in crimes for a variety of personal reasons such as thrill seeking, to get revenge, or to defend territory. Most pertinent is their category of "retaliatory" hate crimes, where people who perceive that there is a wrongful incursion of racial/ethnic minorities into "White" spaces can lash out in an attempt to preserve territory. Given that colleges and universities are traditionally white domains, the increase of racial/ethnic minorities could potentially trigger resistance to their increasing presence through race-based hate crimes and other forms of ethnoviolence. However, retaliation can come in many forms, and Craig (1999) found that when African American students were exposed to a hate crime scenario, they reported being much more likely to come back to the scene of the crime with friends (which Craig interpreted as a desire to retaliate) compared to White students who saw the same vignette. Thus, hate crimes themselves can be a result of racial conflict, or act to spur further conflict.

Although many theorists propose that diversity can cause increased racial tension, the second perspective is that the increased numbers of minority students would begin to foster a campus climate that is tolerant of racial differences . . . .

*****

It is also important to keep in mind that "diversity" is not a monolithic concept and that different racial/ethnic groups trigger different responses from students, faculty, and administrators. In addition, when striving for the condition of "equal status" as outlined by Allport (1954), it is important to recognize that different racial/ethnic groups have different statuses in the educational system. Hurtado (1992) found that the more African American students were enrolled in a university or college, the higher the perceived racial tension among students, whereas higher Hispanic enrollment correlated with lower perceived racial tension. There is also the phenomenon of the "model minority" versus "historically disadvantaged" minorities bringing an additional layer to racial/ethnic diversity. Asians are often perceived as not needing help to get into college (Museus & Kiang, 2009); for example, Asians make up 11% of the population in California, but 40% of undergraduates admitted in the University of California system (Chea, 2009; Golden, 2004), and somewhat ironically, research has increasingly shown admissions standards that make it more difficult for Asians to be admitted. Conversely, Black and Latino students are often perceived as needing extra consideration in the admissions process, and schools often engage in aggressive recruitment and retention strategies that target these populations (e.g., Credle & Dean, 1991; McNairy, 1996). Espenshade and Chung (2005) found that if affirmative action policies were abandoned in higher education Blacks and Latinos would suffer while Asians would see the largest gains in admissions. Thus, model minority students and students who are perceived to have been admitted because of affirmative action may have a different meaning to White students and their sense of "protecting" academia from students of color.

Given that increased diversity has been predicted to either exacerbate or alleviate racial/ethnic tensions, this study was designed to examine whether the racial/ethnic diversity of a college or university is related to the rate of racially/ethnically motivated hate crimes on campus.

METHOD

Although no database exists that contains hate crimes on campuses across the United States, the FBI does collect data from colleges and universities that choose to participate in the annual Uniform Crime Reports. Technically, schools are supposed to report crimes, including hate crimes, to the Department of Education according to the Clery Act of 1992. However, most schools do not appear to realize that they are supposed to be including hate crimes in their

report (Lively, 1998). Thus, at this point the FBI data is the most comprehensive available.

Embedded in each year's report to the FBI is information about race, ethnicity, religion, sexual orientation, and disability based hate crimes that occur on campus. The first step in creating a database about hate crimes on campus was to extract the campus data from the FBI's reports from 1998 to 2008. Because hate crimes are an infrequently reported event and represents an unstable variable, it has been recommended that the reports from multiple years should be collapsed to represent any one geographic location (Alden & Parker, 2005). Thus, 10 years of data were then averaged to create a single variable that was the mean of the number of hate crimes in the reported years to represent the frequency of hate crimes at that institution.

The FBI data contain information pertinent to crimes, but not to universities. Thus, three other sources were utilized for information about the participating schools—the Carnegie Classification website, the National Center for Education Statistics, and the Princeton Review website . . . .

*****

The main hypothesis, consistent with evidence that shows positive outcomes of increasingly diverse institutional environments, is that an increase in diversity as measured by minority student enrollments and the presence of minority faculty will be associated with lower reported rates of hate crime when controlling for other factors. In particular, consistent with prior literature that emphasized the importance of the presence of historically disadvantaged groups on campus, we hypothesize that schools with the highest percentages of Blacks and Latinos will report the fewest hate crimes when controlling for other factors.

Institutional Demographics

A total of 418 baccalaureate degree (or higher)–granting colleges and universities are included in the sample for this article (see Table 1). The mean of the population of enrolled students is 13,027

Table 1   College and University Demographics

Number of reported racially based hate crimes per year	*M = 0.35*	*SD = 0.63*
Schools that reported at least one hate crime	*N* = 228	54.5%
Ratio of race/ethnic hate crime per 10,000 students	23	
School demographics	*M*	*SD*
Population of enrolled students (*n* = 418)	13,027.68	10,689.98
Percent of faculty who are minorities (*n* = 367)	15.94%	12.75
Student racial/ethnic demographics		
Percent of enrolled students—Black (*n* = 416)	12.73%	19.90
Percent of enrolled students—Latino (*n* = 411)	6.83%	11.40
Percent of enrolled students—Asian (*n* = 411)	4.75%	6.98
University characteristics		
School type (*n* = 418)	*N*	Percent
Public	354	84.7%
Private	64	15.3%
The ratio of graduates and undergraduates (*n* = 418)		
Exclusively undergraduate, 2-year duration	8	1.9%
Exclusively undergraduate, 4-year duration	10	2.4%
Very high undergraduate	150	35.9%
High undergraduate	194	46.4
Majority undergraduate	49	11.7%
Majority graduate/professional	7	1.7%
How selective is the school? (*n* = 418)		
Inclusive	86	20.6%
Selective, high transfer	159	38.0%
Selective, low transfer	49	11.7%
More selective, high transfer	48	11.5%
More selective, low transfer	76	18.2%

(Continued)

Table 1 (Continued)

Number of reported racially based hate crimes per year	M = 0.35	SD = 0.63
Degree of students living on campus (n = 418)		
Primarily nonresidential	154	36.8%
Primarily residential	190	45.5%
Highly residential	74	17.7%
Region of the country (n = 418)		
Midwest	84	20.1%
Northeast	87	20.8%
South	185	44.3%
West	62	14.8%
Historically Black universities (n = 418)		
Yes, historically Black	26	6.2%
Policies		
State Hate Crime Law (n = 418)	N	Percent
Yes	368	88.0%
Mandatory law enforcement training	N	Percent
(n = 418)		
Yes	105	25.1%

(SD = 10,689) students. Included in the sample are 354 (84.7%) public universities and 64 (15.3%) private universities. In considering the ratio of graduates and undergraduates, most had more undergraduate students than graduate students. Most were schools considered inclusive or selective with a high transfer rate and most were primarily or highly residential. Of the universities in the sample, the majority were located in states with hate crime laws that included race and ethnicity, whereas the majority of schools were located in states that did not have mandatory law enforcement hate crime training.

Regarding the primary variables of interest, the mean percent of faculty who are minorities is 15.94% (SD = 12.75), enrolled Black students is 13.9% (SD = 20.76), enrolled Latino students is 7.69% (SD = 12.01), and enrolled Asian students is 4.95% (SD = 7.17).

Analysis

Because hate crime data are comprised of count data that is not normally distributed, and the mean is smaller than the standard deviation, a standard OLS regression cannot be used, and instead, nonnegative binomial regression is appropriate. Of those schools in which hate crime data were available, complete information along other demographic variables was available for 347 colleges and universities.

First, a negative binomial regression was run including the eight control variables and the total number of minority faculty and Asian, Black, and Latino students with the variable of interest—the average number of hate crimes per year between 1998 and 2007. In this analysis, diversity did not appear to have an overall effect on reported hate crime rates (see Table 2). Contrary to the hypothesis, the racial/ethnic diversity of the student body and the faculty was not associated with overall hate crime rates. However, in the second model, which separated Asian students from Black and Latino students, an association between hate crimes and race/ethnicity of student body emerges. In this model, partially consistent with the hypothesis, schools that were more successful in being able to admit and enroll Black and Latino students reported fewer hate crimes per year. However, there was still no statistically significant effect for minority faculty. Given the importance of separating out those students who are the most disadvantaged, it is possible that this lack of effect for minority faculty may also be due to collapsing across racial and ethnic groups and further analysis is warranted.

Table 2 Results of Negative Binomial Regressions

	Overall minority enrollment		Enrollment by race/ethnicity	
	Coefficient	Significance	Coefficient	Significance
Cons	−1.49	***	−1.22	***
Number of enrolled students	0.0005	***	0.0005	***
State hate crime policy	−0.275		−0.282	
State police hate crime training	0.780	**	0.640	**
Public/private university	−0.685	*	−0.714	*
Carnegie enrollment profile	0.198		0.184	
Carnegie selectivity	0.203	*	0.157	*
Residentiality	0.434		0.149	
Historically Black college/university	−0.807		−0.162	
Percent Asian, Black, and Latino	−0.008		—	
Percent Black and Latino	—		−2.22	*
Percent Asian	—		01.11	
Percent minority faculty	0.009		0.013	

*$p < .05$. **$p < .01$. ***$p < .001$.

DISCUSSION AND CONCLUSIONS

Given the theoretical literature on the benefits and consequences of a more diverse learning environment in higher education, these results suggest a promising relationship between increased diversity of the student body and a reduced number of hate crimes on campus. Although the percentage of minority faculty and percentage of Asian students were not found to be significant, the percent of students who were Black or Latino at these institutions of higher education had a significant relationship with reported hate crimes, namely, as the percentage of Black and Latino students increased, the overall reported ethnic/race-based hate crimes decreased, even when controlling for a variety of other factors that can influence reporting rates. Although this relationship clearly cannot identify causation and the reasons for this association must be further explored, these results offer increased support for the importance of diversity on college and university campuses.

Rather than setting up a binary between whites and non-Whites, considering a more complex meaning of race is critical, particularly among minority groups are perceived as "struggling" versus those who are "succeeding." Asian students are often perceived as the "model minority" in higher education, having extremely successful rates of entry into college despite historical prejudices and biases barring them access to these institutions. One possible explanation for this association between increased presence of Blacks and Latinos and decreased hate crime rates is the efforts of the university/college itself to provide a more inclusive environment. This is not to say that Asian students and faculty do not matter in the overall diversity and sense of inclusiveness on a college or university campus. All groups make a significant educational contribution as their myriad voices and perspectives can be heard. These results suggest that one possible explanation for the relationship between hate crimes and racial/ethnic diversity is that colleges and universities that are more successful in enrolling students with a current and historical disadvantage may be more successful in part because of the atmosphere and commitment at the university. For example, after the California Board of Regents declared that they were no longer going to consider race in admissions in 1995, the number of Black and Latino applicants declined precipitously (Geiser, Ferri, & Kowarski, 2000). Some have cited the fact that the University of California system was perceived as no longer caring about Black and Latino students, so they would apply to colleges and universities that actually valued their enrollment (Weiss, 1997). Thus, those universities that are the most successful in reaching and enrolling Black and Latino students may be providing an atmosphere that is more inclusive for *all* students and that values diversity more than those that have lower enrollments of Blacks and Latinos.

However, another area worthy of exploration is how students, rather than the institutions, influence campus climate. It is possible that as tokenism is avoided and more Black and Latino students are enrolled and the overall composition of the student body is more diverse and diversity seems more commonplace. In addition, studies of the rural South during the lynching era have suggested that the relationship between increasing numbers of a minority and reported race-motivated bias may not be linear (e.g., Corzine, Creech, & Corzine, 1983), although what that association is has been questioned (Tolnay, Beck, & Massey, 1989). One suggestion is that as the population of a minority group increases, so does the sense of threat for the majority group, resulting in increased bias-motivated crime. However, past a certain point where the minority group moves toward the majority, the rate of bias-motivated crime decreases because of a hypothesized perception of increased threat of retaliation. This could be reflected on campus as well; when the percentage of Blacks and Latinos are too low, then there is actually increased risk of hate crime because of their token status, but when the percentage of Blacks and Latinos goes up, the risk decreases because of the threat of retaliation from Blacks and Latinos. Although these results suggest a relationship between increased Blacks and

Latinos and decreased reports of racial/ethnic hate crimes, it is not clear whether this is due to changes in the institution's climate from institutional sources, or from the students themselves. These results cannot tease apart these two possibilities, but given the multidimensionality of campus climate (Hurtado et al., 1999; Hutchinson et al., 2008), it is likely a combination of many factors outside of percentage of racial/ethnic minorities alone that are contributing to this relationship. However, this research highlights the importance of racial/ethnic minorities' presence on campus as an important starting point for considering how diversity is related to campus safety.

Whenever dealing with hate crime data, there are limitations that are inherent to accurate analysis. First, it has been cited repeatedly that due to collection strategies, there is an undercount of hate crimes, particularly among college/university students (Ehrlich, 2009) . . . . Second, there are some temporal concerns regarding the mismatch between the time frame of the variable of interest (hate crimes) and all those tested. To solidify the fragile hate crime variable, it is recommended that many years are collapsed together, but the independent variables all reflect a static picture of each school since data were collected about size, selectivity, and so on, on 2007–2008 numbers. Third, it is also important to note that this study included only baccalaureate or higher degree–granting institutions . . . . Fourth, other findings have suggested that hate crimes can be a reflection of changing social and community composition (Grattet, 2009), and changes to that composition can elicit prejudicial responses. Undoubtedly, many of these schools underwent changes in racial/ethnic composition, campus climate, and a host of other factors in that 10-year span that is reflected in the hate crime data and not in the demographic data. Thus, future research needs to find ways to capitalize on campus changes while still managing to take into account the instability of any one year's hate crime reports in any one location. Last, the importance of a diverse faculty, staff, and administration could only be touched on in this analysis with one lump evaluation of "minority faculty" provided by the *Princeton Review*. A more complex analysis of the importance of diversity at all levels of the educational institution needs to be examined.

Despite the limitations, these results are promising evidence of the effectiveness and importance of diversity on college and university campuses. Universities and colleges with higher percentages of Black and Latino students reported fewer hate crimes than less racially/ethnically diverse campuses, when controlling for other factors. Further research is needed to explore what factors contribute to the relationship between the increased presence of Black and Latino students on campus and decreased hate crimes. However, in addition to the prior research that suggests the relationship between racial/ethnic diversity and an institution's educational goals, these results suggest that an institutions' increased efforts to recruit minority students is related to campus safety as well.

REFERENCES

Alden, H. I., & Parker, K. F. (2005). Gender role ideology, homophobia and hate crime: Linking attitudes to macro-level anti-gay and lesbian hate crimes. *Deviant Behavior, 26*, 321–343.

Allport, G. W. (1954). *The Nature of Prejudice*. Reading, MA: Addison-Wesley

Anti-Defamation League. (2008). *Retain campus hate crime data collection improvements in Reauthorization of the Higher Educational Act.* Retrieved on February 10, 2010, from http://www.adl.org/combating_hate/letter_campus_hcd.asp

Antonio, A., Chang, M. J., Hakuta, K., Kenny, D. A., Levin, S., & Milem, J. F. (2004). Effects of racial diversity on complex thinking in college students. *Psychological Science, 15*, 507–510.

Boysen, G. A., Vogel, D. L., Cope, M. A., & Hubbard, A. (2009). Incidents of bias in college classrooms: Instructor and student perceptions. *Journal of Diversity in Higher Education, 2*, 219–231.

Chang, M. (1999). Does racial diversity matter? The educational impact of a racially diverse undergraduate population. *Journal of College Student Development, 40*, 377–395.

Chang, M. J. (2000). Improving campus racial dynamics: A balancing act among competing interests. *The Review of Higher Education, 23*(2), 153–175.

Chang, M. J., Astin, A. W., & Kim, D. (2004). Cross-racial interaction among undergraduates: Some consequences, causes, and patterns. *Research in Higher Education, 45*, 529–553.

Chea, T. (2009, April 24). University of California Admissions rule angers Asian Americans. *USA Today*. Retrieved March 1, 2010, from http://www.usatoday.com/news/education/2009–04–24-university-california-asian_N.htm

Choi, C. (2009). Affirmative action in education. *Georgetown Journal of Gender and the Law, 10*, 481–504.

Corzine, J., Creech, J., & Corzine, L. (1983). Black concentration and lynchings in the south: Testing Blalock's power-threat hypothesis. *Social Forces, 61*, 774–796.

Craig, K. M. (1999). Retaliation, fear, or rage: An investigation of African American and white reactions to racist hate crimes. *Journal of Interpersonal Violence, 14*, 138–151

Credle, J. O., & Dean, G. J. (1991). A comprehensive model for enhancing Black student retention in higher education. *Journal of Multicultural Counseling and Development, 19*(4), 158–165.

Duster, T. (1995). They're taking over! and other myths about race on campus. In M. Berube & C. Nelson (Eds.), *Higher education under fire: Politics, economics, and the crisis of the humanities.* New York, NY: Routledge.

Ehrlich, H. J. (1994). Campus ethnoviolence. In F. L. Pincus & H. J. Ehrlich (Eds.), *Race and ethnic conflict: Contending views on prejudice, discrimination, and ethnoviolence* (pp. 279–290). Boulder, CO: Westview.

Ehrlich, H. J. (2009). *Hate crimes and ethnoviolence: The history, current affairs, and future of discrimination in America.* Boulder, CO: Westview.

Espenshade, T. J., & Chung, C. Y. (2005). The opportunity cost of admission preferences at elite universities. *Social Science Quarterly, 86*, 293–305.

Federal Bureau of Investigation. (2009). *2008 hate crime statistics.* Retrieved on February 28, 2009, from http://www.fbi.gov/ucr/hc2008/abouthcs.html

Fenske, R. H., & Gordon, L. (1998). Reducing racial and ethnic hate crimes on campus: The need for community. In A. M. Hoffman, J. H. Schuh, &

R. H. Fenske (Eds.), *Violence on campus: Defining the problems, strategies for action* (pp. 123–148). Gaithersburg, MD: Aspen.

Geiser, S., Ferri, C., & Kowarsky, J. (2000). *Admissions briefing paper—underrepresented minority admissions at UC after SP-1 and Proposition 209: Trends, issues, and options.* Berkeley, CA: Student Academic Services, University of California, Office of the President.

Golden, D. (2004). *Are obstacles created equal?* Retrieved on February 15, 2010, from http://yellowworld.org/academia/203.html

Gottfredson, N., Panter, A., Daye, C. E., Allen, W. A., Wightman, L. F., & Deo, M. E. (2008). Does diversity at undergraduate institutions influence student outcomes? *Journal of Diversity in Higher Education, 1*, 80–94.

Grattet, R. (2009). The urban ecology of bias crime: A study of disorganized and defended neighborhoods. *Social Problems, 56*, 132–150.

Gratz v. Bollinger, 539 U.S. 244 (2003).

Grossett, J. D. (2001). Upholding racial diversity in the classroom as a compelling interest. *Case Western Reserve Law Review, 52*, 339–369.

Grutter v. Bollinger, 539 U.S. 306, 332 (2003).

Gurin, P. (1999). New research on the benefits of diversity in college and beyond: An empirical analysis. *Diversity Digest, 3*(3). Retrieved January 1, 2010, from http://www.diversityweb.org/Digest/Sp99/benefits.html

Gurin, P., Dey, E., Hurtado, S., & Gurin, G. (2002). Diversity and higher education: Theory and impact on educational outcomes. *Harvard Educational Review, 72*(3), 330–367.

Herring, C. (2009). Does diversity pay? Race, gender, and the business case for diversity. *American Sociological Review, 74*, 208–224.

Hurtado, S. (1992). The campus racial climate: Contexts of conflict. *Journal of Higher Education, 63*(5), 539–569.

Hurtado, S., Milem, J., Clayton-Pederson, A., & Allen, W. (1999). *Enacting diverse learning environments: Improving the climate for racial/ethnic diversity in higher education* (ASHE-ERIC Higher Education Report, Vol. 26, No. 8). Washington, DC: The George Washington University, Graduate School of Education and Human Development.

Hussar, W. J., & Bailey, T. M. (2009). *Projections of education statistics to 2018* (NCES 2009–062). Washington, DC: National Center for Education Statistics, Institute of Education Sciences, U.S.

Department of Education. Retrieved from http://nces.ed.gov/pubs2009/2009062.pdf

Hutchinson, S. R., Raymond, K. J., & Black, K. R. (2008). Factorial invariance of a campus climate measure across race, gender, and student classification. *Journal of Diversity in Higher Education, 1*, 235–250.

Levin, J., & McDevitt, J. (1993). *Hate crimes: The rising tide of bigotry and bloodshed*. New York, NY: Plenum.

Lively, K. (1998, May 8). Most colleges appear unaware of requirement that they track hate crimes. *Chronicle of Higher Education* (Students section), p. A57.

Marcus, L. R. (1994). Diversity and its discontents. *Review of Higher Education, 17*, 225–240.

McNairy, F. G. (2006). The challenge for higher education: Retaining students of color. *New Directions for Student Services, 74*, 3–14.

Museus, S. D., & Kiang, P. N. (2009). Deconstructing the model minority myth and how it contributes to the invisible minority reality in higher education research. *New Directions for Institutional Research, 142*, 5–15.

Notes. (1996). An evidentiary framework for diversity as a compelling interest in higher education. *Harvard Law Review, 109*, 1357–1374.

Park, R. E. (1949). *Race and Culture*. New York: Free Press of MacMillan.

Pascarella, E., Edison, M., Nora, A., Hagedorn, L. S., Terenzini, P. T., & Amaury, N. (1996). Influences on students' openness to diversity and challenge in the first year of college. *Journal of Higher Education, 67*(2), 174–195.

Pettigrew, T., & Tropp, L. (2006). A meta-analytic test of intergroup contact theory. *Journal of Personality and Social Psychology, 90*(5), 751–783.

Rankin, S. R. (2003). Campus climates for sexual minorities. *New Directions for Student Services, 111*, 17–23.

Rayburn, N. R, Earleywine, M., & Davison, G. C. (2003). Base rates of hate crime victimization among college students. *Journal of Interpersonal Violence, 18*, 1209–1221.

Regents of the University of California v. Bakke, 438 U.S. 265 (1978).

Schneider, C. G. (1996). Diversity & community. *Liberal Education, 82*, 4–12.

Stotzer, R. L. (2010). Sexual orientation-based hate crimes on campus: The impact of policy on reporting rates. *Sexuality Research and Social Policy, 7*, 147–154.

Tolnay, S. E., Beck, E. M., & Massey, J. L. (1989). Black lynchings: The power threat hypothesis revisited. *Social Forces, 67*, 605–621.

U.S. Department of Justice. (2000). *Responding to hate crimes and bias-motivated incidents on college/university campuses*. Washington, DC: Author.

Weiss, K. R. (1997, February 5). Applications to UC hit a record high: But the number of African Americans and Latinos seeking admission falls for second year in a row. *Los Angeles Times*. Retrieved on February 19, 2010, from http://aad.english.ucsb.edu/docs/UC-apps.html

Wessler, S., & Moss, M. (2001). Hate crimes on campus: *The problem and efforts to confront it*. Washington, DC: U.S. Department of Justice, Office of Justice Programs.

24

Expect Respect Support Groups

Preliminary Evaluation of a Dating Violence Prevention Program for At-Risk Youth*

Barbara Ball

Andra Teten Tharp

Rita K. Noonan

Linda Anne Valle

Merle E. Hamburger

Barri Rosenbluth

Introduction

The prevalence and consequences of teen dating violence make it a public health concern (Eaton, Davis, Barrios, Brener, & Noonan, 2007) that calls for early and effective prevention. Despite recent legislation in multiple states that requires schools to provide teen dating violence education, to date, only three prevention strategies—Safe Dates, the Youth Relationships Project (YRP), and the 4th R (Foshee et al., 1998; Wolfe et al., 2009, 2003)—have demonstrated reductions in dating violence behaviors in rigorous, controlled evaluations. In order to protect young

---

*This article was published in *Violence Against Women*, *18*, 746–762 (2012). We have removed portions of the literature review and method, as well as all the tables.

people and build an evidence base of effective prevention strategies, evaluation of additional programs is needed, including those programs currently in the field (Teten, Ball, Valle, Noonan, & Rosenbluth, 2009).

The Expect Respect program has been developed over the past 20 years by SafePlace, a domestic violence and sexual assault victim service provider in Texas, and offers a comprehensive prevention model, including community engagement; school-wide, universal prevention strategies; youth leadership training; and a selective dating violence prevention program for at-risk youth. In 2003, the Expect Respect program was one of four programs chosen by the Centers for Disease Control and Prevention (CDC) to participate in an empowerment evaluation project that aimed to build capacity in the community agency for program improvement, manual development, and evaluation and to develop a knowledge base of evidence-based prevention efforts (Gibbs, Hawkins, Clinton-Sherrod, & Noonan, 2009; Noonan & Gibbs, 2009).

The empowerment evaluation and the current study focused on a unique component of the Expect Respect program, namely school-based support groups for at-risk youth who have experienced violence at home and/or in their peer and dating relationships. Weekly, separate sex groups, based on a 24-session curriculum (Ball, Rosenbluth, & Aoki, 2008), provide boys and girls a place to share their experiences, give and receive emotional support, and learn skills for healthy relationships. In 2007-2008, SafePlace provided 26 support groups in 16 secondary schools. This preliminary, uncontrolled evaluation is a first step in demonstrating outcomes of a selective, school-based teen dating violence prevention program that is being widely used locally and disseminated nationally. Although violence perpetration and victimization in dating relationships are the targeted outcomes of Expect Respect support groups, this preliminary evaluation asked participants to report on behaviors in

their dating or close peer relationships as these behaviors were considered to be interrelated. Both students who were and were not dating at the time of the intervention were intended to be included in the evaluation.

BACKGROUND: PEER AND DATING VIOLENCE AMONG TEENS

Prevalence

Teens are at risk for experiencing dating abuse, including emotional abuse and physical and sexual violence, beginning with the initiation of dating relationships during early adolescence. A majority of dating 11- to 14-year-olds (62%) report that they know friends who have been verbally abused and one in five 13- to 14-year-olds (20%) say they know friends and peers who have been physically abused by a dating partner (Teen Research Unlimited, 2008). . . .

Risk Factors

A public health approach to prevention suggests targeting risk factors for dating violence that exist at multiple levels, including the individual, relationships, community, and society. Expect Respect support groups target youth with risk factors at the relational level, namely, aggressive or violent family and peer environments. Multiple studies suggest that teens' experiences with violence in their family (witnessing interparental violence; child maltreatment) are linked with the perpetration of dating violence (e.g., O'Keefe, 1998; Wolfe, Wekerle, Scott, & Pittman, 2001) and with the perpetration of peer and delinquency-related violence (e.g., Brendgen, Vitaro, Tremblay, & Wanner, 2002; Resnick, Ireland, & Borowsky, 2004). Furthermore, recent research (Pepler et al., 2006) points to a continuum of interpersonal violence from bullying in peer relationships to teen dating violence. Boys and girls who use power and aggression in their peer relationships, as evidenced by bullying behaviors or conduct problems, are also more likely to sexually harass same- and opposite-sex peers and are more likely to be physically aggressive with their dating partners (Brendgen et al., 2002; Pepler et al., 2006; Williams, Conolly, Pepler, Craig, & Laporte, 2008). Arriaga and Foshee (2004) found that having friends in violent relationships more strongly predicted dating violence perpetration and victimization than witnessing interparental violence. Multiple experiences of violence in relationships across social contexts, lack of positive role models, and violence-supportive peer group norms (Reed et al., 2008) appear to be interacting factors that increase the risk for experiencing or inflicting peer and dating violence.

PREVENTION FOR AT-RISK YOUTH

Prevention approaches for dating violence may be applied universally to all individuals in a population or selective, and more intensive prevention approaches may be developed for those youth who are at increased risk for dating violence perpetration or victimization (Eaton et al., 2007; Pepler et al., 2006; Whitaker et al., 2006; Williams et al., 2008; Wolfe et al., 2003). Universal approaches are often didactic and classroom based, aiming to educate teens about healthy and abusive relationships (e.g., Avery-Leaf, Cascardi, O'Leary, & Cano, 1997; Foshee et al., 1998; Jaffe, Suderman, Reitzel, & Killip, 1992; Schewe, 2002; Wolfe et al., 2009) with the most prominent and rigorously evaluated programs being Safe Dates and the 4th R. In contrast, selective approaches may be tailored to the particular needs of the at-risk group and offered during the school day but outside of a classroom curriculum. Because some students may evidence higher risk for dating violence, the intensity of a selective, in addition to (or in place of), a universal strategy may be needed for these students (e.g., Eaton et al., 2007; Whitaker et al., 2006) . . . .

*****

THE EXPECT RESPECT PROGRAM

The Expect Respect program began in 1988 when school counselors requested services for girls in abusive relationships. SafePlace counselors initially adapted materials and methods from their work with adult battered women to educate girls about abusive and healthy relationships and to increase supportive peer relationships at school. Recognizing the specific needs for preventing dating violence among at-risk youth, SafePlace developed the Expect Respect support group program for girls and then expanded it for boys in middle school and high school. Separate-sex groups are intended to increase participants' sense of emotional safety and comfort, allow them to bond more quickly and more freely explore their expectations for relationships. Groups are led by same-sex facilitators who endorse and model nonviolent, gender-equitable behavior. To maximize accessibility Expect Respect support groups are offered in the school, a social environment where about 40% of the worst dating violence incidents occur (Molidor et al., 2000).

Expect Respect addresses dating violence among at-risk students as a problem that is fueled by gender norms that promote male dominance, the need to control and exert power, negative role models among adults and peers, acceptance and justification of violence, trauma, and a deficit in social skills. The curriculum (Ball et al., 2008) is based on 20 years of experience with implementing boys' and girls' groups and is informed by interviews with group participants and group facilitators. The 24 sessions are structured around five units: (a) developing group skills (5 sessions), (b) choosing equality and respect (5 sessions), (c) recognizing abusive relationships (5 sessions), (d) learning skills for healthy relationships (5 sessions), and (e) becoming active proponents for safe and healthy relationships (4 sessions). Each 55-minute group session consists of a brief check-in (5 min), an educational component (15 min), group activities and discussion (30 min), and a wrap-up (5 min). Group activities include role plays, educational videos, and creative expression through art and poetry and are designed to engage students in a variety of learning experiences. Relationship skills, such as listening, providing emotional support, sharing personal experiences, expressing emotions, and problem solving, are practiced in activities and are also an integral part of the group process. Support group facilitators work creatively with the curriculum, adapt the activities and discussion topics to the specific needs of their group, and allow time for handling crises, individual concerns, and group dynamics (Kendall, Chu, Gifford, Hayes, & Nauta, 1999).

*****

Method

Participants

Students were primarily referred by school counselors and teachers, although self-referrals occurred as well. Expect Respect facilitators provided orientation sessions for school staff to raise awareness about risk factors and warning signs of teen dating violence, to promote the program, and to obtain referrals. The program was also advertised in schools through posters and school newsletters.

*****

Only students who reported being the victim or perpetrator of at least one form of previous violence (domestic violence, child maltreatment, peer violence, including bullying and sexual harassment, dating violence, sexual violence) were eligible for the program and completed a baseline assessment at the end of the intake interview. Expect Respect facilitators explained to students that the group would last 24 sessions, that participation was voluntary, and that the following topics would be covered: developing group skills, defining equality and respect, recognizing abusive relationships, learning skills for conflict resolution, and raising awareness among peers. Facilitators met with students in

weekly group sessions at school, in a private and consistent location.

The program evaluation included Expect Respect support group members from seven middle schools and nine high schools in an urban area in the South Central United States. Because some schools offered more than one group, a total of 26 support groups were provided in 2007-2008. Of these, 14 groups were boys' groups and 12 were girls' groups. A total of 276 eligible students completed an intake interview and a baseline assessment; of these, 20 were referred for a higher level of services and 13 declined to participate in a group, resulting in 243 eligible and enrolled participants.

An additional assessment was completed during the next-to-last group session. A total of 144 students, 59% of the eligible and enrolled students, completed assessments at both baseline and completion and constitute the sample for these analyses. Students who did not participate in the completion assessment were not significantly different on measures of perpetration, $F(1, 272) = 1.22$, $p = .27$; victimization, $F(1, 272) = 2.57$, $p = .11$; or use of healthy relationship skills, $F(2, 272) = 0.08$, $p = .78$, as assessed at intake. Reasons for not participating in the completion assessment included dropping out as a result of changing schools ($n = 52$), unspecified reasons ($n = 10$), conflicts with academic requirements ($n = 7$), arrest or removal to the alternative learning center ($n = 4$), and absence on the day of the completion assessment ($n = 27$).

Of the 144 students with data at both time points, 54% ($n = 77$) were male and 46% ($n = 67$) were female. As much as 65% of students ($n = 92$) were Hispanic, 21% ($n = 30$) were non-Hispanic Black, 5% ($n = 7$) were non-Hispanic White, and 9% ($n = 12$) indicated their ethnicity as "Other" or "multiracial". Forty-two percent of students ($n = 60$) attended groups in middle schools (Grades 6-8) and 58% ($n = 84$) were in high school (Grades 9-12). Groups consisted of students of various grade levels at their respective school.

During the 2007–2008 school year, the average group length for girls was 23 sessions ($SD = 2$) and for boys 18 sessions ($SD = 2$). External circumstances, such as mandated testing days, resulted in a shortened program for some boys' groups. Due to the flexible nature of the curriculum that provides multiple and repeated opportunities for participants to practice new skills, facilitators were able to condense the curriculum while still covering all content areas. Participants in shorter groups, however, may have had less time to engage in personal sharing and group bonding activities. Girls who completed both assessments at baseline and program completion attended an average of 17 group sessions ($SD = 5$; 75% of sessions offered); boys who completed both assessments attended an average of 12 group sessions ($SD = 5$; 71% of sessions offered).

*****

Measures

Measures were selected to reflect the key program goals of decreasing emotional and physical abuse perpetration and victimization and increasing healthy conflict resolution skills. In the process of developing the assessment instrument, we reviewed the Conflict in Adolescent Dating Relationships Inventory (CADRI; Wolfe, Scott et al., 2001) and the measures used in the Safe Dates evaluation (Foshee et al., 1998). The assessment instrument for this study was developed to match the reading level of participants and to be concise enough to be completed in approximately 20 minutes, which was believed necessary to avoid response fatigue.

*****

The instructions for the items in the baseline and completion assessment were: "In the past 3 months, when you had a conflict or an argument with your boyfriend, girlfriend, or a close friend how often did the following things happen?" Each question was asked twice, once in relation to the participant's behaviors toward a boyfriend/girlfriend or close friend and once in relation to a boyfriend's/girlfriend's or close friend's behavior toward the participant. Participants responded on a 4-point Likert-type scale where, $3 = Often$, $2 = Sometimes$, $1 = Rarely$, and $0 = Never$ . . . .

Violence in peer and dating relationships. Violence perpetration/victimization was assessed using a 10-item scale, containing 8 items on emotional violence perpetration/victimization (e.g., "I made fun of them in front of others, I blamed them for bad things I did") and 2 items on physical abuse perpetration/victimization (e.g., "I slapped them, I threw something at them"). At pretest, the perpetration scale had a Cronbach's alpha of .88; the victimization scale had a Cronbach's alpha of .90.

Healthy conflict resolution in peer and dating relationships. Healthy conflict resolution was assessed using 10 items (e.g., "I offered a solution that would make us both happy, I put off talking until we both calmed down"). Behaviors reported for self and boyfriend/girlfriend or close friend were combined in one scale. The Cronbach's alpha for the healthy conflict resolution scale was .90 at pretest.

Data Analysis

A total of 144 participants completed at least part of the baseline and completion questionnaires. Because a few participants did not answer all questions, we utilized listwise deletion, such that for some analyses, the sample population was slightly less than 144. Although only 144 participants completed a posttest, noncompleters and completers did not differ on reports of violence at baseline, though they may have differed on variables we did not assess.

*****

RESULTS

. . . No significant mean difference between pre- and post-tests was identified for violence victimization or perpetration. Support group participants reported using significantly more healthy conflict resolution skills at posttest than at pretest, $t(142) = -3.31, p = .001$.

We then identified participants who reported violent victimization and perpetration means that were at least 1 standard deviation above the group mean at pretest. For victimization, 24 participants had means greater than 2.05, and 24 participants had perpetration means greater than 1.88. These groups were not mutually exclusive, and 15 (62.5%) of the students identified as high risk for perpetration were also at high risk for victimization, $\chi^2 = 43.16$, $p < .001$. Because of the substantial overlap between groups, which indicated many of the students who reported victimization at pretest also reported perpetration, we collapsed victimization and perpetration categories, such that participants with means at least 1 standard deviation above the mean for victimization or perpetration were included in the high-risk group ($n = 33$). . . .

For the exploratory analysis to identify potential mediators and moderators of change, we examined pretest behaviors and participant characteristics that predicted posttest outcomes for the full sample . . . . Victimization at pretest was a positive predictor of victimization at posttest, indicating participants who reported victimization at pretest were more likely to report they were still experiencing victimization at posttest. Perpetration at pretest negatively predicted victimization at posttest, suggesting participants who reported perpetrating at pretest were significantly less likely to report victimization at posttest. Perpetration at pretest and number of sessions attended positively predicted perpetration at posttest, suggesting participants who attended a greater number of sessions and participants who reported perpetration at pretest were more likely to report perpetration at posttest. The effect of sessions on perpetration, though significant, was very small, $\hat{a} = .02$, and may be accounted for by increased awareness and reporting as a result of program participation. Nonetheless, the result bears investigation in subsequent studies. Use of healthy conflict resolution skills at posttest was predicted by the use of healthy conflict resolution skills at pretest as well as by female sex. In other words, girls were more likely than boys to report using healthy conflict resolution skills. Therefore, across

outcomes, reporting a behavior at pretest predicted use of the same behavior 24 sessions later for the full sample and some outcomes varied by sex and attendance.

DISCUSSION

Expect Respect support groups are designed for students who have witnessed domestic violence, experienced child maltreatment and/or sexual violence, or who are involved in abusive peer and dating relationships. The intervention aims to increase healthy conflict resolution behaviors and reduce or prevent dating and peer violence perpetration and victimization by providing opportunities for skill building in a supportive peer group setting. The study showed that among support group participants, there is a subgroup of teens who already experience or perpetrate violence in their peer and dating relationships.

The evaluation of Expect Respect support groups demonstrated that reports of healthy conflict resolution behaviors increased over the course of the intervention for the full sample, indicating that one critical objective of the support group intervention was met. The quantitative results mirror the earlier findings from interviews with support group participants (Ball et al., 2009), who spoke at length about the importance of gaining communication and conflict resolution skills as a result of the program. It appears that the support group format and extended duration of the intervention were successful at increasing the healthy conflict resolution skills of these at-risk students, whereas other prevention programs, including Safe Dates and the YRP, have not consistently demonstrated such outcomes (Whitaker et al., 2006). Interesting questions arise from our finding that higher levels of reported healthy conflict resolution skills at posttest did not appear to translate into less victimization and perpetration.

Contrary to our hypothesis we did not find a reduction in victimization and perpetration over the course of the intervention when considering results for the full sample. Due to the limitations of this study, its reliance on self-report measures and lack of a control group we cannot fully interpret the lack of positive change for the whole group with regard to violence perpetration and victimization. Data from the national Youth Risk Behavior Survey (CDC, 2008) indicate that prevalence rates for dating violence may increase with age. It is therefore possible that though levels of peer and dating violence were unchanged for all the participants, the participants did in fact experience and perpetrate less violence than other at-risk youth who did not receive the intervention. Replication in a larger sample with a comparison group is needed to further understand the nature of these findings

Given our group of at-risk students, it seemed warranted to differentiate participants according to the frequency of perpetration and victimization they reported at baseline. This exploratory analysis offered some critical insights into different profiles of youth and program outcomes. The subgroup of students who reported levels of victimization and perpetration with means at least 1 standard deviation above the group mean at baseline reported significantly less victimization and perpetration after participating in the support groups suggesting that they benefitted most from the intervention. Once a week, confidential support groups may address the unique needs of these students for ongoing emotional support, positive peer relationships, and opportunities to practice new skills in an emotionally safe and supportive environment.

No sex differences in violence perpetration or victimization were found in response to the intervention, but girls were more likely to report using healthy conflict resolution skills at posttest than boys. There was also a small, but significant, effect of number of sessions attended on perpetration reported at posttest. As noted above, the increase in perpetration may reflect greater comfort with reporting perpetration and greater awareness of abusive behaviors as a result of participating in the program, but this finding is in need of further investigation.

The voluntary nature of support group participation and the high mobility of at-risk students contributed to attrition from intake to completion. Although no significant differences were observed between program completers and noncompleters, future studies should include efforts to maintain students in the intervention.

Other limitations resulted from adapting and shortening scales, especially for physical and emotional violence, and given the length of the assessment, the inability to assess context and frequency of violence, impact, and injury, . . .

Finally, we included nondating violence, that is, violence in close, peer relationships, as well as dating relationships. Combining these forms of violence complicates interpretation of results and may have obscured program effects. Future studies may be enhanced by differentiating peer relationship violence from dating violence. Despite these qualifications, our findings begin to lend empirical support to the effectiveness of a support group program that targets students at high risk for violence in peer and dating relationships.

We and others have demonstrated that many students have risk factors that may increase their risk of dating and peer violence. As an alternative or in addition to universal approaches, it may be necessary to tailor programs and resources to the needs of youth with known and modifiable risk factors such as a history of family violence, child maltreatment, and aggressive peer relationships (e.g., Whitaker et al., 2006). This preliminary evaluation of Expect Respect support groups was a step toward building evidence for prevention programs targeting at-risk youth: Expect Respect support groups were useful in increasing participants' healthy conflict resolution skills, and the program appeared to be most successful for the youth who were at the highest risk for future perpetration and victimization.

Funding

The development of the Expect Respect Program Manual and the program evaluation were supported in part by Contract No. 200-2001-00123 from the Centers for Disease Control and Prevention (CDC), an Empowerment Evaluation Project for Programs Designed to Prevent First-Time Male Perpetration of Sexual Violence.

REFERENCES

Arriaga, X. B., & Foshee, V. A. (2004). Adolescent dating violence: Do adolescents follow in their friends' or parents' footsteps? *Journal of Interpersonal Violence, 19*, 162–184.

Avery-Leaf, S., Cascardi, M., O'Leary, K. D., & Cano, A. (1997). Efficacy of a dating violence prevention program on attitudes justifying aggression. *Journal of Adolescent Health, 21*, 11–17.

Ball, B., Kerig, K., & Rosenbluth, B. (2009). "Like a family but better because you can actually trust each other": The Expect Respect dating violence prevention program for at-risk youth. *Health Promotion Practice, 10*(1), 45–58.

Ball, B., Rosenbluth, B., & Aoki, A. (2008). *The Expect Respect Program manual. Part I: Support group curriculum and facilitator guide.* Austin, TX: SafePlace.

Brendgen, M., Vitaro, F., Tremblay, R. E., & Wanner, B. (2002). Parent and peer effects on delinquency-related violence and dating violence: A test of two meditational models. *Social Development, 11*, 225–244.

Capaldi, D. M., Dishion, T. J., Stoolmiller, M., & Yoerger, K. (2001). Aggression toward female partners by at-risk young men: The contribution of male adolescent friendships. *Developmental Psychology, 37*, 61–73.

Centers for Disease Control and Prevention. (2008). Youth risk behavior surveillance—United States, 2007. *Morbidity & Mortality Weekly Report, 57*(4), 1–131.

Cornelius, T., & Resseguie, N. (2007). Primary and secondary prevention programs for dating violence: A review of the literature. *Aggression and Violent Behavior, 12*, 364–375.

Eaton, D. K., Davis, K. S., Barrios, L., Brener, N. D., & Noonan, R. K. (2007). Associations of dating violence victimization with lifetime participation, co-occurrence, and early initiation of risk behaviors among U.S. high school students. *Journal of Interpersonal Violence, 22*, 585–602.

Foshee, V., Bauman, K., Arriaga, X., Helms, R., Koch, G., & Linder, G. (1998). An evaluation of Safe Dates, an adolescent dating violence prevention program. *American Journal of Public Health, 88*, 45–50.

Gibbs, D. A., Hawkins, S. R., Clinton-Sherrod, A. M., & Noonan, R. K. (2009). Empowering programs with evaluation technical assistance: Outcomes and lessons learned. *Health Promotion Practice, 10*(1), 38–44.

Hickman, L. J., Jaycox, L. H., & Aronoff, J. (2004). Dating violence among adolescents: Prevalence, gender distribution, and prevention program effectiveness. *Trauma, Violence, & Abuse, 5*, 123–142.

Jaffe, P., Suderman, M., Reitzel, D., & Killip, S. (1992). An evaluation of a secondary school primary prevention program on violence in intimate relationships. *Violence and Victims, 7*, 129–146.

Kendall, P. C., Chu, B., Gifford, A., Hayes, C., & Nauta, M. (1999). Breathing life into a manual: Flexibility and creativity with manual-based treatments. *Cognitive and Behavioral Practice, 5*, 177–198.

Loseke, D., & Kurz, D. (2005). Men's violence toward women is the serious social problem. In D. Loseke, R. Gelles, & M. Cavanaugh (Eds.), *Current controversies on family violence* (2nd ed., pp. 79–95). Thousand Oaks, CA: Sage.

Molidor, C., Tolman, R., & Kober, J. (2000). Gender and contextual factors in adolescent dating violence. *The Prevention Researcher, 7*(1), 1–4.

Noonan, R. K., & Gibbs, D. (2009). Empowerment evaluation with programs designed to prevent first-time male perpetration of sexual violence. *Health Promotion Practice, 10*(1), 5–10.

O'Keefe, M. (1998). Factors mediating the link between witnessing interparental violence and dating violence. *Journal of Family Violence, 13*, 39–57.

Pepler, D. J., Craig, W. M., Connolly, J. A., Yuile, A., McMaster, L., & Jian, D. (2006). A developmental perspective on bullying. *Aggressive Behavior, 32*, 376–384.

Reed, E., Silverman, J. G., Raj, A., Rothman, E. F., Decker, M. R., Gottlieb, et al. (2008). *American Journal of Men's Health, 2*, 260–271.

Resnick, M. D., Ireland, M., & Borowsky, I. (2004). Youth violence perpetration: What protects? What predicts? Findings from the National Longitudinal Study of Adolescent Health. *Journal of Adolescent Health, 35*, e1-e10.

Schewe, P. (2002). Guidelines for developing rape prevention and risk reduction interventions: Lessons from evaluation research. In P. Schewe (Ed.), *Preventing violence in relationships: Interventions across the life span* (pp. 107–136). Washington, DC: American Psychological Association.

Sears, H. A., Byers, S., Whelan, J. J., & Saint-Pierre, M. (2006). "If it hurts you, then it is not a joke": Adolescents' ideas about girls' and boys' use and experience of abusive behavior in dating relationships. *Journal of Interpersonal Violence, 21*, 1191–1207.

Silverman, J., Raj, A., Mucci, L., & Hathaway, J. (2001). Dating violence against adolescent girls and associated substance abuse, unhealthy weight control, sexual risk behavior, pregnancy, and suicidality. *Journal of the American Medical Association, 286*, 572–579.

Strauss, M. A. (1979). Measuring intrafamily conflict and violence: The Conflict Tactics (CT) Scales. *Journal of Marriage and the Family, 41*, 75–88.

Teen Research Unlimited. (2008, July). *Study on teen dating abuse*. Retrieved from http://www .loveis notabuse.com/statistics.htm.

Teten, A. L., Ball, B., Valle, L. A., Noonan, R., & Rosenbluth, B. (2009). Report from CDC: Considerations for the definition, measurement, consequences, and prevention of dating violence victimization among adolescent girls. *Journal of Women's Health, 18*, 923–927.

Whitaker, D. J., Morrison, S., Lindquist, C., Hawkins, S., O'Neil, J. A., Nesius, et al. (2006). A critical review of interventions for the primary prevention of perpetration of partner violence. *Aggression and Violent Behavior, 11*, 151–166.

Williams, T. S., Conolly, J., Pepler, D., Craig, W., & Laporte, L. (2008). Risk models of dating aggression across different adolescent relationships: A developmental psychopathology approach. *Consulting and Clinical Psychology, 76*, 622–632.

Wolfe, D. A., Crooks, C. V., Jaffe, P., Chiodo, D., Hughes, R., Ellis, W., et al. (2009). A school-based program to prevent adolescent dating violence: A cluster randomized trial. *Archives of Pediatric and Adolescent Medicine, 163*, 692–699.

Wolfe, D. A., Scott, K., Reitzel-Jaffe, D., Wekerle, C., Grasley, C., & Straatman, A. (2001). Development and validation of the Conflict in Adolescent Dating Relationships Inventory. *Psychological Assessment, 13*, 277–293.

Wolfe, D. A., Wekerle, C., Scott, K., & Pittman, A. (2001). Child maltreatment: Risk of adjustment problems and dating violence in adolescence. *Journal of the American Academy of Child and Adolescent Psychiatry, 40*, 282–289.

Wolfe, D. A., Wekerle, C., Scott, K., Straatman, A., Grasley, C., & Jaffe, D. (2003). Dating violence prevention with at-risk youth: A controlled outcome evaluation. *Journal of Consulting and Clinical Psychology, 71*, 279–291.

25

RISK ASSESSMENT WITH VICTIMS OF INTIMATE PARTNER VIOLENCE

Investigating the Gap Between Research and Practice*

LAUREN BENNETT CATTANEO

ALIYA R. CHAPMAN

The question of how best to assess danger has received significant attention in recent research on intimate partner violence (IPV) and has great potential relevance to victim services. However, despite increasing knowledge about risk factors and optimism about professionals' ability to assess dangerousness with improved tools, a gap remains between research and practice in risk assessment. Recent reviews suggest that the current research on risk assessment has focused too exclusively on the prediction of future violence rather than on the management of risk, and that this focus is problematic because the aim of practitioners who intervene in cases of IPV is to prevent future

abuse, not to predict it (Bennett Cattaneo & Goodman, 2007; Kropp, 2004). Instruments that rate the level of danger based on the presence of risk factors certainly could be a component of an overarching strategy for managing risk, but research to this point has not focused on the development of best practices toward such an end (Bennett Cattaneo & Goodman, 2007; Campbell, 2005; Dutton & Kropp, 2000).

This exploratory study describes the current thinking and practice of a small group of professionals with respect to IPV risk assessment. Given the consensus that there is a gap between research and practice in this area, a better understanding of practitioners' work in the field may guide research

*This article was published in *Violence Against Women, 17*, 1286–1298 (2011). We have omitted some information about the methodological approach and most direct quotes from participants in the results section.

in a practice-relevant direction. We suggest that the present study sets a precedent and direction for such research. We begin by reviewing the literature on the science and practice of IPV risk assessment, and then describe the study and its findings.

Kropp (2004) identified three models of risk assessment: actuarial, unstructured clinical assessment, and structured professional judgment. Actuarial tools have received greatest attention from researchers. Roehl, O'Sullivan, Webster, and Campbell (2005) examined the predictive accuracy of several such instruments, and found that although the Danger Assessment (Campbell, 1986, 1995) performed best in most analyses, other instruments performed better than chance. Hilton and colleagues considered the ability of several instruments to predict reported recidivism, and found that their own instrument as well as several others predicted at a level greater than chance (Hilton, Harris, Rice, Houghton, & Eke, 2008). Studies like these are accumulating evidence that actuarial instruments can provide useful information toward the prediction of future violence. We do not know, however, if and how they are used.

There are some jurisdictions, such as British Columbia, where the use of particular actuarial instruments is mandated (Kropp, 2004). In others, partnerships have been developed between researchers and law enforcement to standardize risk assessment. For example, in Maryland the state domestic violence coalition is working with law enforcement to institute a lethality assessment protocol where first responders use a version of Campbell's Danger Assessment, and then link high-risk victims with services (Campbell, 2005; Maryland Network Against Domestic Violence, n.d.). These are important efforts. But even in these examples where an actuarial tool is being administered consistently at one level, it is not clear how such risk assessment scores are used once a case is referred to victim services.

Scholars assume that unstructured clinical assessment, in which practitioners rely on their intuition, experience, and agency training to conduct assessments of danger, is currently standard practice in victim services (Dutton & Kropp,

2000). This approach has been widely criticized and has less predictive accuracy than actuarial models (Hilton et al., 2008), though its utility for practitioners and victims has not been explored (Bennett Cattaneo & Goodman, 2007). As a middle ground, some have called for a model of risk assessment that integrates professional experience with empirically based risk factors. Toward this end, Kropp and colleagues developed the Spousal Assault Risk Assessment (SARA; Kropp, Hart, Webster, & Eaves, 1999) to guide practitioners in terms of which risk factors to consider, while leaving the question of how to combine these factors to professional judgment. In a similar vein, the authors of the instrument validation study described earlier concluded that

The ideal would be a well-validated instrument specific to domestic violence in the hands of a practitioner who is expert in domestic violence by virtue of training and experience, who listens to a victim who is expert in her particular situation, and who has access to other sources of information. (Roehl et al., 2005, p. 16)

Bringing together client, practitioner, and research-based expertise is an excellent ideal. However, in moving toward defining best practices in detail, some of the assumptions in the literature need to be examined. How good is the fit among these three perspectives? This study begins to explore this question by investigating the nature of the gap between practice and research. Specifically, we interviewed practitioners, asking four central questions: First, what do practitioners actually do when they assess risk in IPV cases? Second, how do they use that assessment once they have completed it? Third, what are practitioner perspectives on the usefulness of their practices, both for them and (fourth) for their clients?

METHOD

Participants

Recruitment. Because this study is the first of its kind, we cast a broad net with regard to types of services offered, rather than looking in depth at one kind of service provision. We obtained a list of contacts at 22 local agencies that serve domestic violence victims from the county domestic violence coordinator. We also pilot tested the interview with a participant in a different county, and because the interview did not change substantively, added the pilot interview to our pool. Criteria for inclusion were as follows:

1. Interviewees must work within an agency whose mission is to serve victims of intimate partner violence (or an agency that contains a division with this mission).

2. Interviewees must have direct contact with clients.

3. Interviewees must have contact with clients at a time when risk assessment is salient. After removing from our list three persons whom we were unable to reach, and seven who after providing more information did not fit the study criteria, we retained a total of 13 interviews for analysis.

Sample description. All participants but one were female, and all but one worked near a major metropolitan hub. Participating agencies included two shelters, two courts, one law enforcement agency, two county programs providing services to families, one agency supporting military families, one hospital, and four nonprofit organizations providing a broad range of services to individuals or families. Seven of these agencies focused exclusively on IPV and sexual assault victims, whereas six had just one division or set of services dedicated to IPV. Six provided individual counseling and five of these six also offered support groups. Four agencies provided emergency shelter, and three also focused on transitional or longer term housing needs. In terms of legal services, two agencies were courts, two had one or more attorneys on staff to serve their clients, and six offered court advocacy and accompaniment. Staff at the hospital provided testimony in court when necessary. Five agencies offered services specific to parenting, and three offered case management services.

Procedures

Methodological approach. Procedures for this study were derived from McCracken's (1988) qualitative long-interview methodology, which is applicable when researchers conduct a critical analysis of a topic familiar to them. This study qualifies as such a situation: The first author has researched risk assessment for 10 years, and the second author managed a shelter for abused women where she supervised all aspects of practice including risk assessment.

*****

Interview protocol. Interview sessions, conducted by three doctoral students and transcribed by a research assistant, ranged in length from 30 to 75 min, and included four questions. First, we asked the interviewee what he or she does to assess risk. Prompts included the following: "Is there a particular instrument that you use? Is there a particular set of questions?" Second, we asked how information is used once gathered. Prompts included the following: "Does information gathered in the risk assessment shape what you do to help the victim? How?" Third, we asked about perspectives on the utility of risk assessment. Prompts included the following: "To what extent do you have your own sense of how dangerous a case is, without any formal assessment?" "Are there ways in which risk assessment could be more useful to you?" Finally, we asked whether victims benefit from the risk assessment. Prompts included the following: "To what extent do you believe victims know more about their level of risk after they meet with you? What makes you think so?"

Data Analysis

There are five stages in McCracken's procedure for data analysis. First, we read each transcript twice, noting observations. Second, we organized observations into preliminary categories according to interview content and the literature review. Third, we connected observations and modified categories. Fourth, we identified patterns and themes among the connections, and finally, we identified predominant themes. The authors collaborated at each stage, independently observing and identifying connections, and then resolving disagreements through discussion and recoding until consensus was reached. The three other members of the research team, whose primary responsibilities were interviewing and transcription, also read transcripts, wrote memos about emergent themes, and participated in discussions. This more informal process provided an additional perspective on the data that assisted us in evaluating and minimizing the influence of our frames of reference (Yeh & Inman, 2007).

RESULTS

How Do Participants Assess Victim Risk? How Useful Do They Find Their Assessment?

It was immediately evident from our interviews that most participants do not differentiate risk assessment from the rest of their work with clients. Only two described a distinct method of assessing risk. For most, assessment structure is part of a broader level of structure in the interaction with the client. Consequently, we divided participants into groups according to level of structure in their practices. Because participants' perceptions of the utility of risk assessment were related to level of structure, we include responses to that question here as well.

High structure risk assessment. Two participants reported that they use a standard risk-assessment tool with all clients. In an interview with clients who are injured due to interpersonal violence, Participant 15 uses Campbell's (1986, 1995) 20-item Danger Assessment, which yields a numerical score. Participant 15's interaction style is thus highly structured, employing the same procedures for each client. Participant 3's agency recently completed a year-long process

of refining its risk-assessment procedures. It now uses "a situational risk assessment form" that yields a rating of low, moderate, or high risk, in addition to a less formal procedure in which staff is trained to "glean" risk factors from "the storytelling process." Although this is a high structure version of risk assessment, it has more flexibility than the first case where the Danger Assessment is used in the same way with each client.

Perceived utility of high structure risk assessment. Both high structure participants said that their risk-assessment practices were useful. Participant 3 noted that, at the end of the year spent focusing on risk assessment, "I'm not sure I can think of a way that it would [be improved]." Aside from wishing the Danger Assessment was available in more languages, Participant 15 felt that "it's very well done . . . . In order to use it you have to go through a training program . . . it really does cover the scale so well and it prepares my nurses well to use it."

Medium structure risk assessment. Three participants (1, 4, and 11) fell in the middle of the structure spectrum because they have access to structured risk-assessment tools but do not use them consistently. Two of these three work in a court context where they help their clients to complete a standard document designed to feed specific information into the judicial system. They also have access to a checklist that assesses risk factors. However, they use the checklist only as they perceive the need and do not use it to derive ratings of danger.

*****

Perceived utility of medium structure risk assessment. Medium structure participants had more suggestions for improving risk assessment than did the high structure participants. Participant 1 felt that lethality checklists are useful because they allow "two or three different opportunities to try to get the information that's correct," and can be updated consistant with changes in the field. For example, "the first worksheet that we had when I got here maybe didn't have a huge portion on strangulation . . . [Now] we have a whole separate worksheet if someone says . . . that there was an attempted strangulation." Participant 4 wished for greater use of structured tools, while also saying that the tools could be better validated, more consistent, have more detail and be more often updated. Participant 11 was not aware of a good tool: "[if] I knew that there was a real structured risk assessment tool, I would be using it every time."

Low structure risk assessment. Eight participants conduct unstructured risk assessment, eliciting a narrative from the client and asking spontaneous questions that are guided by their professional experience and by their sense of each individual client. These participants cumulatively mentioned three primary "tools" of risk assessment. The first is their own professional experience, the second the professional judgment of their colleagues . . . .

*****

Participants 5 and 9 reported that consultation with colleagues took place both on an ad hoc basis and at regular intervals, for instance at the time of referral.

Personal and collective experience is often combined with a third tool—a "gut feeling" about which direction one should move to assess the victim's danger level. . . .

Perceived utility of low structure risk assessment. A frequent explanation for the low level of structure was the opinion that the interaction should be driven by the client. Although some participants said that they might find a standardized tool useful, particularly as a training tool, and two of the eight (Participants 6 and 16) noted that they may refer to a written list of questions when interviewing clients, most did not want a structured instrument to guide the interaction. Participant 4 said, "I don't want . . . that first or

second visit to be all about a piece of paper." Similarly, Participant 16 said, "I find in the moment when I am actually talking to somebody on the phone, the last thing I consider . . . is pulling out a piece of paper to go off a list of questions." Some participants suggested that use of a structured form would actively harm a victim by taking away control. For example, Participant 7 said, "I don't want to contribute to taking that power, any power and control away from her" by using a structured instrument.

How Do Participants Use Information About Risk?

In discussing how the nature of a client's risk informs what a participant does for that client, another continuum emerged. Most participants noted that imminent danger would prompt some kind of immediate action (such as calling 911 rather than continuing a conversation), but in the absence of such an extreme situation, participants varied a great deal in their use of information about risk. Again, because most participants did not separate their discussion of information about risk from the rest of the information they gathered, these responses overlapped with participants' general approach to providing services. The continuum ranged from participants who felt the particulars of a client's situation could completely change their work with that client to those who said that their services are relatively standard across clients.

Four participants described an orientation toward tailoring work to the specific needs of each client: "[My] primary goal with the information that I get is to give them the proper resources . . . whether it be shelter, whether it be 911, whether it be getting them to a support group" (Participant 1). This group described the importance of risk assessment in tailoring both services and safety planning. Participant 4 said, "My idea of effective safety planning is to make that plan pertinent to [the victim]."

*****

Seven participants described risk assessment as having some impact on their work, but each also described some fixedness in his or her approach. For three participants, this involves adherence to a standard safety plan; however, the amount of time spent working with the client increases when risk assessment indicates a high danger level. Two participants consistently focus on moving the client from the abusive situation: "somebody who is at high risk they need to leave right then and there, as soon as possible. And the ones at low risk, maybe you could spend a little more time working with her to get her mentally ready" (Participant 10). In these cases, level of risk does not change the practitioner's goal but does affect how it is pursued.

The final two participants in this group explicitly noted the consistency of their intervention across clients, but left room for flexibility, particularly in the intensity of work with the client . . . .

*****

Finally, Participants 11 and 16 fell on the far end of the continuum in reporting that risk assessment does not affect what they do for the client, but for very different reasons. Participant 11 assisted clients in petitioning for an order of protection, and this work did not vary according to level of risk. In contrast, Participant 16 emphasized the primacy of the client's preferences:

For the most part what shapes the services . . . really depends on them . . . even if it sounds to me like you know the individual is in a lot of danger and they tell me that they don't want to come to shelter but they'd like counseling services, that is their choice . . . if that is the service that they are interested in receiving then that's one I'll refer them for.

What Do Victims Gain from the Risk-Assessment Process?

Interviewers asked participants whether they felt that victims know more about their level of risk after meeting with them, and then asked their reasons for these perceptions. Six of the 13 participants responded with certainty that their clients know more when they leave. Three felt that clients already know about their level of risk when they come for assistance. For example, Participant 6 said, ". . . most of the callers . . . are fairly aware of how risky it is and that's why they're calling." Four participants were more equivocal in their responses, making comments such as "I would like to think that they know more" (Participant 1).

A theme that emerged repeatedly across participants was the impression that clients minimize the level of danger they face. Practitioners felt that victims may benefit significantly from education on this front. For example, Participant 8 noted that "what we try to do most of all is to bring awareness to the client of the level of danger she might be in . . . sometimes clients are not aware of that." Participant 16 added, "Maybe they minimize their danger level to an extent because they don't want to think that someone they love could hurt them like this." Comments also reflected the perception that clients may not be "ready to hear" practitioners and that this level of readiness affects the helpfulness of intervention. Participant 1 remarked, "I think because of typical victim behavior it's not that they don't know; it's that they don't want to see."

Participants also discussed evidence that clients learned more about their risk. Participant 3, whose agency reviewed its risk assessment procedures, was the only participant who reported collecting data on this question. For others, evidence for increase in victim knowledge was found in the client–practitioner interaction, the victim's subsequent actions and the ways the victim labels the abuse.

*****

DISCUSSION

This exploratory study investigated the correspondence between assumptions in the research literature on IPV risk assessment and the perspective of a group of practitioners who work with IPV clients. Our results highlight important areas of overlap and disconnection. We now review these areas and identify implications for research and practice in each.

How Do Participants Assess Victim Risk? How Useful Do They Find Their Assessment?

In a jurisdiction where, to our knowledge, there is no external pressure (in terms of policy or collaboration with researchers) to adopt a standardized risk-assessment instrument, only one of our participants incorporated an empirically validated instrument into standard practice. The research literature, including writing by the first author, assumes that it is a difference between the emphasis on prediction versus management of risk that presents the biggest obstacle to using risk assessment instruments. In this sample, participants' comments were related to a different obstacle—an objection to structure in and of itself. The majority of these participants explicitly did not want their interaction with clients constrained by a structured instrument, and some felt that to ask a structured list of questions could actually be harmful to clients. Although research suggests that it is beneficial for victims to have voice in IPV interventions (e.g., Bennett Cattaneo & Goodman, 2010; Zweig & Burt, 2007), studies have not explored whether structure in general or in the form of standard instruments may be disempowering to victims. Future research may explore this question and may also develop and validate approaches integrating some degree of structure with client-driven conversation.

Within this sample and in the research literature, there are examples of ways to move toward this middle ground. Participant 3's agency engaged in a year-long review of their risk-assessment procedure. Interestingly, this resulted not in the adoption of any particular instrument from the literature, but in a customized—and highly standardized—procedure for her organization that combined a checklist with storytelling.

This procedure is reminiscent of recent work in British Columbia, where practitioners gather information about empirically derived risk and protective factors, and then work with clients to discuss potential situations in which violence may recur. Safety planning is then conducted using this information, in explicit collaboration with the client (British Columbia Institute against Family Violence, 2004). Research on the impact of such procedures is needed, including an examination of how comfortable both practitioners and clients are with their level of control over the interaction.

How Is Risk-Assessment Information Used?

There were some stark differences in the ways that practitioners in our sample use information gleaned from risk assessment. Participants either reported that the assessment fully shapes their work with clients, shapes it primarily in terms of the intensity of work toward a fixed goal or in a standard format, or does not shape it at all. These findings support the assumption in the research literature that risk assessment can serve a variety of purposes (e.g., Kropp, 2004) and point to the need for different risk-assessment techniques across contexts. In developing and evaluating such techniques, research should consider the extent to which services may vary across clients. More specifically, an assessment yielding detailed information is warranted if services are likely to vary, and research may identify the specific information that should be gathered. If service options do not differ according to risk, and it is only urgency of service provision that varies, then a briefer form of risk assessment may be appropriate. Evaluation of such instruments should then include assessment of service intensity.

What Do Victims Gain from the Risk-Assessment Process?

Researchers and practitioners know little about how victims experience risk assessment.

In our sample, one agency collected data on client gains over the course of service provision. Where possible, such monitoring may yield useful data that may improve practice.

A discrepancy between research and practice is particularly apparent in the concept of victims who minimize their risk. Research suggests that victims are relatively good assessors of their risk of future IPV, and it has not yielded evidence that help seekers have biased perceptions about their level of danger (Bennett Cattaneo, Bell, Goodman, & Dutton, 2007; Bennett Cattaneo & Goodman, 2003; Heckert & Gondolf, 2004; Roehl et al., 2005; Weisz, Tolman, & Saunders, 2000). However, our participants tended to believe that victims do minimize their danger, and many participants emphasized their role in educating the victim in this regard. Research should explore what victims actually gain from such conversations, and how, in hindsight, they view their perceptions about risk. Do they believe that they minimized danger? If their perceptions shifted over time, how do they understand these shifts?

LIMITATIONS

This exploratory study was designed to be a first step in bridging the gap between practice and research on risk assessment, and its results should be viewed as preliminary, requiring replication. The study is limited in ways typical of qualitative work. First, our interpretation of these data is not the only one possible. As suggested in the long-interview approach and in best practices in qualitative research in general (McCracken, 1988; Yeh & Inman, 2007), we were explicit about our pre-existing assumptions and attempted to reduce their influence through self-examination, alternating between independent and collaborative analysis, and through the input of three other members of the research team. Notably, we did not confirm our original expectations of the data. A strength of our approach is that one of the authors comes primarily from a research background, and the other (at that time) primarily practice, which provided a good balance in

perspectives. A limitation was our inability to recontact our participants to request that they check the validity of our interpretations.

Limitations to generalizability are also typical of qualitative work (Yeh & Inman, 2007). Our sample size was similar to many qualitative studies, and because it included the majority of IPV-focused organizations in the county known to the domestic violence coordinator, our participants are likely to well represent local practice. However, because it is drawn from an area very close to a major city, our sample may well have characteristics that differ from many other IPV workers in our nation. Besides gender, we did not collect demographic information about our interviewees, and although we may have accomplished our aim of increasing participant comfort with confidentiality, in hindsight, we also limited our ability to consider generalizability. This omission again highlights the need for replication of these findings.

CONCLUSION

Risk assessment in IPV is a prime example of an area where ongoing practice may differ from assumptions and data in the research literature. For best practices to be developed and implemented, practitioner perspectives must be taken into account. This study raises some specific ideas about ways to move in this direction. An equally important perspective to be explored in the future is that of clients who have experienced IPV. An understanding and integration of these three perspectives is key to maximizing the efforts of all concerned.

REFERENCES

Bennett Cattaneo, L., Bell, M., Goodman, L., & Dutton, M. A. (2007). Intimate partner violence victims' accuracy in assessing their risk of re-abuse. *Journal of Family Violence, 22*, 429–440.

Bennett Cattaneo, L., & Goodman, L. (2003). Victim-reported risk factors for continued abusive behavior: Assessing the dangerousness of arrested batterers. *Journal of Community Psychology, 31*, 349–369.

Bennett Cattaneo, L., & Goodman, L. (2007). New directions in IPV risk assessment: An empowerment approach to risk management. In *Intimate partner violence* (pp. 1–17). Kingston, NJ: Civic Research Institute.

Bennett Cattaneo, L., & Goodman, L. (2010). Through the lens of jurisprudence: The relationship between empowerment in the court system and well being for intimate partner violence victims. *Journal of Interpersonal Violence, 25*, 481–502.

British Columbia Institute against Family Violence. (2004). *Aid for safety assessment and planning.* Vancouver, British Columbia, Canada.

Campbell, J. (1986). Nursing assessment of risk of homicide for battered women. *Advances in Nursing Science, 8*(4), 36–51.

Campbell, J. (1995). Prediction of homicide of and by battered women. In *Assessing dangerousness: Violence by sexual offenders, batterers, and child abusers* (pp. 96–113). Thousand Oaks, CA: SAGE.

Campbell, J. (2005). Commentary on Websdale: Lethality assessment approaches: Reflections on their use and ways forward. *Violence Against Women, 11*, 1206–1213.

Dutton, D., & Kropp, P. (2000). A review of domestic violence risk instruments. *Trauma, Violence, & Abuse, 1*, 171–181.

Heckert, D., & Gondolf, E. (2004). Battered women's perceptions of risk versus risk factors and instruments in predicting repeat reassault. *Journal of Interpersonal Violence, 19*, 778–800.

Hilton, N. Z., Harris, G., Rice, M., Houghton, R., & Eke, A. (2008). An in-depth actuarial assessment for wife assault recidivism: The domestic violence risk appraisal guide. *Law & Human Behavior, 32*, 150–163.

Kropp, P. (2004). Some questions regarding spousal assault risk assessment. *Violence Against Women, 10*, 676–697.

Kropp, P., Hart, S., Webster, C., & Eaves, D. (1999). *Manual for the spousal assault risk assessment guide* (Vol. 3). Toronto, Ontario, Canada: Multi-Health Systems.

Maryland Network Against Domestic Violence. (n.d.). MNADV Lethality Assessment Project: Learning to read the danger signs. Retrieved from http://www.mnadv.org/lethality.html

McCracken, G. (1988). *The long interview.* Newbury Park, CA: SAGE.

Roehl, J., O'Sullivan, C., Webster, D., & Campbell, J. (2005). *Intimate partner violence risk assessment validation study, final report* (Document No. 209731). Available at www.ncjrs.org, NCJ 209731

Weisz, A., Tolman, R., & Saunders, D. (2000). Assessing the risk of severe violence: The importance of survivors' predictions. *Journal of Interpersonal Violence, 15*, 75–90.

Yeh, C. J., & Inman, A. G. (2007). Qualitative Data analysis and interpretation in counseling psychology: Strategies for best practices. *Counseling Psychologist, 35*, 369–403.

Zweig, J. M., & Burt, M. R. (2007). Predicting women's perceptions of domestic violence and sexual assault agency helpfulness: What matters to program clients? *Violence Against Women, 13*, 1149–1178.

UNIT 6

ADULT AND JUVENILE CORRECTIONS

INTRODUCTION AND COMMENTARY

Correctional psychology represents a broad landscape of opportunities for researchers and practitioners who operate in both institutional and community settings. Jails and prisons are in need of direct services to detainees and inmates, including evaluation of mental status, crisis intervention, counseling, and assessment for making classification decisions. Correctional facilities also need program evaluation and training of staff, among many other things. Psychologists often report the result of research relevant to corrections, such as research on the effects of solitary confinement, crowding, specific treatment approaches, or victimization. In the community, psychologists and other mental health professionals provide a very wide range of services to persons on probation and parole. Additionally, there is a multitude of opportunities in the juvenile equivalent of these adult settings.

Most of the articles in this section deal with the inmates who receive psychological services. The first article, however, focuses on correctional psychology as a career choice. MacKain, Myers, Ostapiej, and Newman (2010) surveyed psychologists in one state's prison system to assess their job satisfaction. The state, like many others, had high vacancy rates in psychology positions. It is sometimes difficult to attract psychologists to this work, for reasons ranging from misconceptions about the prison environment to perceived lack of the skills needed. The researchers hoped to identify the extent and sources of the dissatisfaction. Interestingly, the prison environment itself was not a major source of dissatisfaction, contrary to what might be expected. Rather, economics, perceived lack of organizational support, and interpersonal relationships (particularly with supervisors) created the problems. The economics factor did not refer to base salary but, rather, to broader issues, such as job security and health insurance benefits. Very similar factors are reported by correctional officers when they are surveyed.

The mental health needs of inmates are becoming widely recognized in both jails and prisons. Unfortunately, these needs are too often unrecognized or unmet. Ax and his fellow researchers (2007) begin their article with this acknowledgement, but they also make clear that suicide rates are not as high as sometimes assumed; they are lower than rates in the general population. Still, numerous mental-health–related problems need solving. Ax et al. note that many inmates have dual diagnoses of mental illness and substance abuse, and in many facilities only one or the other is addressed. They also make note of the deemphasis on inmate rehabilitative goals in some prison systems. They offer at least two innovative solutions to meet the needs of inmates: One would require psychologists to have prescription privileges, and the other would require delivery of mental health services from a distance, or telehealth. Each of these solutions is bound to prompt discourse among those who both support and resist such changes.

Mental health needs of prisoners are the topic of the following article as well. Here, Magaletta, Diamond, Faust, Daggett, and Camp (2009) report results of a nationwide survey of newly admitted male and female inmates in federal prisons at all security levels. The authors do not describe here what services are actually offered; rather, they are trying to estimate the needs. They conclude that about 15% of new admissions require mental health services of some type. Those most likely to be in need are female offenders and inmates in medium- and high-security levels. They discuss the implications of their findings and note that future research should strive to identify the needs of specific offenders, such as substance abusers, those at risk of suicide, and those with traumatic brain injuries. Early identification will help in the management and treatment of these offenders.

The last two articles discuss juvenile offenders, specifically programs aimed at their rehabilitation. Many juvenile treatment programs assess the cognitions of young offenders and try to change those that are believed to be distorted. For example, a juvenile may think no one was hurt by his or her actions or may believe that all people are basically evil. McGlynn, Hahn, and Hagan (2013) evaluated one such cognitive intervention program provided to about 500 incarcerated male and female delinquents. Before and after participating in the program, the delinquents filled out a questionnaire that measures cognitive distortions. The program demonstrated some success, measured by lower scores once the program had been completed. Interestingly, younger offenders (some as young as 10–13) had more cognitive distortions, but as the authors note, there is a very logical explanation for this finding. We leave this to readers to discover and discuss. You also may find it helpful to revisit the Steinberg article on risk taking in adolescence (see Unit 4, Article 16), which raises questions about the extent to which the cognitions of adolescents can indeed be changed. The McGlynn et al. study is limited, particularly because it had no control group, but its results are still worthy of contemplation and the study worthy of replication.

Restorative justice (RJ) refers to approaches that try to repair the damage made to a victim and a community after a crime has been committed. In the process, it is hoped that offenders will experience some degree of rehabilitation. RJ programs use such methods as victim–offender reconciliation meetings, teen circles, offender sensitivity training, and role playing to empower victims and challenge the cognitive distortions of offenders. In the final article in this section, Bergseth and Bouffard (2013) offer an excellent summary of these programs. In a section not included in the present text, they also provided a comprehensive review of the research on their effectiveness. The authors note that RJ programs do not necessarily reduce recidivism, but they should not be judged on that factor alone.

Bergseth and Bouffard wanted to examine whether program effectiveness varied depending on demographic characteristics (e.g., age, gender), type of offense, and prior contact with the juvenile justice system. They studied 352 RJ youths and a control group of 353 similar youths who were in the traditional juvenile system. The authors found positive results, particularly for children referred at younger ages but also for older youths and even some with violent charges and prior offenses. Although more research is needed on the specific features of RJ programs and their use with different populations, the RJ approach appears to hold promise for dealing with juveniles, again keeping in mind that the adolescent brain is still developing. A major strength of the juvenile justice system has been its ability to embrace a wide variety of program options, from intensive services for serious delinquents to diversionary services, giving them a second chance before adjudicating them delinquent. Unfortunately, though, programs are often not subjected to careful evaluation; so we simply do not know exactly how they work or, indeed, whether they do work.

Numerous other topics could be covered in this section; one has only to scan the lists of references that accompany the articles in this unit to get a sense of the wide landscape of this field. Correctional psychologists face many challenges, particularly in the institutional setting, but they often report that their frustrations are primarily with the system rather than the inmates. The plight of mentally disordered inmates is particularly troubling, as noted in two of the articles in this unit. Nevertheless, many psychologists find great satisfaction working in correctional facilities or consulting with a variety of correctional agencies. Although the work is demanding, there are numerous opportunities to contribute to significant change in correctional policies and practices, and the lives of individuals.

26

Job Satisfaction Among Psychologists Working in State Prisons

The Relative Impact of Facets Assessing Economics, Management, Relationships, and Perceived Organizational Support*

Sally J. MacKain

Bryan Myers

Lara Ostapiej

R. Arne Newman

The field of correctional psychology has undergone extensive changes through the years (Bartol & Freeman, 2005) and has seen tremendous growth in corrections-specific graduate programs, internship training, and a greater emphasis on research in the field (Ax & Morgan, 2002; Brodsky, 2007). The American Psychological Association has recognized this development, featuring prison psychology as a "growth career," due to trends in available and potential positions in federal prisons (DiAngelis, 2008). A national survey of correctional psychologists employed in federal and state prisons detailed the professional duties and responsibilities of

*This article was published in *Criminal Justice and Behavior*, *37*, 306–318 (2010). We removed segments of the discussion and limitations sections.

prison work (Boothby & Clements, 2000). In addition to providing psychotherapy and psychological assessment services, correctional psychologists engage in a rich variety of traditional and nontraditional tasks such as crisis intervention, inmate classification and community risk assessment, behavioral management of difficult inmates, staff training, developing release plans, and organizational management through consultation with wardens and superintendents (Hawk, 1997; Schwartz, 2003).

JOB SATISFACTION AND STAFFING

Considerable strain has been placed on correctional staff in recent decades as prisons have become increasingly overcrowded. Between 1988 and 2000, the number of state prisoners rose 114.5%, and the rate of mental health service use (i.e., counseling and therapy) increased by 153.2% (Manderscheid, Gravesande, & Goldstrom, 2004). The authors noted, however, that there was a net loss in the proportion of facilities that provide mental health treatment during this period, meaning that prisons fell even further behind in meeting service needs. Psychologists working within correctional facilities already face a variety of demands and expectations not typically encountered by psychologists working in more traditional settings (Milan, Chin, & Nguyen, 1999). The physical plant of many prisons, especially older ones, is not designed to accommodate therapeutic work. Overcrowding creates stress that can exacerbate offenders' needs for psychological services and can result in increased job stress among correctional personnel (Lambert, Hogan, & Barton, 2003). In rural settings, there may be only one psychologist for an institution, and sometimes one psychologist is responsible for the mental health needs of inmates in two or three different institutions. These stressors may present a significant threat to job satisfaction in correctional psychologists.

Job satisfaction represents one of the most widely studied constructs in industrial organizational psychology (Levy, 2006; McShane & Von Glinow, 2007). This attitude can be measured globally as well as tap specific facets such as satisfaction with pay, supervision, and promotion opportunities (Smith, Kendall, & Hulin, 1987). Job satisfaction has been used to predict a variety of work-relevant outcomes such as performance, turnover, absenteeism, counterproductive behaviors, and organizational commitment (Hackett, 1989; Judge, Thorensen, Bono, & Patton, 2001; Lambert, Edwards, Camp, & Saylor, 2005; Tett & Meyer, 1993).

While there are a number of existing measures of job satisfaction already in use such as the Minnesota Satisfaction Questionnaire (Weiss, Dawis, & England, 1967) and the Job Descriptive Index (Smith, Kendall, & Hulin, 1969), these instruments were developed for use across a variety of occupations and may not address important features unique to correctional psychology practice. There has been little systematic investigation into the factors that relate to the employment experiences of correctional psychologists. However, one recent study of federal Bureau of Prisons (BOP) staff reported results from the 2005 Prison Social Climate Survey (Garland, McCarty, & Zhao, 2009). Among noncustody staff, psychological staff (22.3% had less than master's degree) reported relatively higher levels of job satisfaction and commitment to their institution and organization in comparison to teachers and unit management staff. Job satisfaction was measured by a five-item scale that tapped overall feelings toward the BOP job. Of the work-related variables that they assessed, quality of supervision and perceived efficacy in dealing with inmates were strong predictors of job satisfaction (and also significantly predicted institutional and organizational commitment).

The study by Garland and colleagues (2009) was aimed at addressing overall satisfaction rather than assessing satisfaction for individual facets of the job. Moreover, their sample included a relatively high percentage of individuals with no graduate training in psychology— and educational attainment plays an important role in job satisfaction, particularly with respect to the expectations individuals generate regarding job facets such as salary (Judge & Hurst, 2008; Verhaest & Omey, 2009). By contrast, Boothby and Clements (2002) specifically targeted the individual facet job satisfaction among correctional psychologists. They developed a measure of job satisfaction specific to correctional psychologists and surveyed 830 master's- and doctoral-level psychologists working in federal and state prisons. The survey taps 18 different job facets, some of these generalizable to all jobs (e.g., satisfaction with salary) and some unique to correctional psychologists (e.g., satisfaction in relationships with inmates). Respondents gave two separate ratings for each facet, (a) satisfaction and (b) importance; both ratings were on a 5-point scale (see Table 1 for all 18 facets); and a total satisfaction score was derived by summing satisfaction ratings for each facet. Participants reported relatively higher levels of satisfaction with facets related to coworkers and job-specific factors such as safety and lower satisfaction regarding salary and opportunities for advancement. The importance of the individual facets in predicting overall satisfaction was not the goal of the Boothby and Clements investigation. However, an examination of individual facets and their relation with overall satisfaction can be a useful indicator in determining which particular elements of the job are most in need of modification if overall satisfaction is to be enhanced.

The job satisfaction survey developed by Boothby and Clements (2002) asked respondents to rate both facet importance and facet satisfaction to identify gaps between "hoped for and actual working conditions" (p. 311). The benefit of assessing facet importance along with facet satisfaction has come under some debate. According to Locke (1976), the perceived importance of a job facet directly influences satisfaction, such that importance ratings should be treated as a weight (or multiplier) in calculating satisfaction. Boothby and Clements did not use importance ratings as weights in their study, but instead looked at facet importance descriptively. Certainly, there is merit to

the belief that facets rated as more important would play a larger role in overall satisfaction than would facets rated as less important. On the other hand, importance may already be considered when rating satisfaction, as one is only dissatisfied about important facets of the job (Balzer et al., 1997). Some researchers have found that ratings of facet importance are not useful in that they do not play a moderating role in facet satisfaction ratings (Jackson & Corr, 2002), or do so only in particular circumstances (Rice, Gentile, & McFarlin, 1991; Yeoh, 2007). Therefore, the added value of including importance ratings along with satisfaction ratings in a measure of job satisfaction in correctional psychologists merits investigation.

PRESENT STUDY

In an effort to understand what might be contributing to high vacancy rates in psychology positions at prisons in North Carolina (as high as 46% in some regions; Newman, 2008), we administered a job satisfaction instrument based on the one developed by Boothby and Clements (2002) to psychologists currently employed by the North Carolina Department of Corrections (NCDOC). Each of the 79 state correctional institutions has a designated psychologist or psychologists who are assigned a caseload or take on duties as need arises. Unlike psychologists who work for the federal Bureau of Prisons, who are certified as officers as well as licensed psychologists, psychologists working in the NCDOC have a single professional identity, or role. Our goals were to: (a) identify sources of job dissatisfaction and the degree to which individual facets might account for overall satisfaction, (b) identify more general facets among the 18 individual items that would afford greater potential for remedial actions within the organization, and (c) investigate the relative contribution of facet importance in predicting overall job satisfaction.

METHOD

Participants

Surveys were sent to 93 correctional psychologists across North Carolina and were completed and returned by 72 psychologists (response rate = 77%). The majority of respondents (47%, $n = 34$) were women (17%, $n = 12$ did not respond to the question); 73% ($n = 53$) had master's degrees and were licensed psychological associates (LPAs). In North Carolina, master's-level psychologists practice under the supervision of doctoral-level psychologists, although supervision requirements can be as little as 1 hour per month for LPAs who have accumulated at least 7,500 clinical hours and been licensed a minimum of 5 years (MacKain, Tedeschi, Durham, & Goldman, 2002). Service with the DOC ranged from 6 months to 36 years ($M = 10$ years, $SD = 9.81$, $Mdn = 7$ years), although 50% of the sample ($n = 36$) had worked 6.5 years or less. The most frequently reported annual salary range was $51,000 to $60,000 (38%, $n = 27$), and most described themselves as working in a rural area (63%, $n = 45$).

Materials

Our job satisfaction survey consisted of the 18 facets from the Boothby and Clements (2002) scale, which asked participants to rate both satisfaction (1 = *not at all*, 5 = *highly satisfied*) as well as importance (1 = *not at all*, 5 = *very important*) for each facet. We added a single "overall job satisfaction" item, again with rating options ranging from *not at all satisfied* (scored 1) to *highly satisfied* (scored 5). Respondents were also invited to provide written comments at the end of the survey.

Procedure

A DOC Mental Health Services administrator identified all 93 master's- and doctoral-level psychology staff at the state prisons and distributed the survey through DOC interdepartmental mail. Two cover letters were included: one from prison administration encouraging psychologists to participate and assuring them confidentiality and another from the researchers with institutional approval information and instructions to return the survey to the university in the stamped envelope provided. The DOC Human Subjects Review Committee provided a rigorous review to ensure that respondents could not be identified and that they were not coerced in any way to participate. Potential participants were informed that participation was anonymous and voluntary, and all received two reminder e-mails from the DOC administrator, 1 and 2 weeks following distribution. Participants were free to complete the survey at work or at home.

Development of General Facets

Based on theoretical groupings, we developed four composite (i.e., general) facets we felt would be relevant to understanding how aspects of the job might be important to the overall satisfaction as a correctional psychologist. These were economic issues, management issues, satisfaction with work relationships, and perceived organizational support. Each composite was developed by averaging scores for items on the questionnaire addressing this general facet. Economics represents the degree to which the job is perceived as making good economic sense. This general facet is based on averaged scores for: (a) satisfaction with salary and (b) satisfaction with job security. Management represents the degree to which management is regarded as effective (e.g., unambiguous roles, competent supervision). This general facet is based on averaging scores for: (a) satisfaction with supervision, b) satisfaction with level of responsibility, and (c) clear definition of roles. Access to/influence on decision making was not included in this general facet because this item was interpreted to relate to job enrichment rather than to the degree to which an employee felt effectively managed. Relationships as a general facet represents the degree to which one is satisfied with one's work atmosphere and interpersonal relations on the job. This general score was based on averaging scores for: (a) relationships with coworkers, which for this sample includes correctional officers, medical personnel, and others; (b) relationships with inmates; (c) relationships with supervisor; and (d) professional atmosphere. Perceived organizational support represents the degree to which participants believe the organization cares about them and values their contributions (Kinnunen, Feldt, & Makikangas, 2008). This general facet is based on averaging scores for: (a) satisfaction with recognition, (b) achievement satisfaction, and (c) status/prestige of job.

RESULTS

In order to evaluate the degree to which overall job satisfaction was predicted by the individual facets, Pearson product–moment correlation coefficients were computed for each of the 18 individual facets with the single measure of overall satisfaction. As the zero-order correlations show (see Table 1), once the Bonferroni correction for Type I error inflation was employed, all individual facets significantly correlated with the overall measure of satisfaction except for safety, salary, relationships with inmates, and relationships with coworkers.

The relative importance of economics, management, relationships, and perceived organizational support in explaining variance in prison psychology job satisfaction scores was also tested. These four general facets were simultaneously entered into a regression model as predictors using the 5-point subjective measure of overall job satisfaction as the criterion. The analysis revealed that the four composites combined accounted for a significant proportion of the variability in overall satisfaction, $R^2 = .57$, $F(4, 66) = 21.94$, $p < .001$. As Table 2 shows, economics, $\beta = .25$, $t(66) = 2.66$, $p < .01$, relationships, $\beta = .32$, $t(66) = 2.68$, $p < .01$, and perceived organizational support, $\beta = .33$, $t(66) = 2.62$, $p < .02$, all accounted for significant unique variability in the criterion, whereas management, $\beta = .04$, $t(66) = .28$, $p > .05$, did not. Examination of the zero-order correlations among the four

Table 1   Satisfaction Ratings for National Sample of Prison Psychologists and North Carolina Samples

| Item Job Dimension | National Sample[a] | | | North Carolina State Prisons | Zero-Order Correlation |
	M	SD	M	SD	With Overall Satisfaction
1. Opportunity for advancement	2.66	1.28	2.51	1.13	.43*
2. Autonomy	3.72	1.09	3.74	1.02	.44*
3. Recognition	2.94	1.16	2.85	1.12	.52*
4. Appropriate level of responsibility	3.59	1.06	3.75	0.96	.43*
5. Job security	3.91	1.12	4.17	0.93	.54*

(Continued)

Table 1 (Continued)

Item Job Dimension	National Sample[a]		North Carolina State Prisons		Zero-Order Correlation
	M	SD	M	SD	With Overall Satisfaction
6. Salary	3.33	1.12	2.53	1.09	.30
7. Competent supervision	3.12	1.35	3.65	1.30	.40*
8. Relationships with coworkers	3.75	0.97	4.10	0.99	.36
9. Relationships with inmates	3.86	0.85	4.00	0.78	.29
10. Relationship with supervisor	3.61	1.23	3.85	1.31	.50*
11. Achievement or success in job	3.71	0.97	3.85	0.94	.60*
12. Status/prestige of job	3.11	1.07	3.40	0.94	.53*
13. Professional atmosphere	2.85	1.13	3.29	1.29	.50*
14. Clear definition of roles	3.03	1.10	3.38	1.09	.47*
15. Personally meaningful work	3.64	1.08	3.88	0.96	.50*
16. Cooperation among staff	3.26	1.06	3.42	1.03	.42*
17. Access to/influence on decision making	2.91	1.17	2.85	1.23	.52*
18. Safety	3.90	0.94	3.92	1.06	.21

a. From Boothby and Clements (2002).

*Correlation is significant at the .002 level (Bonferroni correction used).

composite facets and the overall satisfaction ratings revealed that each composite, when considered individually, had moderately strong correlations with overall satisfaction (all $rs \geq .52$, see Table 2) and all were statistically significant ($p < .001$). However, there was some degree of overlap among the composite facets (rs ranged from .20 to .71), and this degree of multicollinearity led to the composite management accounting for little unique variability in overall satisfaction.

FACET IMPORTANCE AND OVERALL SATISFACTION

To test the value added by assessing facet importance, we created a score that combined importance and satisfaction for the individual 18 facets and compared that to job satisfaction ratings for the 18 facets as sole predictors of overall satisfaction scores. To combine satisfaction and importance ratings, we recoded satisfaction so that values ranged from –2 (*not at all*

Table 2 Overall Satisfaction Regression on General Facets

General Facet	Zero-Order Correlation With Overall Satisfaction	β	t
Economics	.52	.25	2.66**
Perceived organizational support	.68	.33	2.62*
Relationships	.61	.32	2.68**
Management	.60	.04	0.28

*Predictor is significant at the .05 level.

**Predictor is significant at the .01 level.

satisfied) to +2 (*completely satisfied*), with 0 as the midpoint. We multiplied satisfaction for each facet with importance of facet so that the resultant score represented a combination of these two values. Therefore, these weighted satisfaction scores could range from –10 (*not at all satisfied for an extremely important facet*) to +10 (*completely satisfied for an extremely important facet*). These scores, which reflect a combination of satisfaction and importance, were then correlated with overall satisfaction scores. Presumably, if importance provides valuable information to our facets, the combination of satisfaction and importance would correlate more highly with overall satisfaction than would each individual facet satisfaction score by itself. This was not the case. The combined score correlated slightly less than did the satisfaction scores alone on 11 of the 18 facets and negligibly more on the 7 remaining items. For those items in which the combined scores had higher correlations than the satisfaction scores alone, the difference in these correlations ranged from .004 to .018, and none of these differences were statistically significant.

QUALITATIVE MEASURES

Respondents were given the opportunity to provide additional information not addressed in any of the items on the survey. Of the 73 participants, 44 (61%) provided written comments, addressing a number of issues surrounding employee dissatisfaction. In an effort to provide some content analysis to these comments, the first and third authors independently reviewed the comments with the goal of identifying important themes. The two raters then reached agreement on six general themes that the comments articulated. These themes, in order from most frequently cited to least frequently cited, were: (a) salary/benefits, (b) organizational support, (c) advancement opportunities, (d) workload, (e) training, and (f) other. Both authors then reviewed the 44 surveys and independently assigned each survey to one of the six categories. If a survey addressed numerous factors, the first factor addressed was chosen for the purpose of categorization. Kappa was conducted to assess the degree of interrater agreement between the two raters, and the level of agreement was found to be very high (k = .97). Salary/benefits were the most frequently cited concern, with 68% (*n* = 30) of writers mentioning these. Dissatisfaction related to organizational support was evident in written comments of 43% (*n* = 19) of the sample. The tenor of the written comments was consistent with the substantially lower satisfaction ratings on the salary facet (*M* = 2.53) and recognition facet (*M* = 2.85).

DISCUSSION

Individual Facets and Overall Satisfaction

We sought to evaluate the relative importance of the individual job dimensions, or facets, to participants' overall job satisfaction. The satisfaction ratings for the North Carolina sample closely resembled those in the national sample of correctional psychologists (Boothby & Clements, 2002). Table 1 presents the means and standard deviations for satisfaction with the 18 job facets for our sample and also includes the means for the sample used by Boothby and Clements (2002). For our sample, the zero-order correlations among each of the individual facets and the overall satisfaction rating suggests that all but 4 facets emerged as important correlates with job satisfaction. The 4 that failed to correlate significantly with job satisfaction were safety, salary, relationships with coworkers, and relationships with inmates.

Salary satisfaction was a particularly weak correlate with overall satisfaction. This finding is consistent with those of Boothby and Clements (2002), who found salary even more weakly (i.e., $r = .14$) related to their summed total satisfaction score. It was surprising that salary failed to correlate with overall satisfaction because salary received the second lowest ratings on satisfaction ($M = 2.53$), suggesting individuals were particularly dissatisfied with this aspect of their job. Using a solely descriptive approach (i.e., mean satisfaction scores) as a method to target areas in need of improvement may be problematic in this case because increasing salaries may not necessarily affect overall job satisfaction. The zero-order correlations suggest that in comparison to the other facets, salary alone is not linked to overall satisfaction.

In this study, and consistent with the findings by Boothby and Clements (2002), safety received relatively high satisfaction ratings. However, concerns about safety have been rated by prison psychologists elsewhere as a job function associated with high risk (Magaletta, Patry, Dietz, & Ax, 2007). The finding that safety was not a significant correlate of overall satisfaction was surprising given that prisons can be a sometimes violent and chaotic work environment (for a description of psychologists' roles and experiences in correctional settings, see Bartol & Bartol, 2004). The perception among potential prison job applicants that prisons are dangerous places to work may pose real obstacles for recruiting. Nevertheless, safety concerns were not evident in this sample

and did not appear to be associated with overall job satisfaction. It may be that the design and operation of the institutions promote security for employees and this has been recognized by respondents.

General Facets as Predictors of Overall Satisfaction

Whereas the individual salary facet did not significantly correlate with overall satisfaction, a very different picture emerged when we examined the general facet economics. This construct produced a relatively high zero-order correlation with global satisfaction ($r = .52$), and the beta weight indicates this general facet accounts for substantial unique variance in global satisfaction scores. Moreover, the finding that economic considerations were important to respondents is further supported by the fact that the economic/salary issue was mentioned the most frequently among the written comments (68%). Consequently, if we consider both the regression analysis involving the general facet along with the written comments, economic issues emerged as an important predictor of overall job satisfaction. Along with general facets for relationships and perceived organizational support, economics was a significant predictor of overall job satisfaction and produced comparatively low correlations with the other three general facets. This finding suggests that the degree to which one perceives a job as making good economic sense is evaluated not only on satisfaction with pay but also on the level of job security. This is consistent with previous work concerning the perceived economic value of jobs (Koslowsky, Kluger, & Yinon, 1988). When people evaluate their compensation, they consider relevant factors in addition to salary, such as health insurance and the degree to which job security is present.

Two other general facets emerged as important to satisfaction: perceived organizational support and relationships. Of these two general facets, perceived organizational support may be the most amenable to change. Modifications in status, opportunities for achievement, and recognition may represent the easiest path to enhancing employee satisfaction. Indeed, there are a multitude of effective strategies for enhancing the degree to which employees feel valued and supported by their organization, and these have a number of positive consequences apart from increasing job satisfaction (see Rhoades & Eisenberger, 2002, for a discussion). Perceived organizational support has long been identified as an element critical to worker satisfaction (Eisenberger, Huntington, Hutchinson, & Sowa, 1986). The more an organization can foster the belief among workers that the organization cares for them as individuals and values their contributions to the organization, the better the return in terms of organizational commitment, overall job satisfaction, and performance factors such as conscientiousness (Eisenberger, Fasalo, & Davis-LaMastro, 1990). In other words, the belief that one is valued promotes a reciprocal response on the part of the worker, who in turn is motivated to make a greater commitment to the organization (Eisenberger et al., 1986; Gould, 1979). Given the importance of these beliefs to overall satisfaction, and the degree to which these beliefs are malleable, directed efforts on the part of management to enhance perceptions of organizational support represent a practical solution to enhancing overall satisfaction for correctional psychologists working in NCDOC.

Providing training for employees is one way organizations can show employees that their role and contributions are valued (Rhoades & Eisenberger, 2002). Job training, particularly when it is presented as a discretionary practice on the part of the organization, can lead to increased perceived organizational support (Wayne, Shore, & Liden, 1997). Supervision and training needs for beginning and more seasoned prison psychologists differ (Levinson, 1985; Norton, 1990), but corrections-specific continued education is essential to ensure quality practice (Magaletta et al., 2007). In his article describing the evolution of correctional psychology and comparing the experiences of early and modern correctional psychologists,

Stanley Brodsky (2007) notes that prison psychologists are "accustomed to regular, thoughtful, and productive continuing education workshops" (p. 867). Our present data support this notion, as 32% ($n = 14$) of the written comments addressed the need for greater access to continuing education. Most noted that job-specific training was not made available and that psychologists were not reimbursed for travel on the few occasions when the DOC has offered workshops. Addressing these training needs may improve perceptions of organizational support.

Attempts to improve interpersonal relationships in the workplace are less easily controlled by the organization. While management may engage in a variety of interventions to reduce conflict (De Dreu & Beersma, 2005) as well as improve interpersonal relations, the correlations between interventions and perceived interpersonal relations in the workplace remain fairly weak (Berman, West, & Richter, 2002). Thus, while the relationships facet may be a relatively strong predictor of overall satisfaction, it is probably less amenable to modification. Based on an examination of the individual facet zero-order correlations with overall satisfaction, it is likely that efforts at improving relations may be most easily achieved by focusing on the behavior of supervisors. Management could target supervisors' interpersonal relations with subordinates as a reasonable approach to addressing this problem. In North Carolina prisons, some master's-level psychologists are in supervisory positions over doctoral-level psychologists, predating a change in the psychology licensing law, and written comments reflected some frustration with this policy.

The general facet management, which represents job dimensions directly tied to management oversight (i.e., clear definition of role, adequate supervision, and appropriate levels of responsibility), did not predict overall job satisfaction. The low standardized regression coefficients suggest that changes in these aspects of the job are likely to produce little or no changes in overall satisfaction. The individual items that made up the general facet management correlated significantly with overall satisfaction, yet when combined, they accounted for little unique variability (i.e., incremental validity) in overall satisfaction when controlling for the remaining general facets. When using a simultaneous entry procedure, as we did, predictors that correlate highly with other predictors (as was the case with management) fare rather poorly in accounting for unique variability in the criterion. A worthwhile, alternative approach may be to enter general facets into the equation in the order in which they are most easily addressed or modified (e.g., if economic factors are easiest to address and correct, that should be entered first). We did not use a hierarchical entry strategy in the present case because we did not have clear evidence that some problems would be easier to correct than others.

*****

LIMITATIONS

*****

One of the complexities of working as a psychologist in a prison environment is the variability in training and educational background among psychology staff. As mentioned earlier, some doctoral-level psychologists in our sample were supervised by master's-level psychologists, and all are also supervised, albeit administratively, by the prison superintendent, who may have no background in psychology. Therefore, the item "satisfaction with supervision" may be too ambiguous to work well in this context. In the future, researchers might seek ways to operationalize the term *supervision* so that its meaning may be clearer to respondents and to evaluators (e.g., see Garland et al., 2009).

We used no outcome measures in the present study such as voluntary turnover or intent to resign that would have allowed us to assess the value of satisfaction in predicting some outcome measure of significance in the workplace.

The inclusion of an outcome measure such as an expressed intention to resign would have also provided us with a reasonable criterion to judge which overall satisfaction score (summed or single item) is most appropriate. Conversely, there are numerous consequences of high or low job satisfaction other than turnover or intent to resign, and so including these outcomes as criteria can serve to unnecessarily focus the intent of the present study on these particular outcomes. Our basic goal was to better understand how the individual facets of work as a correctional psychologist relate to overall satisfaction.

In conclusion, the measure of job satisfaction for correctional psychologists developed by Boothby and Clements (2002) proved to be useful in understanding respondents' overall measure of job satisfaction in this sample, particularly when we examined some prominent composite facets such as economics, relationships, and perceived organizational support. We found less evidence for the value of including the importance scales for each of the individual facets. The instrument developed by Boothby and Clements provides a useful tool in evaluating job satisfaction in correctional psychologists so as to better identify strategies to improve recruitment and retention.

REFERENCES

Ax, R. K., & Morgan, R. D. (2002). Internship training opportunities in correctional psychology: A comparison of settings. *Criminal Justice and Behavior, 29,* 332–347.

Balzer, W. K., Kihm, J. A., Smith, P. C., Irwin, J. L., Bachiochi, P.D., Robie, C., et al. (1997). *User's manual for the Job Descriptive Index (JDI; 1997 revision) and the Job In General (JIG) scales.* Bowling Green, OH: Bowling Green State University.

Bartol, C. R., & Bartol, A. M. (2004). *Introduction to forensic psychology.* Thousand Oaks, CA: Sage.

Bartol, C., & Freeman, N. J. (2005). A history of the American Association of Correctional Psychology. *Criminal Justice and Behavior, 32,* 123–142.

Berman, E. M., West, J. P., & Richter, M. N. (2002). Workplace relations: Friendship patterns and consequences (according to managers). *Public Administration Review, 62*, 217–230.

Boothby J. L., & Clements, C. B. (2000). A national survey of correctional psychologists. *Criminal Justice and Behavior, 27*, 716–732.

Boothby, J. L., & Clements, C. B. (2002). Job satisfaction of correctional psychologists: Implications for recruitment and retention. *Professional Psychology: Research and Practice, 33*, 310–315.

Brodsky, S. L. (2007). Correctional psychology and the American Association of Correctional Psychology: A revisionist history. *Criminal Justice and Behavior, 34*, 862–869.

Cohen, J. (1992). A power primer. *Psychological Bulletin, 112*, 155–159.

De Dreu, C. K. W., & Beersma, B. (2005). Conflict in organizations: Beyond effectiveness and performance. *European Journal of Work and Organizational Psychology, 14*, 105–117.

DiAngelis, T. (2008). Psychology's growth careers. *Monitor on Psychology, 39*(4), 64.

Eisenberger, R., Fasalo, P., & Davis-LaMastro, V. (1990). Perceived organizational support and employee diligence, commitment, and innovation. *Journal of Applied Psychology, 75*, 51–59.

Eisenberger, R., Huntington, R., Hutchison, S., & Sowa, D. (1986). Perceived organizational support. *Journal of Applied Psychology, 71*, 500–507.

Garland, B. E., McCarty, W. P., & Zhao, R. (2009). Job satisfaction and organizational commitment in prisons: An examination of psychological staff, teachers, and unit management staff. *Criminal Justice and Behavior, 36*, 163–183.

Gould, S. (1979). An equity-exchange model of organizational involvement. *Academy of Management Review, 4*, 53–62.

Hackett, R. D. (1989). Work attitudes and employee absenteeism: A synthesis of the literature. *Journal of Occupational Psychology, 62*, 235–248.

Hawk, K. M. (1997). Personal reflections on a career in psychology. *Professional Psychology: Research and Practice, 28*, 335–337.

Imparato, N. (1972). Relationship between Porter's Need Satisfaction Questionnaire and the Job Descriptive Index. *Journal of Applied Psychology, 56*, 397–405.

Ironson, G. H., Smith, P. C., Brannick, M. T., Gibson, W. M., & Paul, K. B. (1989). Construction of a Job in General scale: A comparison of global, composite, and specific measures. *Journal of Applied Psychology, 74*, 193–200.

Jackson, C. J., & Corr, P. J. (2002). Global job satisfaction and facet description: The moderating role of facet importance. *European Journal of Psychological Assessment, 18*, 108.

Judge, T. A., & Hurst, C. (2008). How the rich (and happy) get richer (and happier): Relationship of core self-evaluations to trajectories in attaining work success. *Journal of Applied Psychology, 93*, 849–863.

Judge, T. A., Thorensen, C. J., Bono, J. E., & Patton, G. K. (2001). The job satisfaction–job performance relationship: A qualitative and quantitative review. *Psychological Bulletin, 127*, 376–407.

Kinnunen, U., Feldt, T., & Makikangas, A. (2008). Testing the effort-reward imbalance model among Finnish managers: The role of perceived organizational support. *Journal of Occupational Health Psychology, 13*, 114–127.

Koslowsky, M., Kluger, A. N., & Yinon, Y. (1988). Predicting behavior: Combining intention with investment. *Journal of Applied Psychology, 73*, 102–106.

Lambert, E. G., Edwards, C., Camp, S. D., & Saylor, W. G. (2005). Here today, gone tomorrow, back again the next day: Antecedents of correctional absenteeism. *Journal of Criminal Justice, 33*, 165–175.

Lambert, E., Hogan, N., & Barton, S. (2003). The impact of instrumental communication and integration of correctional staff. *American Journal of Criminal Justice, 27*, 35–51.

Levinson, R. B. (1985). The psychologist in the correctional system. *American Journal of Forensic Psychology, 3*, 41–43.

Levy, P. E. (2006). *Industrial organizational psychology* (2nd ed.). Boston: Houghton Mifflin.

Locke, E. A. (1976). The nature and causes of job satisfaction. In M. D. Dunnett (Ed.), *Handbook of industrial and organizational psychology* (pp. 1297–1349). Chicago: Rand McNally.

MacKain, S. J., Tedeschi, R. G., Durham, T. W., & Goldman, V. (2002). So what are master's-level psychology practitioners doing? Surveys of employers and recent graduates in North Carolina. *Professional Psychology, Research and Practice, 33*, 408–412.

Magaletta, P. R., Patry, M. W., Dietz, E. F., & Ax, R. K. (2007). What is correctional about clinical practice in corrections? *Criminal Justice and Behavior, 34*, 7–21.

Manderscheid, R. W., Gravesande, A. G., & Goldstrom, I. D. (2004). Growth of mental health services in state adult correctional facilities, 1988 to 2000. *Psychiatric Services*, *55*, 869–872.

McShane, S. L., & Von Glinow, M. A. (2007). *Organizational behavior* (2nd ed.). New York: McGraw-Hill.

Milan, M. A., Chin, C. E., & Nguyen, Q. X. (1999). Practicing psychology in correctional settings: Assessment, treatment, and substance abuse programs. In A.K. Hess & I. B. Weiner (Eds.), *The handbook of forensic psychology* (2nd ed., pp. 580–602). New York: John Wiley.

Newman, R. A. (2008). *Recruiting and retaining correctional psychologists: A comprehensive multifaceted solution that works*. Paper presented at the Correctional Leadership Program (Class IX) North Carolina Department of Correction.

Norton, S. C. (1990). Supervision needs of correctional mental health counselors. *Journal of Addictions and Offender Counseling*, *11*, 13–19.

Reise, S. P., Waller, N. G., & Comrey, A. L. (2000). Factor analysis and scale revision. *Psychological Assessment*, *12*, 287–297.

Rhoades, L., & Eisenberger, R. (2002). Perceived organizational support: A review of the literature. *Journal of Applied Psychology*, *87*, 698–714.

Rice, R. W., Gentile, D. A., & McFarlin, D. B. (1991). Facet importance and job satisfaction. *Journal of Applied Psychology*, *76*, 31–39.

Schwartz, B. K. (2003). *Correctional psychology: Practice, programming, and administration.* Kingston, NJ: Civic Research Institute.

Smith, P. C., Kendall, L. M., & Hulin, C. L. (1969). *The measurement of satisfaction in work and retirement. Chicago: Rand McNally.*

Smith, P. C., Kendall, L. M., & Hulin, C. L. (1987). The revised JDI: A facelift for an old friend. *Industrial-Organizational Psychologist*, *24*, 31–33.

Tett, R. P., & Meyer, J. P. (1993). Job satisfaction, organizational commitment, turnover intention, and turnover: Path analyses based on meta-analytic findings. *Personnel Psychology*, *46*, 259–293.

Verhaest, D., & Omey, E. (2009). Objective over-education and worker well-being: A shadow price approach. *Journal of Economic Psychology*, *30*, 469–481.

Wayne, S. J., Shore, L. M., & Liden, R. C. (1997). Perceived organizational support and leader member exchange: A social exchange perspective. *Academy of Management Journal*, *40*, 82–111.

Weiss, D. J., Dawis R. V., & England, G. W. (1967). Manual for the Minnesota Satisfaction Questionnaire. *Minnesota Studies in Vocational Rehabilitation*, *22*, 120.

Yeoh, T. E. S. (2007). *The Facet Satisfaction Scale: Enhancing the measurement of job satisfaction.* Unpublished master's thesis, University of North Texas, Denton.

27

INNOVATIONS IN CORRECTIONAL ASSESSMENT AND TREATMENT*

ROBERT K. AX

THOMAS J. FAGAN

PHILIP R. MAGALETTA

ROBERT D. MORGAN

DAVID NUSSBAUM

THOMAS W. WHITE

Approximately 9 million people are incarcerated worldwide, with more than 2 million of these individuals being confined in U.S. prisons and jails (P. M. Harrison & Beck, 2005; Seena & Denesh, 2002). Exactly how many of these individuals have mental health problems has been the focus of considerable discussion. Ditton (1999) estimated that between 7% and 16% of the total U.S. prison and jail population (i.e., about 283,000 people) and 16% of individuals on parole or probation status (i.e., about 547,800 people) suffer from mental illness. Beck and Maruschak (2001) indicated that about 10% of state inmates had significant mental health problems. To define mental health problems, the authors of both of these studies used self-report data from offenders who admitted having a mental or emotional condition and/or reported an overnight stay in a mental hospital or program. Karberg and James (2005) noted that approximately 68% of individuals housed in U.S. jails were found to be dependent on or to have abused alcohol or drugs prior to their confinement. P. M. Harrison and Beck (2005) found

*This article was published in *Criminal Justice and Behavior*, *34*, 893–905 (2007). We have removed portions of the literature review on inmate suicides and most of a section on assessing and treating neurological correlates of maladaptive behavior. A concluding section has been left intact.

275

that 53% of federal prisoners and 20% of state prisoners were incarcerated for drug-related offenses. In a review of the literature on the presence of personality disorders in prisons and jails, Rotter, Way, Steinbacher, Sawyer, and Smith (2002) reported ranges from 7% to 35% depending on the particular disorder.

Interestingly, few of the above-mentioned studies considered the issue of co-occurring disorders. However, as Brems and Johnson (1997) and Sacks and Pearson (2003) have noted, most psychiatric disorders do not exist alone but rather in combination with other disorders. Brems and Johnson (1997); Newman, Moffitt, Caspi, and Silva (1998); and Reis, Mullen, and Cox (1994) have suggested that individuals with co-occurring disorders may differ in significant clinical ways from individuals with a single disorder (e.g., have poorer treatment outcomes and long-term prognoses and greater rates of hospitalization and suicidal behavior).

Prevalence research, such as that cited above, has been problematic in several ways. For example, studies have defined mental illness differently (e.g., current symptoms versus lifetime prevalence) and measured it differently (e.g., self-report, record review, structured interview). Studies have also examined the presence of mental illness using different subject pools (e.g., jail versus prison, male versus female, Black versus White versus Hispanic). Clearly, research is needed to clarify the impact that these various definitional, assessment, and demographic issues have on actual prevalence rates.

Despite variable prevalence rates, most studies agree that the number of incarcerated individuals with mental health problems exceed those found in the community and represent a growing population within prisons and jails, both in the United States (Diamond, Wang, Holzer, Thomas, & Cruser, 2001; Fisher et al., 2002; Jemelka, Trupin, & Chiles, 1989; Lamberti et al., 2001) and in other Western countries (Birmingham, Gray, Mason, & Grubin, 2000; Blaauw, Roesch, & Kerkhof, 2000; Fazel & Danesh, 2002). How responsive have correctional mental health practitioners been to the needs of this growing population? Ditton (1999) reported that about 60% of all federal and state offenders, 41% of all jail detainees, and 56% of all probationers with mental illness receive some type of mental health services while in custody or under supervision. If true, then 40% to 60% of offenders with mental health problems are *not* receiving needed services . . . .

CORRECTIONAL ASSESSMENT: ISSUES AND INNOVATIONS

Dimensional Versus Categorical Assessment

Consistent with current correctional practice standards published by the American Correctional Association (1990) and the National Commission on Correctional Health Care (2003), most correctional systems use a multi-step screening process to identify offenders with mental health problems. The outcome of this screening process is to identify offenders with symptoms sufficient to meet the diagnostic criteria of a mental disorder as defined in the American Psychiatric Association's (2000) *Diagnostic and Statistical Manual of Mental Disorders IV–TR* (*DSM-IV-TR*)—a categorical classification system that divides mental disorders into types based on specific defining criteria. Once identified, these offenders move through the mental-health-delivery system of the facility and are offered psychiatric (i.e., pharmacotherapy) and/or psychosocial (i.e., individual and/or group counseling) interventions targeting symptom alleviation. For offenders with a single diagnosis, this process is relatively straightforward. However, for offenders with comorbidity, this process is more complicated. For example, an offender with a diagnosis of both schizophrenia and substance abuse may be required to address the symptoms of the former successfully before being admitted to a substance abuse program. The substance abuse program is not equipped to address the needs of the schizophrenic individual, and the providers treating schizophrenia do not offer treatment programs for substance abusers.

Finally, offenders who report nondiagnosable or subthreshold mental health concerns often receive either minimal or no mental health services. It may be hypothesized that for some of these individuals, symptoms may intensify, reach *DSM* criteria, and result in referral and treatment. For others, symptoms may persist, resulting in alternative, perhaps self-defeating, coping strategies initiated by the offender (e.g., self-mutilation, self-medicating, acting out, social withdrawal), often resulting in disciplinary actions.

Is there an alternative strategy that would address all of the treatment needs of a given offender and the treatment needs of all offenders? Widiger and Samuel (2005) suggested a dimensional approach to diagnosis and treatment. In support of this approach, they assert that the presence of co-occurring disorders is the norm rather than the exception (cf. Kessler, 1995). Putting people in one or more individual diagnostic categories—each with its own treatment regimen—may produce a fragmented treatment strategy that treats problems in isolation rather than in their totality. Widiger and Samuel further noted that the presence of multiple diagnoses may indicate an underlying pathology common to all diagnoses. For example, they suggest the dimension of emotional instability or neuroticism as a potential underlying pathology common to the diagnoses of mood, anxiety, and personality disorders.

Watson (2005) offered two advantages to a dimensional versus a categorical approach. First, he suggests that a dimensional approach to examining underlying pathologies may provide more clinically relevant information. It allows the clinician to assess the severity of dysfunction rather than simply its presence or absence, and as research has suggested, severity of dysfunction is a good predictor of treatment outcome (Clark, Watson, & Reynolds, 1995). A dimensional approach also allows the clinician to measure treatment success incrementally rather than dichotomously (i.e., meet the diagnostic criteria

or not). Ultimately a dimensional approach may be more helpful in developing individualized, holistic treatment strategies.

If a dimensional approach to assessment and treatment is adopted, then the challenge for correctional researchers and practitioners will be to determine which underlying pathologies are found most frequently in criminal offenders. Once identified, a second challenge will be to determine which treatment strategies are most successful at addressing these pathologies.

Suicide Risk Assessment

Although suicide rates differ between local, state, and federal jurisdictions, it has been generally accepted for many years that suicide is a leading cause of death in prison (Lester, 1987) and jail populations (Hayes & Rowan, 1988). A recent study by the Bureau of Justice Statistics (BJS; see Mumola, 2005) confirms these long-standing findings, indicating that suicide is the second leading cause of death in jails and the third leading cause of death in prisons. Many offenders are at risk because they possess symptoms associated with mental illness and/or an increased likelihood of suicide.

*****

More recent studies (Mumola, 2005; White, Schimmel, & Frickey, 2002) raise questions concerning the basic assumptions that practitioners have about correctional suicide, may significantly alter historical perceptions of the problem, and may provide new directions for experimental investigation. These studies have asked whether inmate populations actually are a high-risk group for suicide. To address this question, most researchers have simply calculated suicide rates in jails and prisons and then compared those findings with suicide rates for the general population. For several decades, researchers have used these comparisons to conclude that suicide rates are 3 to 9 times greater for prison and jail inmates, respectively, than for the general population. Despite its simplicity, the appropriateness of that comparison and the accuracy of those conclusions are open to interpretation, and the reasons differ depending on whether prisons or jails are being referenced.

*****

. . . . it is clear that prison suicide rates have been steadily declining over the last 25 years. They have dropped from approximately 24 per 100,000 in the 1980s (White & Schimmel, 1995) to about 18 per 100,000 in 1993 (Hayes, 1995) and to about 14 per 100,000 in the early 2000s (state and federal rates combined; Mumola, 2005). Given the most recent prison suicide rate, we can now compare the rate for general population males of the ages most likely to be incarcerated (ages 25 to 55), and in doing so, we find it is actually higher (approximately 20 per 100,000) than their age-mate prison peers. By using a more accurate basis for comparison, it is clear the suicide rates are lower for prison inmates than for comparable males in the community. In addition, if the leading causes of death in the community are grouped as they are in correctional populations (i.e., placing all medical causes into one category), suicide ranks as the third leading cause of death in the general population, as it does in prison (Mumola, 2005). Thus, appropriate analysis indicates suicide rates for community males are higher than for offenders and cause of death data is equal for both populations, raising questions about the accuracy of the historical assumptions reflected in the opening sentence of this section.

Suicide rates for jail populations, however, are quite different and somewhat more complicated to calculate accurately. The most recent jail-suicide data show that, although jail-suicide rates have also declined since the 1980s when they were as high as 129 per 100,000, today's jail-suicide rate is still quite high, at approximately 47 per 100,000 (Mumola, 2005). This is more than 3 times the prison rate, but far less than 9 times greater than the general population rate. However, Mumola (2005) makes the point that, like prison rates, the jail-suicide rate is also artificially inflated but for different reasons.

*****

Taken collectively, these data clearly suggest that it may be necessary to rethink earlier assumptions about the generally high-risk nature of both correctional populations. For jail populations, it may be more realistic for researchers to think of suicide risk in terms of volume and resource allocation rather than the more typical focus on offender characteristics or the jail environment.

For many of the logistical reasons discussed earlier, most researchers are unable to gain access to national demographic data about the diagnostic, contextual, or environmental factors related to inmate suicide. However, a few studies with access to national suicide data (Mumola, 2005; White et al., 2002) have been able to shed some light on these variables. Recent population trends clearly show a dramatic increase in the number of mentally ill offenders entering the criminal justice system. This demographic shift might explain the finding that seriously mentally ill inmates who evidenced delusional and paranoid thinking were responsible for many federal prison suicides (White et al., 2002). This is quite different from community suicides that are diagnosed more often with mood disorders such as major depression.

One of the serious high-risk populations that these researchers discovered was high-security inmates serving long sentences who were unable to enter or remain in general population. This finding was echoed in the Mumola (2005) study that found long-term inmates with more than 5 years in custody accounted for about 32% of all prison suicides. Some similarities to high-security prison inmates were seen for jail populations as well. For example, violent jail inmates were 3 times more likely than nonviolent inmates to commit suicide, but in contrast to prison inmates, nearly half of all suicides in jails (49%) occurred within the first week of custody (Mumola, 2005). Mumola (2005) and White et al. (2002) found that the majority of prison suicides occurred in individual inmates' cells, with many prison suicides occurring in special housing units where mentally ill inmates are sometimes confined when they are unable to function in general population.

Specifically, White et al. found that about 60% of all suicides were committed in segregated housing, and 40% of those deaths (one third of all suicides) occurred within 3 days of being placed in the unit. Taken collectively, these data offer researchers promising avenues for future investigation. They suggest that although overall suicide rates for correctional populations may not significantly exceed general population data (depending on how they are calculated), suicide is still a fertile area for investigation because it accounts for a disproportionately high number of correctional deaths and is always a high-profile event. Furthermore, it seems clear from this review that jail- and prison-suicide deaths occur in clearly identifiable high-risk subgroups that merit greater attention from researchers and clinicians.

If continued declines in overall correctional suicide rates are to be achieved, research should begin targeting the known high-risk subgroups (e.g., mentally ill offenders, high-security and/ or violent offenders, newly admitted inmates to segregated housing units). There is a need to develop predictive tools to differentiate the characteristics of specific mentally ill offenders that put them at high risk for suicide attempts or death. Because many suicides occur in segregated housing, it seems beneficial to evaluate the effectiveness of screening programs for newly admitted inmates as well as nontraditional housing environments for disruptive mentally ill offenders. For example, diverting selected inmates to a designated treatment or "step-up" observation unit within the general population might be a viable alternative to segregation placement (Magaletta, Ax, Patry, & Dietz, 2005). Similar efforts should be directed toward identifying the unique factors in violent and long-term inmates that increase their likelihood of suicide. Along those lines, Conner, Duberstein, Conwell, and Caine (2003) have suggested a strong link between serotonin levels, impulsivity, and suicide. Application-oriented research that addresses these critical needs by providing practical solutions will make a significant contribution in any correctional setting.

Assessment and Treatment of Neurological Correlates of Maladaptive Behavior

Prisons typically have the twin goals of maintaining a safe and orderly environment and helping inmates make prosocial changes to minimize risk on re-entry to society. To ensure continued progress in both regards, correctional and forensic psychologists must appreciate the neurobiological bases of behavior as they pertain to forensic issues. This section provides several illustrations of this process and suggestions for future research that can transform psychologists' level of understanding and scope of practice in this vital area of public service.

Three different types of aggression identified in the animal aggression literature most significantly impact the criminal justice system (Nussbaum, Saint-Cyr, & Bell, 1997). *Predatory aggression* is marked by a tangible reinforcing goal, lack of emotionality and empathy, and a severity and degree of violence limited only by goal attainment. *Irritable aggression* occurs in response to frustration or insult, it is accompanied by angry affect, it does not have a tangible goal, and the severity is out of proportion to the eliciting stimulus. *Defensive aggression* is a response to threat: Its goal is to permit escape, and it is accompanied by intense fear. Defensive aggression becomes a problem for the criminal justice system when individuals with impaired reality testing perceive a threat where none exists and launch an often-serious preemptive attack. Each type of aggression has been shown to have distinct anatomical pathways with different principle neurotransmitters (Nussbaum et al., 1997). . . .

*****

CORRECTIONAL TREATMENT: ISSUES AND INNOVATIONS

Correctional mental health researchers must not only keep pace with scientific advancements in the public sector but also must anticipate the changing structure of service delivery and develop research programs that investigate the impact, benefit, and potential costs of innovative intervention strategies. Two innovative treatment strategies are discussed in this section.

Psychopharmacology in Correctional Settings

Treating a range of mental health problems with psychotropic medications is common in correctional settings. For example, Beck and Maruschak (2001) reported that nearly 10% of inmates in America's state prisons were taking psychotropic medications. Such demand, coupled with scarce resources (Manderscheid et al., 2004), makes it clear that whether by design or default, nonphysician mental health professionals working in corrections will have fairly regular contact with inmates who are taking or may benefit from psychotropic medication during their incarcerations.

One way in which psychologists might respond to the demand for mental health services in correctional settings is by adding prescriptive authority to their scope of practice. In 1995, the American Psychological Association officially endorsed the right of properly trained psychologists to seek prescriptive authority (Martin, 1995). With the subsequent passage of practice bills in Louisiana, New Mexico, and Guam, the initiative appears generally viable, and data indicate strong support among correctional psychologists for the prescriptive authority initiative (Fagan et al., 2004). Such authority would enable correctional psychologists to provide combined pharmacological and psychotherapeutic interventions where appropriate (Sammons & Schmitt, 2001) and could facilitate psychologists' involvement in outcome research with this understudied and clinically complex population. Prescriptive authority for correctional psychologists could therefore be highly cost-effective for the agencies that employ them.

Correctional Telehealth

Telehealth is a general term for data transmission systems used by health care professionals to deliver health care services over a distance (Bashur & Armstrong, 1976). Within corrections, this often takes the form of "real-time" audiovisual communications that connect agencies with service need populations (*the remote site*) to agencies that have specialist or generalist service providers (*the hub site*). The remote sites are usually mainline, nonspecialty corrections facilities, and the hub sites are resource-diverse facilities that can provide specialty services through external contracts or internal agreements.

Since their inception as pilot programs in the early 1990s (Magaletta, Fagan, & Ax, 1998; McCue et al., 1997; National Institute of Justice [NIJ], 1999, 2002; Raimer & Stobo, 2004; Vitucci, 1999; Zincone, Doty, & Balch, 1997; Zollo, Kienzle, Loeffelholz, & Sebille, 1999), corrections-based telehealth networks and applications have flourished. By the turn of the century, telehealth had won wide acceptance by correctional clinicians and administrators (Krizner, 2002), and correctional telehealth applications accounted for one fifth of all telehealth services offered (Lowes, 2001). In 2001, more than half of the correctional systems in America were delivering services to offenders via telehealth, with mental health services being one of the most frequently used applications (Larsen, Stamm, Davis, & Magaletta, 2004). The technology is used to evaluate offenders and prescribe psychotropic medications to patients where appropriate (Magaletta, Dennery, & Ax, 2005).

In terms of research and evaluation on corrections-based mental health services offered through telehealth, the field has been dominated by cost-benefit evaluations (Brunicardi, 1998; Larsen et al., 2004; Leonard, 2004; Magaletta, Ax, Bartizal, & Pratsinak, 1998; Magaletta, Fagan, et al., 1998; Manfredi, Shupe, & Batki, 2005; McCue et al., 1997; NIJ, 2002; Schopp, Johnstone, & Merrell, 2000; Zincone et al.,

1997). In terms of costs, the studies consistently found resistance from the professional services staff and high initial start-up costs. In terms of benefits, studies consistently pointed to improved security for the community in which the correctional institution is located (via a reduction in the number of times that offenders are escorted into the community or transferred to hospitals to receive services). Other benefits included improved safety for correctional staff within the institution, a reduction in overall cost of services, and quality-care indicators such as expanded access to types of care specialists who are familiar with correctional populations and/or formularies.

A smaller group of studies examined the clinical effectiveness and utility of telehealth. Within this group, several studies examined the reliability of assessments made through telehealth networks and found it to be acceptable (e.g., Brody, Claypoole, & Motto, 2000; Nelson, Zaylor, & Cook, 2004). In an exploration of how diagnosis interacts with telehealth technologies, Magaletta, Fagan, and Peyrot (2000) surveyed offenders with different diagnoses to assess their satisfaction with telehealth technology compared to the live services that they had received prior to their incarceration. They found that offenders with thought disorders had higher satisfaction with telehealth services than those with affective disorders and that those offenders with personality disorders were the most resistant to the technology. Finally, Morgan, Patrick, and Magaletta (2006) reported no significant differences among mentally ill offenders receiving psychiatric and/or psychological services in terms of their post-session mood, satisfaction with services, and perceptions of the therapeutic relationship regardless of the method of service delivery (i.e., telehealth or face-to-face).

Overall, the field is still in its infancy, and many of the studies require replication and methodological extension. In extending earlier studies, greater attention should be focused on measuring the clinical efficacy, utility, and outcomes of telehealth services (Jerome et al.,

2000). The mechanism of telehealth and how it interfaces with different diagnostic groups should also be studied further. From the perspective of the professional services staff, empirical questions remain as to whether training can ameliorate professional resistance. Research in the telehealth area would also benefit from further empirical study incorporating well-defined comparison groups, larger sample sizes, and richer descriptions of relevant historical and demographic variables. Because all of the current research in this area has focused on male offenders, research exploring the impact of telehealth services with female offenders is still needed.

Other telehealth innovations that correctional mental health researchers may also wish to quantify and evaluate are currently being developed. Perhaps the greatest of these innovations is the use of telehealth technology to enhance the continuity of care for releasing mental health offenders. Other areas include expanding the use of specialized mental health assessments, including competency assessments (Herrick, 1999; Merideth, 1999) and neurological evaluations (Magaletta, Fagan, et al., 1998; Schopp et al., 2000) as well as individual therapy, group therapy, and clinical supervision.

Finally, it remains an open question whether technology itself can indeed provide the treatment as well as be the modality. In this scenario, offenders with the neurocognitive deficits often seen in schizophrenia or the neurological limitations resulting from a traumatic brain injury could be offered computer-assisted cognitive remediation or psychosocial treatments and programs (Bellack, Dickinson, Morris, & Tenhula, 2005; Rotondi et al., 2005). In general, there remains potential for research to determine how computer technology could be developed to provide lifelike scenarios or interactive role-plays that could be used by offenders to develop or demonstrate mastery of core, clinical-change concepts such as empathy building or social skills (Paschall, Fishbein, Hubal, & Eldreth, 2005).

CONCLUSION

With so many seriously mentally ill individuals now incarcerated, the need for innovative and cost-effective assessment and treatment has never been greater. If it is true that change takes place at the margins, then corrections is where clinical psychology may expect to see new and cost-effective ideas implemented. Correctional psychology is moving toward a biopsychosocial understanding of human behavior. Accordingly, psychologists working in these environments should continue to refine and expand the assessment approaches and treatment methodologies discussed here, as is consistent with a holistic conceptualization of the patient.

However, this will be difficult in light of the scarce resources, the obstacles to conducting research, and the eclipse of the rehabilitation mission that characterize the current state of affairs in corrections. To realize this ambitious agenda, psychologists must be mindful of the need to demonstrate that these and other assessment and treatment innovations "add value" to their respective agencies by improving patient care and lowering costs.

REFERENCES

American Correctional Association. (1990). *Standards for adult correctional institutions* (3rd ed.). Lanham, MD: Author.

American Psychiatric Association. (2000). *Diagnostic and statistical manual of mental disorders* (4th ed. text revision). Washington, DC: Author.

Anno, B. J. (1985). Patterns of suicide in the Texas Department of Corrections, 1980–1985. *Journal of Prison and Jail Health, 5,* 82–93.

Bashur, R. L., & Armstrong, P. A. (1976). Telemedicine: A new mode for the delivery of health care. *Inquiry, 13,* 233–244.

Bechara, A., Damasio, H., & Damasio, A. R. (2001). Manipulation of dopamine and serotonin causes different effects on covert and overt decision-making. *Society for Neuroscience Abstracts, 27,* 126.

Beck, A. J., & Maruschak, L. M. (2001). *Mental health treatment in state prisons, 2000* (Bureau of Justice Statistics [BJS] Special Report No.

NCJ 188215). Washington, DC: National Criminal Justice Reference Service.

Bellack, A. S., Dickinson, D., Morris, S. E., & Tenhula, W. N. (2005). Thedevelopment of a computer-assisted cognitive remediation program for patients with schizophrenia. *Israeli Journal of Psychiatry Related Sciences, 42,* 5–14.

Birmingham, L., Gray, J., Mason, D., & Grubin, D. (2000). Mental illness at reception into prison. *Criminal Behavior and Mental Health, 10,* 77–88.

Blaauw, E., Roesch, R., & Kerkhof, A. (2000). Mental disorders in European prison systems: Arrangement for mentally disordered prisoners in the prison systems of 13 European countries. *International Journal of Law and Psychiatry, 23,* 649–663.

Bradford, J. (2006, June). *The biomedical treatment of child molesters.* Paper presented at the Annual Convention of the Canadian Psychological Association, Calgary, Alberta.

Brems, C., & Johnson, M. E. (1997). Clinical implications of the co-occurrence of substance use and other psychiatric disorders. *Professional Psychology: Research and Practice, 28,* 437–447.

Brewer-Smyth, K., Wolbert-Burgess, B. A., & Shults, J. (2004). Physical and sexual abuse, salivary cortical and neurologic correlates of violent criminal behavior in female prison inmates. *Biological Psychiatry, 55,* 21–31.

Brody, B. B., Claypoole, K. H., & Motto, J. (2000). Satisfaction of forensic patients with remote telepsychiatric evaluation. *Psychiatric Services, 51,* 1305–1307.

Brunicardi, B. O. (1998). Case report: Financial analysis of savings from telemedicine in Ohio's prison system. *Telemedicine Journal, 4,* 49–54.

Clark, L. A., Watson, D., & Reynolds, S. (1995). Diagnosis and classification of psychopathology: Challenges to the current system and future directions. *Annual Review of Psychology, 46,* 121–153.

Conner, K. R., Duberstein, P. R., Conwell, Y., & Caine, E. D. (2003). Reactive aggression and suicide: Theory and evidence. *Aggression and Violent Behavior, 8,* 413–432.

Diamond, P. M., Wang, E. W., Holzer, C. E., Thomas, C., & Cruser, D. A. (2001). The prevalence of mental illness in prison. *Administration and Policy in Mental Health, 29,* 21–40.

Ditton, P. M. (1999). *Mental health and treatment of inmates and probationers* (BJS Special Report

No. NCJ 174463). Washington, DC: U.S. Department of Justice (DOJ), National Institute of Justice (NIJ).

Fagan, T. J., Resnick, R. J., Ax, R. K., Liss, M., Johnson, R., & Forbes, M. R. (2004). Attitudes among interns and directors of training: Who wants to prescribe, who doesn't, and why. *Professional Psychology: Research and Practice, 35*, 345–356.

Fazel, S., & Danesh, J. (2002). Serious mental disorders in 23,000 prisoners: A systematic review of 62 surveys. *The Lancet, 359*, 545–551.

Filley, P., Nell, B. H., Nell, V., Antoinette, T., Morgan, A. S., Bresnahan, J. F., et al. (2001). Toward an understanding of violence: Neurobehavioral aspects of unwanted physical aggression: Aspen Neurobehavioral Conference consensus statement. *Journal of Neuropsychiatry, Neuropsychology and Behavioral Neurology, 14*, 1–14.

Fisher, W. H., Packer, I., Banks, S. M., Smith, D., Simon, L. M., & Roy-Bujnowski, K. (2002). Self-reported psychiatric hospitalization histories of jail detainees with mental disorders: Comparison with a non-incarcerated national sample. *Journal of Behavioral Health Services and Research, 29*, 458–466.

Harrison, A. A., Everitt, B. J., & Robbins, T. W. (1997). Central 5-HT depletion enhances impulsive responding without affecting the accuracy of attentional performance: Interactions with dopaminergic mechanisms. *Psychopharmacology, 133*, 329–342.

Harrison, P. M., & Beck, A. J. (2005). *Prisons in 2004* (BJS Special Report No. NCJ 210677). Washington, DC: DOJ, NIJ. Hayes, L. M. (1995) *Prison suicide: An overview and guide to prevention.* Washington, DC: DOJ, National Institute of Corrections.

Hayes, L. M., & Rowan, J. R. (1988). *National study of jail suicides: Seven years later.* Alexandria, VA: National Center for Institutions and Alternatives.

Herrick, S. M. (1999, August). *Forensic applications for telehealth: Assessing competency to stand trial.* Paper presented at the 107th Annual Convention of the American Psychological Association, Boston, MA.

Hoyert, D. L., Heron, M. P., Murphy, S. L., & Kung, H. C. (2006). *Deaths: Final data for 2003. A National Vital Statistics Report.* Washington, DC: DOJ.

Jemelka, R., Trupin, E., & Chiles, J. A. (1989). The mentally ill in prison: A review. *Hospital and Community Psychiatry, 40*, 481–491.

Jerome, L. W., DeLeon, P. H., James, L. C., Folen, R., Earles, J., & Gedney, J. K. (2000). The coming of age of telecommunications in psychological research and practice. *American Psychologist, 55*, 407–421.

Karberg, J. C., & James, D. J. (2005). *Substance dependence, abuse, and treatment of jail inmates, 2002* (BJS Special Report No. NCJ 209588). Washington, DC: DOJ, NIJ.

Kessler, R. C. (1995). The National Comorbidity Survey: Preliminary results and future directions. *International Journal of Methods in Psychiatric Research, 5*, 139–151.

Krizner, K. (2002). Telemedicine still looks for inroads to total acceptability. *Managed Healthcare Executive, 12*, 44–45.

Lamberti, J. S., Weisman, R. L., Schwarzkopf, S. B., Price, N., Ashton, R. M., & Trompeter, J. (2001). The mentally ill in jails and prisons: Toward an integrated model of prevention. *Psychiatric Quarterly, 72*, 63–77.

Larsen, D., Stamm, B. H., Davis, K., & Magaletta, P. R. (2004). Prison telemedicine and telehealth utilization in the United States: State and federal perceptions of benefits and barriers. *Telemedicine Journal and e-Health, 10*, 81–87.

Leonard, S. (2004). The development and evaluation of a telepsychiatry service for prisoners. *Journal of Psychiatric and Mental Health Nursing, 11*, 461–468.

Lester, D. (1982). Suicide and homicide in USA prisons. *American Journal of Psychiatry, 139*, 1527–1528.

Lester, D. (1987). Suicide and homicide in USA prisons. *Psychological Reports, 61*, 126.

Levi, M. (2004). *Aggression subtypes: The role of neuropsychological functioning and personality.* Unpublished doctoral dissertation, York University, Toronto, Ontario, Canada.

Lowes, R. (2001). Telemedicine. *Medical Economics, 78*, 24. Magaletta, P. R., Ax, R. K., Bartizal, D. E., & Pratsinak, G. J. (1998). Correctional telehealth. *Journal of the Mental Health in Corrections Consortium, 44*, 4–5.

Magaletta, P. R., Ax, R. K., Patry, M. W., & Dietz, E. F. (2005). Clinical practice in segregation: The crucial role of the psychologist. *Corrections Today, 67*(1), 34–36.

Magaletta, P.R., Dennery, C. H., & Ax, R. K. (2005). Telehealth: A future for correctional healthcare. In S. Stojkovic (Ed.), *Managing special populations in jails and prisons* (pp. 20–01–20–12). Kingston, NJ: Civic Research Institute.

Magaletta, P. R., Fagan, T. J., & Ax, R. K. (1998). Advancing psychology services through telehealth in the Federal Bureau of Prisons. *Professional Psychology: Research and Practice, 29*, 543–548.

Magaletta, P. R., Fagan, T. J., & Peyrot, M. F. (2000). Telehealth in the Federal Bureau of Prisons: Inmates' perceptions. *Professional Psychology: Research and Practice, 31*, 497–502.

Manderscheid, R. W., Gravesande, A., & Goldstrom, I. D. (2004). Growth of mental health services in state adult correctional facilities, 1988 to 2000. *Psychiatric Services, 55*, 869–872.

Manfredi, L., Shupe, J., & Batki, S. L. (2005). Rural jail telepsychiatry: A feasibility study. *Telemedicine Journal and e-Health, 11,* 574–577.

Martin, S. (1995, September). APA to pursue prescription privileges. *APA Monitor, 26*, 6.

McCue, M. J., Mazmanian, P. E., Hampton, C., Marks, T. K., Fisher, E., Parpart, F., et al. (1997). The case of Powhatan Correctional Center/Virginia Department of Corrections and Virginia Commonwealth University/Medical College of Virginia. *Telemedicine Journal, 3,* 11–17.

McLure, S. M., Laibson, D. I., Loewenstein, G., & Cohen, J. D. (2004). Separate reward neural systems value immediate and delayed monetary reward. *Science, 306*, 503–507.

Merideth, P. (1999). Forensic applications of telepsychiatry. *Psychiatric Annals, 29*, 429–431.

Morgan, R. D., Patrick, A. R., & Magaletta, P. R. (2006). *But does it alter the treatment experience? Inmates' perceptions of telehealth vs. face-to-face treatment modalities.* Manuscript submitted for publication.

Mumola, C. (2005). *Suicide and homicide in state prisons and local jails* (BJS Special Report No. NCJ 210036). Washington, DC: DOJ, Office of Justice Programs.

National Commission on Correctional Health Care. (2003). *Standards for health services in prisons.* Chicago: Author.

National Institute of Justice (NIJ), DOJ. (1999). *Telemedicine can reduce correctional health care costs: An evaluation of a prison telemedicine network* (Report No. NCJ 175040). Washington, DC: Author.

NIJ, DOJ. (2002). *Implementing telemedicine in correctional facilities* (Report No. NCJ 190310). Washington, DC: Author. Nelson, E., Zaylor, C., & Cook, D. (2004). A comparison of psychiatrist evaluation and patient symptom report in a jail telepsychiatry clinic. *Telemedicine Journal and e-Health, 10*, 54–59.

Newman, D. L., Moffitt, T. E., Caspi, A., & Silva, P. A. (1998). Comorbid mental disorders: Implications for treatment and sample selection. *Journal of Abnormal Psychology, 107*, 305–311.

Nussbaum, D., Saint-Cyr, J., & Bell, E. (1997). A biologically derived psychometric model for understanding, predicting, and treating tendencies toward future violence. *American Journal of Forensic Psychiatry, 18*, 35–51.

Nussbaum, D., Watson, M., Levi, M. D., & Ax, R. K. (2005, August). *Four neurobiological hypotheses to explain psychopathy and violence: Pharmacology and psychological treatment implications.* Paper presented at the 113th Annual Convention of the American Psychological Association, Washington, DC.

Paschall, M. J., Fishbein, D. H., Hubal, R. C., & Eldreth, D. (2005). Psychometric properties of virtual reality vignette performance measures: A novel approach for assessing adolescents' social competency skills. *Health Education Research, 20*, 61–70.

Raimer, B. G., & Stobo, J. D. (2004). Health care delivery in the Texas prison system. *Journal of the American Medical Association, 292*, 485–489.

Reis, R., Mullen, M., & Cox, G. (1994). Symptom severity and utilization of treatment resources among dually diagnosed inpatients. *Hospital and Community Psychiatry, 45*, 562–568.

Rotondi, A. J., Hass, G. L., Anderson, C. M., Newhill, C. E., Spring, M. B., Ganguli, R., et al. (2005). Clinical trials to test the feasibility of a telehealth psychoeducational intervention for persons with schizophrenia and their families: Intervention and 3-month findings. *Rehabilitation Psychology, 50*, 325–336.

Rotter, M., Way, B., Steinbacher, M., Sawyer, D., & Smith, H. (2002). Personality disorders in prison: Aren't they all antisocial? *Psychiatric Quarterly, 73*, 337–349.

Sacks, S., & Pearson, F. S. (2003). Co-occurring substance use and mental disorders in offenders: Approaches, findings, and recommendations. *Federal Probation, 67*(2), 32–39.

Sammons, M. T., & Schmitt, N. B. (Eds.). (2001). *Combined treatments for mental disorders: A guide to psychological and pharmacological interventions.* Washington, DC: American Psychological Association.

Schopp, L., Johnstone, B., & Merrell, D. (2000). Telehealth and neuropsychological assessment: New opportunities for psychologists. *Professional Psychology: Research and Practice, 31*, 179–183.

Schutter, D.J.L.G., & van Honk, J. (2005). Electrophysiological ratio markers for the balance between reward and punishment. *Cognitive Brain Research, 24,* 685–690.

Seena, F., & Danesh, J. (2002). Serious mental illness in 23,000 prisoners: A systematic review of 62 surveys. *The Lancet, 359,* 545–551.

Vitucci, N. (1999). Telemedicine utilized in treatment of inmates with hepatitis C. *Corrections Forum, 8,* 52–54.

van Honk, J., Schutter, D. J. L. G., Hermans, E. J., Putman, P., Tuiten, H., & Koppeschaar, H. (2004). Testosterone shifts the balance between sensitivity for punishment and reward in healthy young females. *Psychoneuroendocrinology, 29,* 937–943.

van Honk, J., Schutter, E. J., Hermans, E. J., & Putnam, P. (2003). Low cortical levels and the balance between punishment sensitivity and reward dependency. *Neuroport, 14,* 1993–1996.

Vogel-Sprott, M., Eadson, C., Fillmore, M., & Justus, A. (2001). Alcohol and behavioral control: Cognitive and neural mechanisms. *Alcoholism: Clinical and Experimental Research, 25,* 117–121.

Watson, D. (2005). Rethinking the mood and anxiety disorders: A quantitative hierarchical model for *DSM-V. Journal of Abnormal Psychology, 114,* 522–536.

White, T. W., & Schimmel, D. J. (1995). Suicide prevention: A successful five step program. In L. M. Hayes (Ed.), *Prison suicide: An overview and guide to prevention* (pp. 46–57). Washington, DC: National Institute of Corrections, DOJ.

White, T. W., Schimmel, D. J., & Frickey, R. (2002). A comprehensive analysis of suicide in federal prisons: A fifteen year review. *Journal of Correctional Health Care, 9,* 321–343.

Widiger, T. A., & Samuel, D. B. (2005). Diagnostic categories or dimensions? A question for the *Diagnostic and Statistical Manual of Mental Disorders–5th edition. Journal of Abnormal Psychology, 114,* 494–504.

Zincone, L. H., Jr., Doty, E., & Balch, D. C. (1997). Financial analysis of telemedicine in a prison system. *Telemedicine Journal, 3,* 247–255.

Zollo, S., Kienzle, M., Loeffelholz, P., & Sebille, S. (1999). Telemedicine in Iowa's correctional facilities: Initial clinical experience and assessment of program costs. *Telemedicine Journal, 5,* 291–301.

28

ESTIMATING THE MENTAL ILLNESS COMPONENT OF SERVICE NEED IN CORRECTIONS

Results From the Mental Health Prevalence Project*

PHILIP R. MAGALETTA

PAMELA M. DIAMOND

ERIK FAUST

DAWN M. DAGGETT

SCOTT D. CAMP

In 2005, more than 700,000 men and women were admitted to state and federal prisons to begin serving their sentences (Sabol, Minton, & Harrison, 2007). Within this group, offenders with mental illness will require mental health services during their incarceration. Legal mandates and humanitarian concerns alone require that such services be provided. In addition, the effective, safe, and orderly management of correctional facilities requires that these needs be met.

Although the lessons of the past have typically been forgotten, the impact of mental illness on American corrections has a long history (Morrissey & Goldman, 1986) . . . .

*This article was published in *Criminal Justice and Behavior*, *36*, 229–244 (2009). We have omitted tables and portions of the literature review, measures, results, and discussion.

During . . . 150 years, the correctional population in the United States grew into the millions. Several contemporary studies have provided refined estimates of mental illness and suggest a renewed interest in the mental health of offenders (for a review, see Diamond, Wang, Holzer, Thomas, & Cruser, 2001). Unfortunately, a mature field of investigation has yet to emerge from this renewed scientific interest, and several limitations remain endemic to most studies. For example, most lack specificity regarding important subpopulations, such as female offenders. Others do not capture important risk factors for mental illness such as race, ethnicity, and age. These greatly limit generalizability for population estimates. Equally problematic, few studies make effective use of operations-based data or data systems, thus limiting their ability to link prevalence estimates with real-time prison operations and correctional mental health services (Diamond, Magaletta, Harzke, & Baxter, 2008; Magaletta, McLearen, & Morgan, 2007; Magaletta & Verdeyen, 2005; Mears, 2004; Powitzsky, 2003).

Finally, most contemporary studies have limited their samples to offenders in state jurisdictions, leaving those in federal custody unexamined. This represents a critical omission in several respects. In terms of size, the federal system is currently the nation's largest corrections agency. As of June 30, 2006, the Bureau of Prisons (BOP) held 191,080 (12.3%) of the nation's offenders. In 2005 alone, 56,057 men and women began serving their sentences in various federal facilities (Sabol et al., 2007) . . . .

Few studies have examined the prevalence of mental illness among federal offenders. Among those that have, many have not appeared in peer-reviewed publications (Ditton, 1999; Gaes & Kendig, 2002; General Accounting Office, 1991; Pelissier et al., 1998; Scheckenback & Pape, 1992; Veysey & Bichler-Robertson, 2002), although some have (Koenig, 1995; Koenig, Johnson, Bellard, Denker, & Fenlon, 1995; Roth & Ervin, 1971; Walters, Mann, Miller, Hemphill, & Chlumsky, 1988). Offering an integrated perspective of results across all of these studies, Magaletta, Diamond, Dietz, and Jhanke (2006) noted that studies consistently report prevalence rates in the range of 6% to 9% when using unique, hybrid measures of "mental illness." These measures have typically used or have combined self-reported prior mental health service utilization and reports of having experienced mental health difficulties. This range is notably lower than prevalence rates previously reported from state departments of corrections . . . .

Studies examining the federal population are critical not only to administrators, managers, and clinicians within the federal prison system but also to those within the larger mental health, substance abuse, and general public health and safety communities. In 2005, 47,981 (26.8%) federal offenders returned to their home states (Sabol et al., 2007). Their mental health and substance abuse treatment needs did not dissolve on their release. In fact, needs may have been exacerbated by the stresses of living in the community and the demands of finding employment, reuniting with family, maintaining stable housing, and desisting from criminal activities. It is the community-based mental health and substance abuse treatment providers that assume the treatment of these individuals. The receipt of services in custody, beginning with screening on admission, can subsequently ease the transition to the community and can inform and influence the work conducted by these community-based providers (Lamberti, 2007).

Examining the major indicators of mental illness among federal offenders holds promise for advancing both science and practice by adding to the extant literature on state offenders. Although many factors maintain the need for mental health services in federal prisons, what is clearly needed to guide contemporary services is a thorough examination of the prevalence of mental illness, one that addresses the limitations of previous studies.

The purpose of the present study is to meet this need by examining multiple sources of data on a contemporary, nationally representative group of male and female federal offenders . . . .

METHOD

Participants

A purposeful sampling procedure was used to try to maximize the representativeness of the sample while minimizing the costs associated with collecting data from a system with prisons located across the nation. A nonprobability continual sampling strategy was developed. Specifically, gender and security level were stratified, and from five geographic regions 14 institutions were selected: 4 high-, 5 medium-, and 3 low-security male prisons and 2 low-security female prisons. Females and high-security males were oversampled to ensure representation from those groups. Offenders from administrative units, detention centers, and minimum-security camps were not included in the current study.

When final approval from the national institutional research review board was received for the MHPP, on-site research coordinators from each institution were selected and provided with standardized training to identify and enroll offenders. Sampling was coordinated with the psychology services intake screening process, which occurs at every institution for all offenders who enter the institution (e.g., transfers from other federal institutions, revocations, new court commitments). This coordination established a recurring mechanism for identifying and enrolling offenders and collecting operational mental health data. The only enrolled offenders for the present study were new court commitments who were new to federal custody, including those who had left custody but returned on a new charge. In addition, they spoke either English or Spanish fluently, could read at a fourth-grade level, and were physically and mentally able to complete self-report instruments.

Definitions

The prevalence estimate in this study was based on a combination of three major indicators of mental illness: diagnosis of a serious mental illness, history of inpatient psychiatric care, and psychotropic medication use. The following defines these terms as used in this study. A diagnosis of a serious mental illness was defined as schizophrenia or schizoaffective psychosis, bipolar disorder, or major depressive disorder. Current and lifetime diagnoses were differentiated depending on the data source. Inpatient psychiatric care was defined as evidence of psychiatric hospitalization as a youth or adult. This was coded as distinct from admissions for substance abuse treatment. Psychotropic medication use included the major categories of antipsychotics, mood stabilizers, and antidepressants. Text fields from the different data sources were matched to lists of medications commonly included in these general categories. Two separate coding schemes were used: One was more liberal, where medication use was coded as yes if there was evidence of any of the three types of medications in the data source, and the second was more conservative and was coded yes only if there was history of antipsychotic and/or mood stabilizer use. This was done to acknowledge the widespread prescription of antidepressants by primary care physicians for minor depression and other conditions that are not commonly considered serious mental illness (e.g., smoking cessation, pain management).

Measures

Psychology Services Inmate Questionnaire (PSIQ). The PSIQ is a fill-in-the-blank self-report form that is currently in use at all BOP facilities as part of the psychology services intake screening process. The majority of the items request a yes–no response, and the instrument assesses past mental health service use and current evidence of psychological problems (Diamond et al., 2008). The language used on the PSIQ is normed to a fourth-grade reading level. For the current study, the PSIQ was used to record any offender's self-reported prior or current psychotropic medication use. Items from the PSIQ are described in the tables as "offender self-report."

Psychology Intake Interview from the Psychology Data System (PDS). The PDS is part of the electronic mental health record for all BOP offenders. The psychologist who conducts the clinical intake interview with the offender records the results of this interview in PDS. The PDS format includes a set of specific response categories that generally guides the intake interview process. For the present study, a subset of these intake screening variables was used. These variables include any lifetime history of inpatient psychiatric hospitalization, a current diagnosis of serious mental illness, and any reported or known history of psychotropic medication use. Items from the PDS in the tables are described as "psychology intake interview."

*****

Pre-Sentencing Investigation and Coding Form (PSI-CF). The PSI is a report ordered by the judge after an offender has been found guilty or has pleaded guilty to the presenting charge or charges. Its purpose is to provide the history of and information about the defendant to aid in the disposition of the case. The investigation is conducted by trained probation officers and ordinarily follows a standard format that includes but is not limited to an interview of the defendant and corroboration of information through interviews with family members and/or requests for past public health and safety records. The final report typically includes detailed narrative information about the nature of the defendant's offense and criminal record. In addition, verified and self-report family, personal, physical and mental health, substance use, and employment histories are included.

*****

SENTRY. SENTRY is the BOP's national offender tracking and management data system. It includes sentencing, demographic, and classification information for all offenders in BOP custody. Data retrieved from SENTRY included demographics (e.g., citizenship, ethnicity) and relevant criminal history (e.g., number of prior arrests, sentence length). Several criminal history variables from SENTRY were used to describe the current sample. An offender was considered to have a prior record if he or she had ever been in the custody of any criminal justice system for any length of time. Severity of current offense was coded in an ordinal manner ranging from lowest (which includes white-collar and some property crimes) to greatest (including homicide and kidnapping). Violence history was also an ordered categorical variable that varied in both the level of violence of the prior act and the recent occurrence of the act. In addition to providing a profile of the offenders in the current study, demographic variables from the SENTRY data system were used to develop sampling weights that were used to weight sample findings to the target population of offenders.

Analysis

Both MHPP sample and weighted prevalence estimates were calculated and are presented in a disaggregated fashion, by gender, using individual indicators of mental illness defined above and by data source. In addition to this, these indicator variables were aggregated to provide an overall estimate of the prevalence of mental illness among newly committed federal offenders.

RESULTS

The final sample for the present study ($N = 2,855$) consisted of the offenders correctly identified as new commitments. . . .

Table 1 [not included here] provides a demographic breakdown for the MHPP sample as well as the weighted MHPP sample by gender and for the total. The average age of offenders in the sample was 33.6. The racial distribution for males was higher for Whites than non-Whites, and this difference was somewhat more pronounced for the females. Of both the males and females, 30% were identified as Hispanic. In all,

20% of the males and 38% of the females were non-U.S. citizens, and the largest group within the non-U.S. citizens for both males and females was from Mexico, at 14%.

Table 2 [not included here] provides information on the criminal history of offenders in the MHPP sample as well as the weighted MHPP sample by gender and for the total. In the MHPP sample, only 28% had no history of prior commitments, whereas 72% had either a minor or a serious prior record. Overall, males were defined as having more violence history than females. Only 36% of the males had no history of violence, whereas 81% of the females had no violence in their history. Overall, the average sentence length in the sample was 161.94 months (excluding 54 offenders with life sentences).

Table 3 [not included here] provides our estimates of mental illness for each of the individual indicators. The individual indicators are further delineated by the source of the data. In addition, overall prevalence estimates—indicated by the presence of any one of the indicators—are presented. Data for the MHPP sample as well as the weighted MHPP sample are presented by gender and for the total. In addition, the indicator defined by psychotropic medication use is presented for both liberal (with the inclusion of antidepressant medications) and conservative (not including antidepressants medications) estimates.

Using the combination of current and lifetime verified diagnosis, inpatient psychiatric care, and the more conservative medication criterion, we found that the weighted MHPP sample estimate of newly committed offenders potentially requiring some level of mental health service during incarceration was 15.2%. Disaggregating this figure, it appears that the lifetime diagnosis and inpatient psychiatric care indicators are carrying the majority of the weight in this estimate. It is surprising that 9.3% of the population is estimated to have experienced at least one inpatient psychiatric care episode prior to the current incarceration. As an individual indicator, medication accounted for only 3.6% of the conservative overall estimate. It is important to note that the impact of medication is quite different and more pronounced in the more liberal estimates. When psychotropic medication use includes antidepressants, it reaches an estimate of 12.3% as an individual indicator, and the overall prevalence rises to 19.0%. Finally, because the Psychology Intake Interview provides a *current* diagnosis, it may provide the closest link to immediate mental health service need. It is therefore important to note that the current diagnosis of serious mental illness for the total weighted MHPP sample is estimated at 3.1%.

In terms of gender, some large overall frequency differentials are seen . . . . These differentials find the female offenders having, on average, twice the rate on various indicators compared to the males. The largest overall difference appears under liberal psychotropic medication use. For male offenders, 11.4% of the weighted MHPP sample is estimated to have a history of psychotropic medication use, compared to 24.3% of the female offenders. This gender difference is reduced to 1.8% when the more conservative psychotropic medication use variable, which does not include antidepressants, is used.

In a separate analysis conducted to examine male offenders at the three different security levels, it was revealed that the overall prevalence rate estimates differed by security level. Those in lower-security facilities had consistently lower rates than did those in medium- or high-security facilities. For example, in terms of inpatient psychiatric care, MHPP male sample frequency was 11.5%. Disaggregated by security level, however, the figure was 4.4% for low and 11.3% and 13.6% for medium and high security levels, respectively.

DISCUSSION

Offenders with mental illness remain an important component of the correctional population that requires services during incarceration. Estimating the need for mental health services among this group requires examination of multiple indicators, including prior mental health service use as well as past and current diagnosis of serious mental illness. The present study was able to examine such data and begin to answer pertinent mental health questions that, to date, have remained unexplored. Combining each of the major indicators that were measured, our conservative estimate for the mental illness component of potential service need in a federal population of newly committed offenders was 15.2%. Here, we use the word *potential* because the degree to which prior or lifetime mental health events indicate present-day need in the correctional environment has yet to be determined.

The present work clearly extends prior research on federal offenders in several ways. In terms of diagnosis, it offers a unique perspective by incorporating either verified lifetime diagnoses or a current diagnosis provided by a mental health professional. This approach moves the field beyond synthetic estimates of diagnosis (Veysey & Bichler-Robertson, 2002), offender-based self-report of problems (Ditton, 1999; James & Glaze, 2006), or samples limited to one sampling site or gender (Koenig et al., 1995; Pelissier et al., 1998; Walters et al., 1988). Although the current study did not use a more rigorous structured diagnostic interview, this work clearly adds to the extant literature.

The majority of prior large-scale prevalence studies in the federal system have exclusively relied on one measure tapping only one reporting source (typically offender self-report) or time frame (lifetime). The use of multiple measures, multiple reporting sources, and multiple time frames provides the present study with a range of major indicators to be used additively or independently. From a mental health services perspective, this is important. Among studies of federal offenders, it has been noted that "studies consistently indicated that rates of diagnosis were higher than the rates of service utilization. To only consider diagnosis in the study of mental health prevalence in federal offenders may lead to an over representation of those who eventually need or choose to receive services. Conversely, only measuring service utilization may under

represent those who have a diagnosable and potentially treatable mental health condition" (Magaletta et al., 2006, p. 261).

By producing comparable estimates across both gender and security levels in this population, several important trends are noted. For example, there are very clear differences between male and female offenders. Across most indicators, female offenders have higher rates of mental illness. In a group of newly committed male offenders seen at intake, a clinician can expect to find mental illness in nearly one in seven offenders. The comparable figure for female offenders is one in four. In addition, within the male sample, there appears to be more mentally ill offenders housed in high- and medium-security facilities than in low-security facilities. Overall, these findings suggest that although the entire system bears the weight of treating the mentally ill offender, the volume of chronic offenders with mental illness may reside in three distinct parts of the system: female facilities and medium- and high-security male institutions. Therefore, increased mental health staffing levels should be considered at female and at medium- and high-security facilities to accommodate the overall need within these segments of the correctional system.

*****

Prior research comparing federal and state offenders has suggested a difference in overall rates of mental illness between the two groups (Ditton, 1999; James & Glaze, 2006; Veysey & Bichler-Robertson, 2002). Although the estimates provided in the present work do not generalize to offenders within state departments of corrections, our overall estimates suggest that the populations may actually be more similar than previously thought. Although the two jurisdictions (i.e., federal and state) do house correctional populations that are dissimilar along certain demographic and criminological dimensions, mental health might not be one of them. Of course, this remains an empirical question that awaits further exploration.

Several limitations of the current study must be noted. The first relates to external validity. Because we sampled from an incoming cohort of newly committed offenders housed in general population facilities at three security levels, we cannot generalize our findings to offenders from other parts of the system, such as minimum-security camps or administrative units, nor can we be confident that our findings generalize to the general population of federal offenders who have been incarcerated for some time. Although this limits our ability to make statements about the system as a whole, the offenders in our sample do reside in the types of facilities and at the types of security levels that house the vast majority of offenders and employ the majority of the mental health professionals in the system. In addition, it is worth noting that newly committed offenders eventually transition to become the larger proportion of the general population of offenders. Future research should examine the congruence between the present estimates in the newly committed and estimates generated as they begin this transition.

A second set of limitations relates to construct validity. We were able to make use of measures from a variety of sources, including interview data and self-report data. Although some of the information included in the interview documentation was confirmed through external sources, much of it did rely on the inmate as the primary reporting source. . . .

A final consideration relates to the specific indicators chosen as markers of mental illness in this study. All but one (current diagnosis from the Psychology Intake Interview) are distal indicators of mental illness. Although many of these indicators have been used in the community (Regier, Narrow, Rupp, Rae, & Kaelber, 2000), the degree to which they suggest current need or represent constant or episodic demands for service in this system has to take into consideration the unique features of correctional mental health (Ax et al., 2007; Magaletta et al., 2007; Mears, 2004; Powitzsky, 2003). For example, barriers to care traditionally encountered in community mental health settings—such as lack of transportation, no insurance, no local pharmacies—are typically not barriers to care in corrections. Other challenges that are seen in the community, such as problems with treatment engagement or adherence, not only are present in correctional populations but also gain additional momentum and complexity by interacting with criminal risk, lifestyle, and thinking.

Clearly, the demands placed on mental health professionals practicing in corrections are intense and varied. The development of frameworks to inform correctional mental health services remains a critical building block for the future if research is to guide the administration of these complex, multitiered mental health systems. Absent a shared understanding of such frameworks, critical questions regarding the degree to which individual lifetime indicators share a nexus with actual mental health service need in corrections will remain unanswered.

In terms of future correctional mental health services research, it is important to note that numerous other offender groups might require mental health services (Magaletta & Verdeyen, 2005; Soderstrom, 2007). In fact, the next steps planned for exploration with these data ought to be an examination of the rates of substance abuse. As it currently stands, the issue of how substance abuse has influenced these prevalence rates awaits completion. In addition, offenders with histories of suicide attempts, Axis II disorders, traumatic brain injuries, and sex offenses are all components of the correctional population who regularly receive correctional mental health services. As such, an empirical understanding of these different offender groups will provide the raw material needed to inform correctional policies. Finally, future research is also recommended to compare those who are in these various component groups to those who are not, both in cross-sectional designs and longitudinally as they serve out their sentences. The degree to which diagnostic prevalence rates can inform the longitudinal trajectories and outcomes of this newly committed cohort holds much promise for the development of criminological theory, the practice of corrections generally, and the treatment and management of offenders with mental disorders specifically.

Across gender and security level, this study points to the same conclusion: A component of the correctional population has significant mental health histories. The corrections system containing these offenders requires mental health professionals to screen, assess, manage, treat, and organize services and programs to meet their needs. It also requires these professionals to determine the degree to which mental health histories warrant current and/or later (i.e., episodic) levels of mental health care. Although the present work begins to fill in our understanding of these issues, much work remains. Behind the door of the mental health professional's office and within the walled perimeter of the custodial system, treatment continues. Correctional administrators plan systems of care with the resources they are provided. The developing science in this area must flourish in support of the public service professionals who, on a daily basis, are meeting the challenges of providing a level of care expected by the public and entrusted to be delivered by the correctional system.

REFERENCES

Ax, R. K., Fagan, T. J., Magaletta, P. R., Morgan, R. D., Nussbaum, D., & White, T. W. (2007). Correctional assessment and treatment: Issues and innovations. *Criminal Justice and Behavior, 34,* 879–892.

Barnes, H. E. (1968). *The evolution of penology in America.* Montclair, NJ: Patterson Smith.

Diamond, P. M., Magaletta, P. R., Harzke, A. J., & Baxter, J. (2008). Who requests psychological services upon admission to prison? *Psychological Services, 5*(2), 97–107.

Diamond, P. M., Wang, E. W., Holzer, C. E., III, Thomas, C. R., & Cruser, D. A. (2001). The prevalence of mental illness in prison: Review and policy implications. *Administration and Policy in Mental Health, 29,* 21–40.

Ditton, P. M. (1999). *Mental health and treatment of offenders and probationers. Bureau of Justice Statistics bulletin.* Washington, DC: U.S. Department of Justice.

Gaes, G. G., & Kendig, N. (2002, January). *The skill sets and health care needs of released offenders.* Paper presented at the From Prison to Home conference, Bethesda, MD.

General Accounting Office. (1991, November). *Mentally ill offenders: BOP plans to improve screening and care in Federal prisons and jails* (GAO/GGD-92–13). Washington, DC: Author.

Hiller, M., & Narevic, E. (2007). The validity of self-reported information from prisoners in a modified therapeutic community. In K. Knight & D. Farabee (Eds.), *Treating addicted offenders: A continuum of effective practices* (pp. 7–1, 7–4). Kingston, NJ: Civic Research Group.

James, D. J., & Glaze, L. E. (2006). *Mental health problems of prison and jail offenders.* Washington, DC: U.S. Department of Justice, Bureau of Justice Statistics.

Koenig, H. G. (1995). Religion and older men in prison. *International Journal of Geriatric Psychiatry, 10,* 219–230.

Koenig, H. G., Johnson, S., Bellard, J., Denker, M., & Fenlon, R. (1995). Depression and anxiety disorder among older male offenders at a federal correctional facility. *Psychiatric Services, 45,* 399–401.

Kroner, D. G., Mills, J. F., & Morgan, R. D. (2007). Underreporting of crime-related content and prediction of criminal recidivism among violent offenders. *Psychological Services, 4,* 85–95.

Lamberti, J. S. (2007). Understanding and preventing criminal recidivism among adults with psychotic disorders. *Psychiatric Services, 58,* 773–781.

Magaletta, P. R., Diamond, P. M., Dietz, E. F., & Jhanke, S. (2006). The mental health of federal offenders: A summative review of the prevalence literature. *Administration and Policy in Mental Health and Mental Health Services Research, 33,* 253–263.

Magaletta, P. R., Dietz, E. F., & Diamond, P. M. (2005). *The prevalence of behavioral and psychological disorders among an admissions cohort of federal inmates* (Bureau of Prisons, Research Review Board 01–038). Washington, DC: U.S. Department of Justice.

Magaletta, P. R., McLearen, A., & Morgan, R. D. (2007, December). Framing evidence for mental health services research in corrections. *Corrections Today,* pp. 38–40.

Magaletta, P. R., & Verdeyen, V. (2005). Clinical practice in corrections: A conceptual framework. *Professional Psychology, Research and Practice, 36,* 37–43.

Mark, T. L., Levit, K. R., Coffey, R. M., McKusick, D. R., Harwood, H. J., King, E. C., et al. (2007). *National expenditures for mental health services and substance abuse treatment, 1993–2003.* Rockville, MD: Substance Abuse and Mental Health Services Administration.

Mears, D. (2004). Mental health needs and services in the criminal justice system. *Houston Journal of Health Law and Policy, 4,* 255–284.

Milazzo-Sayre, L. J., Henderson, M. J., Manderscheid, R. W., Blacklow, B. G., Evans, C., & Male, A. A. (2004). Selected characteristics of adults treated in specialty mental health care programs, United States, 1997. In R. W. Manderscheid & M. J. Henderson (Eds.), *Mental health, United States, 2002* (DHHS Pub. No. SMA 3938, pp. 243–279). Rockville, MD: Substance Abuse and Mental Health Services Administration.

Morrissey, J., & Goldman, H. H. (1986). Care and treatment of the mentally ill in the United States: Historical developments and reforms. *Annals of the American Academy of Political and Social Science, 484,* 12–27.

Pelissier, B. M., & Saylor, W. (January, 1998). *TRIAD Drug Treatment Evaluation Project six-month interim report.* Washington, DC: Federal Bureau of Prisons.

Powitzsky, R. J. (2003). A useful management tool for understanding correctional mental health services. *Correctional Mental Health Report, 4*(5), 65–66, 77–80.

Regier, D. A., Narrow, W. E., Rupp, A., Rae, D. S., & Kaelber, C. T. (2000). The epidemiology of mental disorder treatment need: Community estimates of "medical necessity." In G. Andrews & S. Henderson (Eds.), *Unmet need in psychiatry: Problems, resource, responses* (pp. 41–58). New York: Cambridge University Press.

Roberts, R. O., Bergstralh, E. J., Schmidt, L., & Jacobsen, S. J. (1996). Comparison of self-reported and medical record health care utilization measures. *Journal of Clinical Epidemiology, 49,* 989–995.

Roth, L. H., & Ervin, F. R. (1971). Psychiatric care in federal prisoners. *American Journal of Psychiatry, 128,* 56–62.

Sabol, W. J., Minton, T. D., & Harrison, P. M. (2007). *Prison and jail inmates at midyear 2006. Bureau of Justice Statistics bulletin.* Washington, DC: U.S. Department of Justice.

Scheckenback, A., & Pape, M. (1992). *Psychology Data System 1992 summary report.* Washington, DC: Federal Bureau of Prisons.

Soderstrom, I. R. (2007). Mental illness in offender populations: Prevalence, duty and implications. *Journal of Offender Rehabilitation, 45,* 1–17.

Veysey, B. M., & Bichler-Robertson, G. (2002). Prevalence estimates of psychiatric disorders in correctional settings. In *The health status of soon-to-be-released offenders: A report to Congress* (Vol. 2, pp. 57–80). Chicago: National Commission on Correctional Health Care.

Walters, G. D., Mann, M. F., Miller, M. P., Hemphill, L. L., & Chlumsky, M. L. (1988). Emotional disorder among offenders. *Criminal Justice and Behavior, 15,* 433–453.

29

THE EFFECT OF A COGNITIVE TREATMENT PROGRAM FOR MALE AND FEMALE JUVENILE OFFENDERS*

ADREA HAHN MCGLYNN

PHILIP HAHN

MICHAEL P. HAGAN

There has been significant discussion regarding the purpose of corrections and the utilization of it very recently in the United States. Glaze (2010) described the ongoing drop in crime in the United States. Earlier, Levitt (2004) described the significant drop in crime in the 1990s in the United States, including a drop of 43% in homicides from 1991 to 2001, 34% for violent crime overall, a 25% drop in rape, and 4% drop in burglary. Victimization dropped along with it and crime dropped in all major categories. This drop was unexpected and crossed all demographic groups and geographic boundaries. The United States Department of Justice, Federal Bureau of Investigation (2009) reported a drop in violent crime of approximately 2% between 2007 and 2008. This drop surprisingly continued into the recession, and several states have in reaction adopted programs that provide for early release of inmates to reduce state budget deficits and reduce the cost of incarcerating the highest numbers of prisoners in the history of the United States. Michigan, Illinois, Wisconsin, and California have worked to release some inmates prior to the end of their initially imposed sentence. The trend continued

*This article was published in *International Journal of Offender Therapy and Comparative Criminology*, 57, 1107–1119 (2013). We have removed parts of the literature review as well as a section on data analysis.

in 2010 according to the United States Department of Justice, Federal Bureau of Investigation with a drop of 6% in violent crime. The most recent data for the first half of 2011, which is preliminary, indicate the trend continues and there was a 6.4% drop from the same time in 2010.

*****

In addition to the number of adults involved with correctional systems, the number of juveniles involved in delinquent activities is significant. According to FBI 2007 arrest statistics, juveniles comprised 15.3% of the total number of arrests, 16.2% of violent crimes, and 26% of property crimes (Puzzanchera, Adams, & Kang, 2009). Analyzing juvenile delinquency and its prevention is especially important provided that involvement in delinquent activities at an early age contributes to increased crime and other difficulties in adulthood. Colman, Kim, Mitchell-Herzfeld, and Shady (2008) write that the connection between delinquent boys and adult criminal behavior is well documented in the literature.

To reduce costs to society by increasing safety and preventing future criminal activity, correctional intervention programs are utilized and are especially important for juvenile offenders. More specifically, intervention is important for serious juvenile offenders. It has been found that serious delinquents can be helped to desist in offending behavior and avoid incarceration or supervision (Lipsey, Wilson, & Cothern, 2000; Merwe & Dawes, 2007; Wilson, Attrill, & Nugent, 2003). A meta-analysis of the available research conducted by Lipsey et al. (2000) discovered that the 200 intervention programs studied produced significant positive effects averaging a 12% reduction in recidivism. Many types of programs were reviewed, including ones that focused on building interpersonal skills, increasing anger management skills, milieu therapy, behavior management, and individual counseling. The best programs they analyzed, including a cognitive mediation group for institutionalized male and female juvenile delinquents, reduced recidivism by as much as 40%.

Delvin and Gibbs (2010) found significant behavioral changes to coincide with cognitive changes for community-based offenders completing a cognitive intervention program. The Responsible Adult Culture (RAC) program was utilized with 104, three quarters men, offenders at a community-based correctional facility. Using the How I Think (HIT) Questionnaire as a measure of change, the authors correlated cognitive change with behavioral changes. RAC participants were found to have a "greater reduction in risk for offending behavior, longer latency before recidivating, and a lower likelihood of recidivism" during a 12-month follow-up and as compared with residents at a comparable facility.

Correctional intervention programs have also been demonstrated to be cost-effective.

*****

Within the juvenile population, the number of female delinquents, relative to male delinquents, seems to be rising as does their adjudication for violent crimes. Female juvenile arrest rates increased from 20% to 29% between 1980 and 2003 (Snyder & Sickmund, 2006). This is meaningful because it represents a 69% increase in delinquent behavior of girls. In addition, it has been reported that female adolescent involvement in delinquent behavior results in poorer future outcomes than it does for males. The negative consequences of female juvenile offending are broader and more enduring than the immediate impact of the offense and the cost of incarceration or other intervention . . . .

To date, there has been very little research that investigates the effectiveness of intervention for female juvenile offenders. The majority of the interventions designed for offenders have been developed for men, and there may be significant gender differences in response to treatments for conduct-disordered behaviors (Hipwell & Loeber, 2006). For all of these reasons, it is important to evaluate the effectiveness of interventions for female juvenile delinquents as well as those for males.

*****

Cognitive therapy has been demonstrated to be effective in reducing externalizing behaviors (Leeman, Gibbs, & Fuller, 1993; Wilson et al., 2003). The belief is that the correction of cognitive distortions will result in behavioral improvements. Cognitive programs are based on the theory that a lack of thinking skills such as interpersonal, problem solving, social perspective taking, and self-control contribute to offending behavior (Wilson et al., 2003). Cognitive intervention is intended to restructure cognitions and develop and make more flexible the offender's cognitive skills so that he or she can develop more adaptive patterns of reasoning. This change in reasoning or thinking may change the offender's reaction to situations, which may trigger delinquent behavior.

Based on the available research, it can be concluded that interventions that target cognitive distortions not only improve cognitions and behavior but also reduce recidivism (Lipsey et al., 2000; Wormith et al., 2007). A meta-analysis conducted by Lipsey et al. (2001) reviewed the research to examine the effects of cognitive-behavioral programs on the reoffense rates of offenders. They limited their review to studies that were the most methodologically credible, focused centrally on cognitive change, applied cognitive-behavioral therapy (CBT) to general offender populations, and utilized reoffense recidivism as the outcome variable. They discovered that the studies showed that CBT is clearly an effective intervention. The offenders who completed treatment recidivated at a rate of about two thirds that of the offenders in the "treatment-as-usual" control groups used for comparison (Lipsey et al., 2001). In fact, the most effective treatment programs reduced recidivism to about one third the rate of the control group. Moreover, the treatment programs applied to juveniles resulted in a similar reduction in recidivism rates. The treated offenders demonstrated between one third to two thirds the recidivism rates of nontreatment control groups (Lipsey et al., 2001).

The State of Wisconsin Department of Corrections, Division of Juvenile Corrections (DJC) operates three secure juvenile correctional facilities.

Youth in these facilities have been adjudicated delinquent and committed by a Wisconsin juvenile court. The facilities include two institutions for boys, Ethan Allen School (EAS) and Lincoln Hills School (LHS), and one for girls, Southern Oaks Girls School (SOGS), ages 14 through 17. One of the many programs offered by DJC is the Juvenile Cognitive Intervention Program (JCIP). The program is based on the premise that if we can change how someone thinks, we can change their behavior. Many delinquents have cognitive distortions, and attribute their problems to others, and in addition have the belief that they can not change what happens to them. In addition, they often ignore information that may mitigate their propensity for acting out. The JCIP works at helping them recognize cognitive distortions they make, changing the distortions to a more appropriate thinking pattern, and practicing this so that they can use these new skills in finding better ways of dealing with their problems and finding more positive solutions to their concerns. More detailed information on the theoretical foundations, development, and specific lessons can be found in Bogestad, Kettler, and Hagan (2009).

In an effort to ensure the effectiveness of JCIP, the DJC has implemented the use of a number of different performance measures, including the HIT Questionnaire. Prior to starting Phase I of JCIP, youth are required to complete the HIT Questionnaire, the Pride in Achievement Scale, and the JCIP Concept Survey. At the completion of Phase I, youth are required to again complete the JCIP Concept Survey. Before youth successfully complete Phase II of JCIP, they are required to take a final knowledge test on the material presented over Phase I and II of JCIP. If they do not earn a passing grade on the test, they are required to repeat Phase II. Once a youth has completed Phase II of JCIP, they are required to again complete the HIT Questionnaire, the Pride in Achievement Scale, and the JCIP Concept Survey.

In sum, JCIP is founded on the conceptualization that delinquent or maladaptive behaviors are a result of dysfunctional thought processes or cognitive distortions. Therefore, the program follows a cognitive-restructuring approach that aims to positively modify cognitive distortions associated with negative behaviors. JCIP is designed to assist youthful offenders who are at a high risk of reoffending in developing cognitive skills that allow them to make prosocial choices. In JCIP, youth are taught to identify and challenge negative thought patterns that result in poor decisions and antisocial behaviors. JCIP is delivered in a group setting by trained facilitators, typically social workers, using highly standardized instruction materials that are detailed in a manual.

The HIT Questionnaire is utilized to measure the effectiveness of JCIP in targeting cognitive distortions. The HIT Questionnaire specifically examines self-serving cognitive distortions as they are related to externalizing problem behavior (Liau et al., 1998). The HIT Questionnaire is considered a reliable and valid measure (Barriga & Gibbs, 1996). The research conducted by Bogestad et al. (2009) investigated the effectiveness of JCIP in improving cognitive distortions. They discovered that JCIP effectively targets and reduces cognitive distortions that are associated with antisocial behaviors. They also reported in their findings that the program appears to have a broad impact thereby improving cognitive distortions across multiple areas.

The HIT Questionnaire was developed by Gibbs and Potter (Gibbs, 1991, 1993; Gibbs, Potter, & Goldstein, 1995) and formulated a four-category typology to describe self-serving cognitive distortions:

Self-Centered: According status to one's own views, expectations, needs, rights, immediate feelings, and desires to such a degree that the legitimate views, etc., of others (or even one's own long-term best interest) are rarely considered or are disregarded altogether.

1. Blaming Others: Misattributing blame to outside sources, especially another person, a group, or a momentary aberration (one was drunk, high, in a bad mood, etc.), or misattributing blame for one's victimization or other misfortune to innocent others.

2. Minimizing/Mislabeling: Depicting antisocial behavior as causing no real harm or as being acceptable or even admirable, or referring to others with a belittling or dehumanizing label.

3. Assuming the Worst: Gratuitously attributing hostile intentions to others, considering a worst-case scenario for a social situation as if it were inevitable, or assuming that improvement is impossible in one's own or other's behavior. (Barriga et al., 2001, p. 4)

*****

PURPOSE OF THE STUDY

Despite research that demonstrates the effectiveness of cognitive treatment for juvenile offenders, there remains a strong need for additional evidence that treatment can be widely disseminated and effectively implemented with different populations of high-risk offenders. The purpose of this study is to evaluate the effectiveness of the JCIP program in targeting cognitive distortions as evaluated by the HIT Questionnaire. It advances the knowledge obtained in an earlier study because this is a much larger study that allows for the review of the initial findings in Bogestad et al. (2009). Moreover, this study included a significantly larger study than did Bogestadt et. al (2009), which allowed for additional analyses of the data. This included the ability to assess differences based on gender, age, length of incarceration, resistance to programming, and first time versus second time completers. These factors will provide for a better understanding of the nature of cognitive changes in juvenile delinquents and the generalization of cognitive intervention as provided in this program to different groups of delinquents. It is documented that cognitive distortions contribute to delinquent and externalizing maladaptive behaviors. It is proposed that modifying these distortions will result in decreased negative behavior and will reduce the rate of recidivism for those who complete the program.

METHOD

Participants

The participants in this study were 518 youth incarcerated in one of three juvenile correctional facilities in Wisconsin all of whom completed both pre- and posttreatment assessment of cognitive distortions using the HIT Questionnaire. Sixteen potential participants were not included because they did not successfully complete the program within the time frame of this study. In this study, there were 197 participants who participated in JCIP a second time or repeated the program. Noncompletion of the program can be due to several factors, including missing group due to being in disciplinary status or refusal to participate in programming. Of the 534 youth, there were 431 male and 103 female participants. The participants ranged in age from 12 to 18, with a mean age of 16.31. All participants were adjudicated delinquent and would have faced a minimum of 6 months of incarceration if they had committed the same offenses as adults. Most youth had been in several treatment programs in the past and had numerous acts of violent delinquency on their records.

Procedure

All youth in the study were administered the HIT Questionnaire and then participated in the first two phases of the JCIP. These are the two phases which are designed to be completed during incarceration. After completing the first two phases, the youth were once again administered the HIT to determine whether their cognitive thinking patterns improved as measured by this instrument. Some of the youth repeated the program, including pre- and posttreatment assessment, because of a failure to complete it the first time. In the cases where youth were repeating the program, practice effect on the HIT was controlled for by comparing their progress to a new pretreatment administration of the HIT to a new administration of it at the end of treatment. The results were evaluated to determine which areas assessed by the HIT were found to improve and which were not. The data was collected in each institution and provided to the DJC central office where it was stored.

*****

RESULTS

The JCIP program was found to significantly reduce the overall HIT ($t518 = 17.65, p < .0001$) with all participants pooled into one analysis. The mean HIT before the program was 3.24 ($\pm0.97, SD = 1$) and dropped to 2.52 ($\pm0.81, SD = 1$) after the program. The gender by JCIP program (before/after) interaction was significant, $F(1, 482) = 9.1; p = .003$. Both genders had a highly significant reduction in overall HIT following the JCIP, although the reduction effect was different between genders. The reduction was larger for males ($M = 3.30, SE = 0.06$ before to $M = 2.55, SE = 0.06$ after; $p < .0001$). The reduction was smaller for females, although still highly significant ($M = 3.07, SE = 0.14$ before to $M = 2.61, SE = 0.15$ after; $p < .0001$).

Age had a weak, but significant, effect on the overall HIT scores, with younger participants performing worse, $F(1, 564) = 6.46; p = .01$. Age reduced the overall HIT at a rate of -0.08, 95% CI = $[-0.14, -0.02]$ per year of age increase. The time incarcerated before starting the JCIP program had no significant effect on the overall HIT, $F(1, 546) = 0.07; p = .79$.

The participation main effect was significant, $F(2, 719) = 4.09; p = .02$, as was the gender by participation interaction, $F(2, 718) = 8.80; p = .0002$. However, the effect of participation level was only significant for females, not males (all male comparisons $p > .1$). Overall HIT scores for females with minimal participation were not different from females who were cooperative and involved ($p = .95$), but both had significantly improved HIT scores than females who actively resisted (resisted: $M = 3.77, SE = 0.38$;

minimal: $M = 2.45$, $SE = 0.13$, $p = .01$; cooperative: $M = 2.32$, $SE = 0.08$, $p = .003$; p values are when compared with resisted). The sample size for females who actively resisted was small ($n = 5$) and thus there is limited confidence in making conclusions about them.

The JCIP by participation by gender ($p = .63$) and JCIP by participation level ($p = .42$) interactions were not significant, so they were pooled into the residual error before the final model was run. For participants who repeated the program ($n = 200$), there was no difference between their first and second time, $F(1, 388) = p > .77$, and the JCIP by the number of repeats interaction was nonsignificant, $F(1, 390) = 2.71$; $p = .10$.

Total time incarcerated did not affect overall HIT, $F(1, 545) = 0.00$; $p = .96$, so it was not included as a covariate. Age at the start of the JCIP program decreased the HIT with increasing age, although this trend was very weak and highly variable: slope $= -0.055$, r2 $= .005$; F(1, 579) $= 4.24$; p $= .04$. Therefore, we did not include age at the start of the program as a covariate. Overall HIT scores for individuals with minimal participation were not different from individuals who were cooperative and involved (p $= .99$), but both had significantly lower HIT scores than individuals who actively resisted (resisted: M $= 4.06$, SE $= 0.29$; minimal: M $= 2.46$, SE $= 0.11$, p $< .0001$; cooperative: M $= 2.34$, SE $= 0.07$, p $< .0001$; p values are when compared with resisted). Unfortunately, the sample size for individuals who actively resisted was small at all institutions ($n = 35$ at EAS and $n = 13$ at LHS), and particularly small at SOGS ($n = 7$). When these seven observations were deleted, the participation effect and interactions were no longer significant ($p > .1$). Although this information is interesting, the small sample size of those who resisted prevented us from generating robust inferences based on participation level. Therefore, we removed participation from subsequent analysis. The Institution by Period interaction was significant, $F(2, 562) = 61.42$; $p < .0001$. All institutions had a highly significant reduction in overall HIT following the JCIP.

Of the people who repeated the program ($n = 197$), there was no difference between their first and second time, $F(2, 400) = 0.01$; $p = .91$, and all interactions were nonsignificant ($p > .05$).

DISCUSSION

Similar to the previous study by Bogestad et al. (2009), the statistical analysis in this study demonstrates the overall effectiveness of JCIP in reducing juvenile offenders' scores on the HIT Questionnaire. This change implies an improvement in the cognitive distortions of the participants, which are associated with conduct-disordered behavior. The analyses also demonstrated a reduction in scores across all areas. This indicates that the program appears to broadly improve cognitive distortions of different types. It provides more evidence that cognitive distortions are amenable to change in a group treatment setting with individuals who are more severely delinquent and at a higher risk of reoffending.

Similar to the previous research article by Bogestad et al. (2009), a significant difference was found between the levels of reduction of male and female HIT scores. This could be attributed to research that has discovered that in general, adolescent males have a higher deficit in cognitive skills associated with more conduct-disordered behavior. Larden et al. (2006) reported a finding that adolescent girls made more mature moral judgments, demonstrated more empathy, and reported less antisocial cognitive distortions than their male counterparts. In addition, there is research that reports that female offenders have specific criminogenic needs that differ from those of males. For example, it has been suggested that low self-esteem associated with victimization may be a priority for treatment programming with females but not with males (Shearer, 2003; Wilson et al., 2003). There is more research on the treatment needs of male juvenile offenders than girls, and this study provides more evidence in this area. In this study, the males' higher scores on their pretreatment HIT implies that they had more room for a reduction than did females. Therefore, the results support that JCIP in this study was as effective at reducing scores for female delinquents as it was for male delinquents.

The finding that age has a significant effect on change in HIT score was not predicted. The results indicate that younger offenders have higher HIT scores associated with more cognitive distortions. Younger juvenile offenders demonstrated more cognitive deficits in that their cognitive skills are not as developed as their older counterparts. It is also possible that the younger adolescent's cognitive schemas are not as flexible resulting in more concrete and problematic thinking. It needs to be kept in mind, however, that younger youth are likely to be more problematic than relatively older youth who are sent to juvenile correctional facilities. In Wisconsin, every effort is made to try to work with youth in the community and younger youth who are incarcerated, although in the authors' experience, they tend to be far more behaviorally problematic in general as compared with older youth.

The clinical implications of this study support the use of cognitive intervention programs with delinquent youth. This is critical as there has been a significant decrease in the population of incarcerated youth in Wisconsin. When this study was commenced, there were three facilities, but at this point, due primarily to a very significant drop in the juvenile population, there is one site that works with boys and girls, although there is sight–sound separation. With the reduction in resources, it is more important than ever to use programming that is effective in making changes that will translate into transition to the community.

A limitation of the current study is the lack of a control group for comparison, which of course is a common concern in field research. The authors are confident, however, that due to the robust results across ages and genders, the results do evidence the effectiveness of cognitive programming in changing cognitive distortions associated with delinquency. It is thought

that future research in this area that includes a control group would enhance our understanding of this subject.

Future research needs to be conducted to further examine the differences between female and male offenders' response to treatment. Further research looking at adjustment and recidivism post release is indicated; the primary objective of the program being to make lasting changes in thinking and behavior. For all of these different populations, future research should investigate whether and how decreased HIT scores affect an individual's conduct-disordered behavior. In this regard, more long-term studies need to be conducted to examine outcomes of the individual's successful reintegration to the community to determine the effectiveness of JCIP. It is this examination that will determine the overall benefit to the juvenile and society.

REFERENCES

Barriga, A. Q., & Gibbs, J. C. (1996). Measuring cognitive distortion in antisocial youth: Development and preliminary evaluation of the How I Think questionnaire. *Aggressive Behavior*, *22*, 333–343.

Barriga, A. Q., Gibbs, J. C., Potter, G. B., & Liau, A. K. (2001). *How I Think (HIT) questionnaire manual*. Champaign, IL: Research Press.

Barriga, A. Q., Landau, J. R., Stinson, B. L., Liau, A. K., & Gibbs, J. C. (2000). Cognitive distortion and problem behaviors in adolescents. *Criminal Justice and Behavior*, *27*, 36–56.

Bogestad, A., Kettler, R., & Hagan, M. (2009). Evaluation of a cognitive intervention program for juvenile offenders. *International Journal of Offender Therapy and Comparative Criminology*, *20*, 1–14.

Cauffman, E. (2008). Understanding the female offender. *Future of Children: Juvenile Justice*, *18*, 119–142.

Census of State and Federal Correctional Facilities. (2005). Retrieved from http://bjs.ojp.usdoj.gov/index.cfm?ty=pbdetail&;iid=530

Colman, R., Kim, D. H., Mitchell-Herzfeld, S., & Shady, T. A. (2008). Retrieved from https://www.ncjrs.gov/pdffiles1/nij/grants/226577.pdf

Delvin, R., & Gibbs, J. (2010). Responsible Adult Culture (ROC) cognitive and behavioral changes at a community-based correctional facility. *Journal of Research in Character Education, 8*, 1–20.

Fergusson, D. M., Horwood, J., & Ridder, E. M. (2005). Show me the child at seven: The consequences of conduct problems in childhood for psychosocial functioning in adulthood. *Journal of Child Psychology and Psychiatry, 46*, 837–849.

Gibbs, J. C. (1991). Sociomoral developmental delay and cognitive distortion: Implications for the treatment of antisocial youth. In W. M. Kurtines & J. L. Gewirtz (Eds.), *Handbook of moral behavior and development: Vol. 3. Application* (pp. 95–110). Hillsdale, NJ: Lawrence Erlbaum.

Gibbs, J. C. (1993). Moral-cognitive interventions. In A. P. Goldstein & C. R. Huff (Eds.), *The gang intervention handbook* (pp. 159–185). Champaign, IL: Research Press.

Gibbs, J. C., Potter, G., & Goldstein, A. P. (1995). *The EQUIP program: Teaching youth to think and act responsibly through a peer-helping approach.* Champaign, IL: Research Press.

Glaze, L. (2010). *Correctional Populations in the United States 2010.* Retrieved from http://bjs.ojp.usdoj.gov/index.cfm?ty=pbdetail&;iid=2237

Hipwell, A. E., & Loeber, R. (2006). Do we know which interventions are effective for disruptive and delinquent girls? *Clinical Child and Family Psychology Review, 9*, 221–255.

Larden, M., Melin, L., Holst, U., & Langstrom, N. (2006). Moral judgement, cognitive distortions and empathy in incarcerated delinquent and community control adolescents. *Psychology, Crime & Law, 12*, 453–462.

Leeman, L. W., Gibbs, J. C., & Fuller, D. (1993). Evaluation of a multi-component group treatment program for juvenile delinquents. *Aggressive Behavior, 19*, 281–292.

Levitt, S. D. (2004). Understanding why crime fell in the 1990s: Four factors that explain the decline and six that do not. *Journal of Economic Perspectives, 18*, 163–190.

Liau, A. K., Barriga, A. Q., & Gibbs, J. C. (1998). Relations between self-serving cognitive distortions and overt vs. covert antisocial behavior in adolescents. *Aggressive Behavior, 24*, 335–346.

Lipsey, M. W., Chapman, G., & Landenberger, N. A. (2001). Cognitive-behavioral programs for offenders. *Annals of the American Academy of Political and Social Science, 578*, 144–157.

Lipsey, M. W., Wilson, D. B., & Cothern, L. (2000). *Effective intervention for serious juvenile offenders* (Juvenile Justice Bulletin). Washington, DC: U.S. Department of Justice, Office of Juvenile Justice and Delinquency Prevention.

Merwe, A., & Dawes, A. (2007). Youth violence: A review of risk factors, causal pathways and effective intervention. *Journal of Child & Adolescent Mental Health, 19*, 95–113.

Moffitt, T. E., Caspi, A., Rutter, M., & Silva, P. A. (2001). *Sex differences in antisocial behavior.* Cambridge, UK: Cambridge University Press.

Pajer, K. (1998). What happens to bad girls? A review of the adult outcomes of antisocial adolescent girls. *American Journal of Psychiatry, 155*, 862–870.

Pulkkinen, L., & Pitkanen, T. (1993). Continuities in aggressive behavior from childhood to adulthood. *Aggressive Behavior, 19*, 249–263.

Puzzanchera, C., Adams, B., & Kang, W. (2009). Easy access to FBI arrest statistics 1994–2007. Retrieved from http://ojjdp.gov/ojstatbb/ezaucr/

Shearer, R. (2003). Identifying the special needs of female offenders. *Federal Probation, 67*, 46–56.

Snyder, H. N., & Sickmund, M. (2006). *Juvenile offenders and victims: 2006 National Report.* Washington, DC: Department of Justice, Office of Justice Programs, Office of Juvenile Justice and Delinquency Prevention.

Spilke, H., Piepho, P., & Hu, X. (2005). Analysis of unbalanced data by mixed linear model using the MIXED procedure of the SAS system. *Journal of Agronomy and Crop Science, 191*, 47–54.

United States Department of Justice, Federal Bureau of Investigation. (2009). *Crime in the United States, 2008.* Retrieved from http://www2.fbi.gov/ucr/cius2008/index.html

Welsh, B. C., & Farrington, D. P. (2000). Correctional intervention programs and cost-benefit analysis. *Criminal Justice and Behavior, 27*, 115–133.

Wilson, S., Attrill, G., & Nugent, F. (2003). Effective interventions for acquisitive offenders: An investigation of cognitive skills programmes. *Legal and Criminological Psychology, 8*, 83–101.

Wormith, J. S., Althouse, R., Simpson, M., Reitzel, L., Fagan, T. J., & Morgan, R. D. (2007). The rehabilitation and reintegration of offenders: The current landscape and some future directions for correctional psychology. *Criminal Justice and Behavior, 34*, 879–892.

Yochelson, S., & Samenow, S. E. (1976). *The criminal personality: A profile for change* (Vol. 1). New York, NY: Jason Aronson.

30

Examining the Effectiveness of a Restorative Justice Program for Various Types of Juvenile Offenders*

Kathleen J. Bergseth

Jeffrey A. Bouffard

In the three and a half decades since their development (Okada, 2011), restorative justice (RJ) programs have become relatively commonplace in the United States and elsewhere especially as a response to minor, and sometimes more serious, forms of juvenile delinquency or even adult criminal behaviors (Bazemore & Umbreit, 2001). These programs attempt to create nonadversarial dialogue among victims, offenders, and other affected individuals to address the harms caused by crime and promote offender accountability. RJ programs have increased in popularity because they hold promise for achieving several goals, including increased community and victim involvement in the justice process, greater victim and community satisfaction with the case outcomes, improved offender compliance with restitution, increased perceptions of procedural fairness (Latimer, Dowden, & Muise, 2005; Leonard & Kenny, 2011), and to some extent recidivism reduction (McCold & Wachtel, 1998).

Although there is debate among RJ advocates over the centrality of the goal of recidivism reduction, a number of existing evaluations have in fact demonstrated that RJ programs can reduce the likelihood of reoffending (Bonta, Wallace-Capretta, & Rooney,

---

*This article was published in *International Journal of Offender Therapy and Comparative Criminology*, *57*, 1054–1075 (2013). We have deleted portions of the literature review summarizing past studies, including meta-analyses, a section on analyses, and all tables in results.

1998; de Beus & Rodriguez, 2007; Hayes & Daly, 2004; Luke & Lind, 2002; Maxwell & Morris, 2001; McGarrell, 2001; Rodriguez, 2005; Wong, Cheng, Ngan, & Ma, 2011). At the same time, others have shown less success in meeting this goal (McCold & Wachtel, 1998; Niemeyer & Shichor, 1996; Roy, 1993; Umbreit, 1994). Whereas individual evaluations have produced an inconsistent picture in terms of the effectiveness of RJ programs in recidivism reduction, meta-analyses have found consistent support for reduced recidivism among participants in programs that include restorative components, with effect sizes including .03 (Bonta, Wallace-Capretta, Rooney, & McAnoy, 2002), .07 (Latimer et al., 2005), .26 (Bradshaw & Roseborough, 2005), and as high as .30 among studies with stronger methodological characteristics (Nugent, Williams, & Umbreit, 2004).

These recent meta-analyses have demonstrated varying degrees of program success (i.e., in achieving recidivism reductions). In light of these diverse findings, some authors have begun to examine whether RJ approaches are differentially effective for certain types of offenders (Hayes, 2005; McCold & Wachtel, 1998; Rodriguez, 2007; Sherman, Strang, & Woods, 2000). The current study continues this line of inquiry by examining whether an RJ program targeting juvenile offenders has differential impacts on recidivism across various offender characteristics, including age, gender, racial group membership, offending history, and current offense type.

RJ APPROACHES

The term *restorative justice* typically encompasses a wide range of programs, including victim–offender mediation (VOM), community reparative boards, family group conferencing (FGC), and circle sentencing (Bazemore & Umbreit, 2001), as well as some other approaches that use community service

or restitution (e.g., Bonta et al., 1998). The overall goal of these programs is to restore the harm caused by the offense to the particular victim(s) and to the wider community, as well as to eliminate the likelihood of repeated offenses by addressing any underlying issues with the offender that may have precipitated the offense (Smith, 2001).

RJ approaches in general, and those that make use of group conferencing in particular (e.g., FGC, VOM), attempt to bring together affected individuals, the victim(s), community members, and the offender, in a nonadversarial process that promotes offender accountability and repairs the various harms caused by the crime (Bazemore & Umbreit, 2001). There are four basic models of restorative processing (i.e., VOM, FGC, circle sentencing, reparative boards) that share common features, including the development of sanctions that focus on the community, a nonadversarial and less formal process, and decision making by consensus rather than by a single authority (Bazemore & Umbreit, 2001).

Proponents of restorative programs suggest that they differ from traditional justice programs that focus more on retribution (i.e., "an eye for an eye") than restoration (i.e., repairing the harm caused by crime; Bazemore, 1998). In addition, RJ approaches often contrast with the traditional justice system in their definition of crime (as harm to the community or a violation of relationships, rather than a violation against "the state"; Cormier, 2002; Leonard & Kenny, 2011; Zehr & Mika, 1997), the nature of the proceedings (consensus- and community-based), the primary focus of each approach (restoration vs. punishment), and a more active role for victims (Bazemore, 2000; Bonta et al., 1998; Cormier, 2002; Kurki, 1999; Leonard & Kenny, 2011; Pranis, 1998; Smith, 2001; Zehr & Mika, 1997). Those who advocate for these programs claim these features make RJ processing superior to typical juvenile or criminal court processing, because the RJ process is better at meeting victim needs, strengthening the community, and reducing offender recidivism.

Effectiveness of RJ

Some RJ advocates suggest that recidivism reduction is not the central goal of such programs, rather that they are intended to "meet the real needs of victims, offenders, and their communities created by the criminal act" (McCold & Wachtel, 1998, p. 73). There are numerous potential benefits of RJ programs, and while some supporters may not agree that recidivism reduction is one of the most important goals, the programs' potential for reducing reoffending is a paramount concern for policy makers who may wish to consider restorative programming as an alternative to traditional juvenile or criminal court processing. In any case, high levels of victim and offender satisfaction and compliance with restorative agreements have been demonstrated in numerous RJ program evaluations (see, for example, Braithwaite, 2002; Latimer & Kleinknecht, 2000; Leonard & Kenny, 2011). As noted previously, empirical studies of the effectiveness of RJ on recidivism have been somewhat mixed, however . . . .

*****

Studies of Differential Effectiveness

While meta-analyses have demonstrated varying degrees of success for RJ approaches in terms of reducing reoffending outcomes, another group of studies (including at least one meta-analysis, Latimer et al., 2005) has emerged that attempt to examine the differential effectiveness of RJ approaches across various offense and offender characteristics (de Beus & Rodriguez, 2007; Hayes, 2005; Hayes & Daly, 2003, 2004; Kirby Forgays & DeMilio, 2005; McCold & Wachtel, 1998; Rodriguez, 2007; Sherman et al., 2000). These studies have examined this issue as one possible explanation for the sometimes mixed results observed in existing research. Rodriguez (2007), in particular, has called for research into the possibility of differential effectiveness,

because as she states, such efforts "advance(s) research by moving beyond the question of whether restorative justice programs can be successful at reducing crime and addressing the circumstances under which programs can be most effective" (p. 363).

At the same time, critics of RJ programs often suggest that the programs can only be used with less serious offenders (see McAlinden, 2011 for a discussion of this issue). Most research into the potential for individual factors to moderate the effectiveness of RJ programming has examined current offense type, for instance, examining whether RJ interventions work "better" for property offenders rather than those charged with violent crimes. Only a few studies have specifically examined the potential moderating effect of individual demographic factors or prior offending (see Rodriguez, 2007 for an example), despite the fact that many individual-level risk factors may have such moderating effects, particularly when considered in relation to the Risk, Need, and Responsivity (RNR) principles outlined by Andrews and Bonta (2003).

Specifically, given that RJ programs often involve low-intensity, short-term interactions (i.e., a single VOM meeting), one might suspect that these programs would only work well for low-risk offenders (the risk principle). Increased risk of offending is often related to factors like the individual's age, gender, and racial group, as well as a history of prior offending (although Andrews & Bonta, 2003, would also argue that more dynamic factors, like antisocial attitudes, would be better predictors of risk). Regardless, the impact of such legal (criminal history) and extralegal (demographic) factors has been the subject of considerable attention as they may indirectly affect traditional justice system processing, but as Rodriguez (2007) notes, similar research on differential effectiveness in RJ outcome studies is just emerging. The current study attempts to address this shortcoming in the literature . . .

*****

CURRENT STUDY

. . . (T)here have been few attempts to examine the potential for differential impacts of RJ programming on offenders who vary in their risk levels, as indicated by demographic and criminal history measures. Most of the attempts to examine potential moderating effects have involved studies of these programs' differential effectiveness across groups of offenders based on the current offense (i.e., violent or not)—a factor often used by RJ program personnel to select individuals for participation in the program itself. A few studies have examined the potential moderating effects of individual, risk-related characteristics (i.e., participant demographics), or prior offending history. As these various factors are common correlates of, or risk factors for, crime and delinquency, it is important for those interested in the effectiveness of RJ programming to understand whether these factors moderate the impact of the intervention. Results indicating that this type of intervention works only for individuals characterized as low risk would suggest limited potential to apply the program to a broad range of juvenile offenders. Conversely, if the program is similarly impactful among higher risk individuals, the prospects for widespread application of the approach are increased. The current effort is designed to address this gap in the existing literature by exploring the possible moderating effects of age, gender, race/ethnicity, and prior offending behavior.

METHOD

Sample

The sample consists of 352 youth referred to the RJ program operating in a small city in the Upper Midwest see (Bergseth & Bouffard, 2007 for a complete discussion of this RJ program). Participants entered the RJ program between 1999 and 2005, and they are compared with a sample of 353 similar youth who were referred for traditional juvenile justice system. The study

was reviewed and approved by the Institutional Review Board at the primary author's institution. The comparison group was developed by selecting youth referred to standard juvenile court processing during roughly the same time period (2000–2005). Specifically, the juvenile probation office for the jurisdiction being studied provided a list of all youth referred to traditional court processing during the specified years (additional demographic information on this population of juvenile probationers is not available). From this population, the researchers identified a group of 353 youth for inclusion in the study based on referral offense type (e.g., property, violent, public order) in an attempt to select a group of youth whose referral offenses were similar to those in the RJ intervention group.

Measures

Basic demographic and referral offense information was provided by program staff for the 353 youth referred to the RJ program. This information was used to select a group of comparison youth (using simple, aggregated matching procedures) with similar instant offenses referred to traditional juvenile court processing. The names of youth in both groups were then entered into the local juvenile court database from which demographic and offense history information was retrieved. All official contacts occurring after the date of referral (to either RJ or traditional processing) were also recorded, including the date, level (i.e., status, misdemeanor, felony), and type (e.g., status, property, violent) of each offense.

Sample Characteristics

An examination of both groups revealed that 67 youth referred to the RJ program were actually referred to RJ and traditional court processing for the same offense. Approximately, half of these youths ($n = 33$) were referred to RJ as a condition of their traditional sentence (i.e., a condition of their probation); the reason for dual referral (e.g., failure in RJ and then referral to traditional processing; successful restorative processing but traditionally processed anyway) was less clear for the remaining youth ($n = 34$). The focus of the current study is on restorative processing as an alternative to traditional court processing; thus these 67 cases were excluded from analyses. Missing data resulted in the exclusion of an additional 18 cases. The final sample of 551 includes 284 youth referred exclusively to RJ processing and 267 youth referred exclusively to traditional juvenile court processing.

The sample includes primarily young, White males from the small urban area, many of whom had no prior official contact and who were referred for property-related misdemeanor offenses. As presented in Table 1, 71.5% of the sample are non-White and 72.8% are male. Youth averaged 14.95 years of age on referral; those referred to RJ were approximately 16 months younger than those referred to traditional processing ($F = 56.42$, $df = 1$, 549, $p = .000$). A total of 69% of youth in the sample came from the small urban area in the county, although youth referred to RJ were more likely to come from the small urban area (74.6%) than youth referred to traditional processing, 62.9%; $\chi^2(1, N = 551) = 8.82$, $p = .003$. Most youth were referred to their respective program for a misdemeanor offense (84%) and while the most serious current (referral) offense for the majority of youth (67.2%) was property related (e.g., theft, vandalism), the comparison group included a larger number of youth referred for violent offenses (e.g., assault, threats; 19.9%) than the RJ group, 12%; $\chi^2(1, N = 551) = 6.43$, $p = .04$. The remainder was referred for "other" offenses, including curfew violations, alcohol- or tobacco-related charges, drug possession, traffic offenses, or disorderly conduct.

Most youth in the sample (73.7%) had no prior contact with juvenile justice authorities; however, youth referred to traditional processing were more likely to have had prior official contact (38.2%) than those referred to RJ, 15.1%; $\chi^2(1, N = 551) = 37.75$, $p = .000$. The average number of prior official contacts was .53 (range = 0–13); youth referred to traditional processing experienced significantly more prior contacts (average .84) than youth referred to RJ processing (.27; $F = 25.88$, $df = 1$, 549, $p = .000$). The most serious prior charge for most youth was a property-related charge (66.2%), although youth in the comparison group were more likely to have experienced one or more violent (i.e., persons-related) charges, $\chi^2(2, N = 551) = 15.02$, $p = .001$. Finally, the average follow-up period (post-program referral) was 3.5 years; comparison youth were followed for approximately 6 months longer than youth referred to RJ ($F = 11.53$, $df = 1$, 549, $p = .001$).

Treatment/Intervention

The study presented here incorporated an intention to treat (ITT) design (Sherman & Strang, 2004) to eliminate potential confounding effects of treatment motivation (or offending propensity) that occurs when cases are analyzed based on the treatment actually delivered. Individuals were retained in treatment (RJ) and comparison (traditional juvenile justice) groups based on referral to those interventions, regardless of whether they actually received the assigned intervention. In other words, the RJ group includes all youth referred to RJ processing regardless of whether they were deemed appropriate for the program, or whether victims were willing to participate. For some youth, the RJ intervention was limited to initial referral and discussions with RJ staff, which may itself produce some therapeutic benefit. As a result, the research reported here represents a conservative estimate of the impact of RJ programming, given that not all individuals examined in the RJ group actually received a "full dose" of such programming.

The details of interventions received by youth in both groups are important, however, when comparing results across studies and in the interpretation of any demonstrated impacts (e.g., to put any "treatment effects" into context).

Complete information on various program components (e.g., RJ agreement details or probation conditions) was not available; however, some key information was available.

Nearly all (95%) of the youth referred to traditional juvenile court processing received a term of probation as a result of their referral. Most of these youth were placed on supervised probation (79%); dispositions of unsupervised probation (17%) and dispositions other than probation (4%) also occurred. Nearly one third (29%) of youth placed on probation received a disposition of 90 days or less, 40% received a disposition of 91 to 365 days, and 31% were placed on supervision indefinitely.

The vast majority (99%) of youth referred to the RJ program received at least an initial in-person conversation with an RJ facilitator. A total of 7% of cases ($n = 19$) concluded after this initial meeting, as the offender was deemed inappropriate for program participation (program inclusion criteria include admitting the offense and willingness to "make things right" with the victim). An additional 11% of RJ-referred cases ($n = 30$) concluded because victims were unwilling to participate in the program. Direct victim–offender dialogue (including conferences with support people in attendance) occurred in more than half of RJ-referred cases (55%). In all 12% of RJ-referred cases resulted in a victim or community panel (rather than face-to-face interaction between the victim and offender) and 15% were resolved via discussions with the facilitator (indirect mediation; no actual meeting of victim and offender). Agreements were reached in all the cases for which some form of RJ intervention (e.g., victim–offender dialogue, panel, or indirect mediation) was determined appropriate; in some cases, the meeting itself was sufficient. When an agreement was reached, in 95% of cases, the agreement was fully completed as intended. Unfortunately, the details of agreement reached were available for only a subsample of 153 cases (approximately 66% of agreements). Most of these agreements specified multiple conditions, including verbal and written apologies (64% of agreements), a written report or presentation (24% of agreements), community service work (39% of agreements resulting in a total of 804 service work hours), and financial compensation (37% of agreements, including more than US$12,000 in compensation).

*****

RESULTS

Overall Impact of RJ

The relationship between program participation and time to reoffense was examined for all youth in the sample using Cox regression. The key independent variable in this model was the term representing RJ participation. Other predictor variables included age at referral, race/ethnicity, gender, residence in the urban part of the county, number of prior official contacts, and two indicators of most serious offense type (property or violent vs. other). The model was statistically significant, $\chi^2(8, N = 551) = 79.83$, $p < .000$ .... RJ participation was significantly and negatively related to survival time ($\chi^2 = 10.43$, $p < .01$). Youth who were referred to the RJ program remained offense-free significantly longer than similar youth who were referred to traditional juvenile court, even after controlling for initial group differences.

Moderators of RJ Effectiveness

A series of separate Cox regression analyses was computed to examine the potential differential impact of RJ referral on youth based on demographic-related (age at referral, gender, race) and offense-related variables (offense history and most serious offense type). Appropriate control variables...were retained in each model .... First, analyses were conducted to examine the impact of RJ referral on youth who were younger (14 or younger) or older (15 and older) at the time of referral to their RJ or traditional processing. Controlling for other factors, youth who were referred at a younger age (14 and younger) to the RJ program remained offense-free for significantly longer periods than similar youth who were referred to traditional processing ($B = -.52$, $SE = .23$, $\chi^2 = 4.96$, $p < .05$). Youth referred to the program at an older age (15 and older) remained offense-free longer than similar youth in the comparison group, but this difference was not statistically significant ($B = -.26$, $SE = .20$, $\chi^2 = 1.63$, $p > .10$).

. . . . Males referred to the RJ program remained offense-free significantly longer than did males in the comparison group ($B = -.53$, $SE = .19$, $\chi^2 = 8.22$, $p < .01$), controlling for other factors. Females referred to RJ processing remained offense-free longer than comparison females; however, this difference was not statistically significant ($B = -.38$, $SE = .29$, $\chi2 = 1.69$, $p > .10$).

The impact of RJ referral on White and non-White youth was also examined . . . . Controlling for other factors, White youth referred to the RJ program remained offense-free significantly longer than White youth in the comparison sample ($B = -.49$, $SE = .19$, $\chi^2 = 6.69$, $p < .05$). Non-White youth who were referred to the RJ program remained offense-free longer than non-White youth in the comparison group; however, this difference was only marginally significant ($B = -.57$, $SE = .30$, $\chi^2 = 3.66$, $p < .10$).

Cox regression was also used to explore the differential impact of RJ processing by offense history . . . . Separate analyses were computed for youth with no prior official charges and for youth with one or more prior official charges. Youth with no prior official contacts who were referred to RJ processing remained offense-free significantly longer than their counterparts who were referred to traditional court processing ($B = -.52$, $SE = .19$, $\chi^2 = 7.47$, $p < .01$). Youth with one or more prior contacts who were referred to RJ processing also survived longer than their counterparts who were referred

to traditional processing, but this difference was not statistically significant ($B = -.19$, $SE = .26$, $\chi^2 = 0.51$, $p > .10$).

Finally, the impact of RJ referral was examined among youth referred for violent, property, and other offenses . . . . RJ referral was significantly negatively related to survival time in two of the three models. Specifically, controlling for other factors, youth who were referred to RJ processing for property ($B = -.60$, $SE = .20$, $\chi^2 = 8.84$, $p < .01$) and violent offenses ($B = -.94$, $SE = .43$, $\chi^2 = 4.87$, $p < .05$) remained offense-free significantly longer than their counterparts who were referred to traditional court processing. Conversely, controlling for other factors, youth who were referred to RJ for "other" types of offenses recidivated *more* quickly than youth referred to traditional processing for similar offenses, although this result was not statistically significant ($B = .33$, $SE = .36$, $\chi^2 = 0.84$, $p > .10$).

*****

CONCLUSION

RJ programs have become much more common in recent decades, at least partly because individual studies, and some meta-analyses have demonstrated their success at reducing recidivism (although advocates often stress other program benefits). At the same time, an emerging body of research suggests that these programs may not be equally effective for all types of participants. Existing research has only begun to examine the potential for RJ programs to be differentially effective based on the characteristics of the individuals who participate in them. Some research has examined the moderating effect of current offense type on RJ effectiveness; however, fewer have examined the role of various offender demographic or criminal history factors. Understanding these potential moderating effects is important, because the results will speak directly to the ability of RJ programs to be used with a wide range of offenders, rather than being useful only for low-risk individuals.

The current study's results suggest that RJ programming may be effective for a variety of youth. Referral to RJ relative to traditional juvenile court processing was associated with greater survival time in 11 of the 12 analyses. Split-sample models revealed that RJ referral was related to longer survival time regardless of age at referral, gender, racial group membership, presence of prior offending history, and among those currently charged with either property or violent offenses. Practically speaking, 10 of these differences were also quite sizable (i.e., differences of longer than 4 months) and 8 of these differences were statistically significant in multivariate models. Only youth referred for "other" offenses recidivated more quickly when referred to RJ than traditional juvenile court processing (and this difference was not statistically significant in the multivariate model). Consistently, positive results observed across various groups of youth suggest that RJ may be appropriate for a broader population of youth than it has been used with in other jurisdictions. In particular, the results suggest that RJ does not have to be limited to the least serious youthful offenders and that it may be appropriate for more serious offender populations (e.g., older youth, those with prior offenses, those with property and even violent crimes).

Although this analysis adds to the literature in a number of ways, some limitations should be noted. Youth were not randomly assigned to treatment conditions; therefore, the possibility of selection effects remains (alternate models controlling for group propensity yielded similar results, however). The use of control variables to account for initial differences between treatment and comparison groups strengthens our conclusions; however, some potentially important control variables were not available for inclusion (e.g., socioeconomic status, family status, education-level, and community-level variables). We were also unable to examine the effectiveness of the RJ program across groups based on more dynamic indicators of risk (e.g., antisocial attitudes), instead using static factors such as criminal history and individual demographic factors, nor were we able to examine the combination or interaction of these potential moderating influences (e.g., gender and prior offending) on RJ effectiveness. In addition, some of the analyses include small samples (e.g., females), which may have masked significant differences in effectiveness across groups (although this may be a minimal concern given that a number of significant differences was found). Finally, the authors would suggest caution in attempting to generalize the results of this study, particularly to communities or contexts that are considerably different from the small urban area examined here.

It will be important for future research on the effectiveness of RJ programming to examine differential effectiveness of specific types of RJ intervention (e.g., reparative boards, face-to-face mediation). Although some basic data regarding the type of RJ services received by participants in this program were available, we did not examine the differential effectiveness of various types of RJ programming (e.g., direct vs. indirect mediation). In addition, it is possible that different RJ interventions may interact with individual characteristics to further moderate program effectiveness. For example, the current results suggest that individuals referred to RJ programming for "other" (e.g., minor traffic offenses) did not fare as well as those referred for property or violent offenses. Many of these "other" offenses lack a clear victim and as such RJ programs may need to improve their ability to help the offender understand how these behaviors (e.g., underage smoking or traffic violations) really produce harm to the wider community. In line with the risk principle proposed by Andrews and Bonta (2003), that low-risk offenders should be targeted for low-intensity programs, it may also be that these individuals would benefit from some specific kinds of lower intensity RJ interventions (e.g., indirect mediation) rather than full-fledged conferences.

Future research, involving larger samples (and possibly even using random assignment to various types of RJ intervention), is needed to fully examine these kinds of intervention type/individual characteristic interactions. Research should also examine whether several favorable, but nonsignificant, results observed here (e.g., among older youth, females, those with one or more prior charges) might meet the threshold of significance in larger samples (although in this study, these nonsignificant findings also related to some of the comparatively smaller between-group differences). If research using larger samples concludes that RJ programs do not produce benefits among older individuals or those with prior offenses, then the potential to expand their use to "more serious" offenders (at least without program modifications) may be limited. Likewise, if research with larger samples indicates that RJ participation does not provide benefits for female researchers will then need to examine whether females might experience RJ-related interventions differently than males and whether/how those programs might best be altered to address gender differences.

The current study demonstrated remarkably consistent RJ effects across a number of potential moderating factors. At the same time, the current results suggest that a challenge for RJ program administrators might be to modify their programs to be more effective when offered to more serious offenders. The benefit of referral to RJ processing was not as strong among youth with one or more prior offenses (the difference was only 1.2 months on average, and the result did not reach statistical significance). Some existing research (Rodriguez, 2007) had found significant increases in recidivism among those with more prior offenses, so it is possible that among some populations (e.g., urban Maricopa County vs. relatively rural Upper Midwest), RJ programming is more or less effective for "serious" offenders. Future research is needed on the effectiveness of innovative RJ strategies for higher risk offenders that may be more intensive than existing RJ approaches. For example, an individual with a number of prior offenses (and presumably more entrenched criminal propensity) may require a combination of typical RJ interventions (e.g., mediation, restitution, community service), and participation in relevant and potentially more intensive offender rehabilitation programs (e.g., cognitive-behavioral skills training).

The current study set out to examine the potential for differential effectiveness of RJ programming across several individual characteristics (age, gender, race, prior offending, and current offense type). The results provide evidence supportive of RJ programming for a variety of youthful offenders and they begin to fill important gaps in our knowledge regarding the applicability of RJ-style interventions for various types of offenders categorized as low or high risk. The authors hope that this initial investigation, and our suggestions for future research on these issues, will spark others to continue in this important line of inquiry.

REFERENCES

Andrews, D., & Bonta, J. (2003). *The psychology of criminal conduct* (3rd ed.). Cincinnati, OH: Anderson Publishing Company.

Bazemore, G. (1998). Restorative justice and earned redemption. *American Behavioral Scientist, 41,* 768–813.

Bazemore, G. (2000). Community justice and a vision of collective efficacy: The case of restorative conferencing. In J. Horney (Ed.), *Criminal justice 2000: Policies, processes, and decisions of the criminal justice system* (Vol. 3, pp. 225–298). Washington, DC: U.S. Department of Justice, National Institute of Justice.

Bazemore, G., & Umbreit, M. (2001). *A comparison of four restorative conferencing models (Juvenile Justice Bulletin).* Washington, DC: U.S. Department of Justice, Office of Juvenile Justice and Delinquency Prevention.

Bergseth, K., & Bouffard, J. (2007). The long-term impact of restorative justice programming for juvenile offenders. *Journal of Criminal Justice, 35,* 433–451.

Bonta, J., Wallace-Capretta, S., & Rooney, J. (1998). *Restorative justice: An evaluation of the restorative resolutions project*. Ottawa, Ontario, Canada: Solicitor General Canada.

Bonta, J., Wallace-Capretta, S., Rooney, J., & McAnoy, K. (2002). An outcome evaluation of a restorative justice alternative to incarceration. *Contemporary Justice Review, 5*, 319–338.

Bradshaw, W., & Roseborough, D. (2005). Restorative justice dialogue: The impact of mediation and conferencing on juvenile recidivism. *Federal Probation, 69*, 15–21.

Braithwaite, J. (2002). *Restorative justice and responsive regulation*. New York, NY: Oxford University Press.

Cormier, R. (2002). *Restorative justice: Directions and principles*. Ottawa, Ontario, Canada: Public Works and Government Services Canada.

de Beus, K., & Rodriguez, N. (2007). Restorative justice practice: An examination of problem completion and recidivism. *Journal of Criminal Justice, 35*, 337–347.

DeLisi, M., Beaver, K. M., Wright, K. A., Wright, J. P., Vaughn, M. G., & Trulson, C. R. (2011). Criminal specialization revisited: A simultaneous quantile regression approach. *American Journal of Criminal Justice, 36*, 73–92.

Hayes, H. (2005). Reassessing reoffending in restorative justice conferences. *Australian and New Zealand Journal of Criminology, 38*, 77–101.

Hayes, H., & Daly, K. (2003). Youth justice conferencing and reoffending. *Justice Quarterly, 20*, 725–764.

Hayes, H., & Daly, K. (2004). Conferencing and reoffending in Queensland. *Australian and New Zealand Journal of Criminology, 37*, 167–191.

Kirby Forgays, D., & DeMilio, L. (2005). Is teen court effective for repeat offenders? A test of the restorative justice approach. *International Journal of Offender Therapy and Comparative Criminology, 49*, 107–118.

Kurki, L. (1999). *Incorporating restorative and community justice into American sentencing and corrections*. Washington, DC: U.S. Department of Justice, National Institute of Justice.

Latimer, J., Dowden, C., & Muise, D. (2005). The effectiveness of restorative justice practices: A meta-analysis. *The Prison Journal, 85*, 127–144.

Latimer, J., & Kleinknecht, S. (2000). *The effects of restorative justice programming: A review of the empirical research*. Ottawa, Ontario, Canada: Department of Justice Canada, Research and Statistics Division.

Leonard, L., & Kenny, P. (2011). Measuring the effectiveness of restorative justice practices in the Republic of Ireland through a meta-analysis of functionalist exchange. *The Prison Journal, 91*, 57–80.

Luke, G., & Lind, B. (2002). *Reducing juvenile crime: Conferencing versus court* (Crime and Justice Bulletin No. 69). Sydney, Australia: NSW Bureau of Crime Statistics and Research.

Maxwell, G., & Morris, A. (2001). Family group conferences and reoffending. In A. Morris & G. Maxwell (Eds.), *Restorative justice for juveniles: Conferencing, mediation, and circles* (pp. 243–266). Oxford, UK: Hart Publishing.

McAlinden, A.-M. (2011). "Transforming justice": Challenges for restorative justice in an era of punishment-based corrections. *Contemporary Justice Review, 14*, 383–406.

McCold, P., & Wachtel, B. (1998). *Restorative policing experiment: The Bethlehem Pennsylvania, Police Family Group Conferencing Project*. Pipersville, PA: Community Service Foundation.

McGarrell, E. (2001). *Restorative justice conferences as an early response to young offenders (OJJDP JJ Bulletin)*. Washington, DC: U.S. Department of Justice, Office of Juvenile Justice and Delinquency Prevention.

Niemeyer, M., & Shichor, D. (1996). A preliminary study of a large victim/offender reconciliation program. *Federal Probation, 60*, 30–34.

Nugent, W., Williams, M., & Umbreit, M. (2003). Participation in victim-offender mediation and the prevalence and severity of subsequent delinquent behavior: A meta-analysis. *Utah Law Review, 137*, 137–166.

Nugent, W., Williams, M., & Umbreit, M. (2004). Participation in victim-offender mediation and the prevalence of subsequent delinquent behavior: A meta-analysis. *Research on Social Work Practice, 14*, 408–416.

Okada, D. (2011). Editor's note. Special issue: Essays celebrating the 35th anniversary of Restorative Justice. *Contemporary Justice Review, 14*, 365–366.

Pranis, K. (1998). *Engaging the community in restorative justice*. Washington, DC: U.S. Department of Justice, Office of Juvenile Justice and Delinquency Prevention.

Rodriguez, N. (2005). Restorative justice, communities, and delinquency: Whom do we reintegrate? *Criminology and Public Policy, 4*, 103–130.

Rodriguez, N. (2007). Restorative justice at work: Examining the impact of restorative justice resolutions on juvenile recidivism. *Crime & Delinquency, 53*, 355–379.

Roy, S. (1993). Two types of juvenile restitution programs in two Midwestern counties: A comparative study. *Federal Probation, 57*, 48–53.

Sherman, L., & Strang, H. (2004). Verdicts or inventions? Interpreting results from randomized controlled experiments in criminology. *American Behavioral Scientist, 47*, 575–607.

Sherman, L., Strang, H., & Woods, D. (2000). *Recidivism patterns in the Canberra Reintegrative Shaming Experiments (RISE) (Final Rep.)*. Canberra: Australian National University, Research School of Social Sciences, Centre for Restorative Justice.

Smith, M. (2001). *What future for "public safety" and "restorative justice" in community corrections?* Washington, DC: U.S. Department of Justice, National Institute of Justice.

Umbreit, M. (1994). *Victim meets offender: The impact of restorative justice in mediation*. Monsey, NY: Criminal Justice Press.

Wong, D. S. W., Cheng, C. H. K., Ngan, R. M. H., & Ma, S. K. (2011). Program effectiveness of a restorative whole-school approach for tackling school bullying in Hong Kong. *International Journal of Offender Therapy and Comparative Criminology, 55*, 846–862.

Zehr, H., & Mika, H. (1997). *Fundamental concepts of restorative justice*. Akron, PA: Mennonite Central Committee.

About the Editors

Curt R. Bartol was a college professor for more than 30 years, teaching a wide variety of both undergraduate and graduate courses, including *Biopsychology, Criminal Behavior, Juvenile Delinquency, Introduction to Forensic Psychology, Social Psychology,* and *Psychology and Law.* He earned his PhD in personality/social psychology from Northern Illinois University in 1972. He was instrumental in creating and launching Castleton State College's graduate program in forensic psychology and served as its director for 6 years. As a licensed clinical psychologist, he has been a consulting police psychologist to local, municipal, state, and federal law enforcement agencies for over 25 years. In addition to *Current Perspectives in Forensic Psychology and Criminal Behavior,* he has written *Introduction to Forensic Psychology* (now in its 4th ed.), *Criminal Behavior: A Psychosocial Approach* (now in its 10th ed.), *Juvenile Delinquency and Antisocial Behavior: A Developmental Perspective* (3rd ed.), *Criminal and Behavioral Profiling,* and *Psychology and Law: Theory, Research, and Application* (3rd ed.). He served as editor of SAGE's *Criminal Justice and Behavior: An International Journal,* for 17 years.

Anne M. Bartol earned an MA and a PhD in criminal justice from State University of New York at Albany. She also holds an MA in journalism from the University of Wisconsin-Madison. She taught criminal justice, sociology, and journalism courses over a 20-year college teaching career and has worked as a journalist and a social worker in child and adolescent protective services. In addition to *Current Perspectives in Forensic Psychology and Criminal Behavior,* she has coauthored *Introduction to Forensic Psychology; Juvenile Delinquency: A Systems Approach; Delinquency and Justice: A Psychosocial Approach; Psychology and Law: Theory, Research, and Application; Criminal Behavior;* and *Criminal and Behavioral Profiling.* She co-edited *Current Perspectives,* has served as book review editor and managing editor of *Criminal Justice and Behavior* and has published articles on women and criminal justice; rural courts, and the history of forensic psychology.